THE WEAVERS OF TRAUTENAU

HBI SERIES ON JEWISH WOMEN
Lisa Fishbayn Joffe, General Editor

The HBI Series on Jewish Women, created by the Hadassah-Brandeis Institute, publishes a wide range of work at the intersection of Jewish Studies and Women and Gender Studies by and about Jewish women in diverse contexts, disciplines and time periods.

The HBI Series on Jewish Women is supported by a generous gift from Dr. Laura S. Schor.

For the complete list of books that are available in this series, please see https://brandeisuniversitypress.com/series/hbi

Janine P. Holc, *The Weavers of Trautenau: Jewish Female Forced Labor in the Holocaust*

Paula J. Birnbaum, *Sculpting a Life: Chana Orloff between Paris and Tel Aviv*

Susan Weidman Schneider and Yona Zeldis McDonough, editors, *Frankly Feminist: Short Stories by Jewish Women from Lilith Magazine*

Tamar Biala, editor, *Dirshuni: Contemporary Women's Midrash*

Marjorie Lehman, *Bringing Down the Temple House: Engendering Tractate Yoma*

Tamar Ross, *Expanding the Palace of Torah: Orthodoxy and Feminism, Second Edition*

Hadassah Lieberman, *Hadassah: An American Story*

ChaeRan Y. Freeze, *A Jewish Woman of Distinction: The Life and Diaries of Zinaida Poliakova*

Chava Turniansky, *Glikl: Memoirs 1691–1719*

Joy Ladin, *The Soul of the Stranger: Reading God and Torah from a Transgender Perspective*

Joanna Beata Michlic, editor, *Jewish Families in Europe, 1939–Present: History, Representation, and Memory*

Sarah M. Ross, *A Season of Singing: Creating Feminist Jewish Music in the United States*

Margalit Shilo, *Girls of Liberty: The Struggle for Suffrage in Mandatory Palestine*

Sylvia Barack Fishman, editor, *Love, Marriage, and Jewish Families: Paradoxes of a Social Revolution*

Cynthia Kaplan Shamash, *The Strangers We Became: Lessons in Exile from One of Iraq's Last Jews*

Marcia Falk, *The Days Between: Blessings, Poems, and Directions of the Heart for the Jewish High Holiday Season*

Inbar Raveh, *Feminist Rereadings of Rabbinic Literature*

Laura Silver, *Knish: In Search of the Jewish Soul Food*

Sharon R. Siegel, *A Jewish Ceremony for Newborn Girls: The Torah's Covenant Affirmed*

THE WEAVERS OF TRAUTENAU

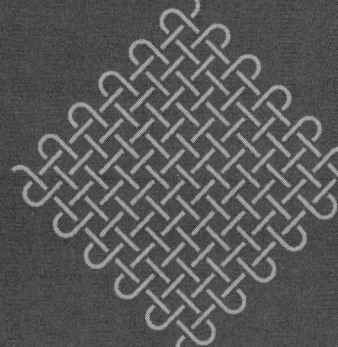

JEWISH FEMALE FORCED LABOR IN THE HOLOCAUST

JANINE P. HOLC

BRANDEIS UNIVERSITY PRESS

Waltham, Massachusetts

Brandeis University Press
© 2023 Janine P. Holc
All rights reserved
Manufactured in the United States of America
Designed by Richard Hendel
Typeset in Minion type by Rebecca Evans

For permission to reproduce any of the material in this book, contact Brandeis University Press, 415 South Street, Waltham MA 02453, or visit brandeisuniversitypress.com

Library of Congress Cataloging-in-publishing Data

paper ISBN 978-1-68458-170-2
cloth ISBN 978-1-68458-169-6
e-book ISBN 978-1-68458-171-9

5 4 3 2 1

CONTENTS

	Maps	vi
	Acknowledgments	ix
	Introduction	1
1	Jewish Girlhood and Jewish Survival in Zagłębie	40
2	The Local Logics of Coerced Labor	81
3	The Social World of Coerced Labor	97
4	The Conflicted Pathway to Survival: A Study of Three Peripheral Camps	136
5	Auschwitz Arrives in Trautenau	152
6	Ethics of Care and Prisoner Society	180
7	Desire and Space in the Coerced Labor Experience	205
8	The Violence and Losses of Liberation	225
9	Conclusion and Coda	247
	List of Testimony-Givers	255
	Archives Consulted	265
	Notes	267
	Bibliography	311
	Index	327

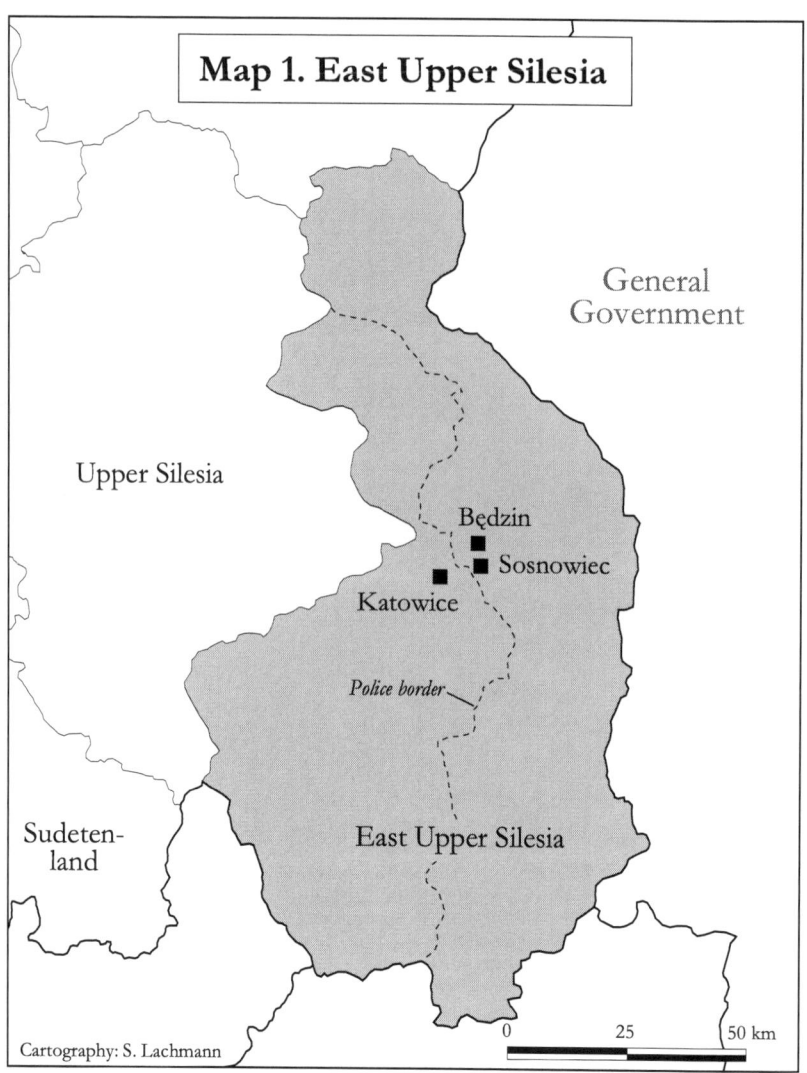

MAP 1 East Upper Silesia

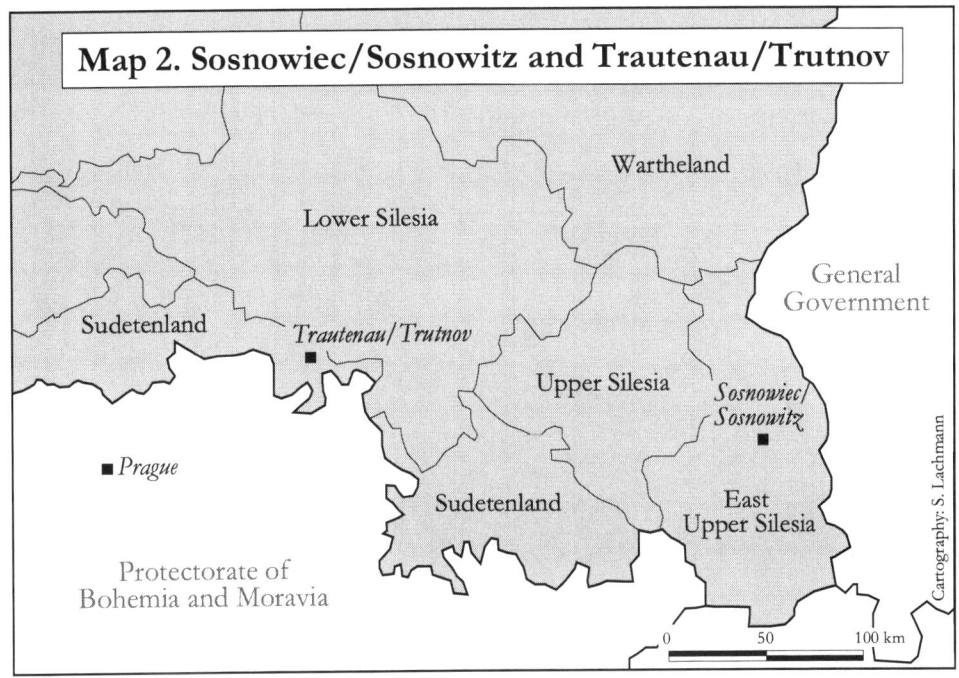

MAP 2 Sosnowiec/Sosnowitz and Trautenau/Trutnov

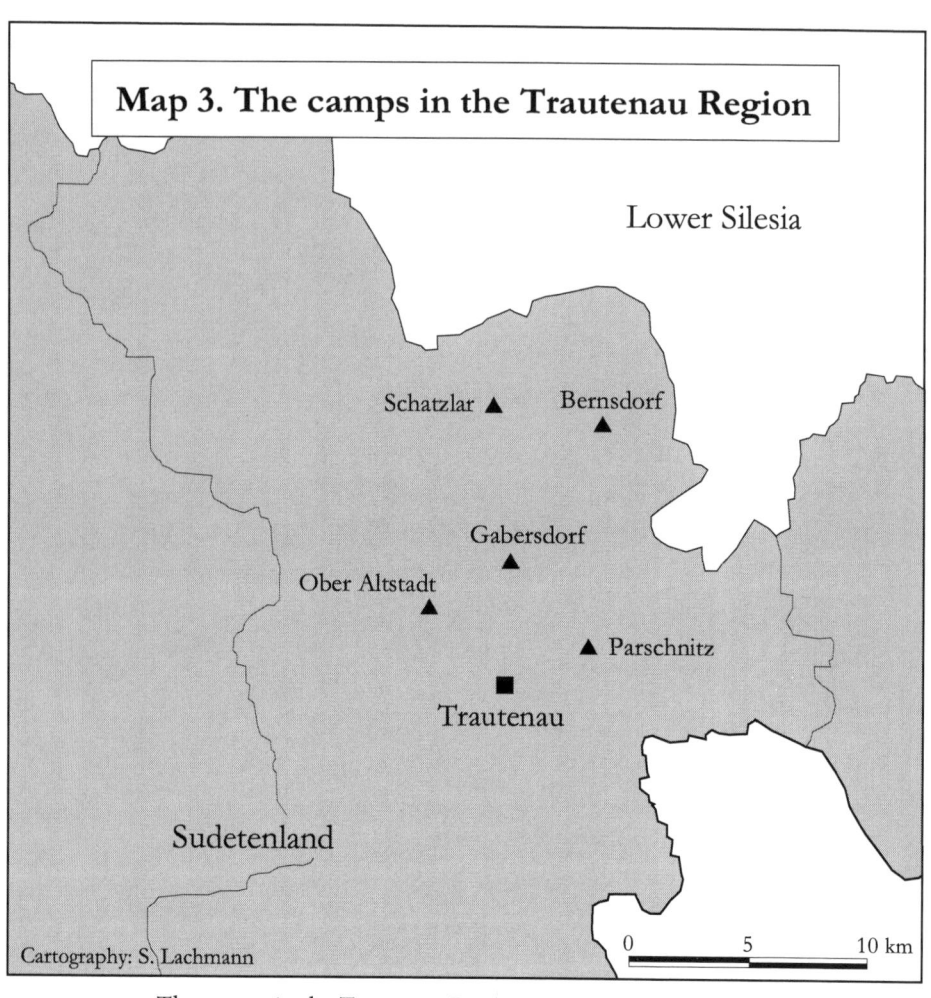

MAP 3 The camps in the Trautenau Region

ACKNOWLEDGMENTS

This book took shape while I was a Ben and Zelda Cohen Fellow at the United States Holocaust Memorial Museum. The time I spent at the Mandel Center for Advanced Holocaust Studies allowed me to listen and re-listen to the courageous testimony-givers who told their stories for the Shoah Foundation's Visual History Archive and who agreed to make the recordings available for researchers and the public. The Mandel Center offered support, expertise, and space for my work. I especially thank the skilled reference librarians and archivists: Ron Coleman, Megan Lewis, Vincent Slatt, and Elliott Wrenn. Elizabeth Anthony, Suzanne Brown-Fleming, and Jo-Ellyn Decker also provided invaluable support. I was lucky to be among talented and delightful co-fellows, many of whom gave me helpful comments on the work in progress: Elissa Bemporad, Michael Berkowitz, Erin Corber, Charles Gallagher, Alexis Herr, Stefan Ionescu, Assia Kovrigina, Vojin Majstorović, Meredith Oyen, Caroline Sturdy Colls, and Anna Veprinska. I am also grateful to Andrew Kloes, Jürgen Matthäus, Kyra Schuster, and Susan Snyder for their help and generosity of spirit.

This book was completed with extensive support from Loyola University Maryland. The Loyola College of Arts and Sciences supported archival research in the United Kingdom, Germany, Poland, and the Czech Republic; a Loyola University Peace and Justice Grant supported the end stages. Amanda Thomas, Michael Franz, and Carsten Vala provided financial and administrative backing for travel to archives. I also thank Tracy McMahon, Robin Smith, Jill Hanson, and Julie Ryder for technical and logistical help. Working at a predominately undergraduate institution means that secondary scholarship is often unavailable. I thank the tremendous work of the Interlibrary Loan department at the Loyola Notre Dame Library, specifically Mallory Walker and Zach Gahs-Buccheri, for enabling me to read relevant work published in Czech, Polish, German, and English.

The wonderful and distinguished scholars Natalia Aleksiun, Anna Hájková, Pamela Nadell, and Laura Levitt each separately stepped up at

ACKNOWLEDGMENTS

just the right time to move the book forward. Anna Hájková also pointed me toward additional sources and helped restructure the argument. Without her I would not have known about the crucial work of Irena Malá and Ludmila Kubátová on death marches (detailed in their book, *Pochody Smrti*) as well as so many additional references, insights, and corrections of claims gone astray. I am also grateful for the Association of Jewish Studies Women's Caucus Cashmere Subvention Grant and the supportive environment of the AJS during the height of the pandemic.

The structure of the Gross-Rosen subcamp system, its relationship to the Schmelt Organization, and the role of the local business in northern Bohemia was challenging to research. A truly transnational historical phenomenon, the task of tracking down documents (and ruling out possibilities) took me to many locations. The journey started at the Gross-Rosen archives in Wałbrzych, when I thought my project would be about the Gross-Rosen camp itself. Archivist Aneta Małek pointed me to the Parschnitz files, provided other supporting documentation, and allowed me to follow up with requests as the book was being completed. I am indebted to her. This book also benefited from archivists at the Wiener Library, the Muzeum Podkrkonoší and the Státní Okresní Archiv in Trutnov, the staff at Bundesarchiv-Lichterfelde and at the Státní Oblastní Archiv in Zámrsk, and Anna Maria Boss at the German Historical Institute in Washington, DC. I am grateful to Andrea Schneider-Braunberger of the Gesellschaft für Unternehmensgeschichte and her confirmation of the role of small family firms in the Nazi coerced labor system.

Many other individuals contributed to this project as it evolved over the years; they have given critical feedback, helped me overcome obstacles, and provided information. Erika Burns first intrigued me by documenting the unusual situation of the Sosnowiec Jewish community. I thank David Barnet, Anna Beaulieu, Natka Bianchini, Donata Blobaum, Robert Blobaum, Chauna Brocht and family, Crispin Brooks, Patrick Brugh, Cal Bullers, Imogen Dalziel, Debórah Dwork, Daina Eglitis, Benjamin Frommer, Tomasz Grząślewicz, Nina Guise-Gerrity, Dagmar Herzog, Cindy Hill, Astrid Holc and family, Jennifer Holt, Bianca Ingram, Jesse Kauffman, Adam Knowles, Robin Kolodny and family, Bjorn Krondorfer, Beatrice Lang, Emily Marquardt, Joanna Michlic, Michelle Morris, Aleksandra Namysło, Brian Norman, Susan Pearce, Robert Jan

ACKNOWLEDGMENTS

van Pelt, Luu Pham and family, Andrea Rudorff, Willeke Sandler, Nancy Wingfield, Donella Woods, and the students in my "Poland and the Holocaust" seminar. Julia Jordan-Zachery was a sustaining presence and the perfect writing accountability partner. Marta Kubiszyn in Lublin and Cherie Marvel in Baltimore were always there for me as I worked through the long course of research, writing, and revising. The resources they provided were absolutely essential. I am grateful for their friendship and unwavering confidence in me and in the project. Wendy Lower pointed me toward the Heine poem and the title for the book during a delightful conversation in Evanston. I thank Sabine Lachmann for the excellent maps. I reserve special thanks to Atina Grossmann for taking time away from her many commitments to help bring the manuscript over the finish line. Sylvia Fuks Fried of Brandeis University Press not only shepherded the project through reviews and publication, but also understood early on how the voices of these testimony-givers mattered. I would also like to express my appreciation for the support of the director and series general editor of the Hadassah-Brandeis Institute, Lisa Fishbayn Joffe, and her keen interest in including this book in the HBI series.

I thank Marisa Fox for introducing me to Harry Birnholz, son of survivor Sally Birnholz. Harry generously shared his mother's documents and photos and never forgot to ask me how the book was going. Jeffrey Cymbler and his group of Zagłębie survivors and descendants helped me stay connected to the experience of growing up in the region and to the powerful need to know more about this history and what had happened to loved ones. I thank Ze'ev Kaftori for a generous conversation about his mother, survivor Bela Kaftori, and for providing context for the photo he donated to Yad Vashem—one of the only photos available of the textile machinery at Parschnitz. I also thank Alan Steinweis and his mother, Rosalie Steinweis, for speaking with me about Parschnitz.

Interviewing Fay B. for hours in her home was an unforgettable experience. I am in awe of her courage and strength and deeply grateful for the opportunity to hear her story. Thank you, Fay and family. Listening to Fay and Rosalie Steinweis also gave me insight into the great listeners of Holocaust history: David Boder, Geoffrey Hartman, Lawrence Langer, and Dori Laub. They are joined by hundreds of interviewers across the globe. Their commitment to a deeply held receptivity and deferral of assertion in the presence of pain and confusion—as well as in the presence of moments of great clarity—is a difficult practice. Through their work I have a deeper understanding of the connection between listening and grief.

There are also other scholars and writers whom I have not met but whose work I read at times when I had to take breaks from note-taking and listening to the Shoah Foundation testimonies. These theorists of knowledge, loss, and recovery in contexts of oppression were crucial to allowing me to hear what the testimony-givers were trying to tell me. Central was the work of Édouard Glissant, who identified the importance of retreat, opacity, and refusal in creating space for imagining oneself differently. The context of his work is Caribbean decoloniality, placing it far afield from Polish Jewry, but this distance was crucial in helping me see what was unique about the coerced labor experience in the territories annexed to the Reich. In addition, I was influenced by the writings of Saidiya Hartman, Tiya Miles, Trinh Minh-ha, and Xine Yao, who take up the themes of who is allowed to speak, whose experience emerges from the archives, and the function of opacity (in Glissant's sense of the term) as a creative, space-making response to systems of displacement and persecution. I am grateful for their work, while at the same time acknowledging that the structures they grapple with are specific to contexts very different from the Nazi project of the Holocaust.

The aim of this book is not to have the last word on the coerced labor experience for the Jewish girls and women from Zagłębie (as well as their camp sisters from Hungary and elsewhere). Indeed, even within the Shoah Foundation narratives I listened to, there were many topics that fell outside the scope of this book or that could not be contained within its narrative structure. I hope that scholars take up these topics for further research. They include the issues of linguistic, religious, and economic differences among the prisoners; relations with townspeople; the perspectives of the non-Jewish Czech workers; the activity of Czech partisans, especially in 1944–45; a more systematic study of interactions of Jewish camp prisoners with prisoners of war; reasons for the absence of a death march; the displaced-person camp experience; issues surrounding memory, family, and second- and third-generation reactions; the role of affect in both perpetrator strategies and resistance; and how these particular testimonies, recorded in the twentieth century in the main, function in the twenty-first century for families, scholars, and archivists. A more

ACKNOWLEDGMENTS

challenging topic is why certain aspects of experience are withheld inside the testimony practice, kept private or shelved for another day.

My hope is that this book brings the experiences of these girls and women into the historical record. I remain in awe of their tenacity, self-awareness, and simply their choice to speak while being filmed. These were people whose families of origin were lost to them, who came into adulthood with no parents, having lived through harrowing conditions that called on them to save the life of a sibling or provide for others by working in dangerous settings. Thank you to all of the girls and women who worked and wove in Trautenau and then labored as adults to share their truth—to give the best testimony they could for history.

My most heartfelt thanks goes to Anthony Holc, my deepest and most nourishing relation, whose open boat into the unknown inspires and challenges me every day.

THE WEAVERS OF TRAUTENAU

INTRODUCTION

And I will come home and sit with my people
and tell them what I went through.
— Nettie S.

In the autumn of 1940, residents of the mountain city of Trautenau in the Sudetenland watched as hundreds of Jewish girls and women between the ages of eleven and twenty-five began to arrive at the local train station. Trautenau—today in the Czech Republic—was small and picturesque, a quaint Central European city with a central square surrounded by homes and businesses. It was also a busy center for the textile trade. Nestled in a valley among fields of flax, the main material in linen, it was modernized in the mid-1800s by German industrialist families who sold refined cloth to the Hapsburg elite in Vienna. Trautenau was, by the 1900s, home to several major exporting companies, which were also the main employers in the region. Its local railway station was typically busy, often bringing migrant workers or foreign buyers to town for temporary stays. But this was something new. Starting in 1940 and continuing to the end of 1943, wave after wave of frightened and disoriented young people disembarked from passenger trains in groups every few months. Some were holding tightly onto sisters, cousins, or friends. Others were alone. Dressed in their own clothing from home, carrying a few belongings or nothing at all, they spoke only Yiddish or Polish—certainly not Czech and only rarely German, Trautenau's local languages. They had been brought to this specific location to live and work as forced labor.

These girls and young women were all from the same location: the Zagłębie region in Poland, a part of East Upper Silesia with a substantial Jewish population and the city of Sosnowiec at its center.[1] It is well known that Upper Silesia was a part of Germany before the end of World War I and was populated by many people who considered themselves ethnically German; reattaching it to the German Reich was a priority for the Nazi regime. Less well known is another region just to the east, which the Nazi regime called "East Upper Silesia," where Germans were a small minority, Gentile Poles a majority, and Jews a significant presence in clusters of Jewish communities in and near the city of Sosnowiec.[2] Before the war, Sosnowiec was a thriving city with more than 20,500 Jews; out of a total population of 129,000, that was about 16 percent.[3] Many were engaged in trade or owned large manufacturing concerns. Just a few miles away were Dąbrowa, Olkusz, Chrzanów, Zawiercie, and several other small towns with sizable Jewish communities. The 21,000 Jews of Będzin—just adjacent to Sosnowiec—made up half the population of that city. Initially the target of Nazi policies to move all Jews and Gentile Poles to the east to allow for ethnic German resettlement, East Upper Silesia (and Zagłębie) was quickly recognized as a source for greater economic exploitation if its Jews remained.[4]

After a period of violent occupation by the German army—during which life in the greater Zagłębie region was transformed by public hangings and street harassment as well as laws forcing Jews to restrict their movements, end schooling, and register with the newly established Jewish Council of Elders—Sosnowiec was made the headquarters of a labor exploitation system in 1940 called "Operation Schmelt," after the SS officer by the same name who was placed in charge.[5] As documented by historian Sybille Steinbacher, the Schmelt organization—staffed by SS and Gestapo—reconstructed Zagłębie as a "labor reservoir" for private companies engaged in war production as well as large-scale public works projects such as road building.[6] Schmelt and his staff, working with a Jewish council created by the Kattowitz Gestapo in October 1939, used a combination of incentives and intimidation to force Jewish families to surrender at first only one family member, then others, most often those without children to care for.[7] By the summer of 1942, the Schmelt SS and Gestapo were ordering all able-bodied young people to report for labor. By the time it was dismantled in late 1943, the Schmelt organization had transported more than fifty thousand Jews to forced labor sites throughout Silesia and the Sudetenland.[8]

This book is a reconstruction of the forced labor experience for young Jewish women in the Trautenau region, as told by those who survived. Of the approximately three thousand girls and women who were caught up in these particular work camps—which became concentration camps in 1943—most did survive. More than six hundred chose to share their testimony with the Shoah Foundation, now archived as the Visual History Archive (VHA) for use by researchers as well as families. In these testimonies, adult survivors of the work sites in the Trautenau region shared memories of their girlhoods in Zagłębie, the pathways by which they came to coerced labor while still in their teens, the effects on their families, their survival strategies on the factory floor and in the barracks, their encounters with the SS, the impact of the Soviet troops on their liberation journeys, and how they coped with learning of the deaths of their families and the damage done to their prewar Jewish worlds. While it was possible to survive in the Trautenau region's camps, threats of illness and being sent to Auschwitz were ever-present; girls and women coped by believing their families would be waiting for them at the end of the war. In their testimonies, they remember realizing of the extent of the Nazi project to murder the Jews of Europe as a simultaneously personal but also communal rupture of the Jewish world that had sustained them. As Nettie S. puts it in the epigraph at the beginning of this chapter, they imagined, fantasized, and anticipated a restored family life in which their persecution as coerced laborers would be extreme and unusual, something to be told at the table. They assumed that their strength and resourcefulness would have meaning once shared with their people—their families, local communities, and the wider Jewish world. This book assembles these testimonies to bring to light the particular aspect of the Holocaust that was the Schmelt system of coerced labor as it was experienced by Jewish girls and women, individually and collectively.

These testimony-givers went through the same persecution journey at the same time, subject to the same perpetrators, and trapped in the same barracks. Yet, they were individuals who brought their own insights and coping strategies to their situations as girls and who made their own meaning of their survivals as adults. To communicate this history—one that is shared and interconnected yet at the same time was experienced in distinct ways and expressed through distinct voices in the testimony process—this book presents similarly themed excerpts from more than one interview serially, one after the other. The source of each quotation is indicated by the first name and last initial of the speaker, with full names usually available in the endnote citations. Assembling excerpts of many testimonies rather than presenting the full, continuous narratives of a few select survivors, is a method that allows particular moments of nuance and precision to come to the foreground. It centers the voices of the testimony-givers in both their similarities and dissimilarities, avoiding the imposition of an overly integrated story. These excerpts—grouped together or, at times, presented singly—provide insight into the importance of family in structuring identity and choice during Nazi persecution, the possibilities and limits of social relations inside camps, and the challenges of moral and emotional repair in the face of indescribable loss.

Examples of this approach to testimony are offered here. The textile factory owners in Trautenau and its suburbs had requested only young Jewish females from the Schmelt organization; women and girls had long been their traditional labor force. The excerpts from the testimonies of the Jewish survivors, placed together, communicate the sense of disruption in their memories of the journey to coerced labor. At the same time, their individual voices remain distinct.

> Phyllis Y.: They put us on a train. Nobody told us where we were going. We didn't know where we were going. And I think we were on that train for—maybe fifteen hours? Twenty hours?[9]
>
> Rita R.: I was taken away 1941 February. I was fourteen years old... I was, right away, I was crying a lot and, you know, I missed my parents.[10]
>
> Shoshana G.: We didn't have what to wear because they didn't let us take nothing. We didn't know where we were going, that we wouldn't come back. It was just overwhelming for a nineteen-year-old. It was just unbelievable.[11]

In these excerpts, each speaker offers slightly different details, meaning that different aspects of the journey from Zagłębie to Trautenau left an imprint on their memories. Yet, together, these short passages communicate the disorientation of separation from family and the awareness of one's young age. In fact, the Schmelt system left many families intact and did not create a ghetto in Sosnowiec until the second half of 1942.

Because of the design of the Schmelt system, the Jewish girls and women assigned to labor and then later imprisoned in their barracks shared both a common regional background—Zagłębie—and a common pathway to persecution; and because the Jews in the Trautenau sites were not sent on death marches at the end of the war, they shared a common experience of liberation. As is the case with any study of Holocaust persecution, there were always exceptions to those experiences and events held in common. This book places testimonies at the center of historical analysis to also allow these exceptions to the shared patterns to emerge in their specificity and in their relation to what was experienced in common. The perceptions and observations of these survivors offer information about the very precise forms in which violence was delivered and received, evaded or countered, and about the wide range of coping strategies that were used in response to that violence.

An example is the following segment from the Shoah Foundation testimony of Lena M., born in 1927 and fifteen years old when she was separated from her family in 1942. As was the case with most of the girls and women, Lena M. worked in a factory that processed flax into thread for use by the German military.

> Lena M.: It was a take and give, too. You know, I was very—very good, I was knitting. I used to, we used to steal. Not take—some of this yarn. I used to make, I used to be very good in it. At night I used to be up and I used to make shoes, I used to—
> Interviewer: [*interrupting*] What did you knit with?
> Lena M.: Well, I got, we got something, somebody brought us, in the, in the what do you call it? In the factory. We had some nice Russ—from Sudeten, you know, people. And we had asked them and they brought us.
> Interviewer: Knitting needles?
> Lena M.: Yes, knitting needles. Yeah, yeah. Wooden knitting needles, wooden. And I used, I used to make a sweater. And I used to make socks. Socks was the most important. And gloves. So I used to be up at night. And sometimes I used to make them and sell them. Sell them for a piece of bread or whatever. So, uh, that sometimes which helped us along.[12]

It is not unique to the Trautenau region's camps that prisoners acquired materials to make and exchange objects; this occurred even in the more violent and brutalizing sites such as Auschwitz. But Lena M. paints a precise picture of the process of acquiring the materials and making the objects as socially mediated, in that she negotiated with the civilian co-workers for tools and knitted along with others. The wooden needles, the socks made of yarn, the well-earned bread, and even the barracks at night palpably invoke a carved-out world of creativity, exchange, and social relation that Lena M. is proud of ("I used to be very good"). She created, in fact, an economic system in which work had restorative meaning. At fifteen years old, Lena M. evaded—and, one could say resisted—three forms of perpetrator deprivation: lack of food, lack of clothing to ward off the cold, and despair.

Thus, this study positions testimony-givers as producers of knowledge. They are not only witnesses to persecution but also often astute observers of the motivations of others, archivists of what occurred to their own families and their campmates, and creators of their own strategies of survival. They document aspects of contradiction and tension in persecutory practices, moments of their own emotional and physical collapse, and shifts in their shared awareness (and at times, shared denial) of the impact of the Nazi regime on the Jewish communities of Poland. In light of these potentialities, this book organizes the testimonial material thematically, to address four key questions in the study of the Holocaust at large. The first is the status of testimony itself as a text that is open to interpretation; performs multiple functions for the testimony-giver; and is expressed via a technical testimony practice that includes interviewers, cameras, and curation. The second is the influence of the age of the testimony-givers on their experiences and their narratives, with "age" treated as an intersubjective self-understanding of how one fits into a family, culture, and moral universe experienced as Jewish. The third addresses the dynamics of social relations inside the barracks and the factory, given the all-female workforce and continuous presence of female Gentile coworkers, as well as the arrival of new Jewish laborers from Hungary in 1944, a transport of Jewish men on a death march in early 1945, and the encounter with Soviet troops in May 1945, which included sexual assault. The fourth is a contextualization of the Schmelt labor system as a part of the wider Nazi use of coerced labor but also as a persecutory system embedded in East Upper Silesia, a region annexed to the Reich and organized as a labor pool for private companies by 1940. These themes are threaded through chapters and organized chronologically, as they were experienced by the testimony-givers themselves.

THE POSITION OF TESTIMONY AS TEXT

It is challenging to approach testimony as a unique, personally voiced experience without reducing testimony-giving to a personally motivated journey toward an integrated identity. The psychological and emotional lives of survivors are inextricably bound up in their testimony-giving practice, as the major scholars of testimony—Lawrence Langer, Annette Wieviorka, Dori Laub, and Geoffrey Hartman—have demonstrated.[13] Until recently, survivor or witness testimony has been positioned in Holocaust scholarship as supplemental to the main purposes of historical research, in large part because it incorporates emotion, trauma, and personal motivations. Saul Friedländer's call for an integration of testimony and history was a significant contribution to addressing and even overcoming the tension between the two, in that he finds both necessary for historical truth-telling.[14] Christopher Browning used testimonies extensively to document individual reactions to and perceptions of persecution in his work, *Remembering Survival: Inside a Nazi Slave-Labor Camp*.[15] However, as Zoë Waxman argues, assumptions about survivor identities—especially women's—can potentially overdetermine how testimonies are read and how they are used in relation to the historical record.[16] She finds that memories that do not "tally with the concerns of collective memory," such as testimonies that mention causing harm to others or sexual activity, are at times discounted as appropriate sources of historical meaning.[17] The resistance to including gay and lesbian Holocaust experiences in historical research, analyzed by Anna Hájková in a recent text, can be viewed in part as an expression of the continued preference for personal narratives that fit an implicit archetype of the Holocaust survivor.[18]

Lena M.'s interaction with the interviewer in the previous excerpt is a reminder that testimonies may function as a working through of trauma or personal identity, but also as texts that can be explored for meanings that are generated through the process of their creation. The interviewer's skepticism about the knitting needles prompts Lena M. to go into detail about selling items that she made, communicating the texture of daily camp life working in the Trautenau region's textile factories. In just a few words we learn about the need for socks and their availability, the ease of unsanctioned nighttime activities, and the presence of sympathetic

Gentile coworkers. At the same time, Lena M.'s specific word choices, affect, and presentation of the knitting project as a part of her identity as a resourceful survivor make clear that this is her unique story and that it has emotional content. The excerpted passage is both a personal narrative and an archival artifact necessary to historical understanding.

In her study of Holocaust diaries, *Numbered Days*, Alexandra Garbarini approaches diaries as multidimensional forms that are simultaneously texts and objects. They communicate what she calls the "perspective" of the writer but also become imprinted with a range of emotions, projections, and material traces of the persecution journey.[19] Garbarini resists any generalization about Jewish experiences in the Holocaust. She uses a careful, precise attentiveness to the differences among diaries, taking into account the motivations for diary-writing, differences in setting, vulnerability to persecution, textual content, and material form to communicate the "heterogeneity" of the Jewish experience. Garbarini aims to honor not just distinct journeys inside and sometimes through the Holocaust but also what she sees as the writers' convictions that "without becoming familiar with the complexity of the Jews' emotional responses, people in the outside world would never come to understand what it was like to be a Jew during this period and thus remain ignorant of the full range of human experience."[20] Emotions and emotional content in texts are crucial to historical research and understanding.

Through this lens, survivor testimonies can, like diaries, reveal their insights if they are treated as complex, intentional expressions of the lived experience of the Holocaust. Like diaries, they are a specific modality of representation that has emerged from a cultural and social context. Noah Shenker's work on the larger institutional context of Holocaust testimony collections remains a key text on this issue.[21] He calls attention to the Shoah Foundation's specific history as an organization, its mission, and testimony-giving process, which includes pre-interview interactions with the interviewer and choices about the conditions of the filming. In his words, "Testimonies emerge from an individually and institutionally embedded practice framed by a diverse range of aims that cannot be reduced to their empirical historical content or visceral impact . . . Examining Holocaust testimonies involves looking at these infrastructures and the labor of the interview process, extending to moments that never make it to the video screen."[22] For the Shoah Foundation testimonies at least, the act of testimony-giving begins before the filming starts, as the interviewer undergoes training; the interviewee prepares a pre-interview questionnaire and meets with the interviewer to establish a rapport; and the interviewer does research on the specific place and events relevant to the interviewee.[23] The interview takes place in the testimony-giver's home, with family members often waiting in other rooms to be introduced near the end of the filming. These elements are intended to create a sense of both comfort and legacy for the interviewee.

The testimonies themselves exist inside an archive as distinct videos cataloged by name of interviewee. Many scholars have written about video as a modality with specific effects on the viewer experience, linking it to theories of film and television.[24] Regarding the Shoah Foundation videos in particular, Jeffrey Shandler has explored issues related to their curation and archival presence, topics Shenker also addressed.[25] Shandler stresses "digitization," which includes the archival interface, usually accessed on a computer or other digital device but at times at a museum, and which presents us with tools such as labeled segments. In other words, testimonies are received by the viewer and/or researcher after technical and cultural mediation; they are shaped by the archival infrastructure and the means by which they appear as representation.

Even given the importance of testimony curation, it is still the case that testimonies are texts with their own narrative strategies, expressed in relation to other texts. This is the approach taken by Hannah Pollin-Galay in her nuanced treatment of testimonies, *Ecologies of Witnessing: Language, Place, and Holocaust Testimony*.[26] In comparing patterns of representation across three national contexts—Israel, Lithuania, and the United States—Pollin-Galay draws attention back to the words, but situates those words in context. She points out which acts of violence testimony-givers single out, when they choose "direct human depiction" and when they generalize, under what conditions they invoke Yiddish or other means to create a bond with the interviewer, and in which moments they invoke a collective "we" and in which they remain an isolated "I."[27] She also points out the importance of place. The choice to depict with a name or a face, or to indicate a perpetrator (for example) with a general term, are responses, in part, to cultural expectations that exist in specific countries, nations, and cities, and influence testimony beyond the discrete event being recalled in its own time and place.

Like Pollin-Galay's work, this book approaches testimony as an act that unfolds in real time on camera and cannot avoid being permeated by what the testimony-giver understands testimony to be. Yet, as Pollin-Galay and Shenker both suggest, testimony can get away; it can escape the intentions of both interviewee and interviewer. It includes unrehearsed, unscripted, and spontaneous elements. Moving somewhat away from the "testimony infrastructure" approach, Pollin-Galay writes that "rather than abiding by a top-down, restrictive set of guidelines, interviewers and witnesses negotiate meaning as they go along, based on a fluid cluster of shared expectations"[28] and that these shared expectations can rupture. Survivors become angry, lose their ability to speak, ask to stop the camera, disagree with the interviewer. This "getting away" can be the outcome of an emotionally charged memory that has not been fully processed, as the work of Lawrence Langer has demonstrated,[29] or it can simply be grief; it can occur after an interviewer mispronounces a loved one's name or refuses to validate an unconventional coping strategy. It can occur simply because a person is nervous speaking on film. These instances generate as much meaning as the story told with expertise and eloquence.

Like the works cited previously, this book seeks to stay attentive to the specificity and contours of testimony practice, including interviewer-interviewee dynamics, choices by testimony-givers to diverge from expected chronologies, disruptive emotional moments, and the mediating role of the technologies used to record and then present testimony to audiences. The Shoah Foundation archive of survivor testimonies referencing Trautenau and Parschnitz, and the related smaller camps of Ober Altstadt, Bernsdorf, Schatzlar, and Gabersdorf, is the central source for this book's analysis of the fluidity of the coerced labor systems and the adaptation required of Jews—specifically Jewish girls and young women—living within them. The characteristic of the archive that is worth noting here is its use of the questionnaire, given to the interviewee prior to the testimony event, with the same questions for all participants.[30] The questionnaire's function as a limiting technique that channels testimony in a specific direction has been criticized, especially in comparison to the more open-ended techniques of the Fortunoff archive, for example. However, the questionnaire's structure allows listeners to receive the testimony as an historical narrative and in this way hear, integrate, and remain present with aspects in ways that are productive. For example, all interviewees are asked about their memories of childhood, family members' names, sites of persecution, emigration or hiding, the experience of the end of the war, and life after the war. But the Shoah Foundation process of imposing specific themes and a chronology is not determinative; survivors frequently subvert or exceed this structure. As people tell their stories, they often ignore the boundaries of the question posed, or share significant aspects of their experiences outside of the circumscribed topic. The ability of the speaker to insert remembered material outside of the assigned structure of the interview can generate as much meaning, if not more, than the material that defers to the interviewer's boundaries.

For example, in her testimony, Nettie S. shared family photos at the very end of the interview, as everyone interviewed as part of the Shoah Foundation is invited to do. She began with a 1941 photo of her father and a 1939 photo of her mother, both expressive images. The interviewer stopped her and asked, "How did you get these photos?" With this question the interviewer wonders how Nettie S., who had been sent to the Walzel barracks in 1942, and which evolved into the Parschnitz concentration camp in 1944, could have either acquired them or, more likely, could have kept them with her throughout her confinement.

> Nettie S.: Oh, when I was in concentration camp I write every time, from the beginning. I say, please—send me some—thing, pictures. My sister sent me the pictures.[31]

Here Nettie S. documents the practice of allowing correspondence in the coerced labor setting, "from the beginning" through to some later period; that her sister in Zagłębie had the resources and ability to respond and send not just a postcard but also a sealed envelope with contents; and that Nettie S. was able to store these photos safely throughout her persecution and postwar journey. The "please" is rendered with emotion; her memory of her pain at the distance from family is palpable. Yet these two short sentences are in the wrong place: she brings them up in the last tape, under the archival keyword "photographs," which is supposed to be an addendum to the Shoah Foundation process.

The importance of the interviewer in mediating the emergence of meaning has been well documented by scholars, including Shenker, but also Dori Laub on the cocreation of knowledge and Geoffrey Hartman on the restorative power of the "testimonial alliance" between interviewer and interviewee.[32] In the Shoah Foundation videos, the interviewer introduces themselves at the onset of the tape, holds the speaker's gaze, clearly poses questions, and intervenes in technical issues such as the end of a tape or a misplaced microphone. This is not to say that the "testimonial alliance" is necessarily stable or productive. The interviewer's alliance is on the surface primarily with the survivor giving the interview, but at times it shifts to an alliance with the imagined audience, such as when the interviewer decides more clarity is necessary, or an alliance with sound or camera technicians. It is the case that the interview-interviewee alliance can break down. A misunderstanding is never clarified or the survivor refuses a specific response the interviewer attempts to incite. These ruptures may be failures on a certain level, but the testimonies presented in this book show that the tensions they generate can give rise to important material. At times the interviewer gives up and changes course; at times they continue forward in confusion; at times it is the interviewee who is dissuaded from saying more on a topic.[33] Attending carefully to these moments allows us to see where our assumptions about the Holocaust experience—which we may share with the interviewer—fall short.

While this book emphasizes testimony as text, the material drawn upon is, of course, also visual. Setting aside the impact of video as a form, the visuality or visual staging of each testimony is intertwined with the spoken content. First, the Shoah Foundation went to lengths to create a system in which survivors were interviewed in their homes.[34] After viewing just a few, the commonalities are striking: the testimony-giver has clearly been directed to choose a formal room in her home, is seated in a large chair or sofa, and has meaningful objects at arm's length. Because lighting and sound are a priority in creating the artifact, and because there is usually only one videographer present (in addition to the interviewer), the interviewee is asked to stay limited in her movement.[35] Even arm motions can dislodge the clip-on microphone. Yet they move—they wave their arms, hold their faces in their hands, roll their eyes, call out to family members in the next room. While staged as a fixed setting, the testimony process is clearly embodied and in motion. Second, the camera remains focused on the interviewee only. Her body language and facial expressions are centered in the frame and her affect can seem legible and heightened. It becomes part of the testimony itself. When a gesture or expression is significant to the meaning of the text, I included it in the transcript. However, the interpretation of affect is itself not only culturally mediated, gendered, and ethnicized but also implicated in broader hierarchies of modernity, as is the choice to present a specific affect or withhold it.[36] As Xine Yao has elaborated in her analysis of the emergence of affect regimes in the nineteenth century, the absence of a specific affect or expression of emotion—or of affect itself—is not an indicator of a shallow investment.[37] Expressions apparently familiar to viewers from other contexts may not be similarly legible in Holocaust testimony; a nervous laugh may function to hold overwhelm at bay, to keep a memory private, or to prevent the next question from coming. With this in mind, observations about gestures, movement, and tone are noted at times but in the main kept secondary to the words themselves. And yet, these narratives are memories of trauma and loss. There are frequent moments of overwhelm, in which the testimony-giver loses her composure; these are integrated into the textual presentation.

It is a challenge to organize an analysis of testimonies such that individual choice as well as shared, collective responses are both present. In much of the scholarly work on the Holocaust, the experience of the individual is sectioned off as an anecdote, functioning, as Joel Fineman and others have argued, to present a complex historical reality through a short, very particularized moment in time and space.[38] As such, it does the work of disrupting the overarching pretense of the narrative to unity. In the Holocaust historical work in which testimony is used, the anecdote is crucial to communicating extreme episodes and cathartic memories, often moments of realization or de-idealization at the time of occurrence or the time of testimony-giving. However, an exclusive reliance on the compelling anecdote can also lead to a misreading of the shared, common experience, in that it potentially presents an event that is atypical. Alternatively, moving away from anecdotes and presenting the full life stories of a select few risks replacing historical reality with the singular life circumstances of individuals. With these issues in mind, the approach taken here identifies portions of multiple testimonies, each documenting a similar or collective event or practice, and places them adjacent to one another in the text. The aim is to give space to the unique voice of the speaker while developing a multilayered understanding of an incident or a setting.

Throughout the text the testimonies are identified by the speaker's first name and last initial, an atypical choice in books using survivor testimonies. This method of citing the speaker honors her specific voice and her specific choices in representation while resisting an overemphasis on her full identity. It is a citational practice that is aligned with the book's purpose: to present the Jewish response to coerced labor as a multivocal, differentiated phenomenon that nonetheless was experienced alongside others and in relation to others. Their words are presented verbatim. Thus, the reader can remain present with the flow of the collective experience while noticing distinctions among speakers and receive testimonies as individual memories with gaps and flaws. The notes also indicate the year the testimony was given and its location. Almost all of the testimonies included here were conducted in Australia, Canada, Israel, or the United States, the result of choosing those given in English. While English was not the native tongue of any of the speakers, their English-speaking families (living in those countries) were often the prioritized audience for the testimony-givers. The result is that there are frequent shifts to correct oneself, find another word, or substitute a Yiddish, Polish, or German term.

Three additional aspects of the testimony archival infrastructure are worth noting. A few survivors appear more than once, either in the Shoah Foundation archive or across multiple archives. There is only one interviewee whose two videos, four years apart, are both used in this book: Regina S., who remarried and became Regina G.[39] Each of Regina G.'s two testimonies contains material that enhances the understanding of the experience of the Schmelt system. A second, clarifying note is that the Shoah Foundation interviewing began in 1994 and continues to the present. However, several testimonies appear in the record as completed prior to 1994. This is because the Foundation began acquiring videotaped testimonies conducted earlier, by other institutions, and has integrated them into its archival structure. Finally, this study includes three interviews conducted or archived by the United States Holocaust Memorial Museum, one conducted by the Midwest Center for Holocaust Education, and one conducted by the University of Michigan-Dearborn.

INTRODUCTION

AGE, GENDER, AND THE LOSSES OF FAMILY
SEPARATION IN THE PATHWAY TO COERCED LABOR

The girls and young women at the center of this book did not pursue survival strategies identical to those that someone with responsibilities for children would have, nor did they make choices that a full adult disconnected from family may have. Although the Schmelt organization formally restricted the age of laborers to fifteen and over, those in the Trautenau sites were mainly between the ages of eleven and twenty (with a few exceptions), unmarried, still emotionally attached to family and living at home, and immersed in the world of conservative Judaism and the complex social landscape of Zagłębie, itself a vibrant network of Jewish communal life. As testimony-givers, they describe themselves as children in the many senses of that word in prewar Jewish Poland: sexually naïve, unaware of politics, living in a home with authority figures of father and mother, and inexperienced in the world of work. At the same time, they had responsibilities at home, such as raising siblings, shopping, and helping in a family business. As they see it, they were on the cusp of adulthood inside their extended family system but also in terms of their wider Jewish world. Thus, "age" in this sense is intersubjective and part of a sense of who one is, rather than the number of years one has lived. Testimony-givers remember their birth order (frequently asked for by the Shoah Foundation interviewers) and explain their childhood experiences in reference to older or younger siblings.

Moreover, their thoughts and actions were shaped by the trauma of their separation from their parents. The violent separation was a rupture of deep emotional attachments but also of their understandings of their place in the Jewish past, present, and future. Of the few survivors who do not fit into this picture—those alienated from their parents, older, or orphaned—their experiences are helpful counterpoints and noted as so throughout. Testimony-givers speak consistently about the importance of imagining a family reunification as the driving force behind their survival. It drives their choices and shapes their ability to overcome the lack of food and isolation at the work sites. They conceived of themselves as part of an extended family, an extended Jewish community, and imagined a Jewish future; their lack of information about what was happening to their families, the specific persecution Jews in Poland underwent, or the larger Nazi project of killing all the Jews of Europe allowed them to sustain this dream.

> Interviewer: What do you think kept you going? Was there a, was there a feeling—
> Berta P.: I was, I was lying to myself. I was thinking that my parents are alive, that my family was alive.[40]

This fierce persistence continues through the period of liberation in May 1945. Trautenau was one of the very last locations to be liberated; some of the girls and women had spent almost five years there. The survivors report a confusing mix of emotions—of being at a loss, unsure of what to do next; they rushed back to their prewar homes in Poland. The realization that, for most, the Nazis had murdered their extended families only hit them at the moment when they saw the empty streets or the family home now occupied by a non-Jewish Pole. The confrontation with this reality was shattering.

Thus, the entirety of this experience was thoroughly inflected by gender, of course, but also powerfully by age. For a girl in her teens called up for labor in this historical context, the rupture of parental, sibling, and grandparent relationships constituted the frame through which she viewed her persecution at the time it occurred and how she recalled it as a testimony-giving adult. In fact, many adult interviewees lose their composure when narrating the first moments of separation. Yet the same young person who cannot stop crying on the train to Trautenau (as Rita R. at the beginning of this chapter recalls herself doing) may have been put in charge of a set of huge looms, responsible for a significant stage in the thread production process. Within the context of overall grief and despair, many survivors (not all) remember feelings of pride at their work, in that they mastered physically demanding processes in settings of extreme deprivation. Ann F., born in 1925 and seventeen when she was forced to work at Alois Haase's company, is one example:

> Ann F.: [*pauses for a moment and smiles to herself*] For a little girl who was seventeen years old—at that time, yeah, I was seventeen—and uh, they put us—they were making thread from raw materials. . . . I myself had three machines that I attended. Most Czech men—we worked with Czechoslovakian people—

that most people in that factory—men!—had had two machines. We girls had three machines that we tended to.⁴¹

Here Ann F. remembers her sense of being too young and unprepared for the situation, because she was "a little girl," having never worked outside of the home. But she quickly turns this into an expression of accomplishment, doing so by contrasting her responsibilities with the prewar assignments of "men" in a reversal that is gendered. It is also presented as a contrast between childhood and adulthood. Ann F. speaks with an immediacy, as if she can still access the emotion as well as remember the actual machinery. She was a "girl" and aware of herself as such.

The testimony-givers' memories of being aware of their age at the time of persecution and of the specific harms of family separation manifest frequently throughout the narratives, as will be seen in the chapters that follow. However, it is hard to say that the interviewees consistently *enact* the tension between their age at the time of testimony (in their sixties and seventies) and their age at the time of the remembered event, either in words or through body language and affect. One exception is Dasha R., whose testimony is characterized by an ongoing strong association with her younger self. She had been close to her father growing up and idealized him. In her interview, she remembers being deeply affected by the moment of separation from him, which occurred at age thirteen when the authorities arrived to take her away for work.

> Dasha R.: My father ran to get me a coat. And he ran after me as I was walking down the stairs. And he put his coat around me—it was November. And his last words were to remain a Jewish child [*begins to cry*]. I had no idea what that meant.⁴²

As the testimony continues, she refers to the embrace of the coat as a symbol of her father's protection and care. This is the case even at a moment when one could say her father's protection failed her. Dasha R.'s sense of being in her father's care continued to be vivid for her in 1995.

Age remains a complicating category for historians.⁴³ Dominant definitions of "childhood" vary by culture and historical time period. Even within cultures "childhood" is a contested category, often interpreted to reinforce ethnic and class hierarchies. It can be problematic to consider those under the age of "adulthood" to have agency; some categories of children are presented as "acted upon" rather than actors, while others' agency is overemphasized. Certainly, the Nazi regime "acted upon" Jewish as well as non-Jewish infants, children, and those who at the time were called "young people" or "youth." With the age of the victims specifically in mind, Nazi perpetrators created family camps, targeted some children for "Germanization," targeted others for medical experiments or euthanasia, and organized child slave labor. Children were objectified and instrumentalized by rescuers, those involved in the postwar reconstruction of societies, and even states, as Gabriel Finder has shown in his work on the Central Committee of Polish Jews in postwar Poland.[44] But we also know that Jewish (and non-Jewish) children were active in resisting the Holocaust, smuggling goods into and out of the ghetto, as couriers, helpers in hiding, as willing participants in disguising themselves, and as coerced laborers. In one of the first systematic treatments of children in the Holocaust, the historian Debórah Dwork collected a vast range of childhood experiences, encompassing death camps, ghettos, hiding, and forced labor.[45] Taking the words of survivors as direct representations of what occurred, she demonstrates that most viewed their childhoods as taken from them. Underlying the pain and humiliation of Nazi tactics are acutely felt memories of being forced into adult roles beyond their capacities, meaning that they knew at the time of persecution that they were supposed to be treated differently, as children. This knowledge retained its emotional charge, which in turn found its way into Dwork's interviews.

Testimonies, diaries, memoirs, and essays by young people in wartime often exhibit the tensions of self-understandings of themselves as children while needing to survive using adult strategies. A recent collection edited by Joanna Beata Michlic illustrates the multidimensionality of children's agency in the Holocaust by contextualizing their choices within family relations. She notes that the "war forced young Jews to suppress critical aspects of their own identity in order to survive," aspects that either reemerged in moments of safety or were grieved as unrecoverable.[46] Often this suppression is remembered positively, as an essential contribution to the survival of the family, even as it is marked as exacting a great psychological price.[47] Rebecca Clifford extends the frame of psychological conflict in her study of child survivors and their difficulties in recreating stable identities in the face of family fractures after the war.[48] She shows how children refused or even subverted newly constructed or recovered familial relationships. In Clifford's work in particular, exact chronological age is important but mediated by events to which the individual was exposed; people who were hidden for years made sense of their postwar world differently from others the same age but who had worked in camps on their own. Johannes-Dieter Steinert takes a sweeping approach in both of his recent volumes on children in World War II, including older teenagers in his definition of children and arguing that their political, social, and sexual choices cannot be commensurate with those of adults.[49]

Like these works, this book's exploration of the experiences of the survivors of the Trautenau-region camps takes us beyond the dualism of children as either objects or actors. Their testimonies (mostly recorded in the 1990s) contain multiple frameworks of self-identification coexisting in a single narrative: experiencing again the feeling of being a child; the recall of those feelings as an adult, with an adult's perspective; the adult awareness that one's naïveté at the time of persecution influenced what occurred; the consciousness that the testimony itself will be viewed by others and the consequent impulse to control the narrative; and competing urges to express emotionally charged responses that are still unprocessed. These coexisting elements of a remembered episode express the contemporaneous, often contradictory, elements of childhood and young adult subjectivity.

A compelling example is Sonia S.'s memory of the labor selection process at the Trautenau train station. Sonia S. was a vibrant, outgoing child who grew up in Dąbrowa and Będzin. She tells vivid prewar stories of a new theatrical company in town and begging her mother to let her join at age thirteen: "I wanted it so much!" She initially evaded the attention of the SS by working in small workshops in Sosnowiec. In the summer of 1942 the Schmelt authorities implemented a mass deportation in Będzin, including Sonia S., then fifteen. She and several others were selected out for coerced labor. After a harrowing series of events she found herself at an open plaza near the Trautenau station:

> Sonia S.: From Sosnowiec they took us to Parschnitz. Parschnitz was a concentration camp but it was also a transit camp. And at that transit camp, there was a big, big space where they brought

in from the whole Zagłębie—girls. At that time, it was only girls. . . . And the *Lagerführers* [sic] from all kinds of camps came. And they looked us over. To see if we are strong enough. Like you look over a cow or a, a—if it's going to be good. Our *Lagerführerin* liked the pretty girls. And she picked five girls. There was me, one was from Zagórze, three was from Sosnowiec I think. Five girls. . . . There was another one coming, she wanted to take me, but she says, "No, she's coming with me."[50]

Via this anecdote, Sonia S. inserts a positive, idealized view of herself as an attractive young person into a description of dehumanization. Given her words and affect, it is almost as if she can still feel the rush of emotion at being chosen from among a hundred others of her same age. Yet the adult Sonia S. giving testimony in the 1990s as well as the fifteen-year-old Sonia S. in 1942 were both well aware that this selection would lead to extraordinarily difficult conditions. Sonia S.'s story as she tells it, unedited, reminds us that that young people's experiences in situations of stress may be influenced by desires and self-understandings that differ from those of adults. It also reminds us that those giving testimony may find it important to mark moments in which they had been able to sustain a sense of themselves as youthful, that is, their actual age.

There were a few "older" women in their late twenties or thirties interwoven among the young people at the coerced labor sites (including a handful of mothers with teenaged daughters). The testimonies of these survivors offer added insight into the dynamics of the Schmelt labor system because they were more aware of what was occurring—they could decode the power structures that they observed. Helena K. was born in 1914 and already twenty-five when she arrived in Trautenau in 1942.

Helena K.: First of all, there were young, almost children. Thirteen, twelve. Because they choose to send the young ones. Because they were easy, easily frightened. And they worked unbelievable.[51]

Helena K.'s observation reminds us that the factory owners and staff targeted young people intentionally because they could be forced to work longer hours with less resistance, something the survivors who were twelve at the time might not have been aware of. From her position as an adult, she could attempt to decipher the relationship among the private companies, the SS and Gestapo, and the girls and women:

> Helena K.: The owner was not a Nazi. He was, uh, he was supposed—he hired us from, uh, from Gestapo. We belonged to Gestapo. Not to Gestapo, to [*pauses*]—well, we were hired. He paid to the authorities for our job . . . He was not a Nazi, but he wanted money, he wanted work. And he complained that we don't work properly.[52]

By "not a Nazi," Helena K. could have meant that she had information about the factory owner's party affiliation, but more likely she meant that he did not share the brutalizing or dehumanizing motivations of the Schmelt officers or SS guards. Later in her testimony she offers another analysis, explaining that food was limited because intermediary camp staff (probably *Lagerführerinnen*) were stealing what the owner had allotted for the Jewish laborers.

Throughout the testimonies, the interviewers' unfamiliarity with the survivors' young age generates ruptures in the flow of the interview. The Schmelt system sent Nettie S. to a work site near Trautenau—Hannsdorf —in 1942 before they transferred her to the Parschnitz camp in Trautenau.

> Interviewer: Who were you with? When you went to Hannsdorf camp?
> Nettie S.: Yeah . . .
> Interviewer: Who were you with? Who was with you?
> Nettie S.: Who was with me? [*loudly*] A bunch of kids!
> Interviewer: From your town, or . . .
> Nettie S.: Yeah, from my town!
> Interviewer: Did you know them?
> Nettie S.: Yes, they were the kids from my town!
> Interviewer: Where was your family?
> Nettie S.: My family was . . . home![53]

Nettie S. seems to interpret the interviewer's requests for clarification as challenges, perhaps because she does not remember her experience as something that required such clarification or perhaps because she herself is still shocked, years later, that such young people would be sent for labor. The interviewer's questions indicate that children being sent for labor unaccompanied by family was not the expected narrative. However, the back-and-forth allows Nettie S. to keep her description of the coerced laborers as "kids" intact and clear in the resulting testimony artifact.

In another example, the testimony-giver attempts to accommodate the interviewers' misunderstandings regarding the meaning of "children." Gitla T. was forcibly taken from her home at age fourteen. There are two interviewers present, one male and one female; the man's name is listed as the official interviewer and he takes the lead in asking questions in English. Gitla T. uses Polish, Yiddish, German, and English throughout her interview. At some moments the second, female, interviewer translates for the first interviewer, and at other moments she asks questions herself. As the interview continues, Gitla T. pauses and looks off camera (apparently at the second interviewer) for help when she is searching for a word. Gitla T. has referred to her campmates as "children" throughout the interview.

> Gitla T.: [*speaking about the last days of her detention*] And they threw out every child . . .
> Interviewer 1: You said "children." Were there children working in the camp?
> Gitla T.: We was working all, those kids were, was together. All, we was working . . .
> Interviewer 2: What ages are you referring to? What age children are you talking about?
> Gitla T.: [*pauses in thought*] One child was [the] youngest child. She was maybe twelve years old. She was I think from Germany. Around the Śląsk [Silesia].[54]

At first Gitla T. seems to believe the interviewer is asking about "working" rather than "children" and she begins a long sentence about which "children" actually did the labor, including herself in this group. The second interviewer compels her to change her interpretation. This interviewer shifts the category of "children" such that Gitla T. is not included, with "what ages are you referring to?" Gitla T. accepts this revision and tries to document the age of one of the younger laborers.

Minnie W. corrects herself, changing "children" to "girls" midway through a sentence, but still including herself in the group:

> Minnie W.: They had an order. They needed young children, young girls, to the, to, to take us to the camp to work in *Spinnerei* [textile factories].⁵⁵

Yetta P. offers a description of herself in which age is measured in terms of life experience. In her case, she is speaking of an interaction after the war with a Soviet soldier and his sexual proposition.

> Yetta P.: [born in 1923] It's really amazing, because we were very naïve. We, you know before the war I hardly went on a date. I belonged to this, uh, Zionist organization so we used to meet and read books and talk about, you know, politics and books and lectures by older girls from us. But we never, I never had a date . . . But still I knew, what this soldier want."⁵⁶

Yetta P. was already nineteen when she was sent to a Schmelt camp, but she still recalls herself as young in the sense of her exposure to physical intimacy or to another's interest in her physically. She was knowledgeable about literature and politics and at the same time still "naïve." At the end of the excerpt, she asserts that she knew what soldiers wanted, but holds on to her sense of not-yet-adulthood.

These moments of misunderstanding and revision are central to this book's argument: that the coerced textile workers at the Trautenau factories thought of themselves as children, and as children of someone, a contextually embedded self-understanding that shaped their responses to persecution. Gitla T. seems to have in mind not just age measured in years but also how she and her cohorts were situated within their understanding of their life journeys as young Jewish women. This self-understanding, crucial to sustaining the identities of the survivors, also enabled a range of local actors—Nazi and civilian, German and non-German—to systematically exploit their specific mix of vulnerability and strength for both state and personal ends. As we will see in the chapters that follow, Nazi authorities, the Jewish Council of Elders, the factory owners and the *Lagerführerinnen* knew how to manipulate the girls and young women. The Council of Elders and the Schmelt staff coerced them to work by threatening their families; the factory owners assigned them to specific machinery; the camp guards bartered with them in specific ways. But while their sense of obligation to parents and siblings was powerful, they did not have children of their own (or responsibility for elderly relatives) and so often took risks that others would not, at times in anticipation of a postwar future for themselves.

THE QUESTION OF SOCIAL RELATIONS INSIDE SPACES OF PERSECUTION

The postwar model of "testimony-giving" has changed over time but was initially (that is, during and immediately after the war) structured as a legal and documentary technique, meaning a witness testified as an individual to document crimes and create an historical record; through the work of David Boder and others, it quickly took on psychological elements, in that survivors were given space to speak to (or avoid) their own personal pain and trauma.[57] Testimony has many more purposes than these (and many more meanings for the testimony-giver than can be listed), but the individual positioned to give voice *as an individual* remains a central assumption. In contrast, survivors of the work camps in Trautenau shared a common yet intimate and sustained persecutory experience—as did, of course, others in other sites of detention or hiding. The coerced labor experience was social and thus has a social history and social dynamics.

However, many analyses of social relations in camps use extremity as a reference point; in other words, the issue of social relations is posed as a question of how people in camps related to others in spite of overwhelming deprivation, humiliation, arbitrary violence, and threats of death. The books by Marc Buggeln and Felicja Karay, focused on coerced labor camps, document a social dimension that emerges, in distorted fashion, as a reaction to extreme persecution. They detail socially based coping practices (as opposed to concern exclusively with the self) under extreme conditions and the emergence of social hierarchies that at times further disempowered some prisoners.[58] Coerced labor camps and work sites were characterized by harsh conditions and the threat of death. But posing social relations as emerging from a ground of extremity can obscure questions of how contexts that were persecutory but less extreme, such as a factory site or a barracks-based camp with no execution practices, shaped social life.

It is well known that the displacement, trauma, and physical harms experienced by those targeted by Nazi persecution distorted social life in specific ways. Perhaps most well documented in memoirs and testimonies is the practice of creating pairs or small groups for mutual support, especially support in acquiring and hiding food and dealing with injury and illness. Survivors across a range of Holocaust settings document practices of finding a camp partner, creating exclusive groups of three or four, or forming into a consistent set of the five frequently demanded by authorities (so that placement could be switched or weaker members could be held up by the others).[59] Survivors also describe transactional arrangements with others, such as trading types of food, which some scholars label "reciprocity" and which Terrence Des Pres argued was an extension of a human moral impulse—even an instinct—to survive as human and resist Nazi aims of debasement.[60]

Maja Suderland's study of prisoner society goes further than "instinct" to document the persistence of social relations even in the face of Nazi aims of dehumanization and atomization. She noted the influence of perpetrator organization of camp life, but also the creation of a "social shadow zone" in which prisoners engaged in "hidden social practices," and the impulse of prisoners to retain a sense of themselves as social beings.[61] While Suderland chose to focus on settings of extreme violence, recent scholarship by Anna Hájková shifts the ground from which camp and ghetto social life is observed from extremity to a focus on the continuities of prewar social categories and newly created, complex social networks that manifested in Terezín/Theresienstadt. She shows that practices typically considered as most meaningful when violence and confinement are absent, such as status hierarchies, political affiliations, and consensual intimacy, retained some of their continuity with the pre-Holocaust past, even while confinement generated new dynamics. Her study reconstructs the modes by which "society in Terezin was both deeply divided and interconnected, based on ethnicity, time of arrival in the ghetto, age, and social capital" while also honoring the voices of singular individuals.[62]

The camps in the Trautenau region were certainly characterized by a social life. Many testimony-givers mention status differences based on educational background, language ability (with German fluency being a prized skill), and physical appearance; the fact that almost all were from the Zagłębie region meant that prominent family names were well known. Privileges and preferential treatment were carefully tended and revolved around food acquisition, although as a later chapter will show, favored status with the guards allowed one to visit sisters at other camps. However, in taking the testimonies together, a picture emerges in which these distinctions fade in the face of monotonous menial labor, shared naïveté and disorientation at being far from home, and constant hunger. At the same time, socializing, social relations, and connecting with others (at times in anger) frequently appear. Social relations only partially coalesced into stable social categories.

For these camps in particular, social life fluctuated between carefully constructed small groups or dyads who supported each other exclusively, on the one hand, and moments in which behaviors and choices became relational in a wider sense, on the other hand. By "relational" is meant intersubjective connections to others and collective self-understandings that emerge situationally, rather than from a fixed social position or a protective small group. "Relationality" is a term that has been used in theology, psychology, and ecology in a variety of contexts but always to denote practices in which the self is embedded in a network of relations not defined by self-interest, but by action aimed at "the flourishing of the other," in Marcia Pally's words.[63] While Pally draws this ethics from a covenant theology, Édouard Glissant, a social theorist of postcolonial diasporas, finds "relationality" to be an anti-hierarchical way of proceeding in the world in which social exchange and interactions are open-ended and not motivated by a transaction that would at some future point be completed.[64] Certainly there are many instances of self-sacrifice and heroism in the Holocaust, but "relationality" captures something else: a more personal, everyday choice in which one's perception of one's own survival is extended to encompass a wider group. Examples of this type of social relation can also be found throughout camps during the Holocaust, especially when it was possible to share religious practices, rituals, or objects outside of the view of guards and kapos, as in Suderland's "social shadow zone."

Even after their barracks were consolidated into the Parschnitz and Ober Altstadt concentration camps in early 1944, the girls and women from Zagłębie continued to create and sustain a social world within what Anna Hájková calls "the logic of the forced community."[65] Here are the words of Gerda F., born in 1925 and aged sixteen when the SS delivered her to the Ignaz Etrich barracks:

INTRODUCTION

> Gerda F.: There were some very Orthodox girls in our camp. They made sure that we had a calendar. And they made sure that we knew when the different holidays came. We would go down when the ss went to sleep and the lights went out. We would go down from our bunk beds and whoever remembered the prayers, we would have a little ceremony, a little service. And we finished by whispering the Hatikvah. Until today when I hear the Hatikvah I see myself, standing in the dark, and singing it, in a whisper.[66]

Gerda F. describes her own unique memory of a group experience. It is deeply personal ("I see myself, standing in the dark") and at the same time a shared event ("We would go down from our bunk beds"). This fragment is also simultaneously broadly observational ("we knew when the different holidays came") but includes the details of her environment of confinement ("the ss went to sleep," "bunk beds," "we whispered"). For Gerda F., her memory interweaves her own interior feelings with her sense of how her campmates experienced their own feelings while noting each separately.

Lena M. uses different terms but her memory extends Gerda's account.

> Lena M.: [There was no religious] service. But what we had, we had, we knew when the holidays were.
> Interviewer: How did you know this?
> Lena M.: We had five sisters. Which were very, very Orthodox. They were together. They lived by us, below us, next to us. And somehow—their name was Halbersztajn—and somehow they knew when this was. So we used to pray. They knew when the holidays. They knew when [it was] Saturday. They didn't eat on Saturday.[67]

These short fragments also speak to the specific deprivations of the lack of space or time for religious practice and the lack of access to knowledge of the Jewish calendar for that year. As Alan Rosen has shown, Jews in spaces of persecution devised ways of remaining conscious of time passing and of marking holidays in some way, to combat the phenomenon of "camp time," that is, the sense—intentionally cultivated by the camp system to disempower inmates—that time has no meaning.[68]

Rosen moves this refusal to allow Jews knowledge of calendars and dates to the forefront of Nazi persecution. He also shows how Jewish calendars functioned to sustain a "continuity" of a "Jewish world" in the face of its denial.[69] In light of Rosen's work, Gerda's evocative memory of finding the "very Orthodox girls in the camp" and arranging a furtive ceremony with them and Lena M.'s vivid depiction of "five sisters" informing others of the holiday are expressions of this very impulse to continuity.

The excerpts from Lena M. and Gerda F. offer a different type of "social life" from practices documented by many scholars of social relations inside camps and ghettos during the Holocaust. Gerda F. and Lena M. reference a broader community, a "we" that was able to recognize and receive gestures supporting an unsanctioned Jewish world inside the barracks. This is not to say that religious observance was frequently or easily accessed; it was instead partial, improvised, and dependent on proximity to particular campmates. However, their testimony speaks to their capacity (as they remember it) to sustain their awareness of Jewishness as more than a personal identity and as more than a reference point for transactions and allies.

COERCED LABOR, PERPETRATION, AND LIVED EXPERIENCE

Historians have long known about the specific dynamics of Nazi forced labor policy from the perspective of the perpetrators. Marc Buggeln and Michael Wildt, for example, have demonstrated how the course of the war opened up more possibilities of using Jewish, Soviet prisoner-of-war, and Gentile Polish labor more extensively and strategically by 1942.[70] Adam Tooze showed that Hitler's insistence on rearmament restructured the German economy and created demands for labor—and compulsory labor requirements—long before 1942.[71] Several foundational studies of individual camps emphasize the camp itself as a specific vehicle for perpetrator intentions, actions, and sources, while taking the experience of the victims of persecution into account, as in work by Marc Buggeln, Wolfgang Kirstein, Karin Orth, and Felicja Karay and the Auschwitz study by Deborah Dwork and Robert Van Pelt.[72] Works by Wolf Gruner, Jörg Osterloh and Markus Nesselrodt analyze coerced labor as policy with sources and effects inside and beyond the camp as a site of persecution, that is, affecting Jewish communities beyond those forced into labor.[73]

Most significant is Christopher Browning's pathbreaking work *Remembering Survival: Inside a Nazi Slave-Labor Camp*.[74] Browning interweaves survivor testimony together with perpetrator documents to trace how a specific camp, Starachowice, functioned. Methodologically sensitive to the nature of testimony, Browning's book positions lived experience as recalled by survivors to not just enhance but at times challenge accepted historical understandings of events.

While the Schmelt system based in East Upper Silesia with its camps throughout Silesia and the Sudetenland should be viewed within this historiography of camp labor, at the same time it constituted an atypical form of Nazi forced labor persecution. As Christopher Browning noted in *Nazi Policy, Jewish Workers, German Killers*, Jews in Sosnowiec and its surrounding towns had a greater degree of mobility than those in the Generalgouvernement and even than those in Warthegau, with implications for the attitudes of local police.[75] Stephan Lehnstaedt argues that the Schmelt system until mid-1943 is best thought of as an institutionalization of a "hybrid type" of coerced labor, in which Jews had access to a small amount of compensation, an unusual degree of physical mobility, and social welfare services through the Jewish Council of Elders while being required to work.[76] Wolf Gruner shows that the Schmelt system operated separately from the *SS-Wirtschafts- und Verwaltungs-Hauptamt* (WVHA) in maintaining a coerced labor regime that controlled more than fifty thousand Jews by 1943.[77] An important context is geographical location: scholars have shown that the annexed territories, which gave German speakers citizenship but which were not governed identically to the Reich itself, have their own complex dynamics.[78] Relatedly, many of the Schmelt work sites (including those in the Trautenau region) were in the Sudetenland, and Volker Zimmermann shows that the Reich rearmament push led to a massive economic windfall—and consequent demand for labor—for local Sudeten German businesses already in late 1938, that is, after annexation.[79] In sum, the Schmelt system was a very early exploiter of Jewish labor; people were sent away in groups to work beginning in late 1940.[80]

The present book moves forward from this scholarship to understand the Schmelt organization and its transformation into the Gross-Rosen subcamp system through the eyes of those most affected and victimized by coerced labor. How did these girls and young women experience the pathway into coerced labor? How did they respond to separation from family, displacement to a distant location, and surviving in the face of severely limited food and medical care? How did they adjust to work on the factory floor, after growing up with very different understandings of what their future would be? In pursuing these questions, it draws on scholarship that engages with the variety of ways Jews reacted to the unprecedented scale and the specific forms of Nazi persecution. Evgeny Finkel, in his *Ordinary Jews*, demonstrates that survival strategies differed according to situation, from cooperation to compliance to evasion to resistance, and none of these strategies was passive.[81] His comparison of Jews with different political experiences (such as Communist party members in the Białystok ghetto) in different locations shows that past experiences as well as the specific nature of each setting, such as whether a ghetto was open or closed, mattered as Jews "assessed" the risks and benefits of their choices. Elissa Bemporad suggests the Jewish women may have worked with different understandings of risk and benefit than the men in Finkel's study.[82] Natalia Aleksiun, focusing on the experience of Jews in hiding, argues that strategic decisions were embedded in social relations and frequently involved mobilizing social networks; among these were well-organized bodies such as Żegota but also family members and individuals, Jewish and Gentile.[83]

Centering testimonies in the search for a better understanding of the individual choices pursued inside the distinctive Schmelt system and its labor camps in the Trautenau region requires a familiarity with the impact of Nazi occupation on Zagłębie, the region used by Schmelt for Jewish labor. In Zagłębie, what "being sent for labor" meant to Jews differed from what it meant to perpetrators. The Polish historians Aleksandra Namysło and Andrzej Strzelecki as well as the German historian Sybille Steinbacher provide the specifics of how the Schmelt system of local ss officers working with the Jewish Council of Elders created the specific context within which Jewish families sought to survive.[84] Camps such as the factory work sites in the Sudetenland (of which Trautenau and its suburbs were a part) were originally (in 1940 and 1941) not named as such; survivors remember that "I was called for work," in part because the Zagłębie region was home to many small "workshops" inside the cities of Sosnowiec and Będzin from early 1941 to 1942.[85] Jews employed in

INTRODUCTION

these local workshops lived in their original family homes and left every day to work in production supporting war industries or the needs of the SS authorities, such as tailor shops; they received a small wage (which had to be partially given over to the Jewish Council) and could switch workplaces, as Lehnstaedt documents.[86] While some streets in Sosnowiec and Będzin were banned to Jews and a curfew instituted, a substantial number had work passes and could move about. As Lehnstaedt notes, this system (in place until 1943) raises interesting questions about coerced labor, forced labor, and slave labor, categories developed after the war for use in compensation claims.[87] For the Jews in Zagłębie, these processes were experienced initially, in 1939 and 1940, as persecution, as the regime took Jewish property away without compensation, but quickly thereafter as opportunities to earn small amounts of money, remain indoors during the day sheltered from street violence and harassment, negotiate side deals with the owners, and establish oneself as having value for local businesses.

Thus, to offer further conceptual clarity on the Schmelt system, it was a coerced labor system initiated by Himmler and designed as an anti-Jewish initiative to also take advantage of the economic resources and skilled labor in East Upper Silesia (of which Zagłębie was a part) by creating a bounded territory that controlled movement in or out. It is best seen as grafted onto the improvised workshop practices (interwoven with the Treuhandler system, in which ethnic Germans were given Jewish companies and shops, but still used the former owners to manage them) already existing in late 1939 and 1940 and the employment office system already used in the Reich for assigning labor.[88] The Nazi regime's annexation of East Upper Silesia meant that Zagłębie was not subject to the policies of the Generalgouvernement. At the same time, it was not subject to policies identical to the Reich. East Upper Silesia was an "annexed territory" with its own chronology and its own logic of Nazi persecution. Through Himmler's appointment of Schmelt, the Jews of Zagłębie became caught in what scholar Andrea Rudorff calls a net made of camps ("*Netz von Lagern*").[89] Schmelt's organization did not physically build any of these camps; they grew from the establishment of barracks for workers by businesses. These camps then evolved over time, from partnerships with the Schmelt SS to "forced labor camps" and then, in early 1944, to concentration camps that were registered formally as subcamps of the Gross-Rosen concentration camp.

The choice to focus this study on survivors from the Trautenau-region camps is informed by the research of scholars Miroslav Kryl and Ludmila Chládková, who developed the definitive study of this specific collection of camps.[90] Kryl and Chládková were the first to shift from understanding these sites as subcamps of Gross-Rosen to describing them as barracks built (or repurposed) to serve specific factories and businesses that existed prior to the war and that took advantage of the Schmelt system of Jewish labor, clarifying that there was little functional connection to Gross-Rosen itself. The Gross-Rosen Archive lists ninety-seven official subcamps of Gross-Rosen, created at various times between 1940 and 1944; a majority were Schmelt system camps clustered near each other in the territory of the Sudetenland south of the Gross-Rosen camp.[91] This collection includes many beyond those in the Trautenau region specifically. In Kryl and Chládková's approach, camps are organized by the name of the town in which they were located but they are also distinguished by the name of the private companies using Jewish labor. Using their documentation as a basis, it becomes clear that Parschnitz, named after the suburb of Trautenau in which it was located, eventually functioned as one of the largest of these subcamps, housing by 1944 more than two thousand Jewish girls and women who were the labor force for three factories based in Trautenau. It was connected to the smaller Ober Altstadt, a mile and a half away, where girls and women worked for two factories, also based in Trautenau. Prior to 1944, multiple small barracks housing Jewish female forced labor for private companies existed in Trautenau, Parschnitz, and Ober Altstadt, in addition to Schatzlar, Bernsdorf, and Gabersdorf, all within fifteen miles of each other. In spatial terms, the city of Trautenau was an all-female hub for the Schmelt system.

The Trautenau-region firms made military-grade thread or cloth for the German army. Both Jewish and Gentile workers engaged in processing raw material (flax) into usable thread, which required combing, washing, spinning, and other aspects of mechanical textile work. The Jewish girls and women were marched to their work sites early each morning and back to the barracks each evening, one group sometimes passing another en route.[92] As their later testimonies affirm, they became familiar with the names of each of the family firms dominant in the Trautenau region, documented by Kryl and Chládková: Alois Haase, based in the suburb of Parschnitz; J. A. Kluge, based in the suburb Ober Altstadt; the Walzel Brothers, based in the city of Trautenau itself; and Ignaz Etrich, with multiple sites eventually diversifying into manufacturing airplane parts as well as textiles. They worked side by side with the longtime local employees of these firms, non-Jewish women who spoke Czech or German, who continued to earn the low wages characteristic of textile work, and who at times silently left them food in the nooks and crannies of the work site and its machinery.

According to historian Bella Gutterman, by the end of the war, 2,500 girls and women were in coerced labor at Parschnitz, the concentration camp that evolved from the Trautenau work camps, 791 at Ober Altstadt, and 373 at other Trautenau barracks.[93] The Gross-Rosen Archive counts 1,400 in Parschnitz, 950 in Ober Altstadt, and an additional 925 in three peripheral labor camps within a few miles of Trautenau, Schatzlar, Gabersdorf, and Bernsdorf.[94] These numbers do not include the hundreds who were housed in the barracks in Parschnitz and Ober Altstadt while in transit to elsewhere in 1945. By the dates that the Soviet army liberated them on May 8 and 9, 1945—a point at which these work sites had been converted to concentration camps and there was almost no food left—there were more than 3,000 Jewish girls and women living as coerced laborers in the Trautenau region. These numbers also do not reflect the fact that the Schmelt system routinely replaced the many girls and women who, while working, became sick, arrived or became pregnant, or resisted the factory or camp regime. At times the factory directors, working with the Sosnowitz SS and Gestapo, simply sent them back to their family homes in Zagłębie; at other times, the SS sent them to Auschwitz-Birkenau to be selected out again for labor or killed. The precise numbers of Jewish girls and women who were caught up in the work camp system is unknown, but likely much higher than 3,000.

A NOTE ON SOURCES AND LANGUAGE

The Shoah Foundation testimonies taken in the 1990s are the heart of this book, but they alone cannot answer all questions about the various aspects of the journey of the Zagłębie Jews through the coerced labor experience. While testimonies can be quite lengthy—sometimes only one hour, sometimes six hours of tapes—the speaker can offer full context only intermittently. Her priority is her own experience as it matters to her at the time of testimony-giving. Taking this into account, this book provides additional documentation periodically to connect these experiences with findings in the scholarship regarding the Nazi regime in East Upper Silesia, the local social and economic context of the Trautenau factories in the Sudetenland, the external events that prompted changes in the work sites and their conversion into subcamps of the Gross-Rosen concentration camp, and the connection with Auschwitz. It integrates primary perpetrator documents from archives in Germany (Bundesarchiv Berlin-Lichterfelde), Poland (State Archives of Gross-Rosen), Trutnov in the Czech Republic (Trutnov District Archive), Zámrsk in the Czech Republic (Zámrsk Regional Archives), London (Wiener Library), and Washington, DC (United States Holocaust Memorial Museum). While keeping the Shoah Foundation testimony-giving practice at the center, the book also incorporates testimonies from other archives besides the Shoah Foundation, including self-published memoirs (accessed in the New York Public Library), diaries, correspondence, the initiatives in Germany in the 1960s and 1970s to prosecute perpetrators, immediate postwar depositions and witness statements, *yizkhor* books, and nonfiction personal treatments such as *Sala's Gift* by Ann Kirschner. In fact, the cities and towns of Zagłębie, such as Sosnowiec, Będzin, Chrzanów, Zawiercie, Olkusz, Dąbrowa, Czeladź, Jaworzno, and Modrzejów, are the setting for many texts—some well known, some recent—that could not fit into the scope of this study, such as Art Spiegelman's *Maus*; Menachem Kaiser's *Plunder: A Memoir of Family Property and Nazi Treasure*; Rutka Laskier's diary, *Rutka's Notebook: A Voice from the Holocaust*; Tomasz Grząślewicz's historical guide to Sosnowiec; and Bartosz Bednarczuk's documentary, *(Nie)Zapomniani*.

Sustained throughout is the centering of the Shoah Foundation testimony-givers as producers of knowledge, who not only offer "perspective" and "personal experience" but also carefully considered insights that potentially reframe and deepen the understanding of the labor camp in the Holocaust. At times these insights are presented as fully thought out. At other times they emerge in a more fragmented process, from conflict with interviewers, misunderstandings, hesitations, and emotionally charged, unplanned reactions to remembered events. These processes are also affected by the frequent choice of testimony-givers to speak not one of their native languages, but in the language of their children and grandchildren, so that the testimony artifact could be accessed by future generations. All of these aspects of testimony practice are invaluable modes of knowledge creation. Testimony excerpts are presented verbatim and include words and phrases in other languages. The testimonies selected were those in English, with the exception of one in German and one in Hebrew, so that my own translation into English would not be necessary—it would not function as yet another mediating structure influencing meaning. To allow a picture of a collective experience to emerge while retaining individual voice—in other words, to depict the multivocality of the experience—I used first names and first initial of last names only for each testimony-giver. This approach, while unusual, allows the specificity of a particular experience to be expressed while at the same time choosing not to develop full personas.

The position of testimony-givers as knowledge producers also informs this book's approach to place-names. Nazi perpetrators renamed the locations in Zagłębie, but because the survivors themselves used the prewar names in their testimonies, such as "Sosnowiec" instead of the Germanized "Sosnowitz," this study also uses the prewar names. When the topic is a site or practice of persecution, the text uses the perpetrator label, for example, Sosnowitz *Durchgangslager*. A more complex situation are the place-names for the coerced labor and concentration camps. In today's Czech Republic, they have Czech names as well as a majority of Czech-speaking residents; thus, Ober Altstadt is Horní Staré Město. However, in the interwar period these places were populated by both local German and Czech speakers, and German speakers were in the majority. At the time of the annexation of Northern Bohemia as "Sudetenland," Nazi authorities just kept the German versions in place. While not a perfect solution, this book uses the German "Trautenau" instead of the Czech "Trutnov" to describe the region in which most of these coerced labor sites were located, as well as the German Bernsdorf, Schatzlar, Gabersdorf, Parschnitz, and Ober Altstadt. These are also the labels used by the testimony-givers themselves.

ORGANIZATION OF THE BOOK

The first chapter of the book draws on testimonies given by survivors from the Zagłębie region to present Jewish girlhood as they recall it, including their understandings of family and parental love. Because of the ages of the testimony-givers at the moment they were separated from their parents, their strategies of coping, evading, and resisting (in Evgeny Finkel's formulation) were deeply influenced by their complex sense of their position in their family. Between ages twelve and twenty, unmarried, most of them continued to seek guidance and care from parents while simultaneously taking responsibility for younger siblings, the children of older siblings, and food acquisition in 1939 and 1940. Each decision seemed to them, as testimony-giving adults, to be an opportunity to prove themselves, although the Schmelt system defined their options very narrowly in this regard. This chapter also documents the significant function of the Sosnowitz *Durchgangslager* in assembling Jewish labor; as the testimonies indicate, this site of persecution became a site of exchange, illicit transactions, and communication between those leaving and the family that remained at home.

Chapter 2 diverges from testimony to develop the historical and institutional context of the wartime experience of the Jewish girls and women caught up in the Schmelt coerced labor system. The private companies that became sites of persecution were longtime family firms, founders of their city, Trautenau, and its surrounding smaller towns. This chapter presents the position of these firms in the growth of Sudeten German nationalism and the effect of the annexation of Northern Bohemia/Sudetenland to Germany in October 1938. It then turns to Poland, and Zagłębie in particular, and documents the invasion and occupation of East Upper Silesia and the creation of the Schmelt coerced labor system. Drawing on perpetrator documents, secondary literature, and legal proceedings, it explains the transition from work sites with barracks to *Zwangsarbeitslager* (coerced labor camps) and then to concentration camps. Parallel to this process was the increasing influence of the Inspectorate of the Concentration Camps (Department D-II), which took over labor assignment from Schmelt in 1944.

Chapter 3 approaches the work site as a social world, influenced by the presence of Gentile coworkers, the requirements of textile work, and the encounter of young Jewish women with the everyday life of persecution through labor: twelve-hour days, very little food or medicine, tight restrictions on communication and movement, and the constant threat of physical punishment. The small work camps scattered through the

Sudetenland near the border with East Upper Silesia were also places of employment for local Czech and German laborers. The interaction between the Gentile and Jewish women was significant, in that Czech coworkers frequently provided additional food. The complexity of the machinery meant that there were many hiding places and means of surreptitious communication. The design of the Schmelt system—to move labor quickly to where it was needed—created a flexibility and possibility for negotiation, as some girls and women switched camps to be near sisters or cousins.

Chapters 1 through 3 focus on survivors from the main work sites near the city of Trautenau: Parschnitz, Ober Altstadt, and Trautenau itself. These sites would eventually become the concentration camps Parschnitz and Ober Altstadt, and house almost three thousand girls and women by the end of 1944. However, even smaller, peripheral camps existed within twelve miles of Trautenau. The fourth chapter engages with testimony from Schatzlar, Gabersdorf, and Bernsdorf. The testimony-givers from these camps add to the growing picture of how coerced labor and confinement were experienced by young Jewish women. In addition, this chapter pulls from the Shoah Foundation testimonies to examine more closely testimony-giving practice and how techniques of testimony interact with memory and expectations of what a Holocaust narrative should be.

Chapter 5 uses testimony to explore the impact of two significant institutional changes in the camps in the Trautenau region. First, in late 1943 Himmler instituted a shift in the Schmelt system, increasing SS surveillance and control and transforming these *Zwangsarbeitslager* into concentration camps under the administrative purview of Gross-Rosen. For the girls and women living in these camps, the change meant the periodic presence of male SS officers who required them to undress in front of them. Testimony-givers remember this presence as traumatizing; they had been able to wear their own clothes, had been guarded exclusively by females, and had not endured naked selections prior to this moment. Second, in mid-1944 authorities at Auschwitz sent groups of Jewish women from the Hungarian-occupied territories to the camps in the Trautenau region. These "Hungarian girls" had undergone a brutal selection process on the Auschwitz-Birkenau ramp as well as several days or weeks of deprivation, humiliation, and violence inside Birkenau. Their arrival was the first time the girls and women from Zagłębie understood the extreme nature of the Nazi project against European Jews, although not its scope.

Chapter 6 applies the recent scholarship on "prisoner society" and the ethics of care to the social relations inside the labor camps. Care was given and received among those imprisoned, but also among guards, work supervisors, and coworkers and the Jewish girls and women. An ethic of sharing food, requesting favors for campmates, and protecting the fragile and ill developed for some. Additionally, the Schmelt system allowed families living at home in Zagłębie to send letters, postcards, and packages to the laborers. These were cherished as objects symbolizing the connection with parental care and as resources to be traded for nourishment. Some survivors remember cultivated social initiatives such as songs, plays, and knowledge-sharing, possible because the barracks did not have a Gentile guard present in the evenings and at night. Girls and young women created their own objects, including *pamiętniki*, or small memory books in which friends wrote messages and signed their names, as if they were not trapped in a concentration camp but possibly able to sustain some of the practices of "normal" girlhood.

In chapter 7 the themes of maleness, masculinity, longing for intimacy, and the recovery of a Jewish family life are explored through testimony. This chapter is organized around three themes: memories of male work supervisors or maintenance employees as helpful, paternal "uncles"; memories that sexualize the prisoners of war who periodically worked to repair factory machinery; and memories of Jewish men on a death march who spent the night in the Haase factory in Parschnitz, an episode in which the testimony-givers remember their longing for connection with Jewish men in particular and their shock at the inability of these particular Jewish men to communicate in any way. The hunger of the starving men, their degraded condition, and the closeness of death were devastating to observe, especially as many of the young women had been hoping for the possibility of rebuilding family life after the war was over.

Chapter 8 presents the narratives of "liberation" offered by the testimonies of the Zagłębie girls and women, as well as the "Hungarian girls" who were with them from mid-1944 until May 1945. Returning to the theme of separation from family, the testimonies show the conflicted nature of the moment of liberation; the self-sustaining fantasies of an intact family—or any family at all—had to be confronted. The withdrawal of the ss, factory directors and supervisors, and the Czech and German coworkers added up to a disorienting vacuum. There were no death marches for these camps. Instead, the girls and women faced the arrival of Soviet soldiers, who brought food, medicine, freedom, and the threat of sexual assault. Many of the survivors remember retreating back to the barracks, blocking entrances at night for protection. Others went into the local towns and even local homes for food and to acquire any items they could, sometimes along with the soldiers. But the need to know for certain whether family survived exerted a powerful pull. Many testimony-givers experienced yet another trauma at facing the emptiness of the family home or the home occupied by strangers or even former neighbors.

Chapter 9 is a concluding section that reemphasizes testimony-givers' own insistence on themselves as producers of knowledge rather than objects of study or damaged victims. Their narrative strategies, interaction with the modalities of testimony practice, and willingness to allow their emotion and vulnerability to add even more meaning to their words create a rich, in-depth explanation of how coerced labor functioned on the ground, through and with the bodies of real people. Attending carefully to the content of testimony as well as testimony practice provides us with the precise cuts the Nazi project made into the social fabric of Jewish life in Europe. In these testimonies we encounter a complex social world of confinement, rendered by those speaking in terms that are detailed and personal, on the one hand, and expansive and revealing of extended social relations, on the other. It is a world in which fearful and hungry people developed their systems for sustaining a sense of themselves as children, as women, and as Jews. This world has some of the elements we, the present-day audience, have come to expect in survivor testimony: hope and despair, strength and weakness, clever strategies of evasion and heartbreaking admissions of betrayal and fear. But just as importantly, these testimonies also confound our expectations and refuse our easy sympathies.

CHAPTER 1

Jewish Girlhood and Jewish Survival in Zagłębie

In her pathbreaking book *Between Dignity and Despair: Jewish Life in Nazi Germany*, Marion Kaplan directs our attention to the early and mid-1930s in Germany, when Nazi policies gradually undermined the place of Jews in Germany's social fabric.[1] Delving into the life stories of Jewish women and their families, Kaplan documents the encroachment of Nazism into Jewish private life. Nazi laws, practices, and rhetoric, combined with the indifference of non-Jews, all contributed to an excision of Jewish communities from Germany's moral and social world. In Germany, Jews went through a "social death" prior to their arrests and deportations, facilitated by the rest of Germany's citizens.[2] Kaplan shows us how Jews attempted to sustain a "semblance of their previous daily lives," even as their isolation and displacement increased over time. She also demonstrates the role of emotion in this response. The "despair" of her title is interwoven throughout the memoirs she cites; feelings of abandonment and hopelessness constituted factors shaping behavior.[3]

This dynamic of Nazi intrusion into private life and its implications for how Jews shaped their survival strategies is an apt framework for understanding the early years of the girls and women from Zagłębie who entered into coerced textile labor in the Trautenau region. As the testimonies show, the Jews who lived in this region of Poland along the German border were aware of what was occurring in Germany in the 1930s. Friends and relatives brought news, the Jewish press covered events, and refugees flowed into Poland when the German government expelled Jews with Polish citizenship who had migrated to Germany in the 1938 "Polenaktion."[4] In fact, the expulsions created a border crisis near Zagłębie because Polish state authorities initially refused to accept the expellees. For the older children in particular, the Polenaktion was their first understanding of the nature of the Nazi regime and its attempts to undermine Jewish senses of place and identity. The Zagłębie basin included some Jewish families with relatives and connections to Germany, who spoke German as their primary language, and who kept careful track of political changes there, but the majority of Jews had backgrounds in Poland and spoke Yiddish and Polish at home.[5]

The Polenaktion suggested a political, systemic anti-Jewishness that was overlaid onto a preexisting antisemitism in Poland.[6] Jewish communities had responded to Poland's antisemitic policies and the attitudes of non-Jewish Poles by creating close-knit neighborhoods with synagogues, schools, and youth organizations. As Kenneth Moss has shown, by 1936 many intellectuals and activists who were not among the youth had begun to withdraw from active political engagement in Poland's political scene.[7] But among the young, Będzin and Sosnowiec were characterized by vibrant Zionist, Bund, and leftist organizations, and organizations such as Hashomir Hatzair, Gordonia, and Betar.[8] Most of the survivors who recalled their childhoods in Sosnowiec, Będzin, and the assorted small towns nearby remember Polish antisemitism in the 1930s as name-calling and playground fights. Some had a number of non-Jewish playmates and neighbors. Others felt quite vulnerable to physical and social ostracism and brutality.

> Sonia S.: [twelve years old in 1937] There was fighting a lot with the, with the non-Jewish girls. They called us "dirty Jew," "go to Palestine."[9]
>
> Berta P.: [thirteen years old in 1937] I was called many times Jew-this or Jew-that. I was told to ignore this.[10]
>
> Brenda R.: [fourteen years old in 1937] And because I was a Jew, they don't like me. They hit me always. In the Polish school.[11]
>
> Masha S.: [nine years old in 1937] When they [Christian Poles] came out from the church we had a lot of trouble. When, because there was a lot of talk. Not nice talk. I don't know what they said there [in the church]. And sometimes were fights and, uh, windows, you know, knocked in, and so.[12]

Rosalie S. remembers antisemitism as an intentional, organized campaign in Poland.

> Rosalie S.: [fourteen years old in 1937] We encountered
> antisemitism in every step of life . . . They were organized.
> In certain places they were marching in front of Jewish stores
> with posters . . . and windows were being broken. It was—
> that's the way it was.[13]

It appears that the urban public life and dense housing of ethnically mixed Sosnowiec led to a day-to-day familiarity among some Jews and some non-Jews in that city in particular—an intimacy that did not preclude antisemitic attitudes. In her interview, Masha S. responds strongly to the term "socialize."

> Interviewer: Did your parents ever socialize with any non-Jewish
> people?
> Masha S.: [*with an animated expression*] Yes! This is it! You see,
> if you got to know the people. If you knew each other on one-
> to-one basis it was completely different.[14]

Shoshana L. recalls relations as collectively "friendly."

> Shoshana L.: We lived with them very, we lived with the Polish
> people. And very, be friendly with each other. Very friendly.
> At that time I didn't under—I didn't feel like they be anti-me,
> you know, how you say, antisemitic, you know? Because we've
> been on very friendly terms with everybody.[15]

The German army's invasion of Poland in September 1939 affected the residents of Zagłębie profoundly, as it did in other regions of the country. These cities and towns were not far from the border points at which the Germans entered Polish territory. Sosnowiec, Będzin, and other communities experienced air bombardment, Polish soldiers in retreat, and civilians seeking shelter, all in the first days of September.[16] By the second week, Nazi authorities were conducting random street killings and other tactics designed to rapidly intimidate the population. In this particular sense, unlike the gradual "social death" of Germany's Jews discussed by Kaplan, the imposition of Nazi laws in September was sudden and shocking. Terror tactics were accompanied by a rapid reorganization of local social understandings, as Jews were immediately demoted by the removal of civil protections, local Germans elevated and placed into civil administrative positions, and relationships with non-Jewish Poles criminalized. As in Kaplan's study, Jews responded by attempting to keep families intact, preserve traditions, and maintain some kind of routine. They did so even as Nazi practices penetrated the synagogue, the home, and even Jewish bodies.

This intense period of trauma put survivor memories of family life prior to the invasion in sharper relief than they perhaps would have been otherwise. Most testimony-givers pose their early prewar years in juxtaposition to September 1939, in part due to the structure of the Shoah Foundation questions. Many recall times of stability and security, marked by the presence of parents and siblings, and shaped by a reliable rhythm of school, holidays, and faith. Some remember migration, either from other parts of Poland or from Germany. For all, the months in 1939 prior to that September day was the last time they were able to take for granted the structure of their family life, in whatever form it was. This knowledge influences how they represent the past in their recorded testimonies. While the Shoah Foundation interview questions are structured to elicit factual information about prewar Jewish life, the interviewees use their answers to express their experience of a specifically Jewish reality prior to the occupation while also honoring—and often grieving—the loss of that reality.

The affect of almost all speakers is pervaded with longing; at least one survivor, Rose B., begins crying immediately at the start of the interview.[17] In the interview with Berta P., the interviewer hopes to capture some of the day-to-day rhythms of prewar home life:

> Interviewer: Do you remember a special food or dish your mother used to make for you that was one of your favorites?
> Berta P.: Ach! My mother was a very good cook. I miss her . . . [*seems to be ready to name a dish but stops*] I miss her . . . Not only her cooking. But I was, I'm missing her forever.
> Interviewer: Do you remember your best friend's name?[18]

In this case, Berta P. resisted the reduction of her memory to food and holidays by first narratively admitting the topic of cooking, but then creating a space for a deeper longing to be articulated. "I miss her [dish]" is replaced with "I miss her." The interviewer redirects the questioning away from grief over the "forever" loss of Berta P.'s mother.

In another kind of shift, testimony-giving in the present (for those speaking) generated a revaluation of their childhood home and family life, marked by vivid images and sensory associations:

> Esther L.: I remember the beautiful tablecloth. It was a, like a plush, only was used on the High Holidays. On the tables.
> Interviewer: Can you describe it? What color was it?
> Esther L.: It was red. With different colors in. Small, like art piece—something—I remember this, everything, every holiday my mother put this tablecloth. It was something that means [something] to her. I didn't understood at this time what this mean.[19]

> Esther S.: My father manufactured hard candy. And, uh, it was a very sweet life, with all those candies [*laughing*].[20]

The details offered in the testimonies do not uniformly idealize family life. The prewar portion of the testimonies emphasize the stability of knowing where one belongs, much more than any imagined lack of conflict or perfect harmony; in some instances, even this sense of belonging is only partial. For example, Ann G.'s mother died when she was five and she grew up being passed among relatives. She ran away from her father and stepmother's home and ended up living with a cousin in exchange for "cleaning and washing and cooking."[21] Ann G. was then ejected from this home once Nazi policies created widespread food shortages for Zagłębie's Jews in 1939 and 1940. The interviewer asks about her specific memories of the holidays, as most Shoah Foundation interviews do.

> Ann G.: [*long pause and slightly disdainful expression*] Sometimes it was nice. But it still—I was missing, we were missing the mother.[22]

Her coerced labor experience is overshadowed by the deep grief and abandonment of her very early years and she makes no effort to hide this.

Frymeta F. remembers a large, caring family that was shattered immediately after the German occupation. She was left caring for younger siblings at age fourteen:

> Frymeta F.: [My] father went out to bring us some food. And he never came home. They caught him in the street and we never saw our father again.[23]
>
> Interviewer: When? When was this?
>
> Frymeta F.: This was, uh, 1939.

In her testimony, Frymeta F. attempts to piece together as an older adult what she had been aware of or not aware of at her age at the time. It appears that at the time, adults in her life kept troubling information from her, leaving her disoriented as the occupation created even more catastrophes for the family. She is still grappling with gaps in information as an adult.

> Interviewer: Where was your mother?[24]
>
> Frymeta F.: My mother wasn't home. She was in the hospital.
>
> Interviewer: What, what happened?
>
> Frymeta F.: I think, hmm, she went to give birth for another child. And she never came home. She died in the hospital. Or something like that.

The interviewer is taken aback until Frymeta F. makes it clear that neighbors had decided to keep the news of her mother's death from her and her older sister, and she had to piece it together on her own from overheard whispers. She and her sister cared for three very young siblings in the family apartment for a few months until the SS arrived and took both Frymeta F. and her sister to the Trautenau-region camps in 1940.

Testimony-givers describe the September 1939 invasion by the German army in ways that remind us that they were children at the time.

> Eta B.: [nine years old in 1939] I thought it would be exciting to see a war.[25]
>
> Shoshana L.: [twelve years old in 1939] It was a sunny day. We could hear music in the street. And everyone ran out! And they said, we could see people marching, people going, you know, with music and soldiers marching in, so easily with, you know, with the banners—what today you even see—with banners, swastikas, and they be, you know, nice dressed black and green with swastikas on their arms, and with confidence they are

> marching in like never. And we just didn't suspect this kind of thing. And everyone was watching.
>
> Interviewer: When was that?
>
> Shoshana L.: That was 1939. 1939. And so easy they marched in. Everyone watched, watched, watched. And we stupid children. I was one of them. I run up to them. . . . They marched to the school where I used to go . . . we children went to the other side, to [secretly] watch them.[26]
>
> Rita R.: [eleven years old in 1939] I didn't understand. About war.[27]

During the first week of the occupation many Jewish families in the Zagłębie region attempted to immediately relocate eastward. Most had relatives in nearby towns, so went on foot or by horse and wagon. Some older siblings attempted to travel alone further eastward as individuals to enter Soviet-held territory. Historians Natalia Aleksiun and Eliyana Adler analyze the experiences of Jewish families who succeeded in crossing the border and who endured the war in the Soviet Union; Adler's book, *Survival on the Margins: Polish Jewish Refugees in the Wartime Soviet Union*, documents not only the lives of Polish Jews who fled the German occupation by traveling into Soviet territory but also those deported by Soviet forces at various points and postwar decisions to return.[28] As Adler notes, the 1939 invasion forced Jews in Poland "to at least contemplate whether to stay or go" and this decision-making was deeply influenced by the precise nature of local violence.[29] For the Jews of Zagłębie, the aerial bombardment of the very first days was a powerful reason to temporarily flee eastward, and the violence of the occupation, detailed in the following extract, was another. Most of the testimony-givers who ended up in the Schmelt labor system were too young to be part of this decision-making, although they remember family members coming and going, hurried packing, movement, overnight stays with unfamiliar relatives, and older siblings who disappeared. Each of the excerpts phrases this moment differently.

> Sonia S.: I got up, and I saw my father, my mother, they were packing fast some clothes, some things, and they said that we have to run because the Germans are coming.[30]

Yetta F.: Chaos! Pure chaos. The minute the Germans came in . . . they took over. Running into houses taking people out.³¹

Esther S.: A lot of people start—ran away from the city. It was like a ghost town. We couldn't go no place. We had a big family. It was very hard to—[*becomes tearful*] to wrap up things and go.³²

Mania R.: On the way, they were bombing. And I remember we were walking together with the Polish soldiers. With the, with the—it was, it was a mess! It was a mess. And the airplanes came. So we laid down in the field.³³

Sonia S.: [*speaking about her brothers*] One of them ran away, to Russia.³⁴

To see more clearly the way age at the time of persecution shapes these memories, it is helpful to compare the testimonies with an adult's version, Paweł Wiederman's *Płowa Bestia*.³⁵ This invaluable documentary text had been neglected until Polish scholars such as Aleksandra Namysło and Jacek Proszyk (among others) redirected attention to it in the 2000s.³⁶ Wiederman was a prominent Jewish educator in Sosnowiec. He worked with the welfare section of the Jewish Council of Elders and later went into hiding when local authorities began a second mass deportation in the summer of 1943. *Płowa Bestia* captures Wiederman's memory of the events of the Nazi occupation as he experienced them, the descriptions vivid and detailed. Rounded up on the street with a group of neighbors in the first week of the occupation, Wiederman writes:

> The armed blonde beasts in their helmets launched an unbelievable roar, and at the same time begin to wildly shoot their machine guns. People were falling over each other; then the wild animals rushed at them, brutally beating them until they lost consciousness. "God," I prayed quietly, "put an end to our troubles." And my neighbor, overhearing my prayer, whispered in my ear, "What we are living today is just a prelude—it is the beginning of great persecutions that will be thrust upon us for many years." Then suddenly a new order: "Turn around and kneel!" Not everyone could understand the command in the chaos.

People again stumbled and fell over each other, and the beast did not get tired of thrashing innocent victims with whips, rubber or leather.[37]

Wiederman's version is one in which adults whisper to each other, attempting to guess the motives of the occupiers. He notices that the German actions and words were designed to cause confusion, thus creating an opportunity for physical violence. The impression left is of an irrational, unpredictable political force that cannot be negotiated with or questioned. Throughout Wiederman's book his adult sensibility presents the occupation as the encounter between an immoral, ruthless force and a shocked Jewish community seeking to sustain its own moral universe in response. In later chapters he details the development of the Jewish Council of Elders as one of these responses.

In contrast, testimonies given in the 1990s by survivors who were children and youth in Sosnowiec, Będzin, Chrzanów, Zawiercie, and other nearby towns viewed the occupation as an intrusion of a new authority rather than an immoral violent impulse. This authority intruded into their communities, homes, and families, displacing the authority of religious and familial authorities and rendering them suddenly weak and vulnerable. Almost all have powerful memories of the Nazi treatment of the male Jewish elders and communal institutions in the first days of the occupation. As Wiederman documented, the Nazis immediately took actions designed to instill complete and total fear in the local population. Within just a few days, they set fire to the main synagogues in Będzin and Sosnowiec; refused to allow anyone to put the fire out, allowing it to spread to surrounding homes; kicked in doors of shops and homes; demanded that Jewish men present themselves for harassment, beatings, or to be shot; and announced a list of regulations severely restricting Jewish life, including a curfew, a ban on economic activity, and a requirement to turn over assets.

Helen P. was born in Chrzanów in 1924. Her family fled to Wieliczka, just east of Kraków, in September 1939. She recalls that when the Nazis arrived (she does not indicate whether they were ss or military) they lined up a group of Jewish elders in the main town square and carefully cut only one curl and one-half of the beard of each. They then forced the men to fill pails with waste from a local public outhouse and run through the square, singing the Hatikvah.

> Helen P.: That was a scene that was unbearable. It would tear your heart out.[38]

The violent force that created the most fear and chaos in Zagłębie was the *Einsatzgruppe*, a highly mobile, armed military organization not accountable to German Wehrmacht officials created to more effectively intimidate civilians and root out partisan (underground resistance) activity. Himmler assigned a brutal ss officer, Udo von Woyrsch, to head the *Einsatzgruppe* in the Upper East Silesian region. Von Woyrsch's forces launched an initiative of random shootings, harassment, beatings, and street violence in Sosnowiec, killing Jews and Gentile Poles.[39] Nazi authorities swarming the area also included military police in the form of gendarmes, ss officers, a separate Gestapo police contingent, and the *Selbstschutz*, a civilian "self-defense" organization composed of locals who identified as German and who were allowed to be armed.[40]

The precise nature of the violence in this period had specific effects on Jewish girls and women. The main synagogues had functioned as the core of Jewish spiritual and social life; their rhythms dictated all other rhythms—spatial, temporal, and spiritual. They were vital, material reference points for the community. Their destruction effectively destabilized social relations, undermined how families existed in time and space, and undercut possibilities for any organized communal response. That an outside force would destroy such revered holy places—such essential places—was shocking to these young people, who had not seen anything like this before.

> Regina P.: They start to burn the sh—the synagogue. And we were living not far from the synagogue. And all the houses beside it was burned mit. They don't care—people, no people. My grandfather and my uncle were burned to death. That night. [*tearful*] And we were running from the houses. We was running whatever we could.[41]
>
> Esther S.: Just the first week when they came into the city they burned down our big synagogue. [*pauses*] We had to close the

windows not to see. But when you moved away the curtains and you looked out, you saw the whole city was like in a fire. Because they were burning not just the synagogue but a whole street. With houses. With people in them.[42]

Fanny W.: The synagogue was roaring all night. Burning.[43]

In the days immediately following the fires, Nazi authorities as well as local German residents accosted Orthodox Jewish men and publicly cut all or part of their facial hair. This focus on hair functioned as a public demonstration of their claimed entitlement of access to Jewish bodies, their disdain for Jewish authority, and their power to emasculate Jewish males, although their effect on Jewish masculinity in general was more complex.[44] In any case, these acts were profoundly shocking to the girls in the family. They had not imagined such acts were possible. Their understanding of the authority of the father in the home and in the community was completely upended. Many sought to restore it by voicing their outrage in their testimony years later, or by remaining just as shocked in their seventies as they were at seventeen.

Eta B.: I saw them cut off the beards, yes, my neighbor's.[45]

It is worth noting separately the effects of the Nazi policy of public hanging in the initial days of the occupation. In Sosnowiec, the German authorities assembled a group of prominent Jewish elders in a public square; it is not clear how they identified these particular individuals. The authorities announced that each Jewish family in the city had to send one member to the square at an appointed time; those who gathered were forced to sing as the men were hanged. That the ultimate authority figures, representing stability, security, and law, were slowly killed with no consequences for the killers was impossible for the onlookers to comprehend.

Regina S.: Then they start taking out the most prominent
Jewish people, for no reason at all. They hanged them. In the marketplace, like. And we all had to go—one from a family had to go watch it.[46]

Regina G.: This is always in my mind. I always see them.[47]

Sonia S.: I threw up.⁴⁸

Recalling the events through the lens of their age at the time, the survivors stress throughout their acute sense of vulnerability, which felt new to them. Interwoven with the vulnerability to dramatic public episodes of brutality was vulnerability to sexualized violence at the hands of almost anyone. The occupation rearranged the ethnic, linguistic, and religious hierarchies of the prewar period. German speakers native to the area were propelled into positions of ethnic preference, the top of a new hierarchy based not on religion, property, or kinship, but ideological racism. They were able to assume the role of enforcers of Nazi laws, even when they were civilians, in part because Jews were deprived of legal protection. Gentile Poles were in an ambiguous position. They had to defer to their German neighbors, and were subject to displacement from their homes, arrests, and shootings, but had access to resources (including political resources) that Jews did not.⁴⁹

Berta P.'s experience illustrates this reordering. As she tells it, she was running in the street after a loose dog without the Jewish insignia she was supposed to wear. A male German civilian stopped her and ordered her to her home, accompanying her into the apartment and confronting her mother.

> Berta P.: He . . . [*she stops to whisper*] . . . pulled up my dress.
>   [in a whisper, *leaning toward the interviewer*] I don't know if I should—
> Interviewer: [*silence*]
> Berta P.: And I had to lay down on the table. And he hit me with a belt. So that was my first bad experience before I went to the camp.
> Interviewer: Yes, continue please, Berta.⁵⁰

Berta P. changes the topic to speak about being hit by a repairman in the Ober Altstadt work site and how she became inured to slaps and hitting while in the camp. The interview is interrupted by the technical need to change tapes. In the new tape, the interviewer asks Berta P. if she would say more about the civilian German entering her home to discipline her for not wearing a Jewish star. (It appears that revisiting this anecdote was agreed to by Berta P. in the break between tapes.)

> Interviewer: Were the civilian Germans allowed to, to hit you?
> Berta P.: I really don't know about it, if they were allowed, but nobody was asking if they were allowed or not allowed. Because they were the masters. They were doing whatever they want. So it just happened that he was passing by and I was grabbing my dog and I had that very bad experience. Which is really was [*shakes her head*] really very bad for me because I, I never—even my parents didn't hit me on my heinie. [*nervous laughter*] So I was very upset about that, and that, that's, that was, um, very outstanding in my life. What I experienced.
> Interviewer: Do you recall if you and your mother were concerned at that time about possible rape?
> Berta P.: Oh, well, my mother was there. And, uh, at this time, you know, it was something very, very new to us. So I really don't know what my mother was thinking. We never discussed it. And I didn't think about any rapes because I was [*shrugs*] very young and I didn't understand that, um, something that would happen ... But I was very upset that a German can do that to me.[51]

Berta P. recalls the incident with a degree of personal shame—"I don't know if I should tell it." Her word choices also communicate the entitlement to public space that German civilians assumed—he orders her home and indeed enters her home with her—and the entitlement to Jewish bodies. Berta P.'s memory is that she had to organize her body—to offer it—such that it was exposed and it could be hit by him. The degree of the German civilian's penetration of her personal privacy, her home, her body, and her self-understanding as a young person who is to be protected, is shocking to her—perhaps as shocking as rape. In fact, the interviewer immediately thinks of the threat of rape and asks directly about it. For Berta P., the ethnicity of the perpetrator was a crucial element of the emotional suffering she endured, but also the nature of the violence: "I was upset that a German could do that to me."

The prevalence of sexual predation on the part of either Gentile local civilians, deputized residents such as *Selbstschutz* members, new investors or "trustees" from the Reich, or German authorities in Zagłębie in particular has not been systematically researched by scholars. Historian

Birgit Beck has shown that German army soldiers engaged in sexual predation generally, not as a part of intentional policy but because it was easy to do so and it aligned with understandings of entitlement in occupied areas, a point also developed by Regina Mühlhäuser in her analysis of territories further east.[52] The Zagłębie region was saturated with German police, army units, ss, and the newly empowered local Germans in the *Selbstschutz*.[53] Alexander Rossino, in his study of the Wehrmacht soldiers' attitudes and experiences with Jewish and Gentile Poles in the first days of the occupation, presents the case of a small group of soldiers going on a looting spree, breaking into homes and raping Jewish women.[54] In the case presented in Rossino's research, one family brought charges and Wehrmacht officials pursued an investigation, concerned about a violation of Nazi racial laws banning sexual relations between non-Jewish Germans and Jews.

Berta P.'s story is important in establishing the availability of the Jewish body to any type of predation or instrumentalization; in this sense, it aligns with the cutting of Jewish beards as well as beatings and killings as an element affecting Jewish social life under occupation. Longtime residents as well as newcomers, soldiers, and civilians all came to realize the new degree of vulnerability of Jews, and the additional embodied, sexualized vulnerability of girls and women, whether they acted on it or not. Perhaps precisely because of her age at the time, testimony-giver Phyllis Y. remembers that Jews had no recourse in the event of sexual assault—or any type of assault—and were well aware of that fact.

> Phyllis Y.: If you came across a guy that, um, wanted to rape you or beat you up, you had to take it and go on.[55]
>
> Anna W.: Once they came. And my mother must have been scared, so she left. And she left me alone with the children. So when the young soldier came, he pushed them off to the other room and left me alone there and said I should undress. Which I refused. I said, "I'm not." And he must have heard the other fellow coming, because they always were in a company, so he really left me alone.[56]

This realization runs counter to the view that the Nazi project essentially repressed sexuality, a view critically analyzed by scholar Dagmar

Herzog.[57] If the remembered experiences of female survivors are to be taken seriously, embodied sexual threat was interwoven into the occupation.

As historians have documented, occupation authorities immediately forbid Jews from interacting with non-Jews, owning property, participating in professions, purchasing food at Gentile Polish shops, and attending school. The Nazis also required anyone Jewish to wear a white armband with a Star of David sewn on. In the case of most of the towns around Sosnowiec and the city itself, authorities did not force Jewish families to relocate into a specific sector; instead, they closed off specific streets to Jewish access, one at a time over the course of months. In this way, the institution of separate legal and economic spheres for Jews and non-Jews was reinforced by spatial limitations that initially fell short of a full ghetto. It meant that Jewish individuals who found themselves on a non-Jewish street (legally or illegally) could not rely on family or community for protection. The person in the family most able to evade all of these rules were the older female children. They knew how to handle money and shop for provisions because they had done so already to help in the family; thus, they were capable of going to a Gentile store. They were agile and aware enough to avoid being caught and could get away with dressing as a non-Jew. Once Jews were forbidden to purchase food and their property confiscated, they had to turn to violating the bans to survive.

> Nettie S.: You have to have permission to bake. And we did not have permission. Everything was closed up ... It was very hard ... We tried to bake. We baked something. Oh, but we make, like, "nobody has to know this."[58]
>
> Esther S.: [speaking about her father] He ran his business and it was illegal to run the business. [He ran it] in the house. There was a black market that you could buy sugar and make those candies. And then my brother and my oldest sister, they were helping out. And that was in 1941.[59]
>
> Mania R.: We were smuggling to, to the, to Kraków. I remember I was, I was going to Kraków smuggling some dollar bills.[60]

Although at times boys also did this, the survivors remember that it was the girls and young women in particular who were propelled into a public world with new rules, running errands for family members who were confined to the private home—to avoid arrest or street harassment or to protect and care for other family members—and often "came across" the range of people.

> Shoshana L.: [age twelve in 1939] One day I said—we run out already of food—and I said, we got the coupons [ration cards], why shouldn't we go and get the food. So matter of fact, it was very dangerous, because we had to wear this with the [*gestures on her arm*]—always they told us if we take it off we would be punished . . . I said, "Daddy, I'm going!" But what happened, a lot of people started to stand in the queues [at the Gentile stores] at nighttime. To get the bread. Hundreds, hundreds of people. So I said, "I am going, so I will go." So I dressed myself like a babushka, you know, no one would recognize me, because it [the stores] were not for Jewish.[61]

The Gentile Polish shopkeeper confronted Shoshana L., asking her if she was Jewish, but in a whisper. Shoshana L. was paralyzed with doubt about how to respond. She finally claimed, no, no, she was not Jewish, was given the bread, and ran home.

> Shoshana L.: The bread! Lovely! You know, the best bread! It was hot! A whole bread that I got. And I warmed up myself. [*hugs herself, smiling*] Because it was so cold, winter. I came home and said, Daddy, Mama, I got the bread! And it was wonderful.[62]

Esther S. also snuck into stores banned to Jews at ages twelve and thirteen.

> Esther S.: I used to sometimes take off that star. I didn't—they said I don't look Jewish—and go to a German store to shop for some food. If they didn't recognize me I was very lucky to buy some stuff and bring home.[63]

In one instance in a store a Gentile neighbor loudly announced that Esther S. was Jewish.

> Esther S.: I started screaming, "What? How can you say I'm Jewish? I'm not Jewish! Maybe you are Jewish!" So the saleslady asked me my name. And I said, "My name is Marisia Antosz." I knew

> a girl by that name. So I right away—so she didn't believe
> that other girl, that I'm Jewish. And I succeeded to buy some
> food. Milk and stuff. And I brought it home. My mother was
> overjoyed![64]

Esther S. was twelve at the time of this incident. She speaks with pride at her resourcefulness.

Both Shoshana L. and Esther S. remember not only evading the law but also negotiating dangerous social confrontations to provide for their families, recalling specifically the reactions of their mothers.

In a surprising moment of testimony, Lola W., who was born in March 1929 and eleven when the German army occupied the region, explains that she not only passed as Gentile to acquire food in 1941, but she also actually joined the local *Bund Deutscher Mädel* (League of German Girls), the female equivalent to the Hitler Youth organization. The *Bund Deutscher Mädel* was active in Silesia as a tool to allow young Gentile German women from the Reich to travel east and participate in socializing German speakers local to Silesia.[65] In other words, it was an aspect of the Nazi policy of Germanization. The fact that a twelve-year-old Jewish girl joined this group emerges obliquely in the testimony-giving event.

Lola W. is reticent from the beginning and she states that she does not remember much from her childhood in Oświęcim. The German authorities forced the entire Oświęcim Jewish population to move to Sosnowiec and Będzin in 1941, which is how Lola W. eventually ended up in the Schmelt system.[66] The interviewer attempts various modes of posing questions, but Lola W. states repeatedly that she remembers little. Since the Shoah Foundation questionnaire was known to the testimony-givers prior to the interview, it is not clear whether Lola W. was restating her "not remembering" or deciding to keep some material to herself, out of the recorded interview, at the last moment. It seemed that the interviewer already knew from the questionnaire that Lola W. had been in the BDM, and she was able to create a narrative environment in which Lola W. could participate by creating space for Lola W. to express pride in helping her family. She begins by asking about the environment for Lola W.'s family in Sosnowiec in 1941.

> Interviewer: How did you survive? What did you do for food?

Lola W.: I, I used to bring in food. [*long pause*] They used to give me, the girls used to give me, they had cards, too, you know, like for certain things. They always said, "We have so many children, and my father is a soldier, we haven't got enough." They were good to, I mean, they thought I'm German, you know!

Interviewer: These are the Bundenmach—? Uh—

Lola W.: *Bund Deutsches Mädchen.*

Interviewer: They say that's the—

Lola W.: I wore the hat. They gave me the thing [*smiles*] from a sister, from [*inaudible*], or whatever. I was good at it.

Interviewer: What did you look like at that time? [*Lola W. looks confused.*] Could you describe yourself?

Lola W.: [*long pause*] Yeah. I looked like a shiksa. [*pause*]

Interviewer: What was your coloring like?

Lola W.: Blue eyes. Light hair. White skin. And a good German [language].

Interviewer: They thought you were German?

Lola W.: Absolutely! Absolutely. I brought home *everything*.[67]

Later the interviewer asks her what kind of food she brought home. She answers, "Nothing but the best."[68]

The Jewish residents of the Zagłębie region realized that the German authorities were entering homes in the very first days of occupation—1939 and early 1940—to arrest Jewish males for short periods of detention, to abduct them for short-term labor, and to loot. Households organized hiding places for fathers and other adult males (as well as for assets such as jewelry). The apprehension of a father extended the shock of the first days of the invasion.

Berta P.: Actually me and my mother were hiding our father and brothers. Because they said they would kill the Jewish men.[69]

Sonia S.: They came, they ripped open the door. "Raus, raus, heraus!" They were screaming, "With your arms up!" They took my father first. And they said to us, "You go up!" And they took my father away. Screaming, pushing him, kicking him. My mother was hysterical. We came home, we were hysterical.

>We didn't know what's happening. We didn't know where they took him. We didn't know what's happening... Now it took about two days, I think. My father came home. I want to tell you... He was a very proud and very, very clean man. And very devoted father and husband. [*pause*] When he came home, I did not recognize him... He looked—that proud man. I never forget. He looked like an old, old man... He was stripped of his dignity. The look in his eyes. And like that he would apologize to us, that he cannot help us.[70]

In this excerpt Sonia S. struggles to keep an idealized memory of her father while being asked to detail the circumstances causing his powerlessness. Her testimony captures the nuances of how gender and age are interwoven with the personal impact of seeing a loved one physically harmed. He had been a "devoted father" but was now unrecognizable, no longer capable of keeping his family safe. Fatherhood itself had been excised from the family, for Sonia S.

In October 1939 the Department of Jewish Affairs in the Kattowitz Gestapo established a new Jewish-led organization to facilitate the Nazi control of Zagłębie's Jews, as was done throughout Nazi-occupied Europe. Gestapo chief Hans Dreier assembled the male Jewish elders of Sosnowiec and requested a volunteer to lead a new Jewish organization that would cooperate with the Nazi occupation to manage Jewish life according to Nazi priorities.[71] When no person volunteered, Dreier picked out a young Jewish man disconnected from Sosnowiec's traditional Jewish elites, Moses Merin. With German financial support, Merin quickly created a functioning organization that eventually had more than one thousand employees.[72] Merin's Jewish Council of Elders solicited resources, information, and people from the Jewish communities under its purview; transferred lists of Jewish residents to local Nazi authorities; and distributed ration cards, operated soup kitchens, and opened an orphanage. Like other Nazi-created Jewish organizations, it created a narrative that it was the only body that could support Jews and enable them to survive at this time because it was able to negotiate with the authorities for better conditions.

Merin's Jewish Council eventually grew from its base in Sosnowiec to cover all of Zagłębie. Philip Friedman counted thirty-seven different

Jewish communities and more than 100,000 Jews under its supervision.[73] It functioned as a partner to the Sosnowitz ss and Gestapo, but also distributed substantial resources back to Jews. For example, in Olkusz, populated by about 750 Jewish families, the Jewish Council provided meals to 141 families daily and distributed coal to 218 between September 1939 and the end of December in that year.[74] Merin developed a strong relationship with the us Joint Distribution Committee and received funds and advice from its representative for Eastern Upper Silesia, Isaac Bornstein; he also cultivated other external donors.[75] For the purposes of this study, the Jewish Council was crucial in that it registered all Jews in Zagłębie, tracked their changes of residence, and identified who would be available for labor and when.

As was the case in other Nazi-established *Judenräte*, the Jewish Council also employed Jewish police, referred to at times in the testimonies as *milicja* or *milits*. They appear in the Shoah Foundation accounts at various moments: when survivors remember being forced to leave their homes for work assignments; when a policeman recognized a neighbor or friend and shared information, a favor, or a warning; and during the implementation of the mass deportations to Auschwitz in the summer of 1942 and the summer of 1943, at which point the ss disbanded it. This complex and contradictory position of the Jewish policeman—who was not always able to protect his own family from deportation—is well analyzed in Dan Porat's study of trials of collaborators in Israel. Using the case of the trial of Hirsch Barenblat, the head of the police in Będzin, Porat documents the difficulties among Israeli prosecutors in establishing harm done, the ambivalence of witnesses, and the reluctance of the courts to create a precedent of jailing "ordinary functionaries."[76]

Testimony-givers remember fragments of overheard adult conversations and public declarations from the Jewish Council.

> Sonia S.: First they put up placards that German and in Yiddish that we have to register. Whoever won't, won't get no bread cards. And we are going to be prosecuted.[77]
>
> Helen P.: Of course, they promised him—why did my younger brother go? Of course ... what we heard later, they promised him everything is going to be wonderful. They are going to work. They are going to get food. They are going to go home

for vacation, for the holidays. And that's how, where a lot of people got lured in not knowing that such a horrible thing [at a forced labor site] could happen, so they went kind of willingly.[78]

Ester R.: [referring to an employee of the Jewish Council] He start to talk to my mom. And when we are w-willingly to go to this, to camp, the parents would be saved. And we stood out like army. And said, "OK! We are willing to go to save our parents."[79]

Nettie S.: And everybody said, one person has to go. When one person goes, that's—your family [will] be safe. Your family will be safe! The other people be safe. [*in a whisper*] But that's not true. They were not safe . . . you were not safe.[80]

Esther S.: There were some well-known people from the city [Będzin] that worked, uh, they arranged everything. If somebody was supposed to get to the hospital or—or they were also talking with the Germans. I knew a guy that worked for the *Judenräte*, that he arranged for the Germans, for the Jewish people to be sent to working camps. Because he knew what was going on.[81]

The case of the Jewish Council of Elders supports scholar Dan Michman's conceptualization of these organizations as "headships" whose functions for the Nazi authorities changed over time and which were not reducible to the personality of one individual.[82] At the same time, Merin, his family members, and his main assistant, Fania Czarna, were largely hated as corrupt and untrustworthy. Fania Czarna was central to compiling and maintaining the paperwork that was the basis for the Schmelt system of matching Jews to work sites. Sonia S. remembers her as the frequent topic of family conversation. She substitutes the Yiddish word for the Polish *czarna*, which means "black," possibly because she anticipates using "black" in her later phrasing:

Sonia S.: Her name was Fania, Felicja, Fania Shvarts. She was a very, very mean person.[83]

In 1940 Jewish families coped in different ways with the Jewish Council's practice of requiring families to "volunteer" one member for coerced labor. Often they hoped to evade the call-ups and letters issued by the Jewish Council by simply ignoring them. This strategy succeeded in postponing the confrontation with authorities, allowing more time to develop additional resources or pathways of evasion. Eventually, however, the ss and Gestapo, working with the Jewish Council's Jewish police, used the lists of names and addresses and went to homes directly. Lucy M. was among the first group of girls and young women assigned to a work site in Trautenau, in April 1940.

> Lucy M.: They picked me up at my house [at] six in the morning.[84]

In 1941, Phyllis Y. was asleep when two ss men knocked on the front door, asking for her by name. "Get dressed and come."[85] They also had the name of a neighbor who was a young teenager. "They knocked on her door, too."[86] It appears that the authorities were targeting a specific type of person, females without children.

Shoshana L. remembers her family trying to hide her older sister. Her father tucked her into an adjacent shop room and covered her with debris.

> Shoshana L.: In the nighttime we could hear the Germans. "Öffnen! Öffnen," banging on the door. "Öffnen, du verfluchte, öffnen!" And we didn't know, we'd just been asleep. We were just like, we didn't know what's happening . . . My mom, she was standing frozen.[87]

In this excerpt, Shoshana L. pronounces the repetitive "*öffnen*" ("open") as a blend of German and Yiddish (*efenen*). The interviewer, perhaps not recognizing the blended term, asks if the family could understand the German demand. Shoshana L. takes time away from the story to explain the closeness in pronunciation (in her experience) of *öffnen* and *efenen*. She continues, again using a blend of German and Yiddish when recalling the ss demand for her sister, Pola Wulc.

> Shoshana L.: Daddy went to open the door. Four ss men coming in and they said, "Wo is Pola Wulc?" They start shouting and they start to look everywhere, under the covers, everywhere. In the room we were standing. In the other room. And then they went into the shop. It was obvious. It was like a big pile. It was obvious that someone was there . . . they saw the pile and they start to dig. They start to dig. And I was peeping, I was peeping because I was next door like that. I can see the ss men pulling out my

sister, like a murderer, the hand up and the gun at her back. Already Mom, Dad, me, standing. Like a murderer, she went past us. Even not saying goodbye to anyone. To anyone goodbye. She went away. She went away. We didn't sleep all night. We had been hypnotized. We'd been stone—there is not such a word. We had been cold frozen.[88]

The practice of local SS, Gestapo, Jewish police, and others working with the Nazi regime of bursting into private homes was common in occupied cities and towns. Here Shoshana L. documents the effect on not just herself but also her family in vivid, evocative terms. In the testimony-giving moment, Shoshana L. shifts to the present tense, from "I was peeping" to "I can see," and shifts from a fast-moving narrative to a repetitive incantation of emotion. First with "SS men pulling out my sister" to "she went past us" to "she went away," Shoshana L. slows time further to describe the paralyzing, time-stopping effect on all those present: "hypnotized," "cold frozen."

The SS, Gestapo, and Jewish police also simply picked up any young female they came across in the street, according to several survivors. They recall a parallel process of unorganized, impulsive seizures that coexisted with the Jewish Council's careful lists and letters. They note that this practice was a response to work site owners' requirements for a specific type of person within a specific period of time. Testimony-givers remember experiencing the "recruitment" into coerced labor as an abduction rather than an unequal transaction.

> Ida G.: They staged "catching parties." They either caught someone for some work they needed or shipped them out.[89]
>
> Ester R.: All the, all the young people. They wanted young people and girls.[90]
>
> Regina P.: They came and took my sister. They said—because we know already, because they took some other children and we know that they are going to send her to a working camp. Not to a death camp, just to a working camp.[91]
>
> Rusia Y.: In the morning, six o'clock, a knock on the door . . . So they take me.[92]

Berta P. had a work permit for a local workshop but was still targeted in a labor sweep.

> Berta P.: After a while everybody had to work in a, for them. And I was working there too, as a—whatever they found for us. Sewing uniforms. At a certain day I was going to work. And they—I was picked up in the street with my friend.[93]

After they were deposited in an empty building, Berta P. noticed that "they were still were picking up people. Most of them—they were, those people were young. . . . This was going on for about two days."[94]

Many of those testifying viewed the anti-Jewish terror as a personal assault on their families and took on the weight of responsibility for not just helping their families survive but also keeping their own fears and emotions in check. Nettie S. left with authorities who came to her home.

> Nettie S.: I tried not to cry. I don't know, I tried not to cry. And I said, "I will be all right. Just you try to stay together." I kissed them, I hugged them, the kids. I was shaking, you know. I never thought this would be the last time, the last one, I would look [at them] in the face. I never thought that's the last time I [would] shake their hands. And I never saw them [again]. I never thought this. Never thought this. [That] I never see them again. Nobody! Nobody.[95]

The Jewish communities of Sosnowiec and Będzin were not organized into formal ghettos until the second half of 1942, although Jews in the small town of Olkusz were forced into a ghetto in 1941.[96] As noted previously, immediately after the German invasion in 1939, specific streets were closed to Jews; gradually throughout 1940 and 1941 more streets were banned, meaning that Jewish families in those particular areas were forced to move elsewhere. This system of allowing most Jews to live in their original homes functioned to help Moses Merin and the Jewish Council of Elders achieve their goal of keeping an accessible population that would cooperate, in the main, with the Schmelt labor system.[97] The Jewish Council and the local ss were attuned to the possibility of organized political resistance. They kept the population in a constant state of heightened vigilance and fear, off-balance. As was the practice in other places (such as the Warsaw ghetto), the ss and Gestapo initiated sudden

Aktionen, or loud, public abductions of Jews, sometimes arbitrarily shooting individuals in the street as they traveled to local workshops, to assigned temporary work such as street repair, or to find food.

Some of the *Aktionen* of 1939, 1940, and 1941 targeted Jewish men specifically. The first requests received by the Schmelt organization were for specifically male labor for large scale, heavy-duty projects such as road-building initiatives.[98] Thus, the labor demands of 1939 and early 1940, the *Aktionen*, and the Schmelt-organized labor roundups focused on adult males ran parallel to the effort to find Jewish girls and young women for specific labor requests, but was much more visible, violent, and extensive. As a result, many households made it a priority in 1939, 1940, and 1941 to keep male family members hidden, which upended the cultural and religious fabric of the home and of religious life, and propelled girls and young women into the role of buffers between the SS and their fathers and brothers.

In Regina S.'s testimony-giving process, the interviewer indirectly challenges her past decision to protect her father. Regina S. had grown up in Sosnowiec and was sixteen at the time of the 1939 invasion. During 1939 and 1940 she regularly reported for local, spontaneous labor call-ups intended for her father. This fact emerged from a series of prompts from the interviewer, who assumed that all Jewish men had to work in response to SS demands.

> Interviewer: Did he [your father] work for a time as a laborer?[99]
> Regina S.: But, well, uh, he was supposed to work as a laborer.
>   One of the family had to go and do a job. All kinds of jobs.
>   What I did, instead of him, I was afraid to let him go. He was
>   a very gentle, delicate person. So I put on a pair of pants and a
>   deep hat—[*pause*] And I was working for him. I tried anyways.
>   So did my brother.
> Interviewer: [*surprised*] How long did you do that?
> Regina S.: As long as I could.

At this point Regina S. seems satisfied with her answer, but there is a long pause as it appears that the interviewer is processing this answer and organizing her next question. The matter-of-fact affect with which Regina S. explained how she substituted for her father reflects her interpretation of her position as the oldest girl in a family in which men were devoted to religious study and teaching. Regina S. dons men's clothing to help her father avoid the brutalization of the labor call-up. While the interviewer finds Regina S.'s actions remarkable and sounds slightly disdainful, Regina S. neatly reverses the transgression by confidently reiterating ownership of her actions: "as long as I could," that is, as long as she could get away with it.

Regina S. gave testimony again four years later, this time as Regina G. because she had remarried. This phenomenon of a second testimony is not uncommon. Local institutions asked survivors in their area to participate in taped testimonies in the late 1980s and early 1990s, and when the more well-known Shoah Foundation initiative gained momentum in 1994, some of those participants decided to do another recording. In the case of Regina G., the Shoah Foundation acquired her earlier testimony for its archives.[100] In this second testimony, Regina G. also tells about taking her father's place for a labor call-up. She adds that her family had moved to Sosnowiec from Radomsko for economic opportunities when she was six years old. In 1939, when the local Treuhandler organization appropriated her father's business, she became "the breadwinner" at age fifteen.[101] To do this she dressed as a man and traveled with her father from town to town selling the soap made at home and esrog for Sukkot.[102] She then restates her decision to substitute herself for her father during a labor call-up. This time, the interviewer (a different person) does not challenge her decision to pass as a male or to work in place of her father. And this means that this time, Regina G. does not have the opportunity to say that she did this "as long as I could."

Through an extended anecdote, Sonia S. vividly relates acquiring food illegally for her family. This episode likely occurred in 1940, when she was fifteen, because she remembers the demarcation of a new police border in Olkusz, which occurred that year. The family had relatives with a farm about twenty-five miles from Będzin, where they lived. Her father initially planned to make a furtive trip, but Sonia S. remembers that "I wouldn't let my father go because we knew that the men were killed every day."[103]

> Sonia S.: My older sister was very shy and very—she was the opposite of me. I was more energetic, more aggressive. She was very, very quiet. So I said, "I'm gonna go!"[104]

Passing as a Gentile, she took a train and then walked to the farm, encountering shooting at nightfall. She hid in a ditch and later found the farm. The relatives sent her back with "flour and sugar and a goose." But in the course of the few days of her visit the German authorities had instituted new rules for travel. Germany demarcated the new eastern border of the "Eastern Strip" and formally annexed it to the Reich.[105] Sonia S. now needed documents permitting her to cross what was a new border right at Olkusz. Local Gentile Poles, including young boys, entered the train to apprehend Jews who had been traveling, to identify them for the local German authorities, going from car to car; they caught Sonia S. and she was made to wait with her huge bag of provisions in a room at the Olkusz train station.

> Sonia S.: I see there was a German. And he looked to me like he had a good face. And I said to him, "Ich will raus gehen. Where is there a door?" I asked him. He didn't say nothing... he showed me with his eyes. I took this [bag] and I start running.[106]

Gentile Poles chased her as she ran; she hid in a cemetery, then approached a house in a rural area away from the town. Sonia S. explained her situation and inquired whether this family knew a distant cousin who lived in Olkusz, a Passelman. The Gentile Polish owner of the house, by coincidence, knew him. "They said, oh, we know Passelman, very well! He is our Jew!" and took Sonia S. in for the rest of the night. When morning came Passelman arrived and brought her home with horse and wagon.

Sonia S.'s story foregrounds a number of elements in the changing social reality for Jews in Zagłębie. First is the physicality of acquiring extra food. Heavy, bulky, difficult to hide, illegally acquired food at times had to be carried long distances. Several survivors speak of holding bread tightly against their bodies or struggling to make sure food does not spill. Sonia S. took the added risk of continuing onward during an episode of shooting. Second is the great risk of her appeal to "the German," whom she does not characterize by official position; we do not know whether he was a local, a Gestapo officer, or a soldier. He violates the law by helping her find the escape route. Sonia S. does not analyze why she took the risk beyond her intuition about his face and body language. Perhaps she interpreted him to be sympathetic to her specifically, because of her youth and attractiveness, although she doesn't say. Another subtext, however, is the difference between the positions of Gentile Poles and Germans in the social order of the occupation. A German guard at a train station in 1941 may not have viewed arresting Jews in particular the same way that Gentile Polish youth did. A Gentile Polish family who employed specific local Jews (in this case, Passelman) may not have offered refuge to just any Jewish fugitive. Finally, even as the Poles threatened her, Sonia approached a Polish home. Her decision-making and risk-taking attest to her specific qualities as a teenager: physically and mentally agile, willing to act impulsively, and at times able to communicate across obstacles.

Helen P. was sixteen in 1940 when the Schmelt organization sent her brother to Sakrau (Zakrzów, near Opole) for labor. The news of the conditions there horrified her family. Helen remembers the family hearing news of a doctor who traveled to the Schmelt labor camps to identify people who were too sick to work and who would be sent home. Helen P. decided she would travel to visit this doctor, although her mother begged her not to go. Her lengthy anecdote attests to the risks she was willing to take as a young woman as well as the permeable, negotiable rules that helped the Schmelt labor system function in this early period.

> Helen P.: So. [*laughs slightly*] I was the one that—I made out papers, we made out papers, like, "Maria Frisch." German-sounding papers. And another friend, another boy's sister, we decided that we're going to go visit that doctor, that German doctor. And speak to him and plead with him that he should bring my brother back to Sosnowiec if possible.[107]

As she recalls it, she and her friend first took a train to see the doctor, but he refused their request. They decide to continue on to actually visit the brothers at the labor site. Helen P.'s affect throughout seems to indicate that she is, at the time of her testimony, surprised at the risks she took at sixteen.

> Helen P.: So there was a guy with a horse and carriage and they took us and we came there. It was winter, in the winter. It was dark. And snowing. And cold. And we didn't know what to do! We stood there in the street. So finally we see—and it was

early in the morning—and finally we see a whole commando of people coming, walking.¹⁰⁸

These men were Jewish coerced laborers assigned to Sakrau. They called out to her because they recognized her from Chrzanów. They informed her that her brother was back at the barracks because he was ill. Helen P. and her friend then entered a bar—a *Bierstube* intended for Germans—and talked the bar owner into having a friend smuggle a message to her brother using one of the suppliers to the camp. At this point two camp guards arrived at the bar, and Helen P. then convinced them to bring the message to her brother, whom they liked because they had been benefiting from the many packages Helen P.'s mother had been sending to her son. Surprisingly, they not only accepted her note but also allowed her to see her brother inside the labor camp. The guards then took both girls back to the train station to return to Chrzanów.

Helen P. expresses pride and amazement at her accomplishment and spends time remembering the significance of her act not only for her mother but also for her community. However, the interviewer, perhaps anxious to document the facts, cuts short her pleasure in the retelling.

> Helen P.: And I can't tell you what it meant for my mother's day, for my mother, for my mother, that we saw my brother. And we talked to him. And we had to tell her every detail, everything what happened. And I can't possibly tell you what happened. The whole city—everybody had somebody there—kept coming to my house, to our house, and asking, "Did you see my son?" "Did you see my brother?" "Did you see my husband?" Did you see this one, did you see this one. And wherever we could—
> Interviewer: [*interrupting*] What was the name of that camp? Do you remember?
> Helen P.: Sakrau!
> Interviewer: Where your brother was. Sakrau?
> Helen P.: Yes. Sakrau. Like I mentioned.¹⁰⁹

Helen P.'s detailed testimony may seem initially to exaggerate the mobility accorded to Jews in the region. However, her experience, as she remembers it, is in line with the early forms of social life "on the ground," in the early days of the occupation. Maren Röger documents the wide range of interactions between German officials and soldiers, on the one hand, and civilian girls and women, on the other, in her study of sexual and romantic interactions. She writes, "Members of the armed forces frequently gave women lifts in their vehicles—a recurrent cause of complaint and admonishment from authorities."[110] While Röger's study covers the Generalgouvernement, the environment of potential sexual access encouraged loosened regulations in the annexed territories as well. The guards seemed not to have bothered thinking about whether Helen P. and her friend were Jews or not; although the girls had German papers, the guards must have realized that if her brother was in the camp, Helen P. must also be Jewish.

In regard to the ability of Helen P. to enter a coerced work site, in the Reich and the annexed regions coerced labor was a policy that took different forms at different time periods and with regard to different populations. As Mark Spoerer aptly puts it, over time "the exploitation of Jewish labor took four, successive, but overlapping forms," beginning with Jews assigned as "forced civilian workers" at work sites that were not necessarily punitive camps and ending with Jews as formal prisoners in concentration camps by 1944.[111] The Schmelt organization had its own specific dynamics grafted onto the forced civilian worker model, in which allowing a degree of mobility in the forms of exchange of workers, letters, and visits home facilitated the maintenance of a responsive, adaptable, and income-generating labor pool.[112] Zagłębie's Jewish families often knew the name of the work site to which a family member had been sent even as late as 1943; at the same time, because Jews were subject to arbitrary arrest and detention, there were certainly many instances in which families experienced simply the sudden disappearance of a relative. Throughout the testimonies there are frequent references to taking risks just to catch sight of a family member or to quickly speak to someone in these years.

Helen P.'s testimony also extends and deepens the description of the Nazi labor system documented by Spoerer as well as many other historians. It is likely the case that Nazi authorities were not unfamiliar with family members traveling to work sites through the region, although Helen P. had to create false documents because Jewish travel required permission, which she did not have. It is her entry into a German drinking house that was an extreme risk here, as these two young women are then out of public view, as well as the agreement to ride in a car with Nazi guards. The ending of Helen P.'s anecdote makes very clear why she took these risks: these brief connections were substitutes for information for the entire community and the presence of the loved one for family.

The initial pathway into coerced labor was different depending on not only the time period and the capacities of the Schmelt organization to find and organize specific types of workers but also the specific strategies of the Jewish Council of Elders as well as the demands of the private firms requesting workers. Work sites such as the Haase textile factory in Trautenau created posters that they put up in Sosnowiec calling for "female Jewish laborers" and listing working conditions (which were not upheld once people were on site). One such poster was titled, "Application and Payments for Long Shift, Long Transit, and Night Workers" [*Antrag und Zuteilung von Zulagefarten für Lang-, Langewege- und Nachtarbeiter*], with the handwritten addition at the top: "Female Jewish Workers!" Dated October 1942, long after the factory had started using coerced Jewish labor, it announced 280 open positions. It is not clear whether the poster's audience was the Jewish girls and women themselves, their families, or the Jewish Council of Elders, nor is it known exactly where it was posted.[113]

> Yetta F.: Right away [there were] big posters in town. And they put down, this, "Girls and boys born in this and this year have to come to this *Durchgangslager* and sign in." So they knew what age—to start taking to the work camps.[114]

The letters received at home also varied in their appeals. Some were simple commands, others were threats to deport the entire family if the girl did not appear, and others were offers of incentives such as wages.

> Chana B.: They sent us a letter. That I have to go to that—assembly. If I am not coming at the time where I had in the letter, so they will send the whole family to Auschwitz.[115]

Many attempted to evade the letters and were caught up in building-to-building sweeps.

> Rose S.: I heard that the Germans are coming and they are looking for girls. I was running down to the basement. But sure enough they went after me. And they grabbed me.[116]

> Estera S.: We hid in the bed covers.[117]

Anna W. remembers an instance in which the Jewish police conducted a raid on her home but intentionally did not "discover" her.

> Anna W.: They knew once that I was there, in bed, under the pillows. He knew that I was there. He didn't take me. So I was safe then.[118]

Rose S. loses her composure as she remembers her separation from her family in 1941:

> Rose S.: And I remember they brought me up to the front of the house, so my mother came out. [*pauses, tearful*] With my older sister. And my chin began to shake. My sister took off a scarf from her head. And she said, "Take it, you'll be cold." [*begins to weep*][119]

Masha S. and her two sisters volunteered for labor duty in 1942 to, in their perception at the time, save their parents.

> Masha S.: They took us to Sosnowiec ... They had such a place, where they put all the people together, before they sent them to the forced labor camps.[120]

The "such a place" was a high school on Składowa street in the middle of Sosnowiec that the authorities commandeered and converted into a transit camp, called the Sosnowitz *Durchgangslager*. It features prominently in most survivor testimonies as the beginning of the coerced labor journey. The SS functionaries who carried out the labor roundups (and who would later carry out the deportations) included Friedrich Kuczynski and Heinrich Lindner.[121] These officials used the high school's numerous separate smaller rooms and long hallways to organize Jewish individuals into groups according to the requests of the companies "leasing" them. The *Durchgangslager* had designated spaces for holding people just rounded up; for segregating people by age, gender, and skills;

for medical examinations; and for the administrative work of managing a coercive labor system. People stayed at the transit camp from one day to three weeks.[122]

The survivors remember their stays at the "*Dulag*" as times of scrutiny of their bodies, although none reported being assaulted there.

> Berta P.: We were selected to which camps we should go. They processed us . . . We had to go through a doctor. And, uh, we had, they were asking us all kinds of questions.[123]
>
> Estera S.: They looked at our hands. The most important thing was to have small hands.[124]
>
> Lucy M.: You stay there 'til certain factories or certain, uh, people have room for you to work.[125]
>
> Anna W.: And at that time we were taken to Sosnowiec, which was called *Durchgangslager*. It was a *durch*, uh, in-between *lager*. Where it was a doctor, examining you, if you were capable to work.[126]
>
> Rose S.: It happened that one [factory owner]—his name was Schindler also [not the Oskar Schindler]. He came to, he had girls also at his camp from our, like from our Chrzanów, Auschwitz [Oświęcim] and Sosnowiec. And they used to come to the *Durchgangslager* to, if they need more workers. So he was really trying to take the girls from these towns like. The same ones.[127]
>
> Esther S.: They took us not far, but to another city. Like, six kilometers from us, to a place it was called *Dulag*. It was called *Durchgangslager*. Short is *Dulag*. In Sosnowiec. And there we stayed for a few days. And then somebody from—um—a factory owner came and they took us out to the backyard and stood us up, you know, in rows. And he chose whom he wants for work. And he chose like cattle, you know. Fifty girls he chose. I was among them. And they took us again by train to that factory.[128]

True to its original purpose as a high school, the *Durchgangslager* (or *Dulag*) had a large yard with a wire fence surrounding it. Family members could stand at the fence and throw parcels over to their loved ones.

Others could ask those assigned to a work site to carry packages to family already there. Those inside could easily look out of windows to gesture to friends and family. For a significant number of the girls and women who survived the Trautenau-area camps, the *Dulag* fence was the last place they saw their parents.

> Estera S.: The next day in the front of that building parents came to see the children. My mother was there, my father. This was the last time I have seen them.[129]
>
> Lucy M.: I can remember my father standing by the fence there and crying and [*pauses*] you know [*silence*].[130]
>
> Yetta F.: People were hanging out the windows.[131]
>
> Regina S.: My father came to the *Dulag*. And he was calling me. And one of the girls in the *Dulag* said, "Your father's here." And I went to the window. And—this was his last words, I heard—he says to us, "Don't obey the kosher laws, whatever, you can eat everything."[132]
>
> Mania S.: [speaking of her mother] And she came. She brought me some food. This was the last I saw of her.[133]
>
> Chana B.: [*very tentative*] Maybe I—my mother came close by just to, to—I think she threw to us something to eat. I remember the little sister was waiting with her.[134]
>
> Anna W.: We were taken to a school. And I have never seen my mother again.[135]

Detention at the *Durchgangslager* was also the last time their parents or siblings saw them—the survivors remember feelings of guilt, abandonment, and frustration at their inability to reassure their distraught relatives across the fencing or through the windows.

> Shoshana L.: They sent me away also to the same, like, *Durchgangslager*. You know, in Sosnowiec was a selection place. Where I went to see my brother there [before]. So they took us then with trucks and girls and they stuck us in a big, on the top, the top floor. They thought we would run away. There was

nothing there, just a long, a long table. And we were all night there.[136]

Interviewer: How many girls were there?

Shoshana L.: I don't know, maybe a hundred. Maybe less, less. Two trucks, we were squashed around. And we didn't get anything there. We got a little bucket if we want to go. They locked us up there. Next morning the children start to scream, scream, what are they screaming, they see someone walking outside. Walking? So I was far away, I said, "So who is there walking?" I want to see someone, too. So I went near to the window. And I can see my mommy is walking. She came to see where I am. So anyhow I don't know if she ever seen me. Because I was short, because she went around, because she has seen the big building, she can see, you know, in the top room. But you couldn't open the windows, you know. But we screamed, I was screaming, I become hysterical, because I said, "That's my mom! That's my mom!" And then she looked, looked. Because she maybe, I don't know, maybe she has seen me. I have no idea if she have seen me. But I have seen her. Then for a short time she looked. But she turned around, resigned. She turned around. That was the last time I have seen her. I remember what she wore. She was so beautiful.[137]

Rusia Y.: You know what? The parents—here is the front from the police. [*gestures*] But in another side, they could come to see us. This was on the second floor. So what did the girls do. Everybody had to give string and she makes a note, yes? She lets it down. And the mother give her, give to the children food or something . . . But when I saw my mother, I didn't recognize her . . . Oh, she was looking terrible, terrible, terrible. But she comes, she brings me. She couldn't talk, she was crying. "Meyn kindl, meyn kindl, meyn kindl." It was very sad. What can you do. [*loses her composure, then puts her hand to her mouth*] I promised myself I will not cry.[138]

Families did not only come to the fence to give packages; often they could switch siblings or bribe the Gestapo authorities to release their loved one. Natan Szternfinkiel, who, like Paweł Wiederman, developed a contemporary account of the occupation in Sosnowiec published after the war, writes:

> Transports of people for shipment to German camps were usually organized on the basis of calls from the Jewish Council, but they were often completed with the help of the [Schmelt] Operation round-ups by [ss officers] Lindner, Kuczynski, Knoll and Ludwig. In the event that a person marked by the Jewish Council did not come to *Dulag*, then the militia forced the family member to deliver a substitute, who was called an "ersatz."[139]

While an "ersatz" was a substitute, the Jewish Council and the Schmelt staff at the *Dulag* also had a practice of holding a family member such as a grandparent hostage, as a "*Geisel*," to force a more desirable potential worker to turn herself in. The possibility of substituting people and the terror of a beloved family member held as a *Geisel* created a new set of wrenching decisions for families. For example, the ss sent Rita R. to coerced labor when she and her parents had attempted a strategy for saving her older sister, who had received a summons from the Jewish Council.

> Rita R.: I was taken away 1941, February. I was fourteen years old ... They took me for my sister ... Because they thought, my parents thought that I was so young, they are not going to send me to concentration camp. I would come home. But meanwhile I didn't come home.[140]

The testimony of Rita R. helps explain why girls who were under the official age for coerced labor ended up in the camps. Age was simply not consistently confirmed; the ss received payments from the companies per female Jewish body.

Rose S., age fifteen at the time of this episode in Sosnowiec, remembers:

> Rose S.: It happens that in that school building which was across the street from us, they kept the people what they send away. So they took [my brother] over there. My mother was very heartbroken because he was a very shy and quiet boy. And I was really like more—tomboy. And I said to my mother, "You know what? Maybe I go for him. Let me go and try. Maybe we will exchange." Because Jewish police was there also, watching them,

and the German police. So I went over. And I packed just a little bag and I went over there to try to just make the switch.[141]

The police agreed, but Rose S.'s brother himself refused her offer.

Regina S.'s recollection from 1942 adds to this emerging picture of the *Dulag*:

> Regina S.: It was a holiday. My father was with my brothers at the synagogue . . . When I came home a neighbor told me that the Gestapo was here and they took my mother, two brothers, and my sister . . . to the *Dulag*. So I was terrified. I start crying. I run out, down the street. And I met a Jewish *milici*—this was like a police. Jewish police. And he was a friend of ours. So I begged him that he should help me. He should do something for me. I want to save them. So he said to me, "What I can do for you, if you go, volunteer, to the *Dulag*, I can try to let your mother out." And that's what I did. He took me to the *Dulag* and they let my mother and the two brothers out. And I was with my sister in the *Dulag*.[142]

What Regina S. remembers as a favor from a Jewish policeman was likely the intended outcome of the detention of her family as hostages—to compel her to arrive for a labor camp assignment.

Taking these testimonies together, a picture emerges of a growing awareness among Jews that the priorities for the authorities in Sosnowiec were bodies capable of labor rather than specific individuals. By 1942, Jews increasingly viewed labor as a means of evading harsher outcomes. The Jewish Council sent a letter requiring Fay B. to report to the *Dulag* in 1942. She remembers her mother standing at the fence "with a shawl and a green suitcase" for her. She was told, "Your mother is here," and they were able to kiss goodbye over or through the fence. Her mother reassured her: "If you work you will be fine, my meydl."[143]

The testimony-givers also make clear that the *Durchgangslager* was a space of negotiation, bribery, sexual exploitation, and the hiding or revising of identities, ages, and connections. It is one instance of many in which corruption, bribery, and skimming were interwoven with persecutory motivations in the treatment of Jews throughout the areas controlled by the Nazi regime.¹⁴⁴ At least one survivor, Fay B., remembers that *Durchgangslager* staff were not only able to be bribed, but participated in sexual barter with the Jewish girls and young women. Fay B.'s family lived in a large building across the street from the detention site. She recounts that a married couple was held at the *Dulag* for assignment to forced labor. As Fay B. remembers it, their teenaged daughter, who had been left at home, came to the *Dulag* offices without their knowledge and purchased their freedom by having sexual intercourse with a Gestapo officer.¹⁴⁵

It is not clear whether the ss, Gestapo, and Jewish militia took every person they arrested to the *Durchgangslager*, or just those assigned to coerced labor. Either German soldiers or the ss arrested Fay B.'s father in 1940 and detained him there. As Fay B. remembers it, her mother went to the *Dulag* to protest. She recalls that he was released because his arrest had been an error, but it could be that her mother did not share with Fay B. that a bribe took place. In 1941 the Gestapo took her father from the family home to the *Dulag* again, but her mother bribed an officer and he was released. Finally, the Gestapo sent him to one of the Gleiwitz labor camps (in Gliwice) for the large road-building projects that absorbed so many Jewish men from Zagłębie.¹⁴⁶ Fay was fourteen and felt the loss of her father's presence keenly. After six months her father was scheduled to return. Fay and her younger brother waited at the *Dulag* as truck after truck unloaded returnees, her father not among them. She suddenly realized he had indeed disembarked, but she had not recognized him. He told her, "I had to build a whole highway to come home."¹⁴⁷

In May 1942 the ss in the Schmelt system implemented the first mass deportations from Zagłębie to Auschwitz-Birkenau. This was a turning point for the Jews in Zagłębie; until May most Jews had the credible hope that their work, either in the workshops that still functioned inside Sosnowiec and Będzin or at work sites elsewhere, would be the extent of the Nazi project to harm Jews. Those with family members who had been leased to factories outside of the region hoped that this agreement would protect them. The Jewish Council of Elders and the Schmelt organization authorities were well aware of these perceptions and took care to mislead the Jewish residents, who were summoned to Sosnowiec's sports stadium in 1942 on the pretext of document confirmation.¹⁴⁸

Eta B.: First of all, we supposed to go and register. And that day. We supposed to go register. But before going to register at that place, we sent somebody to see what's there. So they said, "There are just tables and chairs. And you have to come just to register. And if you don't register, you don't get the coupons for the rations—to get the food. And whoever wouldn't come is going to be shot."[149]

Once hundreds were inside and had been made to wait for two days in the open air, Kuczynski, Lindner, and other Schmelt staff selected out young people for labor, sent some families back to their homes, and forced those remaining onto trucks that would take them to Auschwitz. Several of the survivors arrived at the camps in the Trautenau region in 1942 as a result of this selection.

Regina P.: They said to everybody that all Jews what's left in the city have to go to a stadium. And we have to go, all of the—all Jews went over there. And when we went over there they "select." To go, like, uh, I remember was 1—1A, 1A was to go a camp, to a working camp.[150]

Rosalie S.: [from Modrzejów, near Będzin] They [the ss] brought us to a meadow, where they gathered the entire town. All the Jews from town were gathered on that meadow. Next to the river. And there they kept us for hours and hours and hours. Later on they separated old people from young people. Myself, my sister, and my brother were all taken away.[151]

Shoshana L.: Everyone was saying, "Where's the office? Where can we register?" And no one said where to register. Register? We are just standing! We are waiting. Twelve, one, two, three. No food, nothing. People coming, droves, from the whole Zagłębie area. Everybody—Sosnowiec, Będzin, Dąbrowa, Czeladz, the whole area Zagłębie. All to register but we don't see the office, there is no one to register. And everyone come in droves and thousands.[152]

Tola G.: I worried terrible about my parents. It was killing me inside. All the time. I remember when—seeing my mother the last time on that sport place, when they pushed her away from

> me, she wanted to say goodbye to me ... She was wearing a trench coat. She didn't have the sleeves and it was just thrown over her. And when they pushed her, I remember this trench coat fell to one side on her one shoulder and she reached out like she wanted to grab me in. And this was the last time I saw her.[153]

> Lola W.: All the people went to this place. And we were there for two days. It was raining. Ladies gave birth to little babies in the open. No food. The first day they made—it was raining cats and dogs. They made us stand in line. Thousands upon thousands of people. During the day and a whole night—I don't know how long I took—they told us to stand in line and in front, when we came, it was our turn, it was, uh, German officers. And they waved. Left, right, left, right.[154]

The 1942 sports stadium event also initiated the relocation of some—not all—remaining families into formal ghettos: Środula, for Sosnowiec residents, and Kamionka for those in Będzin. The raids forcing all Jews into these ghetto areas, which were then patrolled, did not occur until mid-1943.[155] After the 1942 stadium event, Zagłębie Jews began to seek out labor assignments instead of evading them. Tola G. explains the family-centered context for these decisions:

> Tola G.: I asked [ss officer] Ludwig, who was a high German official there ... I, I begged him to send me to Ober Altstadt, where my sister was ... I knew that it would give peace [to] my parents, this I knew hundred percent, if I would be with my sister, who—she was a more—uh—pampered girl.[156]

Tola G.'s testimony here centers her effort to "give peace" to her parents, in part because an older sister was less independent and capable of surviving on her own in the same camp.

These instances of Jewish girls and young women revising or completely upending their familiar prewar positions within their families to enable release from detention, obtain food or information, relieve suffering, and support parents emotionally and materially extends the observation by Marion Kaplan in her book referenced at the beginning of this chapter. Jewish women facing Nazi policies "experimented with new behaviors," "taking on 'male' roles both within and outside the family."[157]

Testimonies render these "new behaviors" in vivid specificity, although the testimony-givers do not consider them particularly "male." They share stories of quick intuition, daring, moving forward in the face of fear, and an ability to read people and assess the payoff for taking a risk, but remember these as newly integrated into their identities as young Jewish females. These socially embedded, personal, contextually dependent behaviors are reminders that, as Evgeny Finkel notes in *Ordinary Jews*, familial and social senses of belonging (as well as imposed structures of mobility and immobility) function as independent determinants of choice even when distorted by fear and trauma. Yet as Anna Hájková demonstrates in *The Last Ghetto*, while senses of oneself as a social being, mediated by ethnicity, gender, age, and other factors, continued through and within processes of oppression, these self-understandings were also *produced by* the persecutory setting.[158]

Taking these insights into account and circling back to Kaplan, this chapter documents the constant revision and renegotiation of one's position within the family system required to retain a sense of Jewish meaning inside a genocidal project aimed at dismantling it. It also documents the very specific harms that a coerced labor system imposes on those attempting to survive it, harms that would evade later attempts at healing and repair.

CHAPTER 2

The Local Logics of Coerced Labor

What were the precise contours of the labor system that the girls and women from Zagłębie found themselves in between 1940 and 1945? Historians of the Holocaust have long established that the Nazi regime pursued coerced labor policies in response to changing economic conditions, especially labor shortages in industries crucial to the war effort. Coerced labor was not a single, intentional policy carefully crafted by Nazi elites. Instead, it shifted by time and place, but the number of people affected—Jewish and non-Jewish—steadily increased as private companies shifted to war production demanding more workers and the SS itself developed economic initiatives using concentration camp labor. Jews in Germany and occupied territories, non-Jewish civilians in Poland, prisoners of war—the Nazi regulations and policies that affected all of these groups not only changed over time but also varied according to implementation on the ground.

The coerced labor regime began, as Wolf Gruner has documented, in the Reich itself in the 1930s.[1] The model of creating labor registration offices in each city and town to facilitate compulsory labor policies was established in 1938. These offices (*Arbeitsämter*) were the link between communities of Jews who had suffered a sudden loss of economic resources and private companies or local municipalities seeking to exploit inexpensive labor. The Nazi regime expanded this practice as it annexed Austria, the Sudetenland, and then territories including East Upper Silesia.[2] The Schmelt system grew out of this model, in that private companies initiated the request for laborers who lived at home and were not detained in concentration camps, beginning in 1940.[3] State-run initiatives also requisitioned labor from the Schmelt system, as was the case with Fay B.'s father, who was sent to Gleiwitz (Gliwice) for road-building with the *Reichsautobahnlager* (RAB) labor initiative.[4] German administrators and Jewish staff in the main Schmelt office in Sosnowiec processed the requests, set up financial transfers, and communicated with the ss in Sosnowiec regarding the number, timing, and destination of the workers; indeed, working inside the Schmelt system was yet another labor assignment sought out by Jews as protection from street harassment and starvation in 1940 and 1941 and deportation in 1942 and 1943.[5]

This labor registration model positions the Schmelt system as somewhat out of step with broader developments in the exploitation of prisoner labor controlled by the ss-Wirtschafts- und Verwaltungshauptamt (WVHA), an institution central to much of the historical scholarship on labor in the Nazi regime.[6] The companies that participated in the Schmelt system were different from the huge industrial concerns that were first courted by Hitler and who later partnered directly with large concentration camps, such as IG Farben.[7] Aside from the *Reichsautobahnlager* project, the workshops and factories were small, local concerns; in the Trautenau region, they were family firms. According to policy, these small companies were to partner with a concentration camp or site of detention with an ss presence and share ss personnel for surveillance, guard duties, and punishment.[8] In practice, firms such as those in the Trautenau region, but also those throughout Silesia and the Sudetenland, evaded this requirement. Instead, firm owners identified Gentile employees to deputize as guards. In late 1943 Nazi authorities required these employees to undertake special training and return to the work camps as formal "ss guards."

These guards had a determinative influence on the daily lives of the girls and women in the camps in the Trautenau region. Some were brutal and used violence arbitrarily; others took a transactional approach, using less violence in exchange for objects or favors; and a few protected the girls and women from starvation, disease, and overwork, all aspects of female guard behavior well known to Holocaust scholars.[9] In the case of the Trautenau-region camps, because these guards had been company employees, they were embedded in the social life of the workplace and the local municipality.[10] The main guard for each camp, the *Lagerführerin*, was responsible for escorting the girls and women from barracks to factory and back; the clerical work of tracking each laborer's activities, such as days off for illness or informal assignment to other duties; handing out mail; billing for and acquiring food and supplies; maintaining the barracks; organizing the laborers when the Schmelt ss visited or when, in 1944, SS from Auschwitz or Gross-Rosen came to conduct selections; and responding to correspondence from various parties. Under the *Lagerführerinnen* were other *Aufseherinnen*, who varied in number over time, and some barracks had *Judenältesten*, Jewish laborers who were to oversee barrack life when the guards were absent. Guard violence took the forms of on-the-spot brutality, such as hairpulling; beatings with a truncheon, a whip, or the hands; withholding of food; forcing prisoners to clean human waste; and locking individuals in a cellar or closet. There were no reports of the type of ritualized performances of humiliation and torture in full view of all prisoners—as was the case in Auschwitz and Gross-Rosen—nor were there dedicated spaces for punishment, such as cells, or equipment, such as shackles. A few survivors remember being locked in a closet or observing someone else being punished in this way. Multiple survivors recall that guards resorted to punitive head shaving.

> Rose L.: [The guard] shaved her head and she made a big cross on top [*gestures with hands on her own head*], top of her head. She had hair like an angel, just long, blonde hair.[11]

Several girls and women died on site due to illness compounded by lack of nutrition and preventive medical care, or by exposure or overexertion, although exact numbers are not available.[12] There were no systematic executions at these work camps; ill or resistant laborers were sent home until 1943 and to Auschwitz-Birkenau after that date. There are two exceptions. Survivors who had been assigned to Parschnitz recall one shooting in 1944 by an SS squad escorting a death march through the town. The girls and women had been banned from viewing the march and one person did move paper covering the barracks window to look; she was shot by an SS guard accompanying the march who saw her. Some survivors also recall a hanging in one part of Trautenau or Parschnitz. Testimony-givers do not depict the hanging in detail; some say it was a mother and daughter who tried to escape. It appears that periodically people did indeed escape. There is little documentation available on this topic, but the factors facilitating escape included the ease of interaction with the local Gentile population. As testimony-givers remember it, the girls and women believed that they were working to support and protect their families at home in Zagłębie and did not want to endanger that bargain.

Several aspects of the Schmelt system position these Sudetenland camps as outside of the overall understanding of camp processes. Sending people back to their family homes, for example, is a practice that has not been systematically analyzed by scholars. This raises the question of what to call the sites of detention to which the Zagłębie girls and women were assigned beginning in 1940. As the International Tracing Service's guide notes, they do not fit easily into a single category, and perpetrator documents even refer to them by various labels.[13] As Alfons Adam notes in his discussion of coerced labor in the Sudetenland, these were not coerced labor camps (*Zwangsarbeitslager*), nor were they concentration camps until 1944; some possibilities are "factory camps" (*Betriebslager*) or simply "work camps" (*Arbeitslager*).[14]

To understand the nature of the work sites in the Trautenau region, it may be best to use a company-based approach, in which the choices of the firms themselves shaped the conditions of coerced labor from 1940 through 1942; by 1943 the SS intervened to transform these work sites into coerced labor camps, or *Zwangsarbeitslager*; by 1944, they were consolidated into concentration camps. This approach is supported by Germany's state-sponsored Erinnerung, Verantwortung, Zukunft (EVZ) Foundation, created in 2010 as an extension of the government's attempt to grapple with legal claims from coerced labor survivors. The EVZ documents the various types of persecution not encompassed by the formal concentration camp categories.[15] Using the materials collected by the German courts in the 2000s to compensate forced laborers (Jewish and non-Jewish), the EVZ includes in its lists of sites of detention any company "in which it can be proven that forced labor was performed," even if that company was not directly responsible for "inhumane conditions" of living space. While the EVZ is very clear that it is not presenting historical research and only making evidence available, its work clarifies that coerced labor was a fluid and changing phenomenon linked not only to SS organizations but also to private companies, which themselves had changing relationships to the Nazi regime over the course of the war years.

LOCAL STRATEGIES OF LABOR EXPLOITATION

On July 4, 1942, the floor manager of the Etrich textile plant in Trautenau wrote a letter to the Trautenau Labor Office (*Arbeitsamt*). On the surface, it was an explanation of why the firm was not meeting the production quotas it had promised. But a careful reading of its tone reveals frustrations with the firm's reliance on young people held against their will:

> At the end of last year [1941], I began the successive deployment of Jewish forced laborers in our company, whose number increased to about 300 during the last few months. This deployment, which was necessary due to the increase in production demanded by the highest places, met resistance understandably at the team level, resistance to cooperation especially in the fine spinning room [*Feinsaal*], where attention to detail is demanded . . . so the training of these completely unskilled workers was very slow and a significant increase in production could not be achieved.[16]

The letter is a concrete documentation of what should have been obvious to all: groups of terrified young women kept away from their families and quartered in poor conditions with little food cannot be "managed" into a highly productive workforce. This central contradiction of all forced labor projects is the ever-present subtext of the memos, orders, and bureaucratic processes that moved the exploitation of European Jews forward.

How did Etrich, Haase, Kluge, and the Walzel brothers, long established in this mountain region, view their role in the rise of Nazi Germany and the murder of Europe's Jews? None were put on trial after the war. None are viewed today as war criminals. As individuals, the owners fled westward when the war ended in 1945, blending in with the flood of Sudeten Germans hoping to avoid the Soviet zone of occupation, as did many other firm owners and shareholders. The extent of private company use of Jewish and non-Jewish coerced labor and the precise documentation of company names gained wider awareness only with the legal agreements for compensation reached in the late 1990s and early 2000s between the German government and various parties in the United States and elsewhere.[17] As noted previously, the German government worked with industry to create the EVZ Foundation, through which individual firms still operating today can register their acknowledgment of complicity with Nazi-era exploitation.[18] None of the Trautenau-region family firms appear on the public list, although these names (Etrich, Haase, Kluge, and Walzel) are used by a variety of businesses today. For the purposes of this book, what is revealing is the sensibility Northern Bohemian German speakers brought to their use of local labor and then coerced Jewish labor, and how small and midsize family firms were positioned inside the Schmelt system (later the Gross-Rosen subcamp system) to affect the lives of the girls and women of Zagłębie so deeply.

The industrial families who owned the factories in the Trautenau region had developed their expertise and trading connections in the 1800s as part of the Hapsburg Empire. The Trautenau family firms looked toward Vienna for purchasers and to the surrounding countryside for raw materials, developing what Caitlin Murdock calls a borderland, regional identity overlapping Saxony and Northern Bohemia.[19] Migration was part of this, and the Trautenau region was characterized by labor mobility.[20] World War I and the worldwide depression, including fluctuation in the textile markets, further lowered standards of living and marginalized labor. Many employees supplemented the long and brutal workdays with piecework they took home, which was at times done by younger family members. Not surprisingly, the textile workforce often conflicted with the factory owners, especially in Austria, which saw strikes and ethnically tinged riots pitting German speakers against Czech speakers willing to work for lower wages throughout the late 1800s and early 1900s.[21]

All four of the firms were led by "founding families" in Trautenau, who adapted textile-processing techniques and machinery from Britain in the 1800s to become leaders of industrialization in Bohemia: Alois Haase, the Walzel Brothers, Johann Kluge, and Ignaz Etrich. Because of their prominence in the region's history and importance to the economy, local historians and enthusiasts offer a wealth of detail on the technical development of the spinning and weaving manufacturing, as well as the response of the families to rising labor demands.[22] As was the case elsewhere in the textile industry in the mid- to late 1800s, Haase, for example, employed men, women, and children for fourteen-hour days, but these conditions gradually changed with the rise of social democratic movements in the 1890s.[23] As was the case in the 1844 Silesian weavers' uprising, workers in Trautenau threatened owners with violence.[24] By the 1930s, labor had been unionized, although unions were divided by political party.[25] The four main family firms were socially integrated into the region's elite and collaborated to lobby for preferential tax and trade policies. Their capital accumulation allowed them to survive the global depression, although damaged. J. A. Kluge in particular bought out any new small competitors throughout the early twentieth century.[26]

With annexation to the Reich in 1938 came scrutiny regarding the technological level of all local industrial plants; Haase, Walzel, Etrich, and Kluge were able to ward off absorption into Reich industries and, in fact, acquired new capital and contracts with the Wehrmacht already in 1939.[27] They switched to production for military purposes exclusively, which was crucial to surviving inside the Nazi regime's economic framework. The capital infusion also allowed the Kluge firm to appropriate Jewish firms, such as the K. H. Barthel firm in Gabersdorf.[28] The Nazi authorities did force Kluge to transfer a portion of its physical plant to Siemens in 1944, as well as part of its Jewish and prisoner-of-war coerced labor force, the result of a German government push to relocate war production to the Sudetenland.[29] By 1943, each of the founding families had ownership or shares in multiple concerns throughout the Sudetenland under the names of sons, grandsons, brothers, and nephews.[30]

As the main scholars of Northern Bohemia's radicalization in the 1930s, Volker Zimmermann, Jörg Osterloh, and Caitlin Murdock have shown the interwar period was characterized by sharpened ethnic identification, increased antisemitism instigated in part by Germany, and a strong push for regional autonomy rather than annexation with Germany itself.[31] Earlier in the century the "Sudeten Germans" were not all unified and at times expressed pride in being "Czechoslovak Germans" or "German Bohemians."[32] Yet the possibility of self-rule offered by Konrad Henlein's version of the Nazi party, the Sudetendeutsche Freikorps, was tempting; for example, "Sudeten German" financial organizations allowed themselves to be taken over by banks in Germany proper as a way of achieving ostensible financial independence.[33] Henlein used paramilitary tactics to further destabilize the region and intimidate Czech speakers, Jews, and anyone who was not ethnically German (including migrant workers).[34] The aim was to undermine the ethnic accommodation in the German-majority region of democratic Czechoslovakia.[35] Northern Bohemia became "the Sudetenland," a center of right-wing, anti-modern political activity and the target of an extraordinary Nazi propaganda campaign.[36]

However, the priorities of German speakers in the outer rim of Czechoslovakia in the 1930s was not hatred of Jews. As Jörg Osterloh puts it:

The future elite of the Sudetenland's German community grew up in a climate shaped by hate and intolerance of the Jews. But racial antisemitism was not yet capable of gaining broad support. While tens of thousands of Sudeten Germans tacitly accepted the exclusion of their Jewish neighbors, most of them prioritized the "nationality struggle" with the Czechs.[37]

Moreover, the German speakers living in Czechoslovakia did not agree among themselves what the outcome of that "nationality struggle" should look like.[38] Historians such as Eagle Glassheim and Tara Zahra note that strong ethnic attachments did not necessarily go along with one's linguistic identity; most residents spoke both Czech and German.[39] As was the case for Jewish citizens of Germany and Austria, Czechoslovakian Jewish families in this region were educated and assimilated.

Supported financially and logistically by the Nazi regime in Germany, Henlein had already prepared antidemocratic institutions to be put in place prior to October 1938. The annexation only legitimized his legal proposals, individual administrators, and practices.[40] The prominence of Henlein's political party and street thugs was familiar to all. The effect on the textile factories in Trautenau was mixed. The small city tucked into the mountains with streets called, for example, "Mountain Street," had to change these long-standing, folk-inspired names to Nazi-approved names such as "Adolf Hitler Strasse."[41]

Street naming is just one example of how the annexation worked against the cultural autonomy the Sudeten Germans thought they had been fighting for. Economically, Trautenau companies lost the protection of Czechoslovakian tariffs, lost the markets of those countries not trading with Germany, suffered the costs of readjusting standards and policies to those of the German Reich, and were cut off from trade circuits running through the Czechoslovakian capital, Prague.[42] Yet as Jörg Osterloh puts it, in 1938 most Sudeten Germans viewed the Third Reich uncritically; Volker Zimmermann finds that they looked forward to a "new world" with enthusiasm.[43]

A close look at the family firms in the Trautenau region shows that some actors benefited from the new access to capital, new contracts with the Wehrmacht, and freedom to take over vulnerable companies. J. A. Kluge in particular was an avid Henleinist and from his company's home base in Ober Altstadt strongly supported not only the separatist cause but also Nazism itself.[44] The November 9, 1938 Kristallnacht pogrom in Germany was taken up enthusiastically in Trautenau. Mobs of Freikorps members and other opportunists looted Jewish businesses.[45] They burned down the Trautenau Synagogue, and most remaining Jews fled over the border to what was still, for a few months, Czechoslovakia.[46]

Along with annexation to the Reich came the legal use of coerced Jewish labor. Kluge, Etrich, Walzel, and Haase were not truly short of labor, because their workers had always been women and children; the German army draft cut into labor for other industries, but not textiles. But a new source of coerced labor was made available in September 1939 when the German army invaded Poland and instituted the brutal occupation detailed in chapter 1. The difference between exploiting textile workers prior to World War II and Jewish (and later non-Jewish) labor during World War II is that the former could resist, a resistance made famous by Marx's analysis of the 1844 textile workers' uprising and Heine's poem, "The Weavers of Silesia."[47] Heine's last verse is particularly apt:

> The shuttle flies, the loom cranks,
> We weave feverishly both day and night—
> "Old Germany, we weave your funeral shroud,
> We weave into it a threefold curse,
> We're weaving, we're weaving!"

THE SCHMELT SYSTEM IN UPPER SILESIA AND THE EASTERN STRIP

The overall approach the German state took to the economy between 1938 and 1942 was at times planned, at times improvised, at times the outcome of bureaucratic competition, and at times the result of how the war was proceeding; private companies adapted, strategized, and sought to keep a competitive position among rivals.[48] The Trautenau textile firms had behaved as a local cartel prior to annexation; their goals were to keep textiles within the category of "war production." German economic planners attempted to create incentives for private companies to expand their capacities in the direction of shifting military or foreign exchange needs; at the same time, manufacture for the German civilian market could not be ignored.[49] In addition, Hitler issued and withdrew directives according to his own whims. The implication for small private companies was that demand, labor supply, and the specific skills required shifted unpredictably. They relied on the local labor registration offices (*Arbeitsämter*) for access to coerced laborers. These offices were run by the local civil administration in most places but by the Schmelt organization in East Upper Silesia.⁵⁰

Upper Silesia was an ethnically mixed border region that had been part of Germany prior to the interwar period and whose residents variously thought of themselves as Germans, German speakers, Silesians, Poles, and Jews.⁵¹ Germany had no prewar claim, however, to the adjacent "Eastern Strip," which was populated by fewer Germans and many more Poles and Jews.⁵² The Eastern Strip was home to a vibrant economy based on extensive trade networks and highly skilled labor and anchored by the growing city of Sosnowiec and the larger urban center Katowice.⁵³ The extraction of raw materials such as coal, the manufacturing of finished products, trade, and retail—all of these economic dimensions coexisted in Upper Silesia and also in the Eastern Strip.⁵⁴ In 1940 Himmler had the Eastern Strip annexed to the Reich as a special police-administered territory.⁵⁵ Historians have noted that incorporating the Eastern Strip into Germany meant adding a Jewish population of approximately 68,000; in addition, Jews from other areas were resettled there in 1939 and 1940, including Jews from Oświęcim (the town) and from the territory to the west of the Eastern Strip.⁵⁶ The incorporation of this territory meant that both its Jewish and non-Jewish Polish labor could be contained and controlled. The police acquired extensive governing authority.⁵⁷ But they coexisted with other overlapping local authorities such as the Wehrmacht, the civil administration, auxiliary militias recruited from the local German-speaking population (the *Selbstschutz*), and the *Gauleiter*, the NSDAP official, and his staff.⁵⁸ To maintain control of the borders, the labor, and the economic activity of Upper Silesia, Himmler put the police chief of Breslau (in Polish, Wrocław), SS Oberführer Albrecht Schmelt, exclusively in charge of all "foreign labor" and protected him from the internal competition for influence inside the SS.⁵⁹

Schmelt set up a headquarters in Sosnowiec, where he installed SS and Gestapo originally from Breslau/Wrocław responsible only to him, headed by Heinrich Lindner.⁶⁰ He also allied with first Richard Wagner and then Fritz Bracht, the successive *Gauleiter* for Upper Silesia.[61] Bracht enjoyed more extensive political control than other *Gauleiter* because in the annexed territories power devolved onto the *Gauleiter*; this was also the case for Arthur Greiser in Wartheland.[62] Schmelt also moved to take control of the Jewish Council of Elders in Sosnowiec (which had been created by the Kattowitz Gestapo) and expand its purview into the wider Zagłębie region. The Jewish Council managed the process of coerced labor in the Eastern Strip that a Labor Registration Office (*Arbeitsamt*) would perform in other locations. As was the case in the Altreich, anyone could request Jews for work—businesses, municipalities, private individuals. The Jewish Council of Elders processed the form, used its lists of Jewish residences to summon individuals, delivered them to the location, and charged the applicants a monthly fee per person, or, as the invoice noted, "per head." The Jewish Council kept a percentage and deposited the rest into a Dresdner Bank account under Schmelt's name.[63] As an individual, Schmelt himself was rarely present.[64] He secluded himself in a villa in nearby rural Parzymiechy, using Jewish labor as landscapers and other staff until 1943, when he was forced to relocate to Góra świętej Anny/St. Annaberg.[65]

Because the Schmelt system did not demarcate ghetto housing in Sosnowiec, Będzin, and the other small towns in the Eastern Strip until mid-1942 and did not force all Jews into patrolled ghettos until 1943, most Jews remained in their family homes for a significant length of time and tried to keep family members close.[66] Another factor also increased the mobility of Zagłębie's Jews: the demand for labor *inside* Sosnowiec, Będzin, and other local areas. German trustees (*Treuhandler*) arrived in 1940 to appropriate Jewish businesses, but they needed to hire the former owners to run these businesses; in some instances, the trustee was not even present.[67] In addition, hundreds of small "workshops" employing Jews popped up at this time to respond to immediate demands for goods. Both the long-standing firms and the workshops functioned as centers for licit and illicit exchange, as Jews needed to sell valuables and Germans sought to acquire them.[68] The result was that a significant percentage of Jewish people in the Eastern Strip had labor passes (*Sonderausweise* or "*Sonders*") allowing them to move through public areas before curfew (and after for night shifts).

In a memoir written after the war, Hadassah Rosensaft, a survivor who grew up in Sosnowiec, describes the complex local economy of Jewish labor, German owners, and the workshops. Since Rosensaft had the opportunity to work with others on her memoir and confirm factual evidence, the writing is measured and presented (in this section of the memoir) as historical documentation:

> The Jews in Sosnowiec came up with the idea of establishing workshops that would employ men, women, and even children over ten years old and would thus help them live, at least for a while. The German officials stationed in Sosnowiec were in favor of this idea, first because it would keep them from going to the Russian front, and second, because they could make a lot of money by accepting bribes. . . . A workshop called Braun produced boots for the German army; 1,400 Jews worked there. Another firm, Lande (which also operated a labor camp in Bunzlau, Germany), produced furniture for the German army and employed 600 Jews, including my husband, who was an expert in lumber.
> I worked in this shop's dental clinic three days a week taking care of the workers' teeth . . . [A]lmost half the Jewish population of Sosnowiec . . . worked in these and several other workshops. Every Jew tried to work there; special certificates, called *Sonders*, were issued as guarantees against deportation, but some small shops were liquidated in the second half of 1942 and people lost their *Sonders*.[69]

The possibility for Jews to work in local businesses and continue to live in their homes made the paltry wages offered of secondary importance to the temporary protection from deportation, relocation to the ghetto established in mid-1942, or separation from family that these "jobs" provided.[70]

> Chana S.: They told us if you make it, have a sewing machine, you can stay and make uniforms for the army . . . I started to sewing. And my cousins, aunties, start with the sewing.[71]

> Roza W.: And I found out that whoever gave them a [sewing] machine has a chance to go in to work. As it happened they had two machines in my name . . . and luckily I got this job . . . We were protected. We weren't sent away to camps.[72]

Fanny W.: I had to go look for a job [to avoid detention for labor]. And I found it. They gave—they hired me to sew buttons on the uniforms. In a factory. Used to be a Jewish factory—clothing. And that—I start going there every morning.[73]

In addition to remaining at home, access to others with items to barter for survival, and protection from street harassment and arbitrary detention by the ss, Jews received a small wage.[74] This balance of "coercion and incentives," as Stephan Lehnstaedt describes it, was carefully patrolled by Merin.

The Schmelt system oversaw the workshops in Sosnowiec and Będzin while at the same time matching individual Jews who did not find positions with workshops (most people did not) with firms outside of Zagłębie. Schmelt required employers to only use Jewish labor that had first passed through a "transit center," the Sosnowitz *Durchgangslager*, in which Jews were assembled before transport to work sites. In 1942, Schmelt established a second collection point at Cosel, on the western edge of his jurisdiction, which had a train station on the route from Western Europe toward Auschwitz.[75] His ss personnel stopped trains to pull out people for work, substituting them with dead bodies, a practice that Rudolf Höß complained about in his memoir.[76] The Sosnowitz *Dulag*, the Cosel operation, and the Jewish Council registration efforts together constituted the "wide net" to capture all potential Jewish labor in Upper Silesia. This net was aimed to not only capture labor but also to bring in firms that might be using Jewish labor outside of the Schmelt system. It is telling that the document establishing "Organization Schmelt" is directed at employers, not Jews.[77] "Schmelt Jews" and Schmelt-associated factories were considered separately from Jewish coerced labor sites elsewhere. One private subcontractor even indicated that it was required to keep "Schmelt Jews" and ss Jews working at the same site separated.[78]

THE SCHMELT SYSTEM AND THE INSPECTORATE OF THE CONCENTRATION CAMPS

As the historian of the Gross-Rosen subcamps Bella Gutterman notes, the Schmelt system took some time to dismantle.[79] In 1942 the WVHA, controlled by Oswald Pohl, empowered the Inspectorate of the Concentration Camps, Department DII, located in the Auschwitz administration, to take over the assignment of labor for all of Silesia and the Sudetenland. However, Schmelt successfully resisted WVHA control until he was disciplined for corruption in 1944. Schmelt's ability to maintain autonomy may have been in part due to Himmler's intentional structuring of his position and in part due to his own strategies.[80] Starting sometime in late 1943, any new workers (and new regulations) for the camps in the Trautenau region came from Department DII. At this time Himmler issued directives to deport all Jews out of Zagłębie (to Auschwitz-Birkenau). Private companies now sent their requests to DII instead of Sosnowiec; company staff traveled to Auschwitz to choose workers. Local guards such as those at the Trautenau-region camps had to provide more documentation on conditions in the barracks, facilitate SS visits from Auschwitz for selections, personally inspect workers, and identify groups to be transferred. The logistics were created by Gerhard Maurer, an SS official working under Richard Glücks.[81]

The Nazi regime transferred an increasing number of Jews to Auschwitz throughout 1944. Christian Gerlach, in his sweeping account of the Nazi project of murdering all of the Jews in Europe, documents and contextualizes the culling of people from deported groups across different camps and locations. For Auschwitz he draws on various secondary sources to conclude that the SS diverted about a quarter of the more than 430,000 Hungarian Jews arriving in Auschwitz in 1944 for labor.[82] This gives us an idea of the numbers that were absorbed by the companies. However, as Gutterman points out, it was difficult for DII to oversee Jewish laborers once they were transferred out. She writes, the "WVHA lost more and more control over the prisoner work force and developed into a mere agency that rented out forced-laborers to private firms."[83] While there is no direct confirmation that Pohl's WVHA "lost ... control" over coerced laborers once they left the grounds of Auschwitz-Birkenau, the survivors of the camps in the Trautenau region report that the SS visited to conduct "selections" only a few times. The SS continued to be paid directly by the companies per worker.

In practice, Maurer assigned an Inspectorate representative to each forced labor site and concentration camp.[84] His aim was as much to restrict the autonomy of the companies in their treatment of the prisoners as it was to capture the funds previously received by Schmelt.[85] In 1944 the Trautenau companies of Etrich, Haase, Kluge, and Walzel (as well as the other firms in the Sudetenland and Silesia) had to adapt to the presence of an SS representative of Maurer's office in Trautenau.[86] At the same time, they had access to even more Jewish labor because of the mass deportations in 1944 of the Jews in Hungary and the Hungarian occupied territories, the surviving Jews of Łódź, and smaller groups of Jews from elsewhere. To retain flexibility in meeting changing production quotas and skill requirements, the firms themselves developed a practice of subleasing people among themselves. The entire Sudetenland region of Aussig, where Trautenau was located, became characterized by the frequent forced movement of Jewish people. By late 1944, the Jewish girls and women in the camps in the Trautenau region faced even more crowded conditions as barracks were crammed with temporary additional people, meaning even less food, less access to medical care, and new outbreaks of lice and bedbugs.

In her book *Death Comes in Yellow: Skarżysko-Kamienna Slave Labor Camp*, Felicja Karay analyzes a coerced labor site in the Generalgouvernement, that is, one that was not part of the Schmelt system. She describes a site of persecution that has become unmoored from the values of rationality, productivity, and flexibility, even though the company, HASAG, had carved out room for significant autonomy.[87] Karay documents random killings, regularized sexual assaults, constant prisoner humiliation, little discipline on the part of guards, widespread smuggling and barter between the Jewish and Gentile Polish prisoners (and also between prisoners and the local population), which benefited only a few given the complex prisoner hierarchy, and corrupt local police who were part of the camp security staff. In one incident among many, a camp guard forced a male and female prisoner to engage in sex in the camp yard in front of assembled inmates.[88] Karay's study dismantles the notion that greater autonomy for the private firm necessarily translates into a more humane coerced labor experience.

The camps in the Trautenau region were violent, but nothing like Skarżysko-Kamienna. This may be due in part to the fact that the girls and women of Zagłębie went to small factory sites in which production processes were already underway and in which the Gentile workforce was already part of an established workplace culture. Most importantly, the girls and women lived in small barracks without men present (or intermittently present). They could develop social norms, ethical practices of care, and shared survival strategies in a setting of intense deprivation but only episodic overt violence. Yet while the girls and women were at their sites of detention, Nazi authorities sent their families to be killed in the mass deportations in 1942 and 1943. The local logic of the Schmelt system and the local logic of the Sudetenland factory owners shaped their experiences but did not, in the end, allow a Jewish world to survive.

CHAPTER 3

The Social World of Coerced Labor

The forced labor world into which the girls and women from Zagłębie were thrust was utterly new to them. It was a world created in the nineteenth century with the invention of industrial practices that transformed labor from individuals creating objects, such as clothing, to a series of repetitive movements on an assembly line. Some of the girls and women had done piecework at home or helped with a parent's manufacturing business; none had stood for twelve hours a day at a massive machine. The looms were huge. They required constant tending, correction, and repair. The massive rooms housing the assembly lines and rows of spools, looms, and wetting machinery were dirty with the particles given off by the flax and the water the fibers were soaked in. Their civil coworkers were brusque, uneducated, and initially annoyed at having to train confused teenagers. The floor manager was usually a man—often the only man at the work site. Both managers and employees were accustomed to an all-female workforce.

But the first surprise was the beauty. Trautenau was nestled in what the Czechs called the Krkonoše Mountains.

> Chana B.: It was beautiful. Everything was green. This was in the mountains.[1]
>
> Helena K.: The surroundings were beautiful. In the mountains. And it was summer.[2]
>
> Tola G.: Behind our camp there was a beautiful river, you know, the mountain's river are very shallow and you could see every stone, very pure, very clear. Behind that river was mountains, so gorgeous. Of course, we could see it from our camp. Behind the wall was the beauty.[3]

There were many bucolic settings for camps in Nazi-controlled territory—in this sense, the Trautenau region was not unusual. The survivors' memories of the physical setting speak to the significance of landscape, place, and space in the pathway through persecution, as they remember perceiving it as young people. The acknowledgment of beauty in the midst of fear—and the memory of that perception, many years later—could potentially be interpreted as a reconnection with a humanizing, sensory capacity to recognize the value of the natural world. At the same time, natural beauty was set off from the destination, as seen in Tola G.'s words: "Behind the wall was beauty."

Testimony-givers frequently remember finding a sibling, cousin, or hometown friend among the group being transported by train to Trautenau, whether they had been commanded to report to the *Dulag* alone, been forcibly picked up on the street, or were part of the mass roundups in Sosnowiec and Będzin in 1942. The Schmelt system allowed sisters, cousins, and, once in a while, mothers and daughters, to stay together in the same barrack section and at times near each other on the factory floor. Even when they did not know each other personally, the survivors remember they were among others from Zagłębie. The trip together in the passenger train seemed to make them even more aware that they were almost all in their teens.

> Chana B.: We was maybe twenty, maybe twenty-five—I don't remember—girls [traveling together]. The oldest, she was thirty, she was to us old already.[4]
>
> Ann F.: None of us knew what it means to put out a day's work. We were students. I had just finished seven grades when they took me to the camp . . . So we didn't understand, we didn't know, but we did work.[5]
>
> Shoshana G.: It was overwhelming for a nineteen-year-old. It was just unbelievable. And all of a sudden you were all by yourself.[6]
>
> Berta P.: The experience was awful. Because first we were away from our family. We were mistreated. We, um, it—the situation was very bad in that camp. We couldn't wash. We couldn't—they gave us practically nothing to eat. And it was really very depressing, very—it's undescribable [about Ober Altstadt].[7]

> Lucy M.: We were all [of us] all alone but we were all Jewish girls and—we all spoke the same language and we were all in the same shoes. And we were so young! We didn't understand anything. We had lived a very sheltered life, before. And, uh, we didn't understand what was waiting for us.[8]

Several survivors remember an open area near the train station at which company representatives identified which specific groups of girls they had paid for. At times there was negotiation and switching to be with siblings or near food. Masha S. had been in Parschnitz, was sent home because of illness, and then caught in a labor roundup in Dąbrowa and sent to another Schmelt camp (Bad Kudowa). She decided to directly ask for what she wanted.

> Masha S.: I walked over to this German woman. The ones who were choosing people for the kitchen, for the—all kinds of work. What you need, you know . . . I said, "I was already in a camp"—I was standing like a soldier, you had to . . . I am a good worker. I would like to stay in the kitchen."[9]

The production process was one of converting agricultural flax and cotton into military-grade thread. This involved some of the worst aspects of textile processing: combing flax for dirt, wetting it with hot, steaming water, placing thick strands onto special spools for separating, drying and rewetting the ever-thinner material, managing automated spools for breakage. Some were assigned to a stage in the process that required standing in water the entire twelve hours of the workday; the air inside the factory buildings was filled with particulate. Many battled skin and lung conditions during and after the war.

> Regina G.: My hands had holes. My hands had holes everywhere. From the water.[10]
>
> Suzan L.: From lack of vitamin, slowly my whole body was covered with um, with uh, with wounds. I still have some. Not the wounds, the brown spots.[11]
>
> Elizabet B.: I had, the first ten days all my fingers were bleeding.[12]
>
> Bracha H.: [*showing her arm*] I used to have gangrene.[13]

Rose S. worked a flax-combing machine at the Walzel factory.

> Rose S.: Saturday we cleaned the machines. And I stuck—you know, the machine was full of needles. Very, very long needles, pointy. And I got stuck a needle into my—by cleaning, I hurt my knee with such a needle.[14]

The survivors also spoke to the initial strangeness of being a young person placed in charge of massive machinery, which at times turned into pride, as well as disgust at the dirt.

> Rose K.: "Vorspinn" they called it, "Vorspinn." There were spools, big spools with cotton, like. And here was a big [*gestures with arms*], big, like, barrel. And the cotton was going through that barrel electrically. And when it tore the only way to stop it, you had to stop it with your stomach. So I had to fall over it [*leans forward*] and stop it. And then with a certain knot that they showed you to tie it. And let it go again . . . So constantly I had to lay and stop it with my stomach.[15]

> Regina S.: I was in arithmetic very good. And I had a, a job . . . They brought in raw materials. In barrels. On the barrel there was a number. How much the barrel weighs. And they put the material in a big scale. And I have to count—in my head, mind you!—how much, how much the raw material weighs . . . It was considered the best job.[16]

> Anna N.: At first I worked at a scale. And I was the one who weighed the fiber. These things, they were these kind of huge containers, and I had to always lift them onto the scale. . . . Later I had to measure the thread strength of the yarn.[17]

> Rena M.: And I was servicing the machines, about 150—na, maybe not that many, I don't remember exactly how many spools on the machine. And they needed—once the spools filled up, you had to take them off and put empty spools on again, and that's what we used to do. And I, uh, must have been more ambitious because I wanted a machine, I wanted to run a machine. I didn't want to be running from machine to machine. So eventually

SOCIAL WORLD OF COERCED LABOR

I qualified to run my own machine! . . . And I was very proud of myself. [She was fourteen.]¹⁸

Rita R.: They called it "*Spinnerei*." We made thread there. And it was wet. Everything went on water. And it was steamy, it was so hot there. And I, they gave us special wooden shoes, I couldn't wear those wooden shoes so I walked barefoot . . . That machine was bigger than I was.¹⁹

Frymeta F.: I was watching those machines, that the thread will not rip. I was going from one place to the other. It was 120 spools. To look through, will be everything in order.²⁰

Lucy M.: Because I was good in math and I spoke good German, I had a very good job.²¹

Ann F.: If you could see some of the girls! Dragging those bales of cotton. No man could do that!²²

In these portions of the testimonies the consciousness of one's gender and age intervene in the narration of the labor site as degraded and thus degrading. The conditions of the factory are remembered in detail as overwhelming, beyond one's abilities, dangerous and coerced ("I had to stop the barrel with my body"). But the pride and pleasure in demonstrating skills and overcoming even their own expectations of themselves in a setting that they had previously associated with maleness and maturity are interwoven in the memories. Rena M.'s memory of wanting to run her "own machine" is a remarkable commentary on the capacity to create personal meaning inside a setting of dehumanizing coercion.

The ability to cope with these assigned work duties while still experiencing unwanted and, for some, violent, separation from family differed by individual. Some testimony-givers recall nothing but dangerous conditions, physical and mental exhaustion at the repetitive nature of textile processing, long workdays with few breaks for using the toilet, and exposure to arbitrary abuse by factory staff or, at times, the camp guards. The conditions are evocative of the conditions across the textile industry in Germany in the late nineteenth and very early twentieth century, as women and girls were absorbed into factory labor on a broad scale. As Kathleen Canning demonstrated, the process "feminized" labor, while the prevalence of women in labor changed cultural conceptions of sexual difference; both had to be taken into account by the state.[23]

For the Jewish girls and women in coerced labor during the Holocaust, there was no state attempting to manage their welfare and no authorities concerned with their womanhood. Yet the production process itself—one in which each step depended on the one before and determined the one after—generated a type of social alliance. It shaped the interaction of the Jewish girls and women with each other, their interaction with non-Jewish Czech and German employees, and their strategies for survival. Nazi policy forbade any normal conversation between Jewish and non-Jewish workers. But for this manufacturing process to function, communication and coordination were crucial; the technology of flax processing required a factory space of interconnection, interdependence, and feedback. If thread became entangled at one stage of its refinement, those feeding the thread at an earlier stage had to know to temporarily stop the spools.

> Nettie S.: When I see everything, I say, "I can never make this. How can I do this?" Everything goes so fast. The machines. You know, the—everything, you know, the transmission goes so fast. And, uh, the belts, the belts. I say, "I never! How can I do this? I can never stay [at] this." ... Oh, but little by little. There was a German girl. What she showed me. How to—you have [to] every time, every time [something] break ... And she said how to fix it. Every time. To fix it. ... The next week she gave me another machine. I said, "Two machines! I be—that's my finish!" I said. "How can I do this?" But in a couple of weeks I do two machines. I do! I do! [*leaning forward, nodding for emphasis*][24]

Here Nettie S. conveys the almost paralyzing encounter with the machinery as she repeats, "How can I do this?" As her testimony continues, she renarrates her process of working through the fear and ends with something close to a feeling of accomplishment, with the help of a non-Jewish coworker. Nettie S. does not express any memory of fear, hesitation, or transgression in her interaction with the "German girl," nor does she remember gratitude; the formulation here is a matter-of-fact receptivity to training across ethnicity on the factory floor.

Flax, machinery parts, and thread had to be transported from one part of the factory to another constantly, with large baskets or an assembly line.

> Anna W.: I had a small machine. On one side I was, on the other side, the [German] lady. [Who] was called Hubert. That was the first spinning machine. Which had four bands of flax. I laid two bands of flax and she laid two bands and that came out on the other end in one band.[25]

Anna W.'s description of the industrial process is worth noting as a reference to the precision with which the workers had to coordinate their efforts. Working together every day for twelve hours over the course of weeks, months, and years, it is not surprising that interaction would occur. The outcome was an environment of circulating interactions, which is what affected the substance and tenor of worker interactions. Studies of the Holocaust suggest that coerced labor settings were one of the few places that non-Jews could deliver relatively low-risk aid to Jews. The daily routines built up a rapport among workers even when talking was forbidden; movement through a workplace outside of a formal camp, such as a factory (rather than a road-building site, for example), allowed for small exchanges of goods and messages. While Franciszek Piper has noted that "sub-camps were sometimes used to threaten and blackmail civilians working in factories,"[26] this aspect of coerced labor settings—their use as punishment for non-Jews who committed some kind of work-related offense, such as absenteeism—was not relevant for the Trautenau group of sites, in which the barracks were the places of detention and the factories, miles away, were civilian, with many non-Jewish employees working for wages.

The non-Jewish employees of factories in the Trautenau region reflected that area's mix of Czech and German speakers, Northern Bohemia's regional identity, and the long history of female labor in these factories. Most of the Jewish girls and women from the Zagłębie region spoke Polish, which had a small degree of overlap with Czech, making basic communication possible. It is not likely that the Jewish workers could always discern who was "really" German and who was Czech, but the testimonies are filled with references to ethnicity.

> Chana B.: The German girls worked for eight hours, we had to stay another two, three hours for more working.²⁷

Many of the survivors use the words "nice to us" or "kind" to describe the German and Czech workers, which was defined not only in terms of how often they smuggled them food. Help with a problem at the machinery, small gestures of indicating where food and sometimes medicine was hidden, and a general demeanor of sympathy were all recalled by survivors as being important in their mental fortitude and physical survival.

> Ann F.: One in particular—a person, a Czechoslovakian person—would say, "Go to number three barrel." You know, we did our strips of cotton in big barrels . . . There was a sandwich sometimes, under the cotton.²⁸

> Rosalie S.: Since we worked with the Czech and German people in the factory, some of them were very kind. And they would give us a little food.²⁹

> Phyllis Y.: And we were taught by workers, you know, who worked there!³⁰

> Lili T.: Smart Czech-isch people. Can you imagine? They was like a mother. They bring to the toilet—under it, because there was not many toilets and we had to go, too—under the toilet, food. A little paprika, a little fruit. Everything.³¹

Augusta S. is one of the few testimony-givers who worked not at a textile factory but at the Allgemeine Elektricitäts-Gesellschaft (AEG) plant established later in the war in Trautenau.³² She explains her memories of working enthusiastically but often searches for words, even consulting a dictionary during testimony. In this excerpt she means "assembly line" by the phrase "running table."

> Augusta S.: You know the running table. The end of the running table was sitting an old German. I think he was [*inaudible*]. He used to put some food to my friend, who was the last on the running table. To like—[*gestures out of the camera frame*].
> Interviewer: Oh, put some down for him?
> Augusta S.: Put some down for us, yes.

> Interviewer: And so you shared the food.
> Augusta S.: And I was—make—listen to my friend, who was the last. Close to the man.
> Interviewer: And they would share it.
> Augusta S.: We shared it.[33]

Augusta S.'s testimony is full of frustration for her as she tries to make herself clear, and the interviewer also struggles to understand her meaning. Here it is not clear that the interviewer realizes that Augusta S. and her friend at the other end of the assembly line were sharing the food offered by the elderly Gentile coworker. What Augusta S. points out is that the technical organization of the work facilitated the offering of food and the simultaneous ability of the giver to distance himself from the act. In all of these instances, food is not exchanged person to person, but left on a machine or a hidden part of the factory.

Yetta F. communicates a number of insights in this very short section of testimony referring to coworkers, which begins with the identification of the civilian coworker not as a Czech or German (as most other survivors did) but as a "Christian:"

> Yetta F.: So I had a sitting job. And I was working with a Christian lady opposite me. And we were like pulling through cotton, cotton to make the linens. It's called *Spinnerei* ... And when I was doing this, this lady used to bring me two pieces bread and butter every day. From a large, round bread. I must tell you. I think because of her I'm still alive. But if they would have—she was maybe ninety. Maybe eighty. But they if they would have grabbed her, seen doing this, she would have been dead. Definitely. But she was such a nice bubbe lady. That she would do this every day![34]

Here Yetta F. invokes a concrete and particular sense of place and labor ("sitting" "opposite" and "pulling through cotton" together) to ground her memory of receiving a nourishing supply of a small amount of food, important to her because of its regularity ("every day!"). She also identifies her helper as ninety years old, adding to the picture of a work site populated by locals who were often longtime employees. Most tellingly, however, is that she uses her testimony to bring her helper into her Jewish moral world by reidentifying her at the end as a "bubbe lady." In a sense, Yetta F. converts the woman in her word choices from one religion to another, giving her this gift of entry into Jewishness in exchange for the life-sustaining bread and butter.

Frymeta's testimony is similar, up to a point. She developed a skin disease on her hands; cuts from the thread became infected and her hands constantly bled. Her Gentile coworker noticed.

> Frymeta F.: She said she worked in the company for seventy years. And she never saw this in her life.[35]
>
> Interviewer: Did she do anything about it?
>
> Frymeta F.: She did help me a lot. She went and brought me a piece of good soap. And she told me I should put with water, warm, wash my hands. And then she brought me a piece of fat from a duck. And she said, "Smear it with this. Now don't tell nobody. Even your sister. Don't tell her. I can get killed for it." And I did. I did what she told me. And thank god for her. I healed my hands. She did this to me a couple times. She told me, "Don't worry, I will help you, don't tell no one."

Frymeta F. knows her well enough to understand her ethnicity, how long she had been employed, and to receive an accurate diagnosis and treatment for her condition; in turn, the older woman creates a bond of secrecy with "don't tell no one." The perspective these non-Jewish workers brought to the Jewish forced labor experience seems, from the survivors' testimonies, to have been a mix of solidarity and hard-edged realism, which manifests itself in the reported contradictory words of Frymeta helper: "I can get killed for it" and "Don't worry, I will help you."

Genuine, sometimes intimate relationships also developed, generated by the daily routine of long hours spent working side by side.

> Ida G.: There were some German women. In the, in the factory, too. But we were not allowed to converse with them. It was forbidden to converse with them . . . Once in a while a German woman would take a liking to us. And there was one woman, not far from me, who obviously liked me. And one day—we had a little basket next to the machine where we put our aprons . . . One day she sort of motioned to me across two machines to say I should

look in the basket. And sure enough, there was some food for
me.³⁶

Shoshana L.: One lady even told me to run away with her.³⁷

It is unclear how sexualized the relationships presented in this extract were; sometimes older women developed familial or motherly attachments to the young Jewish workers. In Helena K.'s case, the woman working across from her was direct in her offer to help her:

Helena K.: I had a woman. Because when we came, you were
 trained. By a German woman. And she was very good to me,
 I didn't know why. She was a lesbian. This is, was there a lesbian
 woman are very frequent. And she always, you know. [*half-
 shrugs*] And when the, things got very bad, she said, "I, I want to
 save you. I have a brother who is in the ss. But he will do it for
 me." . . . I said, "Don't do anything, you risking your life when
 you will help me." And she was telling me [about the war], not
 to frighten me but to give me information.³⁸

In some instances, workers left food for a specific person because of a personal connection. As Ida G. stated, "One liked me." At other times, food was left for anyone who might encounter it. The distance in just leaving food without indicating who it was for may have allowed the workers more safety.

Threaded throughout the testimonies is an expressed awareness of the economic and social positions of the non-Jewish coworkers. Testimony-givers remember realizing what it meant for a Gentile Czech- or German-speaking girl in Trautenau to grow up working in a textile factory. One of the *Aufseherinnen*, Anna Hrda, had been working at Walzel since the age of fifteen.³⁹ The Jewish girls and women saw that the "lunch" these workers brought with them was mainly bread and that there were tensions between the Czech and German employees. Estera S. did not remember being aided by Gentile coworkers. She explains:

Estera S.: They didn't help us much with food or anything in
 the factory. Because the Czech had a limited amount of food
 themselves.⁴⁰

Elizabet B. offers her own analysis of the economic and political position of the Gentile Czech coworkers in her testimony:

> Elizabet B.: I suppose the people in the village were not Nazis, because they really tried to help us. They were very, food was very scarce . . . very little food in Germany, there were really problems and everything was rationed. And in spite of that they brought us—not a lot of food—it was very often a small piece of bread with margarine on it. It was so little margarine that you couldn't really see the white of it. But it was a terrible help. Because in Parschnitz we didn't get almost anything to eat. It was a terrible help. They knew it. And they really shared their very poor rations, their very hard rations, with us. And it was not one or two men or three men. It was the whole factory, you know, helped us. So it seems to me that they were never Nazis. They were in the Republic or Communist or Social Democrats. Very—
>
> Interviewer: [*interrupting*] Can you tell us about the journey from Birkenau to Parschnitz?[41]

In this case, Elizabet B. seems to be ready to continue with her observations of the political context of the Trautenau region, but the interviewer firmly redirects her.

Frymeta F. offers a different analysis of the motivations of the Gentile coworkers, one that emphasizes their moral response to the ages of the Jewish girls and women. Her sentence structure and word choices shift to Yiddish at times:

> Frymeta F.: We came there so young. And how they was handling mit us, the Czechs, the Czechs wasn't liking this kind of thing, what they done to us. What kind of life they did to us. "This is wrong," they said. Children so young, to cut away from their mothers and fathers, this is absolutely brutal.[42]

It is important to note that not all coerced laborers had access to help. Some survivors remember no help whatsoever. Fay B., at the Kluge factory in Ober Altstadt, does not remember help from coworkers, but the factory manager himself gave her a pair of shoes.[43] Furthermore, the food was likely dirtied by where it was left and it was the Jewish workers who were punished if caught with it.

> Aranka T.: One of the Czech boy—men—brought us some apple. And he put some apple in everybody's drawer. And I saw [on] the other side, the *Lagerälteste* started to hit the girls because they had apple.[44]

Lucy M. discusses a coworker that she remembers was German, who kept Lucy M.'s family photos for her and saved them from damage until after the war in exchange for two rings Lucy M. had given her. The interviewer asks how this understanding between them developed.

> Lucy M.: One time she put a carrot on the floor for me. And I, uh, and then the next time she put a little salt on. You know, we had everything without salt . . . And then I thought, well, she must feel sorry for me, she must be a good person. So I started trusting her. And I, uh, and then I asked her for the pictures, to hold the pictures for me.[45]

Survivors tell of transactional relationships that were limited but nevertheless deeply appreciated. The inadequate amount of food distributed to the girls and women was a constant source of suffering, so much so that a person leaving food on the floor is narrated as a positive, helpful action. What Lucy M. may have meant to communicate was that the Gentile employees had to find unusual places to leave anything at all.

The factories themselves were economically integrated into Trautenau and its environs. They depended on local suppliers and local government, and local businesses depended on the demand for services from the coerced labor sites. Some of the girls and women did errands for the factories or the barracks at town shops, the railroad station, or the homes of the guards.

> Frieda W.: This was in the city. So the people cannot say that they didn't know, because they saw us marching during the daytime to work and in [rows of] five to march in the street. They saw what's going on.[46]

> Anna W.: It belonged to a Mr. Walzel. He owned the factory. He paid the ss for the work we did. The ss collected the money. He supplied the food.[47]
>
> Magda-Madeleine F.: We had to go to pick up this horsemeat [she worked in the kitchen] in the next village—not village, town. The Trautenau. To the butcher, we went there.[48]

The girls and women threaded through the streets of Trautenau or its suburbs in the early mornings and again in the evenings; night shifts were added in about 1942. Most remember the long walk as a particularly painful aspect of their persecution. The Trautenau region was subject to frequent snow and rain. Most girls and women had their own shoes but some had to wear the clog-type wooden shoes common in forced labor testimonies and memoirs describing other settings, which would become embedded in wet snow and difficult to lift out.

> Yetta F.: The walking to work was miserable. Because wintertime in Sudetengau is a long time. It is very cold and there is a lot of snow there. And they didn't give you shoes. They gave you wooden shoes . . . And the snow used to stick to the bottoms.[49]
>
> Paula S.: We were marching in wooden shoes. No socks, nothing. And they stick to the, to the snow.[50]

Nettie S. shares an episode that that is telling. She is describing a long walk back to the barracks after a day at the factory:

> Nettie S.: It was wintertime. Cold, I remember. Windy. Dark outside. And I was so hungry. I tell you, I just said, "I don't make it today. I don't make it to my home [the barracks]." And I was the last, it was six girls [in a row]. Six. We going in six. You know, then somebody, somebody . . . I don't know who it was, maybe a miracle, I don't know, an angel. Somebody come after me, after me, and put me under the arm—two rolls! I don't know who was it. I've seen, like, a little woman sent, like straight after [me] and . . . she put me a little package.[51]
>
> Nettie S.: And when I, when I turned to the other girl, I say, "Somebody gave me something." And I feel, in my soul, not

forgotten! Someone remembers me! I feel something, an angel [came] to me.⁵²

The narration's vivid imagery conveys the hungry laborers trudging back to their barracks in public view, probably just as residents are also walking home from work or shopping. In the dark it was likely easy for another female to slip in among those walking. The Gentile woman wants to give them food but must do so furtively. Yet she uses a gesture of intimacy and care, placing something under Nettie S.'s arm almost as someone would give a gift that she wants no acknowledgment for, an act that might be contrasted to leaving a carrot on the factory floor. While Nettie S. never saw the woman directly, she feels strongly that the woman saw her, in the sense of seeing her as a human being and responding to her hunger. Nettie S. says, "What you feel when another person . . . remembers you," meaning, perhaps, a sense of those outside of the world of the factory and the barracks taking her into account. Moving outside of the testimony itself, the episode also tells us that the girls and women were visible—seen but not "remembered" as persons.

Very few survivors talk about feeling preyed upon sexually or threatened with sexual violence from the coworkers and factory staff. The absence of rape or attempted sexual assault is striking in light of the systematic sexual abuse at some camps, such as the HASAG camps as documented by Felicja Karay.⁵³ However, it was clear that the Jewish girls and women in the Trautenau region were without protection and their mobility and intermixing with the Gentile population exposed them. Frances H. relates:

> Frances H.: And it was an old man. A Kutscher [coachman]. He had a, he had a wagon and two horses and he was transporting the food in, and whatever else had to be transported. And once I had an occasion to talk to him and we find out that he was from the same part [region] where my father-in-law, in Mohács. Uh, and uh, somehow I dared to tell him that, "Look, I need some food. If you can give me something to eat I promise you when we get home you'll be, you will be reciprocated." And after that I got sometimes, uh, rotten breads, bread crusts, or apple skins—anyway, whatever it was, it helped, even the rotten bread, with penicillin [*laughs*], it helped me. It happened only once

that I had to tell him that, "Look, what would you say if your daughter would be somewhere else in the same situation as I am, and somebody wants [from] her what you want from me?"
He wanted to, uh, have . . . ya, whatever [*in a quiet voice*].
Interviewer: He wanted to what?
Frances H.: [*pauses, sighs, looks to the side*] He wanted sex.[54]

In this instance the interviewer does not redirect Frances H., change the subject, or accept her implication in silence. It could have been that the interviewer did not know what she was referring to with her tonal gesture. The request for more clarification allows her another chance to say it, and she states it directly.

Each factory work space had a male production manager, the site supervisor for both the Jewish and the non-Jewish workforce. These managers (sometimes called foremen or "Meisters" in the testimonies) seemed mostly concerned with labor productivity; testimony-givers separated their view of him from their work conditions. The latter seemed determined by some distant external force and was unchangeable. The former was a human person who mediated those conditions. The testimonies here fit with Hannah Pollin-Galay's attention to the instances in testimony of "direct human depiction" in contrast to generalized, abstracted processes of persecution (or refuge).[55]

> Regina G.: You could talk to him. He was not bad.[56]
>
> Bella C.: [The foreman was] very good! He, sometime—he [was] scared, too. Sometime he bring bread. He sat at, on the desk . . . The bread was so, that I could take it.[57]
>
> Sonia S.: We had a director which lived in Trautenau who was a very good man, who saved our whole lives.[58]
>
> Edith R.: [at AEG] The foreman was a very nice man. We can talk to him. And sometimes he brings us something to eat.[59]

It was in the factory space that the girls and women had the chance for food scraps and to find sympathetic coworkers. It was in the barracks—separate locations for sleeping and eating—that they were able to talk freely to each other but were also subject to the tyrannies of the *Lager-*

führerinnen and at times other *Aufseherinnen* or even the *Judenältesten*, Jewish women who were given the responsibility for barracks discipline at night. Although these buildings were not yet officially concentration camps in 1940, 1941, and 1942, they had the characteristics of detention: the laborers could only leave with permission, their food was allotted, their sleeping arrangements were restricted, their communication was surveilled, they were subjected to physical harm, and, of course, they were forced to work. In 1943 and 1944 the barracks (although not the factories) became progressively more like the concentration camps elsewhere in several aspects. These barracks were scattered across Trautenau and its suburbs in no organized pattern. They had been constructed in repurposed buildings with no consistency among them; some were not truly self-standing worker housing but unused sections of the factories themselves.

> Lucy M.: [speaking about an early work site in 1940] We lived in a building in the factory, yes. As long as we worked in that factory, this is where we lived. There was one building and the German lady would go home at night and lock the main door and that was it. There was no SS watching us at that time. At that time, I say![60]

Some sites were newly built, but Masha S. says she "lived in an old, old warehouse, which had a lot of bugs."[61] Some were carefully and brutally guarded, some not; some had running water, some not; one had a bathtub; another, no indoor toilets or sinks.

> Lena M.: We didn't have the Germans they should be on top of us. Or killing us. They were more the people who were in camps [referring to *Judenältesten*]. Everybody wanted to be a "Macher." And they did a lot of damage.[62]

> Hela K.: Showers we took. It was a special, a big hall. And there were showers. And how many [girls] goes in, goes in, then we wait for the next [turn.][63]

> Rosalie S.: And there was a lot of German people [living in this region]. And some of these people were recruited into the SS to become our guards. They were guarding us at the factory and at

the camp. Some of these people we knew because previously we worked with them.⁶⁴

The girls and women were organized as workers by their barracks number, which appears on the postcards and letters they received from family. In 1940, 1941, and early 1942 they were not yet formally prisoners and they do not appear on Gross-Rosen transport lists. This is one reason it was possible to negotiate the arrival of a sister or the exchange of a cousin from another work site with someone else who wanted to transfer.

> Ann F.: My little sister, my younger sister, who was at that time twelve years old, was . . . left in Poland . . . by herself. So my sister and I were very good workers—because we had to be— so we asked one of the managers if we could—in those days it was still possible—if we could possibly bring her to us. And that she would be a worker and that she would be a good worker. Which they did. They let her come. She came to us with her little package under her arm and they put her to work.⁶⁵

Several testimony-givers remember that they had to clean the barracks in the evenings and on Sundays, when the factories were closed because the civilian workers and management were Christians. This included cleaning the toilet facilities, which varied from barrack to barrack. Tola G. explains that the girls and women in her barrack did not make the very youngest girls clean.

> Tola G.: The *Judenälteste* would not take to certain work. She would not take the children. The seven [very young] children. In camp [the barracks] they had no work. They were relieved. In camp. In the factory they were working just like anybody else. But at least this was their privilege.⁶⁶

> Yetta P.: [nineteen years old in 1942] There were lots of kids, twelve years old, ten years old kids in our camp. About ten kids. And for them it was very hard and we had to protect them.⁶⁷

In these excerpts, neither Tola G. nor Yetta P. include themselves in the category of "children."

A significant factor shaping the memories of the survivors was illness.

While historians have documented the role of illness in almost all Nazi sites of persecution, few have analyzed its effects on social relations as carefully as Anna Hájková in her analysis of Theresienstadt.[68] Hájková delves into the clinics and medical spaces of Theresienstadt as intentionally constructed by prisoner physicians and their coworkers, as well as the psychological and social impact of illness within the social life of the ghetto. Taking a different approach, Anna Ziółkowska focuses on how vulnerability to not only typhus but also conditions resulting from contaminated food and malnutrition affected Jews in the Wartheland work camps.[69] For the survivors of the Trautenau-region work sites and camps, illness brought the threat of not being able to work, of death, and of displacement, in that a sister or friend would be sent back to Zagłębie in the early years and to the Auschwitz-Birkenau killing center after mid-1942.

Ann F. had organized a plan to bring her younger sister to Trautenau in an effort to save her from deportation.

> Ann F.: [speaking about her younger sister] She became very, very ill. She had breathing problems. And she was, um, running a high fever. . . . There was no medication, there was no aspirin that we could give her . . . They took her out of there. We have never seen her since . . .[70]

She speaks only briefly about what must have been an extraordinarily painful episode of first watching her sister suffer, then separating from her, and finally realizing her efforts to transfer her to Parschnitz may have contributed to her sister's execution. She does not even allow herself to state that her sister died: "We have never seen her since." This brief portion of testimony clarifies the connection of the forced labor work sites with other processes of persecution. For those who did survive, continuing to work functioned as some kind of protection from the extreme brutality of the killing center, the large concentration camp, or the street shooting. But the ability to work was contingent on a host of factors, many of which were out of the control of the young person trapped in this system. With limited nutrition and medical care, a range of physical difficulties interfered with survival, including typhus, sepsis, the flu, any injury to one's limbs at the work site or elsewhere, depression, paranoia, and related physical conditions such as pregnancy or asthma.

Ann F.: [A girl] just, you know, misjudged and cut off a piece of finger. And you know, she put that piece of finger in her pocket and she never said a word about it.⁷¹

Ann's statement captures the specific sadism of the coerced labor bargain. From the adolescents amazed at the giant machinery in their first days to the seasoned teenager running multiple spools, the cost is not just a finger (or a sister) but the space to grieve them.

Factory owners were responsible for food, medical care, and security in the barracks until sometime in 1943. Food content and amounts were similar to other work site camps: black "coffee" and meager bread slices in the morning, intended to be saved for "lunch," and soup with little nutritional content in the evening. There were periods of time in which some margarine or a slice of meat would accompany the bread. It may be the case that food delivery personnel skimmed some of the supplies off for themselves, since there was a thriving black market in food at the border between the Sudetengau (where the Trautenau camps were located) and the rest of former Czechoslovakia (renamed the Protectorate of Bohemia and Moravia by Germany).⁷² Helena K., who had been considered an "older" worker in her mid-twenties, believed this to be the case:

Helena K.: He [the factory owner] was supposed to feed us. As the same rations as the German population had . . . Before we came to the meal, before we came to lunch, it was all stolen. Very little came to the table.⁷³

Since the availability of soap was unpredictable, some of the girls and women used the morning coffee to wash their hair.

Nettie S.: We don't got soap, we don't get towels.⁷⁴

Fay B.: We used leftover flax for the toilet.⁷⁵

The amount of food was so small that the girls and women devised complex strategies and mental bargains with themselves to be able to control their consumption, a phenomenon common in other Holocaust settings.

Berta P.: I don't know how we were existing—because we were getting practically nothing to eat.⁷⁶

> Nettie S.: I got bread, two pieces little bread. Mit marmalade. Or sometimes margarine. This you have to have for tomorrow. Tomorrow to take mit you when you go to work. You know, this was the supper, for the whole day. You have to have for tomorrow to take. There were people eating up everything [right away]. Eating up the supper and the bread for tomorrow . . . I don't eat up the bread. I got a will. I want [to] survive. Everything has a beginning. Everything has to have an end. And I said [to myself], when I eat everything up, everything, I don't see the end.[77]

In Nettie S.'s testimony her shifts from present to past tense creates a sense of her reentry into the past negotiation she had to make with herself every day about whether or not to eat up the small portion of bread. This negotiation becomes intertwined with her hope and fantasy about reuniting with family. In a twist, what "keeps [her] going" is holding the bread as an object not to be eaten, an object that will sustain her another day, not today. Yetta P. also remembers the constancy of this bargain with the self to save food for the next day:

> Yetta P.: Some girls could put their mind to something else and keep it and every day take a piece of bread. And save it for every day. I couldn't resist. Once I knew I had this piece of bread, I ate it.[78]

The ability of the forced laborers to periodically leave the work site to either visit a family member or to switch with another worker is difficult to establish concretely, in part because no formal documents permitting this exist—it was formally banned—and in part because interviewers express surprise when survivors attempt to explain it. This practice by company staff has no equivalent in the ss-run companies, the large firms like IG Farben, or the labor brigades sent out from concentration camps, each so well documented by researchers. The practice speaks to the importance of local context; in other words, the guards lived in these towns and had friends and family nearby, and may have enjoyed handing out the favor of a visit to another camp and perhaps thought of it as low risk.

For example, Ester R. remembers asking the *Lagerführerin* if she might be able to visit her sister, who was in another barracks in Parschnitz—technically in another camp. The *Lagerführerin* agreed to have another guard escort her and even allowed her to spend Shabbat evening through to the next morning with her sister at this other camp. Ester R.'s maiden name was Pardes.

> Ester R.: Once she came over to me. "Pardes, heute, itst du gehen. Today you'll be sent there. But remember, you must not tell anyone about it." I felt so bad—there were girls what got sisters in the same camp. A few, quite few girls.[79]

Estelle C. remembers an arranged visit as a result of being in good stead with the *Lagerführerin* in Parschnitz.

> Estelle C.: My younger sister, no, I managed to visit her. Since, uh, I already was on good terms with my—Hawlikowa, which was in charge. She, I said, I want to see my sister, so she, she, she, she said, "Okay, I'm going to send you to see her. But I cannot send you just as anybody, you know, any prisoner . . . But I will send you as a nurse." So I did see her. I played nurse.[80]

Shoshana L.'s sister was sent to Trautenau in 1940 with one of the first groups of girls and women. Shoshana L. herself was sent to a different Schmelt work camp outside of Opole, Gogolin, in 1942, over 120 miles away from Trautenau. While there Shoshana L. received a note from her sister letting her know that she had negotiated with the *Lagerführerinnen* of both camps to have Shoshana L. transferred to Parschnitz.

> Shoshana L.: The ss woman, the *Lagerführerin*, the German, she took me to the station. We went to the station. On the station was another German ss woman. They say, "Heil Hitler," "Heil Hitler." They are exchanging some words. And she take—gave me over to the other one, lady. The other lady, the German ss woman, she was in charge of my sister's camp. So she took me over.[81]

Shoshana L.'s experience is supported by other survivors who remember female family members negotiating camp transfers, visits, or letters carried by guards. It appears that allowing sisters to join each other was at the discretion of the *Lagerführerinnen*.

In her testimony, Shoshana G. explains the complexity of organizing transfers of sisters and visits in this system. Shoshana G. was taken for labor in 1941, leaving behind younger sisters Hela and Marella. Afterward,

Marella was taken to a nearby camp. In 1943, Hela, still in Sosnowiec, pursued the possibility of assignment to a labor camp, likely to avoid deportation to Auschwitz.

> Shoshana G.: My sister came. After being two years by myself, with my friend, she came. She had a choice where to go. Or to my little sister Marella, [who] was already in camp, or to me.[82]

Hela did indeed arrive at Parschnitz.

> Shoshana G.: My sister actually saved me because she brought everything from the home. There was a gold watch, a gold ring. And there were nice clothes and—it was, my sister came during the night. It wasn't the SS yet. And I could take her in. I was already there two years. So nobody knew what she had. And what we did with that, we sold this to girls who were working in the kitchen. Like a piece of gold, a ring—five breads.[83]

After Hela arrived, Shoshana G. approached the *Lagerführerin* to request that Marella be transferred to Parschnitz, a request that was refused.

> Shoshana G.: She said, "You have Hela." She [the *Lagerführerin*] was supposed to bring Marella to me. I was working all the time on this, since she arrived. I told her she should do me a favor, because other sisters were also reunited. And because Hela came to me [first], she wouldn't do nothing about that Marella should come.[84]

Although Marella could not be transferred, Shoshana G. did visit her once alone and once with Hela. The practice of prisoners visiting family in other camps was not part of the general understanding of the camp system, so the interviewer later returns to the topic and questions Shoshana G. about it again in an extended interchange.

> Interviewer: Now how many times, when you said you visited, um, Marella—[85]
> Shoshana G.: Twice.
> Interviewer: Twice. With your sister, Hela?
> Shoshana G.: Once.
> Interviewer: You were able to leave the camp? The factory?

> Shoshana G.: With somebody. This was on a Sunday. Not when we were working. They wouldn't let you go during the week.

The back-and-forth continues as the interviewer expresses skepticism about the possibility of visits while Shoshana G. responds from the context of her experience. The confusion, while possibly frustrating for the interviewer, allows more clarity on the practice to emerge, especially after the interviewer asks whether bribes to the ss were involved.

> Shoshana G.: We couldn't do that. They would, they would kill us.[86]

Marella did not survive, a fact that Shoshana G. attributes to Hela choosing her camp, Parschnitz, over Marella's and the sisters' ability to support each other.

The *Lagerführerinnen* supervised the girls and women most intensely on the long walks to and from the barracks. They were left alone inside the barracks in the evenings and on Sundays (unless they were on a night shift), most of the time with an order to clean. The female guards were housed close by and inconsistently patrolled the external boundary of the camp in Trautenau and Parschnitz. A few testimony-givers mention a Jewish "camp elder" (*Lagerälteste* or *Judenälteste*) chosen to be in nominal charge (working in exchange for extra food), but most remember times when they were just left to their own devices. It appears that this allowed for bonds of friendship and solidarity, as well as status hierarchies and cliques.

> Lucy M.: But we also wrote poems and we made up songs and we had, in fact we had, sometimes we had shows and dancing and I took dancing lessons even.[87]
>
> Shoshana G.: I took twenty-four girls who were—ballerinas. And, uh, we found in the attic silver sla—flax. And we made dresses for them. They looked like from heaven. Gorgeous. And this was a long time of rehearsing. A long time. But they did a fantastic job.[88]
>
> Berta P.: It was very, I would say a camaraderie lifestyle. We tried to help each other.[89]
>
> Sonia S.: We loved each other.[90]

Regina G.: Oh, we were very close. All of us.[91]

Ida G.: [speaking about the Walzel camp pre-1944] There was leisure time. The leisure time where, we were sitting and writing or, ah—in some instances we even, we even put on a show! For ourselves. We were young, you know.[92]

Magda-Madeleine F.: We actually tried to make once a, a show [*laughing*] to entertain or something, I don't know. They, you know, they tried to—somebody organized some kind of a show, some singing, so there should be—[93]

These dynamics were inflected with the odd feeling of not knowing anything about the "outside world." Unless a person happened to be in a barrack with girls or women who had intentionally documented the Jewish calendar, the rhythms of Jewish life had simply disappeared, leaving a temporal void.

Suzan L.: We didn't know what day it was, how—or very seldom did we know. We didn't know what month it was.[94]

Magda-Madeleine F.: [when asked about Jewish holidays] I don't think they knew what date it was. I don't know. I don't remember this.[95]

The physical space of the barracks also shaped social interaction. The beds were metal "bunk" beds, one on top of another, and each person had her own bed, coarse mattress, and single blanket. A wall of small shelves for storing personal items seems to have been installed in all the barracks, old and new.

Regina G.: We had little spaces to put in a piece of bread, or whatever we possessed.[96]

Estera S.: Next to the bed was a little closet.[97]

The importance of these small spaces, to which each was entitled, was reinforced by the practice of allowing the girls and women to send postcards and to receive postcards, letters, and packages from family and friends in Zagłębie, facilitated by the Jewish Council of Elders. These ended when one's family could no longer send them—in 1942 for those whose families had been deported to Auschwitz in the 1942 stadium event, and in 1943 for all. The testimony-givers remember the ebb and flow of mail as a camp policy, but in truth it depended on the home situation of mothers, fathers, siblings, and cousins.

> Rosalie S.: In the beginning we were able to receive mail. For about I would say maybe a year. We were able to receive mail and packages from home.[98]
>
> Gitla T.: 'Til 1943 we used to write letters. "Dear father, mother, sister, brother." Only those words. "We are working, we are happy, we are good, and we are fine." "But we are lonesome for the bakery"—not the bakery! "For the, uh, Mrs. Greenbaum." Greenbaum was a bakery. Greenbaum. We was lonesome for "Mrs. Greenbaum."[99]
>
> Minnie W.: Me, myself, we had hope . . . When we were still able to receive mail from home. This was practically the last letter from my mother. [She begins a story about her mother.][100]

Minnie W.'s words convey the complexity of how these postcards are remembered by adult testimony-givers. At the time of receipt, they functioned as the fundamental emotional mainstay for many, much like the quick glimpse of a loved one through the *Dulag* window—whatever was written, it was a concrete sign of life. As Minnie W.'s words demonstrate, an adult giving testimony is aware of the desperate conditions faced by families in Zagłębie, which were unknown to the interviewee at the time of her detention. A specific postcard was actually a final goodbye—"the last letter from my mother." In other words, the mail provided emotional sustenance, a cherished memory, but created an illusion of "correspondence": that such sustenance "corresponded" with a parallel ability to survive on the other end. Although German authorities heavily censored the postcards and letters, families managed to communicate some type of information or emotional support. Many of these postcards survive; one collection is the basis for Anne Kirschner's book, *Sala's Gift*.[101]

While *Sala's Gift* treats the postcards as a source of information and as a unique glimpse into the evolution of one person's persecution journey, testimony-givers remember treating the cards, letters, and packets as objects and continued to do so at the time of testimony. These objects were precious, hoarded, hidden, and even curated. They also played a role in the exchanges inside the barracks and work site. Non-Jews hid photos for Jewish coworkers, an exchange that was low risk. The families seemed to realize that the *Lagerführerin* might steal any obviously valuable item and used ingenious methods to communicate how money in particular was hidden. Testimony-givers remember using the money or other objects sent by families strategically.

> Gitla T.: I got a Czech. He brought me such a big bread [*gestures*]. Every Monday. He was from the country. From a farm! And I got money. Why? I [write] to my sister a Brief—a letter . . . And she sent me a shmate and here in the shmate she makes such a thing [*gestures*]. In here she puts in money. And it can help me and I can help other kids, even. I helped other kids, I helped me . . .[102]

This practice was called "organizing" by many Holocaust survivors. "Organizing" is the English version of a Polish term (sometimes identified by scholars as a "camp" term) that means participating in transactions both to achieve an immediate goal and to build a network for future exchange; the network extended through and over boundaries of perpetrator and victim; sometimes the person was an intermediary rather than the giver or recipient. Defined as "stealing" by Israel Gutman and Michael Berenbaum in their study of Auschwitz, it is best described as an ongoing socially embedded practice of acquiring unsanctioned items or services.[103] As Karay's text on Skarżysko-Kamienna documents for that camp, "organizing" can become institutionalized.

As will be detailed in a later chapter, objects became anchors for emotional stability in a setting where the young women had very little concrete remnants of their prewar worlds. Objects were held, examined, described, and exchanged, and attachments to them are interspersed throughout many testimonies. For example, very soon after arrival in the Trautenau region, the girls and women responded to the intense hunger by focusing intently on bread as an object; testimony-givers can describe the bread in precise detail. How big or small, what type, how thinly it would be sliced to be able to pretend it was more than one meal, and the joy when extra was attained in some way, or the despair when it was lost, stolen, or eaten too soon, are details interspersed throughout the testimonies. Bread's important link to hunger and survival can over-

123

shadow its function as an object that symbolizes more than just nourishment. However, reconsidering bread in its concrete form as a symbol demonstrates how the remembered Trautenau experience is in alignment with other memoirs, testimonies, and secondary source analyses of Holocaust sites of more extreme deprivation and violence that support bread's function as a touchable container of symbolic meaning, such as Magda Hollander-Lafon's *Four Scraps of Bread* and Noah Benninga's scholarship on objects.[104]

Frymeta F. shares a short anecdote that brings together the space of the barracks with its small areas for storage, the longing for connection with family, anticipation of exchange, and the power of bread as a symbol:

> Frymeta F.: One girl wasn't eating. She put the bread she saved in a closet. She got a small little closet. She saved her bread. She said, "Maybe I will find a brother or someone." She will have for them the bread. And then all of a sudden one day she died. We opened the closet. The whole bread! [It] was green! And she died. She wasn't eating or drinking. Just like that.[105]

In this excerpt, Frymeta campmate created a sustaining illusion of reconnection with a family member, accumulating bread to make the possibility concrete in some way. Her investment in her bread as an object signaling life was more powerful than her own nourishment.

Another object of exchange was the potato, a food that can be transported, buried, stored, and easily grown. Town residents grew food in household gardens, which the Jewish girls and women passed by. Practices of burying harvested potatoes in the dark soil to last through winter extended toward the grounds of many of the barracks. Testimony-givers report instances in which a Jewish laborer would discover a cache of buried potatoes, and then face the dilemma of how to carry them into the barracks without notice. Ann F. describes working in the factory building where a cafeteria as well as a vegetable cellar existed for the Gentile workers, and where the Jewish girls and women wore burlap aprons for various jobs. At times the Jewish workers might be called in to peel potatoes.

> Ann F.: We would put some potatoes in these [aprons] . . . We got a few slashes [if they were caught] and mostly what they did to the women is shave their heads . . . But we didn't give up. We'd

> go down in the evenings, they had a warehouse with all the vegetables that they were picking for this cafeteria. So we would go down at nighttime, some of us, and unlatch the window. And then when everyone was asleep we would crawl into the little window, jump down—sometimes you jumped down and you didn't know if the potatoes are going to keep you up or you, know, fall down. And [we would] "organize" the potatoes and brought them up to the camp. And there was a woman who was heating the, uh, the camp with coals, and she would sneak in some things for us and cook them, put cabbage in.[106]

The extent of coordination required, as well as Ann enjoyment of the risk-taking, successfully subverting the rules, and even jumping through a window, is apparent in her testimony.

Chana B.'s memory of the importance of a single apple demonstrates the emotional dimension of its function as both symbol and food. In her testimony she is quite reserved until she comes to this anecdote, during which she is quite expressive:

> Chana B.: [her friend] Ala got typhus. I remember. She got typhus. And they didn't allow to go in to that area where the sick people were there. So I, I went, I don't know how. I wanted to see her, just to say hello. So she says, "Chana," she says, "If I will have an apple, I will survive." So next day, I went to the washroom. And somehow I found an apple, [it] was big, like a ping pong ball. And I found it. [*smiles*] So I said, this I'm going to give to Ala! I just smelled that that apple was—in springtime! I smell it. And I went over there and I give it to her. She bite in that green apple. [*enacts amazement*] "Oh," she said, "I think I feel better right away." She had a dream of an apple. She survived! [*smiles, tearful*][107]

The apple functions in multiple ways in this story. Ala offers Chana B. a way to save her, via the apple, creating a pathway for Chana B. to cope with her fear and grief. She is able to locate one and give it to her, no easy task because visitors were not permitted. The apple holds the promise of healing Ala and is itself the object of Chana B.'s own desire as she smells it, but she is able to refrain from eating it. Her triumph is not just in finding it and smuggling it to Ala, but also in resisting her own consumption of it—a temptation she only indirectly admits to.

Another type of object that circulated through the barracks was clothing. Dresses, coats, shoes, and, importantly, socks were all very valuable and subject to transaction. In her testimony, Minnie W. begins by explaining the possibility of making clothing from factory yarn, using language that suggests a wide range of objects that met specific needs:

> Minnie W.: We would steal the yarn in the factory. And girls would knit. One would make a, herself a sweater, one a pair of stock—socks. One a kerchief, a hat.[108]

The tape ends (interrupting the interview) and when the new tape begins, she recalls how she transformed knitting for personal use into a camp business. She describes a system of exchange in which she sold clothing she knitted from stolen fibers. She soon was taking orders for more items from one of the camp guards and the Jewish and Gentile kitchen workers, and eventually hired her campmates to knit for her.

> Minnie W.: And I was able to pay the girls, which I employed. I paid them with bread.[109]

Rita R. remembers her sister trading for a specific dress.[110] Many testimony-givers spend time discussing their shoes, describing them in detail as important to survival, as was the case for shoes in other Holocaust persecution settings.

Testimony-givers almost never mentioned sabotage. One exception was Helen F., who worked at Ober Altstadt, the suburb of Trautenau, in an Etrich factory that began to manufacture aircraft parts later in the war. She states that "sometimes I tried not to make it accurate."[111] However, subversion of camp rules was common, mostly in the forms of stealing and acquiring forbidden items. Food was not the only item that was stolen. The discarded remnants of the threads turned out to be a desirable commodity in the right hands, as noted by Minnie W. here and Lena M. in an earlier chapter. While most girls stopped menstruating while in custody, Phyllis Y. did not. She stole flax from the factory to use as padding to absorb her menstrual blood.[112] The *Lagerführerin* Elsa Hawlik brought her cotton pads to use as well. The issue of why girls and women stopped menstruating in concentration camps and coerced labor settings is still an open question for researchers. Many survivors insist that a chemical was added to their food to stop menstruation. In any case, for a few individuals, managing menstrual blood was very challenging.

Like Lena M., who was described in an earlier chapter collecting fibers and selling socks and sweaters, others also created objects out of flax and cotton.

> Frieda W.: I was going just wooden shoes without socks. So, they made thread over there. So a German girl, she saw, she asked me if I knew how to knit. I told her yes. This saved my life. I—she gave me some thread. And on account she gave me, I took a little bit more, made myself a pair of socks.[113]
>
> Fay B.: I took flax. I crocheted belts.[114]

It could be that one reason there was little actual sabotaging of production in the textile factories was that the machines often broke down without any intention on the part of the worker. The girls and women had to repair the spools themselves when the flax became entangled or broke.

Most survivors describe their *Lagerführerin* as overly enchanted with new power over the vulnerable girls, prone to vindictive behavior, overpunishment, handing out favors, and cultivating favorite prisoners. The Haase, Walzel, Kluge, and Etrich barracks in the city of Trautenau and the suburb of Parschnitz were all under the authority of Elsa Hawlik.

> Lola W.: We were lucky because she [Hawlik] was on our side.
> Interviewer: The *Lagerführerin*?
> Lola W.: Yeah. Yeah. She was. She was. She was bad. She was bad. But not to us. Not to me. I even played with her daughter.
> [Lola W. was thirteen in 1942.][115]

Hawlik (also called Hawlikowa, the Czech version of her name) was the staff member who had the most contact with the most women. Many remember moments of brutality from her, while some, such as Lola W. here, developed relationships that protected them from violence. As noted earlier, these factories had their own social world and a work culture that had already been established prior to the war. Hawlik was recruited from this world. While formally she was to oversee only the barracks and the walk to and from the factory, she often entered the work sites, either

FIGURE 1 Photo of a Czech friend of Bela Kaftori and a guard standing in the Walzel factory, 1944. Given to Bela Kaftori at liberation. Item ID 4415506, Yad Vashem Photo Archive, Jerusalem, 7633/8. Reproduced courtesy of Ze'ev Kaftori.

to communicate with factory management or to socialize with Gentile women who were likely her neighbors and friends.

Bela K. was born in Będzin and assigned to Parschnitz. She developed a close relationship with a Gentile Czech coworker who gave Bela K. a photo of herself as a parting memento at liberation.[116] The photo is of a camp guard standing with Bela K.'s Czech helper. This photo is one of very few available that depicts, first, a relationship between guard and Gentile worker and, second, the machinery of the Haase factory. In it, not only are the spools visible, but the Gentile Czech wears the leather apron all workers also wore to be able to stop the machinery with their bodies. The prisoner numbers Jews would be assigned in late 1943 and early 1944 would be made from the scraps of this leather and worn around their necks.

Illness, presented earlier as a part of work life, was also connected to the threat of deportation and death. Many girls and women became ill at some point in their time in Trautenau. Prior to the summer 1943 deportations, those too ill to work could just be sent back to their family home in Zagłębie; alternatively, they might have been assigned to a transport to Auschwitz between 1942 and 1943.

> Yetta F.: They decided because of my foot to send me back.
> So when I came back—
> Interviewer: Back to where?
> Yetta F.: To Sosnowiec. To my parents' house.[117]

Typhus became rampant after 1943. But the laborers had other illnesses as well. The filthy working conditions caused skin and lung infections. Individuals also brought health issues with them, such as epilepsy. Perhaps surprisingly, there was medical and dental care available for the Jewish workers at the Trautenau factories. The factory owners built an infirmary in Parschnitz, to which girls and women assigned to Parschnitz, Trautenau, Ober Altstadt, Bernsdorf, Gabersdorf, Schatzlar, and other local work sites (later camps) were sent when they were ill. By 1943, the factory owners were lobbying the SS to pay for meals for those admitted to the clinic.[118] In the early years of the system, a short illness was a legitimate reason for absence from work. After rest and recovery, the girl or woman returned to her barracks and work site.

> Rose S.: At that time [1941] we had a German doctor in the camp. And he operated on my knee . . . I was unable to work for six weeks, but they kept me in camp.[119]

> Regina G.: I broke a leg. Because, uh—so they took me to the Krankenhaus. This, like, our little hospital. And I stayed. So they took out a piece of wood. And they tore a dress or whatever and they put it on, because, this, while it was broken, and this was the cast. So the *Judenälteste*—she was a Jewish girl but she was looking after the girls in my block . . . So she came into the Krankenhaus and she said to me, "Remember, that tomorrow's gonna come the SS and they are going to pick out the sick people." . . . So I went with a broken leg, I went to work.[120]

Many testimony-givers recall the Jewish doctor from Sosnowiec assigned to the Schmelt camps, Wolf Lajtner (also spelled Leitner or Laitner). His main location was Parschnitz, but he traveled to other infirmaries in Silesia on a regular basis. Most survivors remember Lajtner as an ally and viewed him very positively.

> Sala K.: He tried. He tried his best. And then he went to other camps, he was going from one to the other.[121]

> Masha S.: There was a doctor, a Jewish doctor, very nice man. And he helped me. When there was an inspection to—[see] who is sick, so the sick people they send, the girls they send to Auschwitz, so he hide—he was hiding me. Pretending that I'm not so sick.[122]

He and his nursing staff did not have much medication to give out, but they were perceived as allowing people some respite. Medicalized support was especially needed after 1943, when there was no longer any possibility of being sent home and the ss began to visit the barracks and conduct "selections," meaning that prisoners who were very ill had to appear less so to avoid being sent away. Rose S. remembers attempting a number of strategies with the help of a nurse.

> Rose S.: And she was worried because the ss men used to come and check how long a girl was sick. And if they were too long sick, they take them out, they send them away, at one point one of us, a girl, they sent them to Auschwitz . . . So she used to, she changes sometimes my name. To somebody else's that shouldn't be on the list, that I'm so long sick.[123]

Lajtner had a degree of mobility and access to resources—especially information about what was happening in other camps and which family members were imprisoned where—that others did not. He and his family were from the Zagłębie region and he likely acquired his position through the Council of Jewish of Elders. He seemed to have perceived the Trautenau work sites to be a safe haven from the mass deportations from Zagłębie that Lola W. remembers already beginning while she was still in Środula (the ghetto created in late 1942). Lola W. reports that he arranged to have her, together with her sister and mother, assigned as laborers to Parschnitz. In this excerpt, Lola W. remembers that Lajtner had Elsa Hawlik's cooperation in the transfer.

> Lola W.: My brother-in-law was a doctor in a camp, in the camp.
> Interviewer: What was his name?
> Lola W.: Lajtner. Doctor Lajtner.
> Interviewer: Lajtner? What was his first name?
> Lola W.: Wolf. So somehow, somewhere, I don't remember how it happened, they knew more than we did. In the [Środula] ghetto. He managed to come to the ghetto, took us out . . . And he took us, he came with a *Lagerführerin*. Her name was Hawlik. Frau Hawlik . . . They took us on a train—and I think it took a good day—to get to Sudetendeutschland.[124]

Lajtner may also have helped many girls and women by misleading the factory managers or the visiting ss about whether or not someone was truly ill in order to provide rest and evade a selection. Certainly some survivors think so. But he was also the person who escorted chronically ill workers (and possibly some who were simply being punished) to Auschwitz beginning in 1942. One of his nurses was Lola W.'s older sister, Erna E., a Jewish woman born in Oświęcim who had already been taken into the Schmelt system in 1940 at age eighteen and eventually transferred to the Trautenau-region camps before Lola W. arrived. Lajtner had trained Erna E. as a nurse in Sosnowiec. In Erna E.'s testimony, she remembers that it was she who convinced Lajtner to have her sister and mother sent to Parschnitz, not only saving them from deportation to Auschwitz but also giving them some measure of protection through her position in the Parschnitz clinic.[125] Erna E. offers a horrifying story that sheds light on how the coerced labor in the Trautenau factories fit into the Nazi genocidal project. She states that in 1943 Lajtner as well as herself and two other nurses escorted a group of three hundred Jewish girls and young women who had typhus from the Trautenau-region camps to Auschwitz to be killed. They traveled in open trucks (and were likely accompanied by ss). When they disembarked, Auschwitz officials refused to recognize the status of the Jewish health care workers as exempt from selection and possible death. They forced Lajtner, Erna E., and the nurses into what Erna E. remembers as a cell or possibly a changing room connected to a gas chamber, along with the three hundred ill and dying young people.

The SS guards ignored the doctor and nurses' pleas that they were professional factory staff with privileges. It is unclear what part of Auschwitz they were held in, but it could have been an undressing room. She states that an officer suddenly opened the door to force another prisoner with an infant into the room, and at that point the doctor and nurses were able to exit.[126] Erna E. was forced to remain at Auschwitz.

Lajtner gave a deposition to German prosecutors in 1970 as part of their effort to prosecute Ritterbusch, the SS officer assigned to Trautenau by the Inspectorate of the Concentration Camps in 1944, and Hawlik. In his recollection, he did not escort a group of Jewish girls and women from the Trautenau camps to Auschwitz; instead, he states that he was placed in transport himself while at Blechhammer, where he had gone to check on his parents, who had been assigned there for work.

> Dr. Lajtner: In Birkenau I was already in the gas chamber. But a friend of mine told an SS doctor that I was a doctor. He took me out of the gas chamber. I was then driven to Auschwitz by ambulance, right to Block 13. This was the block where every morning executions occurred. I thought that I would also be executed.[127]

He was made to organize the bodies of those who had been shot, and then he was transferred to Buna, and then Buchenwald, and then Zwieberge.

Whether Lajtner was with Erna E. in this incident or not, this portrayal of what actually occurred when a laborer was "sent to Auschwitz" is available to us through Erna E.'s testimony, but it was not known by the girls and women who remained at what was by then the Parschnitz concentration camp in its specificity—the selections, the death by gassing, the humiliations. Danuta Czech's *Auschwitz Chronicle* lists the arrival of a transport of female Jews "from a Silesian labor camp" in November 1943, but it is difficult to find any other narrative to supplement Erna E.'s story.[128] As Czech's calendar of Auschwitz events documents, it was frequently the case from 1942 through 1944 that small groups of Jews arrived, a few were registered as prisoners, and SS camp personnel sent the others to be killed. Those executed in the incident mentioned previously had typhus and dysentery, illnesses that were difficult to recover from without medicine and nutrition—neither of which the factory owners would provide.

Many testimony-givers share their memories of the group transports of people who became ill out of the camp. They frequently say that these transports went to Auschwitz and that those in them were killed there. However, it is not always clear whether the postwar knowledge of Auschwitz has influenced memories. Lucy M. offers a short anecdote that, in its use of detail, indicates that a deep awareness (but not explicit acknowledgment) of the significance of these transports existed in these camps:

> Lucy M.: There were a few that were sent to Auschwitz. They had TB... There were maybe ten girls from [my] original group that were gone. But there were three sisters. And the youngest one got TB. And she was sent to Auschwitz. And before she was leaving I could see those two sisters making the preparation, like she was going to—uh—a hotel for a vacation. That's how they acted. They probably knew. But she was the youngest one. And that's the one they lost.[129]

Lucy M.'s testimony captures the simultaneous knowing/not knowing that expressed itself in a variety of ways among the girls and women. In an act of love, the sisters withhold the actual information (although it is unclear whether the youngest sister also knows) and create an alternative story that they perform with and for their family member. Lucy M. not only presents this memory with insight ("They probably knew"), but she also extends her compassion for the youngest sister to the others. The excerpt also communicates the reality that loss was both familiar and irreconcilable.

Pregnancy was also considered a physical condition that meant either a return home in 1940 and 1941 or, in later years, a transfer to Auschwitz.[130] Several survivors remembered rumors about a nurse or doctor either performing abortions or refusing to do so.[131] A few remember helping a pregnant coworker, although there is no definitive documentation on pregnant coerced laborers. Zagłębie residents had lived in the family home or with relatives and were permitted a degree of autonomy in mobility and familial and social life; people became pregnant through consensual intimacy, transactional sex, or coerced sex. The girls and women from the Hungarian territories who arrived in 1944 had also lived in family homes or with spouses until their deportation. Helena K. remembers a particular "Hungarian girl" in Parschnitz.

Helena K.: There was one woman. One young woman—I will never forget her face. She was pregnant. And the transport, the transport came to pick her up. And the others. Sick people. And she hid. You know, that was in a courtyard. Everybody was assembled here. One person was me—, was missing. She was hiding. Well, that was at night. These events took place at night. And the lights went on in our dormitory. And everybody was looking. And incidentally she was hiding—I had an upper bed and she was hiding under the lower bed. Just in my view.[132]

. . .

Helena K.: [continuing after an interruption in the interview] And a German SS woman . . . She came to her and she was so gentle with her. She was so good. She took her, she took her hand. And she said, the woman said, the woman said, "I want to live! I am so young!" And she [the SS woman] said, "Don't worry. They will send you somewhere, where you can have your child."[133]

Helena K. states that the pregnant woman was taken with the transport to Auschwitz. In her telling, Helena K.'s tone is slow and precise, her cadence creating space for the complexity of the situation to emerge. Her words and tone express her own compassion for the pregnant woman and recognition of her position, as she claims to have never forgotten her face and lingers on the fact that she was "just in my view." Yet Helena K. also creates space to acknowledge the perpetrator's tactics as possibly compassionate as well, noting that "gentle" interactions with Jewish laborers were certainly possible. Ultimately, while the pregnant woman was sent to Auschwitz, Helena K. documents that this particular SS woman could clearly see the humanity and vulnerability of the person she was sending there.

In these testimonies it becomes clear that the labor itself, in its interaction with machinery, items for transport, the structures comprising the factory floor, and the flax itself, structured the possibilities for support and survival while also creating pain, despair, and hardship. The testimony-givers offer vivid depictions of stolen scraps of fabric, hidden pieces of food, and fear of illness, all conditioned by the specific nature of these sites as technological spaces of production. At the same time, the work experience was gendered in multiple ways. This is not to say that in men's camps there were no favors done by Gentile coworkers, no photos saved or socks sewn; it is certainly true that these interactions occurred in many different camps among many types of people. Rather, these testimonies show that first, the specific persecutory elements of these work sites and labor camps were attentive to and anticipated the coerced laborers as female. And they show that second, the Jewish girls and women conceived of and enacted strategies for survival and connection *as* girls and women, that is, they insisted on seeing themselves and their Gentile coworkers as female; femaleness was, as they remember it, inseparable from the acts of leaving food and receiving that food, sending a postcard and receiving a package.

Interwoven with these gendered logics was the awareness of themselves as simply young. For some this registered in their memories as naïveté, for others a longing for parents, and for others a delight at selling a handmade item to a Gentile. Mediating all of these memories was the knowledge that the transport trucks leaving the medical clinic were bringing people to Auschwitz. Their youth offered them no protection.

CHAPTER 4

The Conflicted Pathway to Survival

A STUDY OF THREE PERIPHERAL CAMPS

The collection of barracks in the city of Trautenau and its suburbs, Parschnitz and Ober Altstadt, would eventually become the concentration camps Parschnitz and Ober Altstadt in 1944. However, within twelve miles of Parschnitz were three additional small work camps that were also part of the Schmelt system: Bernsdorf, Gabersdorf, and Schatzlar. These also began as work sites, also housed Jewish girls and women from Zagłębie and later "Hungarian girls," were subject to the same Schmelt policies, required uncompensated labor in factories operated by private companies, and used female guards chosen from among local women who had themselves worked in the factories. These small work camps have been the subject of little scholarly attention in their particularity as sites of persecution. Since they all became subcamps of Gross-Rosen administratively in late 1943, the main scholars of Gross-Rosen subcamps—Andrea Rudorff, Bella Gutterman, and Isabell Sprenger—include them in more general histories of women in the subcamp system.[1] The authoritative source for the camps in their Sudetenland/Northern Bohemia context, Mirolav Kryl and Ludmila Chládková's study, places these three in close relation to the Trautenau, Parschnitz, and Ober Altstadt camps as self-standing sites of persecution.[2] After the war the names used by the Nazi authorities to signify these camps reverted back to the names of the towns in which they were located: Bernartice for Bernsdorf, Libeč for Gabersdorf, and Žaclér for Schatzlar.

Like the testimony-givers who survived Parschnitz and Ober Altstadt, survivors of Bernsdorf, Gabersdorf, and Schatzlar also donated their time and testimony to the Shoah Foundation Visual History Archive. This chapter presents selected aspects of the individual experiences of survivors from these camps in light of what previous chapters have established regarding the coerced labor experience initiated by the Schmelt system. Testimony-givers who survived these particular work camps remember patterns of persecution that mirror closely the experiences of those in the Trautenau-area camps: the amount and content of food, the marches to and from the work sites, the relationships with Czech- and German-speaking Gentile coworkers, the unsanctioned visits and errands, and the repetitive and dangerous work itself. However, at times differences and distinctions appear. The unique voice and memory of the survivor remembers a detail or an event that others chose not to foreground or that simply did not leave an imprint. The approach taken in this chapter is to present those narrated portions of testimony from survivors of these camps that add an extra dimension to the insights and documentation in the previous chapters.

The Gabersdorf work site opened in January 1941.[3] It was located only three miles north of Trautenau city. Approximately 360 Jewish girls and women (in addition to the non-Jewish employees) worked at textile factories owned by the Trautenau families of Haase and Etrich as well as at a firm that had originally been Jewish—K. H. Barthel—but was appropriated by the Kluge family.[4] A Siemens munitions factory was added in 1944, taking over part of a Kluge building. A hand-drawn map submitted by survivor Sara Helfgott to an International Tracing Service query in 1950 conveys the small-town feel of these sites and the proximity of Jews, civilians, and guards, in her memory.[5]

Titled "Camp Map of the Gabersdorf Camp," the drawing depicts the remembered spatial organization of Helfgott's coerced labor experience at the Barthel factory. There are strong horizontal lines bisecting the page, labeled as a "main street" with the homes of "Germans and Czechs" on one side and the camp on the other. The effect speaks to the simultaneous senses of closeness to local residents in their everyday lives and the violent camp border of barbed wire, the latter rendered in carefully spaced marks. The map also conveys information about the relative importance of specific aspects of camp life. A main barracks building sits almost centered on the page. Helfgott lists its crucial functions: it contained a kitchen, a dining hall, a toilet, and the apartment of the *Lagerführerin*, and then seven stories occupied by "prisoners," the official name given to the laborers in 1944 (*Häftlinge*). A second barrack is off to the side.

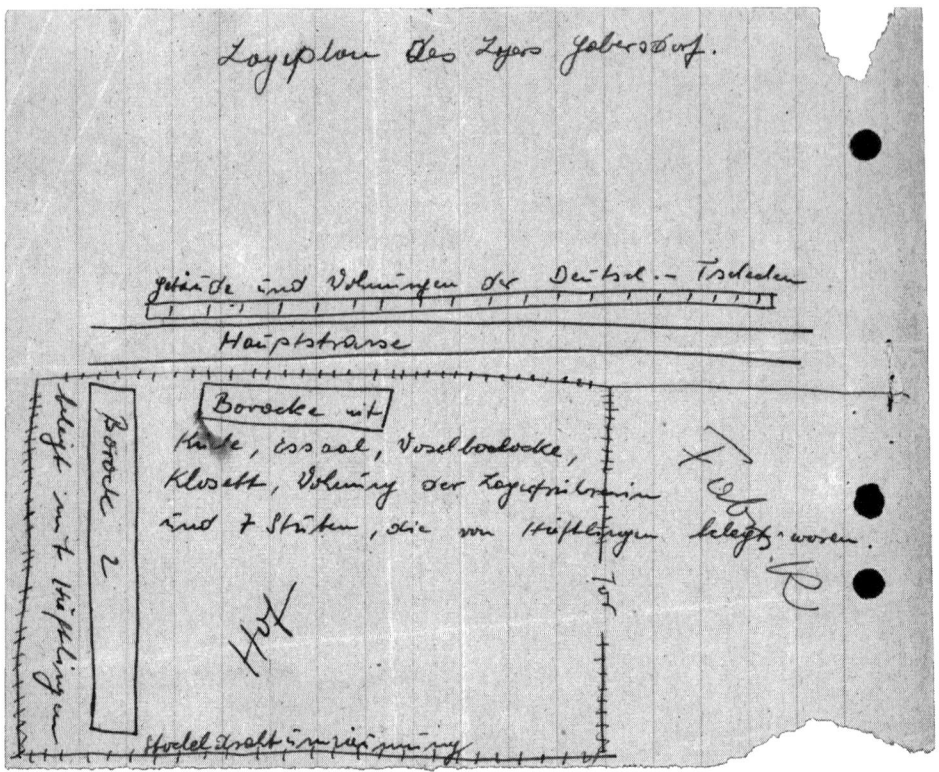

FIGURE 2 "Camp Map of the Gabersdorf Camp." Concentration camp Groß-Rosen and commands. 1.1.0.7, Document ID 87764678, ITS Digital Archive, Arolsen Archives.

These two buildings and the square of barbed wire around them frame a courtyard of empty space. There is one small opening in the wire frame that leads only to the factory building, adjacent to the square. The effect of the drawing is that the laborers lived in a small, tight enclosure but with "normal" life easily in sight, just across the street.

The Bernsdorf work site and camp was five miles further north from Gabersdorf. Its barracks held more than four hundred Jewish girls and women. It was also opened in 1941, by the Etrich family.[6] Etrich shared coerced Jewish labor with another firm called Berko, although it is unclear in which year this arrangement began.[7]

The Schatzlar work site was nine miles north of Trautenau and began using coerced Jewish labor in November 1942.[8] The main Schatzlar work site was a textile-processing concern owned by Gustav Adolph Buhl & Sohne, who also operated a camp in the Auschwitz subcamp system in Lichtewerden, 120 miles east.[9] Some of the Jewish girls and women assigned to Schatzlar had been among the very first females to be recruited by the Schmelt system in 1940; they were initially sent to Geppersdorf in Upper Silesia to support a mostly male work camp in road construction, part of the string of camps comprising the RAB camps.[10] This early group of girls and young women faced frequent transfers from camp to camp between 1940 and 1942, including time at Blechhammer, a notoriously violent labor camp for Jewish men, to do kitchen or clerical work, which allowed them some protection from malnutrition.[11] They arrived in Schatzlar along with girls and women selected in the Zagłębie deportation events of 1942 and 1943, and then more from the Hungarian territories (via Auschwitz) in 1944. The total number of Jewish laborers was only approximately 150, and as Nazi-coerced labor policies shifted to require a consolidation in 1943 the factory owners struggled to keep Schatzlar open. In 1943 Himmler required camps to consolidate Jewish workers. Because of this, the girls and women from Schatzlar were moved to the Bernsdorf barracks in 1944, although they still walked to their original factories for work. In 1944 Bernsdorf/Schatzlar and Gabersdorf received new formal administrative identities as subcamps of Gross-Rosen and as satellites of the Parschnitz concentration camp under the authority of the Trautenau Kommando, the title of the new SS office in Trautenau.[12]

Schatzlar has entered the current-day Holocaust memory consciousness through the popular book *Sala's Gift: My Mother's Holocaust Story*, by Ann Kirschner.[13] Kirschner is the daughter of a survivor and Shoah Foundation testimony-giver, Sala Kirschner. Ann Kirschner collected her mother's correspondence from Schatzlar and added historical and familial information in light of what she knew as well as interviews with family members and historical research. Debórah Dwork and Robert Jan van Pelt worked with Ann Kirschner to publish additional correspondence in the same year.[14] While Schatzlar was much smaller than Parschnitz, Kirschner's representation of the Schatzlar experience has become the route by which many readers have become familiar with the Schmelt camps generally. Sala Kirschner had shared her testimony for the United States Holocaust Memorial Museum in 1996 and the Shoah Foundation in 1997, approximately ten years prior to the publication of these books, meaning that there are at least four "memory texts" that express her experience of prewar Zagłębie, the Schmelt system, and life in the Schatzlar camp.[15] Other audiences may have encountered Dasha Rittenberg, also a Schatzlar survivor, who became a frequent speaker and participant at Jewish community events in the United States in the 1990s and 2000s.[16] Along with other Schatzlar survivors, these two voices position the Schatzlar experience as a powerful source of knowledge for not only the Schmelt camps but also for the wider Holocaust itself, even though it was one of the smallest camps in the Nazi system.

Dasha Rittenberg was one of the youngest Jewish girls at Schatzlar. Born in Będzin in 1930, she was thirteen when an employee of the Jewish Council of Elders arrived in November 1942 at her family home to collect her sister for coerced labor. At the time of her testimony, Dasha R. had already reflected on and spoken about her Holocaust experiences. Her words are more composed and detailed than other interviewees, many of whom were speaking about their persecution for the first time.

> Dasha R.: [speaking at first about her sister] When they hid Hana, into a box, and they [the authorities] said, "Where is she?" And my mother and father said, "She's away." "Where is she?" "She's away! We don't know, she's away!" So I was there. They said, "Then we'll take her." [imitates someone pointing] So my mother threw herself at this murderer. She grabbed his feet, his boots. She put her arms around his boots. Begging him not to take me. To take her. That she is much healthier. That she has worked. That she has still energy and why take me, they'll have no use of me, they'll have more use of her. And he kicked her back and he said, "I'm taking her."[17]

Dasha R.'s earlier testimony described an unhappy childhood with little affection and after this excerpt she remembers that her attachment to her mother fundamentally shifted.

As Dasha R.'s testimony indicates, the pathway to these three camps involved the same perpetrator processes documented in previous chapters: the Jewish Council demanding "volunteers," ss and Jewish police bursting into homes, ss separating families in the 1942 stadium deportation, and assembling people at the Sosnowitz *Dulag*—leading to agonized decision-making for families. Fela G., from Będzin, was awakened at night in 1942, in a door-to-door initiative prior to the mass deportation that would come in the summer:

> Fela G.: [Schatzlar] And I'll never forget that my father was crying. [*loses composure*] He wanted to give them money to leave me home. But they wouldn't listen, they just took me away.[18]
>
> Regina B.: [Schatzlar] They catched me on the street and I never went home.[19]
>
> Fryda F.: [Gabersdorf] One day they came at night and they took everybody out from their homes and they took us to a big field and [they] decide which, where everybody will go. To concentration camp. Or to Auschwitz. Or back home. Because the city [Chrzanów] was still there for Jewish people. I went to concentration camp.[20]
>
> Eda R.: [Gabersdorf] I tell you, they came in the house, and they tell you, Germans with trucks and they tell you, in the morning, and they have already a list and they took me from the house and they took lots, from that where they saw my age people. And they put us on the truck. There was, the people went crying after—the mothers—after the truck.[21]
>
> Esther R.: [Bernsdorf] They were going [through Chrzanów] with those loudspeakers and said all the Jews that are in the bunkers, if they don't come out now—if they [do], they still have the chance to go to camps, to working camp.[22]

Rosa S., sent first to Blechhammer and then later to Schatzlar, offers testimony that expresses the deep contradictions of a seventeen-year-old separated from her family by the Schmelt system. She had already shared a heartbreaking story of SS taking her from her family home by force, bloodying her protesting father in the process.

> Interviewer: Do you remember the feelings you had when you were in that cattle car [on the way to Blechhammer]?
> Rosa S.: Hungry. Depressed. Crying all the time. Nobody wanted really to talk to me because whenever they looked at me I was crying. And everybody had his own problems. A lot of problems.

> Until one day in Blechhammer I said, that's it. I have to stop with that crying and talk to people. But I wanted my parents. And I couldn't forget the picture—what I saw when I walked out.
>
> Interviewer: [changing topic] Did you receive any mail from the camps you were in?[23]

In this excerpt, Rosa S. begins with a story of hope and resilience as she describes conquering her emotional paralysis through her own will. It is a strongly resonant depiction of a victimized person refusing the despair created by the camp system. But she quickly reverses the impression of the coherent, integrated young person who learns to overcome this despair and strongly asserts her longing for parental protection. She also refuses to move past the earlier story of her father's pain. The simultaneous grief over losing one's place in an intact family and pride in overcoming one's limitations takes a specific form for the Jewish girls and women in Rosa S.'s age range. The excerpt also demonstrates her resistance to the imposed format of the Shoah Foundation questionnaire as she shifts the topic from the cattle car to Blechhammer and then back to her family home, a shift the interviewer does not accommodate.

Sala K., the "Sala" of *Sala's Gift*, was one of the very first girls from Zagłębie to be assigned to forced labor in a camp away from her hometown, in 1940 at age sixteen.

> Sala K.: Then we got a, uh, they, actually, there was a card sent, not for me, for my sister. To be this and this day at a certain place. And they told us we are going to go to work, we're going to get paid, and if one member of a family goes to work, then the rest of the family is going to be left alone. It's for one year. And they need workers and they are going to pay for it.[24]

Sala K. volunteered to take the place of her sister, whom she remembers in her Shoah Foundation testimony as important to running the household. Sala K.'s is one of the only testimonies in which the survivor leaves the family home in the very first months of the Schmelt system. Her explanation corresponds with what contemporary sources and the secondary literature claim was the standard process of the Jewish Council of Elders.[25] It attests to the widespread practice in the towns and villages of Zagłębie (she was born in Cieszyn) of Jewish coerced labor that

CONFLICTED PATHWAY TO SURVIVAL

began quickly after the German occupation, the painful separations that appeared at first to be the condition for the survival of the entire family, and the payment that families received in the early months of the Schmelt system.

> Sala K.: They really made it look so real, that it's to go to work for a little time, you know. That it just fooled everybody.[26]

The Jewish police did not bring Sala K. to a *Durchgangslager*, but directly to the train station, probably because the *Dulag* system had not been created at this early point, nor had the large-scale transfer of girls and women to textile factories. Sala K. was sent to Geppersdorf (one of the RAB camps) for kitchen and clerical duties. The bulk of the labor force was composed of Jewish men.

> Interviewer: Can you assess about how many people there, were there—
> Sala K.: Hundreds. Hundreds. Hundreds, because they divided us, I think it was two camps. Hundreds of men. A lot of men. The women was just, like, I don't know, maybe I would say fifty, sixty, something like that.[27]

By the time Sala K. arrived at Schatzlar in 1942, she and the other girls and women who had been transferred among various camps for two years had developed an awareness of how these small camps functioned within the context of the war. Here Sala K. chooses to share her analysis of the position of the factory managers in this context.

> Sala K.: It was the factory director that really kept us going. They said later on you know, if not him—and I can't remember his name, which I would love to, but I really can't. The work wasn't needed so much. As much as, for him, not to have to go to the front, he had to keep the factory going. So we were his ticket to freedom, too. And he lived like across the street from the, uh, from the factory. With a wife and two children.[28]

Sala K. not only presents an explanation of how the small Schatzlar camp persisted throughout the war but also comes close to endowing the director with full humanity and inside the circle of those who are given recognition in testimony, as in Hannah Pollin-Galay's conceptualization of

143

depiction. She does not name him but acknowledges the pull of naming: "which I would love to." The tension in this excerpt between empathy, proximity, and a transactional, instrumental relationship also echoes the hand-drawn map of Gabersdorf with its row of German and Czech houses "across the street."

Other testimonies from Schatzlar survivors also echo those who were in Parschnitz, Trautenau, and Ober Altstadt regarding the work itself as dangerous, technically difficult, and unfamiliar.

> Regina B.: But the smell was horrific. In that Feinsaal [a room designed for a specific phase of the textile process] it was choking you . . . It was a long machine . . . you had to attend this machine, later, when she told you. So you see, the spools, the spools went from top and then, the machine was so long, from the spools the little cotton had to go through those things making the thin cotton. Sometimes you had to put your hand in there. Because it was [*makes a circular motion with her hands*], it could knock off the fingers.[29]
>
> Chaya S.: I was getting two big machines. And my work was, I had to pick big bundles—it was this that grows in the fields—they used to make, they used to make—I don't know how they call it in English—they used to put it in the machine, a big bundle. It was very dusty.[30]
>
> Chaya S.: [later in her testimony] I had to work on two machines at the same time. . . . It was a very hard job.[31]

The Gabersdorf experience was slightly different, in that the barracks opened in 1941. The girls and women had left families in Zagłębie who were still living in their homes, and the understanding, perpetuated by the Jewish Council of Elders, that labor was a temporary assignment rather than a pathway to imprisonment and death was still prevalent.

> Irene W.: You see it was a fairly new camp. The barracks and everything. There were already one hundred girls there [in 1941]. Fifty from—the first transport was from Będzin, the second fifty was from Sosnowiec, and we were the third transport.[32]

> Bluma S.: Gabersdorf? Gabersdorf was a heaven. We were treated very, very nice. There were thirty girls in a room. There were all together three hundred girls. In the barracks. And we have, we could take once a week showers. We worked in the factory. And food? You could survive.[33]

Bluma S.'s jarring description of a coerced labor camp as "a heaven" speaks to the shared expectations of testimony-giver, interviewer, and audience that influence testimony, as noted in Pollin-Galay's work. The Gabersdorf experience is only "heaven" in the context of the killing centers of Auschwitz-Birkenau, Majdanek, and Sobibor and the rural ravines and pits into which Jews were shot in Ukraine and Belarus.

Among the Gabersdorf survivors are women from Zagłębie whose testimonies also recall offering to exchange themselves for a sibling, an exchange inside the family that both Dasha R. and Sala K. went through, not anticipating that labor in these isolated camps would keep them out of mass deportations to killing centers. There are several testimonies from survivors of these peripheral camps that develop the nuances of these wrenching decisions and foreground the conflicted nature of the memory as well as the limitations and possibilities of testimony practice.

Tosia J. remembers that she was taken to the Gabersdorf camp in an unusual interview with the Shoah Foundation that proceeded outside of the bounded script of the questionnaire.[34] A series of technical missteps during the interview blend into Tosia J.'s own intentional "misstep" as she recalls substituting herself for her sister at the time the family was confronted with a demand to surrender a member for coerced labor. The interview begins with a few moments of informal banter that is not part of the official interview, in which the interviewer interrupts Tosia J. and does not respond to her attempts to correct a misimpression. Once the interview begins, the interviewer introduces her by mispronouncing both her first and last name. After a few moments, the interviewer asks Tosia J. to pronounce and spell her maiden name, as is the case for all Shoah Foundation interviews. Tosia J. spells out "Jakubowicz." The interviewer asks her current name, which she states is "Jakubowicz-Schwartzbaum," although the archival title of the interview is "Tosia Jakubs-Schwartzbaum."

The interviewer then asks the prescripted prompt, "Tell us where you were born." At approximately two and a half minutes into the interview, Tosia J. begins to lose her composure, almost imperceptibly at first. She speaks carefully, methodically, but quickly, knowing what is being asked of her because she had received the questions ahead of time, but not being able to stop herself from forging ahead emotionally and chronologically:

> Tosia J.: I was born in Zawiercie, Poland. Uh. My parents' name were [*voice begins to tremble*]. My father's name was Joachim. My mother's name was Pesel. Uh. I had some siblings. Some [*gestures with her eyes*]. There were five of us. And I am the only survivor. My oldest brother's name was Mordechai. Uh. My sister's was Sala. Which I took the name for a while. [*begins to weep softly*] I—uh—I—uh—went to camp under her name. I was trying to protect her. That she won't be going to the concentration camp. So I went in as Sala Jakubowicz. And then later on I got back to my own name, Tosia. [*She continues to name siblings.*][35]

The earlier off-track pre-video miscommunication and the problem with Tosia J.'s name seems at first to be jarring and perhaps even offensive to the listener. But the mishearing and misnaming appear to open up Tosia J. to the memory of the intentional misnaming she herself pursued. This particular misnaming was painful to her, because she "took" her sister's name in an effort to save her, but her sister did not survive. In fact, Tosia J. was "the only survivor." The name switch was the pathway by which Tosia J. entered the camp system, surviving and "later on" going "back to my own name." Once she begins to list family names she seems pulled into the wartime decision-making regarding labor facing Zagłębie's Jewish families, even though she knows this moment is not the time to talk about it. As she has been told ahead of the interview, this first "segment" of the Shoah Foundation interviews is intended to introduce the viewers to prewar Jewish life and to document the family names for the record. Material about the Nazi camps is to be discussed in a later segment.

The reality that Tosia J. and the others in this book survived *because* they were separated from their families was at times acknowledged and at times suppressed throughout the testimonies. The notion that one's initial sacrifice and self-understanding as acting to save one's family member was ultimately the action that only saved oneself appears to be extremely painful for most testimony-givers. They only realized the complete truth after the war was over. Until then, they continued to fantasize about reuniting with family.

Bluma S. also tells of a switch with a sister that was meant to be protective but that ended in a reversal. Bluma S. was nineteen in 1941 when the ss came to the family home in Będzin.

> Bluma S.: And they came for me and my sister. And they came there. And we were thinking, they are not going to kill everybody. She was younger. We were pleading. And I said, "I go." And my sister still was—she was younger than me. And she stayed home. I wish [now] she would [have gone] with me. She would be alive.[36]

Bluma S.'s sister was taken two months later and killed in a labor camp elsewhere.

Gabersdorf survivor Irene W. also speaks to the conflicted nature of the desire for survival without one's family, a theme that is echoed in Bernsdorf survivors as well. In 1944 a new group of young women arrived from the Hungarian occupied territories, via Auschwitz, a process detailed in the next chapter. These women had gone through the brutality of that killing center.

> Irene W.: But when [the Hungarian women] got used to us and they saw that in our camp there was no killings and all that, then they started telling us what's going on at home. And that's when we first found out that there won't be any survivors. At that time I started praying to God every night: Please, God, don't let me survive if I am going to be all alone in the world.[37]

Irene W.'s formulation here contains the contradictions in the coping strategies of the girls and women in all of these camps: pushing oneself to persist for the sake of family, longing for information about loved ones, but resisting the truth because it would leave one bereft of any guidepost for continuing onward.

The barrack in Bernsdorf was a repurposed factory warehouse. The Etrich family owned the factory, which manufactured pieces of cloth—mostly sacking—made from natural fibers or paper.

> Dora R.: They put us up in a big hall from the factory. It was a very dirty place because machines must have been there before. And they divided us to work. Some went to *Spinnerei* [spinning], to *Weberei* [weaving]—this is weaving machines, and some worked with flax. They made sacks there. Ordinary sacks.[38]
>
> Roza W.: I did not know [when I arrived] that what they worked there was paper and wood. From wood from Hirschberg [another coerced labor location]—where men were, not women—they made from the wood like you see [into] white cotton. It looked exactly like cotton balls.[39]
>
> Cesia T.: I was working by two big machines. And I was going like from one in to the other, from one end to the other.[40]
>
> Cesia T.: We were making big mattress sheets, like, big rolls of fabric. But I think it was made out of paper. Because they were saying that this goes for mattresses for the army.[41]

Based on the testimonies, there were more men present in the Bernsdorf factories than in the factories in Trautenau, Parschnitz, or Ober Altstadt, although reference sources do not mention them; this is likely because those sources prioritize the barracks themselves, which were officially the "camp," and these quarters were off-limits to men. Survivors report a number of different foremen, work supervisors, and support staff, all Gentile Germans or Czechs, interacting with them at the factories. In the Bernsdorf case, some of these men were quite abusive, a different experience from the memories of those in the other camps.

> Cesia T.: [confronted by a foreman while sick] He slapped me in my face once. And he slapped me the other side second. He gave me a kick. And I fell to the ground. He went to the bathroom. I was lying there and crying and I could not get up.[42]

Similarly to the camps in the Trautenau region, Czech and German Gentile coworkers surreptitiously supplied food to the Jewish girls and women.

> Cesia T.: [speaking about a Czech male worker] [H]is mother came one time and she was wearing a scarf, a big scarf on her.

And she stopped by my machine and she left a little basket with some fruits for me.[43]

In May 1941 Mina J. was fourteen and living in Sosnowiec when the Gestapo and ss initiated a sudden roundup of entire Jewish families from a particular street. Mina J. describes the street in front of her home as filled with soldiers, police, trucks, and blaring noise. Along with Mina J. herself, the authorities took her mother, father, three brothers, and one of her sisters to the *Durchgangslager*. (An older sister was living elsewhere at this time.) Her memory helps sharpen the understanding of the practices of exchange and what could be called the circulating economy of Jewish coerced labor that operated in and through the *Dulag*.

In Mina J.'s telling, a Jewish family friend was working at the *Dulag* to patrol the detainees and happened to be assigned to the area where her family was sequestered. The friend became quite agitated when he encountered the family.

> Mina J.: [*crying throughout*] He was devastated. He walked around, he kept on coming back and finally came back. "The only way I will get your parents, that everybody will get out, you have to volunteer." I have to volunteer. To take me away. I don't know if I was so brave, or was naïve, I don't know. I volunteered. And I saw my mother with all my brothers and sisters released. They let them go. And they took me away. I was wearing a sailor suit. It was May.[44]

Mina J.'s memory deepens the understanding of the exchange approach used in Sosnowiec for coerced labor, which in light of her testimony seems to be best described as a hostage approach, in which volunteers for labor are coerced by holding loved ones. This interpretation is supported by the fact that the family friend targeted Mina J. in particular for volunteering.

Mina J. uses the specificity of the sailor suit to help her anchor the incident among her memories and to stand in for her age and position in the family—as a beloved daughter taken care of by her parents and protected from responsibilities, which she had described earlier in the testimony. She is still uncertain as to how to categorize her action at the time of the testimony-giving and withholds the label "brave" from herself.

Her ambivalence is apparent when she states that "I saw my mother . . . released" rather than taking accountability for the release herself. This moment in the *Dulag* was the last time she saw her mother and siblings, something she only realized at the end of the war; thus, her ambivalence is a present-day emotion that overlays her feelings at the time of the event. The ambivalence and resistance to claiming courage is echoed in this portion of testimony a few minutes later, in which her survival itself is unclaimed by her:

> Mina J.: [*still crying*] But I saw my father. He came to the gates. And said to me these words, which I guide myself all my life with. He said, "Minusia, whatever they tell you to do, do the best you know how. Do the best. And you will survive."[45]

Mina J. does not take this moment in the testimony-giving process to assert a comment such as, "and I did survive." The words remain with the father.

After these words Mina J. continues to cry silently and the interviewer is also heard crying. The tape abruptly stops. The interviewer had not intervened to transition either Mina J. or the viewers into the change in tape, which is the typical protocol. In the next tape, both Mina J. and the interviewer have recovered their composure and begin speaking about Mina J.'s childhood, since she had relayed the *Dulag* incident out of chronological order. All of these aspects of the practice and techniques of testimony-giving leave Mina J.'s feelings about her own survival in ambivalence. Later in the testimony the interviewer asks Mina J. directly about this:

> Interviewer: So did you, you believed that you would survive? Did you have a sense of it?
> Mina J.: [*pauses and sighs*] I think we were not aware what was going on in those camps. We were young. And I think youth has a lot to do with survival. And we were—we felt, we're going to live. But how we're going to live, we didn't know.[46]

Although the interviewer probes—"Did you have a sense of it?"—Mina J. evades the directness of the question, but in doing so provides nuance and truthfulness to the issue of survival. As was the case for Irene W.,

Mina J. remembers the painful contradiction of an urge to live combined with a growing awareness that the Jewish world shaping her childhood that provided a sense of how life would unfold among family and community was no longer intact. This living with no idea of "how we're going to live" was already a palpable rupture for these girls and women.

CHAPTER 5

Auschwitz Arrives in Trautenau

This chapter presents two significant changes in Nazi policy that deeply affected the daily lives and emotions of the girls and women in all of the Trautenau-region camps. The first, in late 1943, was the attempted imposition of newly restrictive and brutalizing regulations on the constellation of small barracks, consolidating them into the concentration camp Parschnitz and forced labor camps (*Zwangsarbeitslager*) Ober Altstadt, Gabersdorf, and Bernsdorf, which absorbed Schatzlar. This period was the formal repositioning of the girls and women as prisoners (*Häftlinge*) and brings a more direct ss presence into their experiences. This direct presence brought with it ss strategies of bodily manipulation and humiliation, processes that scholar Brigid Halbmayr calls "sexualized violence."[1] The second change, in mid- and late 1944, was the addition of a new wave of Jewish female labor: groups of young women mostly from the territories occupied by Hungary, who had been rounded up by Hungarian gendarmes and military authorities for transport to Auschwitz-Birkenau. Amidst these "Hungarian girls," as those from Zagłębie already in the camps called them, were also a few who had been sent to Auschwitz from the dismantled Łódź ghetto and elsewhere. These arrivals were visibly marked by their Auschwitz experience, both on their bodies and in the way they carried the trauma of recent family separation.

Both of these changes have been well documented by historians as manifestations of shifts in the Nazi regime's approach to labor and the camps system. The late-1943 change formally brought the Schmelt work camps under the administration of the Gross-Rosen concentration camp; the 1944 change removed Schmelt and created a more direct link to the *Wirtschafts- und Verwaltungshauptamt* (WVHA) and the Inspectorate of the Concentration Camps. Historians of the camps system such as Daniel Blatman have used perpetrator documents and Nuremberg testimony to piece together the rationale behind these changes and the vagaries of their implementation.[2] For the survivors of the camps in the Trautenau region, perpetrator rationales were secondary; their testimonies centered on how these experiences shaped their ability to cope with perpetrator behavior and their growing awareness of what was happening to European Jewry on a larger scale.

The testimony-givers remember their experiences during the late-1943 imposition of new persecution processes as physically embodied and sexualized. Halbmayr's definition of "sexualized violence" fits well with how the survivors explain what occurred, which is similar to camp processes throughout the Reich, annexed regions, and occupied territories: "Violent acts can be understood as sexualized if they are directed at the most intimate parts of a person and, as such, against that person's physical, emotional and spiritual integrity."[3] In her work, Halbmayr brings practices that were not labeled as "sexual" in past historiography into relation with sexual assault as such by attending to the meaning of the body for the participants, that is, victims, perpetrators, and observers. The foregrounding of "intimate parts" in her definition allows the connection to become clear between forced nakedness, for example, and the feeling of sexual violation. It also allows for a juxtaposition between what might be taken as apparently identical instances of sexualized violence (again, forced nakedness is an example) in different persecutory settings, in this case between the Trautenau camps and the Auschwitz processes undergone by those arriving from the Hungarian territories. By hearing how survivors remember each, the specificity of each institutional context and how that context shaped coping strategies can be discerned more clearly.

In late 1943 Himmler instituted a policy changing the legal status of Jewish workers in camps associated with private firms. All Jews would now officially be prisoners of the German Reich, administratively subject to one of the large concentration camps directly run by the ss.[4] They would not necessarily physically move into these large camps; they would continue to live near and work at the same (or new) factories; factory owners would continue to pay for them. But the conditions they lived in would substantially worsen, including increased vulnerability to tactics of fear and humiliation. In a sense, instead of being sent to a concentration camp, a concentration camp was sent to them.

It is helpful to recall the atypical chronology of the Schmelt labor camps in relation to the evolution of the concentration camp system. The role of camps in ss terror began in the 1930s, as Nikolaus Wachsmann has shown, with the development of specific techniques of persecution aimed at targeting specific enemies of the party and state; over time, the model of a bounded space inside of which mass killings could occur emerged.[5] The war brought additional concentration camp initiatives responding to new goals, such as imprisoning partisans and Soviet prisoners of war. From 1942 to 1944, the use of inmates as labor came to the forefront; the concentration camp system grew alongside and through the development of the WVHA, which, among other tasks, administered the large ss-initiated economic projects.[6] The WVHA institutionalized the use of prisoners already in concentration camps for coerced labor; camps and killing centers became not just sites of detention and execution but also spaces in which ss authorities identified individuals as physically capable of work and held them until they could be sent to a work site. Conditions were brutal. As Daniel Blatman notes, "labor and extermination" "became indivisibly connected."[7]

As noted earlier, the Schmelt system in Upper Silesia and the Sudetenland operated somewhat autonomously from direct WVHA control. The November 1943 order began the process by which Schmelt's system would begin to come under the WVHA's control and by which the small labor camps in Sudetenland would become "concentration camps." Historian and Himmler scholar Peter Longerich argues that:

> In order to pre-empt potential resistance from employers, who might insist on continuing to employ their Jewish workers, Himmler now pursued a policy of transforming the remaining ghettos and camps into concentration camps. This ensured that the inmates were now at last totally subject to the ss and prevented any attempt by other agencies to gain access to them.[8]

Himmler's target appeared to be the factory owners—the "employers"—as well as ss insiders such as Schmelt, who had come under suspicion of skimming the income generated by his system for personal gain.

Consequences of this policy for the Trautenau region included the crowding of some of the girls and women from the smaller barracks in the town of Trautenau into a single large barrack that was part of the

Haase factory building itself; a similar combining of the Schatzlar barracks with the Bernsdorf barracks; SS training for the *Lagerführerinnen*; the end of letters, postcards, and package privileges (although most families were not alive to send them by late 1943); and periodic, terrorizing visits by groups of male SS officers.

> Estera S.: [speaking of late 1943] The whole camp was taken over by the SS and they arranged a team of SS women. These were German girls who started wearing the uniform of the SS ... Things changed completely ... We had to be watched and punished for every little thing.[9]

> Regina G.: I mean, the SS was the worst thing what could happen to us. They were watching us from, from the morning 'til late at night. And during the night. [*pauses*] And you know, we were young kids. The oldest maybe could have been in our camp maybe twenty-five, twenty-six. And we didn't know what's going to happen to us.[10]

> Sally B.: It started out we were just a few hundred [girls]. And from—I think the camp opened at the end of 1940. 'Til, 'til the middle, the end of the summer '43, we were as a working camp. The camp wasn't too bad because it was run by the directors also from the—we were, I don't know whether you knew about it but they were paying, I think to the Gestapo or the SS for each person.[11]

> Phyllis Y.: By 1943 we were transferred. You see, that part of Sudeten, every couple of miles there was a factory.[12]

Phyllis Y. clarifies that those living in the barracks adjacent to the Walzel factory had to move to barracks at the Haase factory, placing them under the supervision of a *Lagerführerin* she remembers as quite harsh.

> Phyllis Y.: They took us out. Not out of the factory. We still worked in the Walzel factory.[13]

> Phyllis Y.: But when we were transferred there [to Haase], we were now in a concentration camp. And that was a hell of a difference.[14]

As her testimony continues, it becomes clear that she had experienced the Haase barracks as violent. By "hell of a difference" she suggests not only "quite different" but that the Haase barracks were "hell."

Himmler's order also demanded an end to the unregulated activities at work sites, such as the interaction between Jewish and non-Jewish workers, the guards using the girls for babysitting and other errands, and the practice of negotiating to switch one sister for another. To achieve these aims, Himmler created an administrative connection between the Trautenau region's camps and Gross-Rosen, the nearest large concentration camp and killing center. Gross-Rosen itself had never been under Albrecht Schmelt's supervision, although it was located in Silesia; it had not been permeable by visiting Sosnowitz Gestapo, the Jewish Council of Elders, or any of the other local actors benefiting from the Zagłębie labor circuit. It was a huge concentration camp near Wałbrzych, forty-two miles north of Trautenau. Gross-Rosen SS administrators contracted prisoner labor out to private businesses, some of whom operated on site.[15] Although the Trautenau constellation of coerced labor sites did not use prisoner labor from people already imprisoned at Gross-Rosen, and Trautenau's coerced laborers did not physically travel there, each laborer was assigned a Gross-Rosen prisoner number for the first time, stamped onto a leather disk and worn as a necklace.[16] In practice, however, Schmelt held on to his control of Jewish labor until March 1944. Only after Schmelt was removed did the WVHA gain a foothold in Trautenau.[17]

Late 1943 was also the beginning of "roll calls," in which every barrack resident was awoken even earlier in the morning (although all the girls and women had been counted every morning and evening prior to 1943) and stood in rows outdoors to be counted and recounted; more negative consequences for offenses like stealing; rules forbidding looking out the windows; and an end to errands into town and postcards and packages. From the testimonies it appears that these roll calls were shorter in duration than those in more brutal sites such as Auschwitz; were not consistent in frequency and form across the different barracks in the Trautenau-region camps; and could be evaded at times.

In practice, the people responsible for documenting that all of this was occurring in Parschnitz, at least, were Elsa Hawlik and the other *Lager-*

führerinnen. Every morning Hawlik needed to create a handwritten list based on roll call, likely relying on the *Aufseherinnen* under her. Every month Hawlik had to track which laborers from the single massive barrack were paid for by Etrich, which by Haase, which by Kluge, and which by Walzel. Finally, it meant that the owners had an opening to make a bit more money: they argued that because the girls and women were now prisoners of Gross-Rosen, Gross-Rosen should pay for their food, medical and dental care, and even the straw for their bedding. Monthly invoices tracking these expenses by company were the responsibility of Hawlik.[18]

Trained at Ravensbrück, Hawlik and her staff began to use violence more frequently.[19] The girls and women found this shift in practice confusing and even resisted it to some degree, because the laborers themselves had not changed their behavior.

> Ida G.: There were SS women who were very eager to show off that they are SS women. And every time they approached you their hands were flying.[20]

Nettie S. was assigned to a job receiving materials and processing them. The employee bringing the work had not yet arrived, so Nettie S. just waited, sitting, as her Gentile coworker did. She remembers being suddenly berated by a guard:

> Nettie S.: She said, "You're Jewish!" She said to me. "Yes, I'm Jewish." "You [are not] supposed to sit." You know, she starts, uh, slapping my face.[21]

Fay B. worked at the Kluge factory in Ober Altstadt. She remembers the stark change:

> Fay B.: The *Lagerführerin* left for two or three weeks. For SS training. She came back mean, and with a black uniform. There was no mail for us.[22]

Thus, in late 1943 two small concentration camps appear in the archival records: Parschnitz, which consolidated the Haase, Etrich, and Walzel workers, and Ober Altstadt, which consolidated the Kluge workers and some of the Etrich.[23] These terms—"Parschnitz" and "Ober Altstadt"—

began to refer to the barracks in which the girls and women lived, rather than the geographical locations, meaning the towns, that they had referred to in the past. The work was the same. The Jewish laborers continued to work side by side with civilians in the textile factories. The head of Gross-Rosen, Johannes Hassebroek, appointed an ss official, Fritz Ritterbusch, to supervise Parschnitz, Ober Altstadt, Gabersdorf, and Bernsdorf/Schatzlar. Ritterbusch set up an office he called *Kommando Trautenau* in Parschnitz. He sent frequent memos exhorting the factory owners and *Lagerführerinnen* to tighten security.[24] And it was Ritterbusch who now received payments from the factory owners instead of Schmelt, presumably forwarding them to an ss account because his living quarters in town were modest.

One new policy that the factories did take advantage of was the creation of scrip, or coupons that the *Lagerführerinnen* or the floor supervisor could give specific laborers as rewards, to increase productivity. The factory owners had to purchase this scrip (officially called a *Prämienschein*) from the Gross-Rosen supply administration and did so frequently in 1944 and early 1945.

> Nettie S.: When you work [well], you got fifty cents. You can buy for this sauerkraut. [*Nettie shows the camera one of the coupons she has saved from that time.*] Fifty cents.[25]

The coupon system was dictated by the ss. It appears to have a few different functions: it was a tool to increase productivity because it was an added incentive, and it was supposed to combat the use of monetary bribes, although almost none of the laborers had access to any money by late 1943.[26]

The implications of the shift to the girls and women becoming prisoners are complex to sort out. It appears that Etrich, Haase, Kluge, and the Walzel Brothers (as well as Buhl & Sohn in Schatzlar) attempted to evade some of the new regulations coming from Gross-Rosen and *Kommando Trautenau*. Ritterbusch himself seems to have been concerned with the restrictions on the mobility of the girls and women—now officially prisoners of Gross-Rosen—and overseeing food supplies and other issues related to finances.[27] There appear to have been at least two ss officers in the Trautenau *Kommando*, one elderly and one in his forties; it is unclear whether the testimony-givers knew which one was Ritterbusch.[28]

Anna W.: [encountering Ritterbusch at a food supply depot outside of the camp] He never said a word, anytime.²⁹

Lola W.: One ss man, an elderly gentleman, who was very nice. He couldn't help us. But he wouldn't hurt us. He was the only one. [*pauses*] He killed himself right, when, at the war's end, when the war ended. And we would never have done anything wrong to him. Just give him our love and our thank you. He was the only one. But he couldn't take it and he killed himself.
Interviewer: Well, what did he do that was good?
Lola W.: He never hurt us.³⁰

Estelle C. was taken to one of the ss in the *Kommando* to be punished for an infraction.

Estelle C.: He didn't remember. He was old. He must have been, I don't know, like I said, to me everybody was old. But he was like, seventy at least. I would say. Very old man.³¹

Survivors tell of periodically encountering a more intimidating ss figure on the premises of either the barracks or the factory; a survivor giving a deposition in 1970 remembers an officer she calls Ritterbusch screaming at, hitting, and kicking a campmate.³²

These members of the Trautenau *Kommando* were the on-site ss, distinct from small groups of ss who arrived periodically for specific purposes. Survivors who had been at the Parschnitz concentration camp take some time in their testimony to share their memories and emotions regarding the unpredicted visits of teams of ss doctors to conduct on-site "selections." Beginning in late 1943, at least once a group of men in uniform visited the camps in the Trautenau region for these "selections." This was the first time the Zagłębie girls and women had gone through the type of "selection" with its veneer of medicalization common in concentration camps and killing centers. The ss commandeered space in each camp; in Ober Altstadt it was a large empty room with a hallway connected to a second room. The girls and women were taken from the barracks (it is unclear which building this occurred in but many report wearing coats, so it is likely it was located away from the barracks themselves), assembled in line, and made to undress completely while waiting. Although they changed clothes in the barracks among their fellow workers, they experienced this type of nakedness as something of an entirely different order. The ss team required each person to slowly walk to a chalk circle drawn on the floor, then slowly turn front to back. The men controlled the length of time each person was to display herself in front of them. They then directed each person to some other part of the building.

> Fay B.: I had to stand outside the room nude. I said, "I'm going to take my coat" and I put on my coat. Five Germans were at a table in the dining room. We have to go into the dining room. I walked in. Men sitting at a table. One saying "right" or "left." Black uniforms. I was given a number. I didn't look. Girls sent to the left were sent away. I only thought about my mother's advice.[33]

In this short fragment Fay B. expresses a range of recalled coping strategies aimed at keeping the sense of violation at a distance from her inner psyche—her "spiritual integrity," as Halbmayr might put it. She directly defies the order to remain naked by taking her coat. She refuses to acknowledge the men as specific human beings or distinguishable individuals—they are only "black uniforms." She refuses to "look" at the number she was given and will not register herself as a number in her own mind. And she chooses to occupy her mind with a loved one expressing protection, again keeping the threat to personal integrity at bay. Suzan L. echoes this mental refusal, attributing it to the cold temperatures:

> Suzan L.: It took all of our effort not to collapse. Literally. It was like, you know, this kind of cold. So that—it was demeaning, but at the same time you, you really could not concentrate on your nakedness.[34]

The testimonies, taken together, communicate the association of nakedness with not only sexual threat but also the possibility of death that this experience represented.

> Ester R.: Every girl must take off as she was born. [*pauses*] There were no questions! No question, why, what? We were so scared, we were so scared—we couldn't even remove—something on us . . . We must not show it! They shouldn't find this [their fear], they shouldn't see it. So one by one, get undressed. We turn

around. The front, and then the back. Everyone tried, tries [*gestures standing up very straight*]. With her bitter feeling! Tried to stay straightened out. Everyone was—itst [now] the moment of life or death.³⁵

Lucy M.: It was, I think, I wasn't the only one that had goosebumps all over, just going there and not from being cold. It—you know, you are so scared, you don't even know how to explain it. [*silence*]³⁶

Regina G.: And they used to make selections. And one on the right side one on the left side. And they put my sister on one side and me on the other side. And by some miracle my sister crawled to my side.³⁷

Sonia S.: They assembled us in a court, you know, where it was like the field there, and we had to strip naked. Nude completely. And there were about three Gestapos.
Interviewer: How many girls do you think—
Sonia S.: Oh, uh, at least 150. And we had to make a [*gestures*], we had to make a circle. And we are not allowed to—you know, we are young girls, we were embarrassed, we are not allowed to hold [*holds arms across chest*]. We had to stay like this. [*holds arms at sides*] They walked around with a cane.³⁸

Phyllis Y.: And they made us stand. Face them. Look at them. Turn around. This is all naked. With not a stitch of clothes on you. Turn around. And they say, they send us aside.³⁹

In these camps the killing of prisoners did not ordinarily occur. The everyday expectation was that violent death was not at hand (although death by disease or lack of nutrition always was). The association of ss or Gestapo officers with Auschwitz changed this understanding. It meant that these episodes of sexualized violence also represented a threat to life. The use of the term "selections" indicates that the survivors realized on some level that those sent in a different direction would indeed be killed at Auschwitz.

The testimony-givers also remember their awareness at the time that this was a ritual with no genuine medical or labor-related purpose. There is an element of ridicule in their descriptions at the time of testimony-giving that functions to reverse the perpetrator's gaze.

> Ann F.: These guys were having one big time. They were sitting and watching us go around the circles.⁴⁰
>
> Bella C.: They made a circus from us.⁴¹
>
> Sonia S.: I think they were degenerates.⁴²
>
> Regina G.: They were laughing from us. And they had a long stick and they used to take to our breasts and say, "Die hat große, die hat kleine." "She has big one, she has nothing." And they used to laugh and make fun of us.⁴³

Here Ann F. categorizes the SS as "these guys," deflating their power; Sonia S. herself uses "degenerates," which retains a sense of violence but adds a certain moral or even sexual inadequacy. This projected inadequacy is well captured in the rhythm of Regina G.'s statement. She emphasizes the length of the stick, as if the SS can use only sticks, that is, substitutes that are potentially penetrative but that in fact keep bodies at a distance.

These testimonies complicate and extend the role of sexualized violence in the Holocaust in significant ways. Halbmayr focuses on the insight that the perpetrator's goal in this violence is a "show of power and demonstration of dominance."⁴⁴ However, the enactment of that violence is received variously by those assigned to be dominated, a reception that is influenced by social factors and institutional setting. Several testimony-givers remember holding the violence at bay and finding the SS officers deeply frightening but limited as sexual beings. At the same time testimony-givers did not always perceive a boundary between sexualized violence and the threat of death; nakedness was not only a precursor to sexual assault but also to being killed, and one was not separable from the other.

By mid-1944 the new rules had once again relaxed—or perhaps had been only partially implemented. Ritterbusch's correspondence indicates that it was the firm owners who pushed back against the regulations. Ritterbusch sent the Haase firm a list of his concerns in mid-April 1944: he stated that there should be no toleration of Jewish women interacting with civilian workers, that Haase should stop sending small groups of women out without supervision, and, tellingly, that the firm should start feeding the prisoners appropriately.[45] "It is the responsibility of the firm to supply food. The company should be interested in the health of the workforce." Later in the month Ritterbusch complains that he has heard that "Jews are working with civilians," and reminds the company that it is responsible for medical care, "since the companies would be responsible if these were civil workers."[46] In November 1944 the commandant of Gross-Rosen sent Alois Haase a memo in support of Ritterbusch, who had apparently complained that his directives were ignored. One of the new requirements was to have male guards, and apparently Haase had claimed difficulty in finding "accommodation" for these men—either while they were working or as quarters.[47] The commandant reminded Haase that the Jewish girls and women "are no longer forced laborers, but prisoners of the Gross-Rosen concentration camp," that the male guards must stay, that civilians can neither be guards nor interact with the girls and women, and that "further protests on your part" would not be appreciated.[48]

Did the girls and women ever try to escape? Did any succeed? This question is often posed by the Shoah Foundation interviewers, part of the questionnaire asked of every participant. The answer is complex. First, very few survivors felt they had the wherewithal to create an escape plan.

> Interviewer: Did you ever think you could escape from the camp?
> Regina S.: No, no. There was no means to escape. No way. No way.[49]

> Regina S.: Well, our thoughts were only if we survive, we want to see our parents. And—period. We never thought about something else.[50]

> Minnie W.: All of a sudden we heard that two girls escaped. But they got caught. There was no place where to escape.[51]

This exchange reminds us of the original implicit or explicit understanding when the girls and women were first taken to the *Dulag*: that in exchange for their work—that is, their obedience—their families would survive. Even when evidence trickled in that the SS was deporting their families, arresting individuals, killing people at camps, the girls and women in the Trautenau factories held on to the belief that their actions might possibly help in their family's case. The belief was also a way of keeping the attachment to their parents alive, vivid, sustaining, to help them continue. An escape might possibly destroy this bargain. Regina S. has to remind the interviewer again, late in the interview, of the ages of the coerced laborers.

Second, it appears that a few individuals did indeed escape. Some instances were remembered in the testimonies as hearsay. In one of these passed-along rumors, a mother and daughter escaped and went to the railway station.

> Ida G.: They got as far as the train station . . . When they tried to purchase a ticket, they were asked for identification. And they had none.[52]

With no legal documents, the stationmaster simply called the police, who arrested them. Escape in general, as we know from other research and memoirs on the Holocaust, required a careful plan, new clothing, safe houses, information, contacts in the "outside" world, and false documents, a project that most of the girls and women in Trautenau could not undertake because of the nature of their imprisonment. However, in 1944 the newly assigned representative of the Inspectorate of the Concentration Camps (part of the WVHA) sent an angry letter to Ritterbusch criticizing the factory owners for lax security. He references "two Jewish females who successfully escaped."[53]

In sum, even when the repression at the Trautenau work sites and barracks increased, the choice of escaping did not make sense. As Evgeny Finkel's detailed study of choices made by Jews in Kraków, Minsk, and Białystok during the Holocaust demonstrates, the specific conditions of confinement, persecution, political experience, and social context all mediated the rationality of decisions to cooperate, comply, evade, or outright resist.[54] For the girls and women in the Trautenau-region camps, escape did not make sense because these particular prisoners did not consider themselves (with a few exceptions) as isolated individuals who could risk only their own lives if they ran into the countryside. They thought of themselves as part of an extended family and rarely as part of a political movement. They weighed each action they took for its impact on their hope of rejoining that family at some future point. This perception of their own persecution was shaped by gender, age, religious identity, and the isolated, enclosed spaces of barracks, factories, towns, and mountain landscapes.

In the summer of 1944 the girls and women laboring at Parschnitz were shocked to see the arrival of a group of people who appeared unlike any human they had ever seen. Most striking were their recently shaved heads, which, combined with the thin fabric or ill-fitting clothing that they were wearing, upended any ability of the "Polish girls" to understand them as gendered. Their ill-fitting garments hung uneasily on their bodies. Deep trauma was etched on their faces and apparent in their movements. Many spoke some German; only a few spoke Yiddish. They were from the territories annexed to Hungary. The testimony-givers recall that only gradually did they realize that these people were also, like them, female, Jewish, and young.

What the "Polish girls" saw were the physical and emotional scars of the Auschwitz experience on the bodies of the new arrivals, carried with them to Trautenau.

> Esther S.: When they came our lives changed completely. [*begins to cry*] From the stories they were telling us. Horror. What they did to the people. [*Unable to speak. Tape ends.*][55]

> Esther S.: [*composed*] They came in. Long dresses. With no hair. With shoes from the other century. With left, uh, not even pairs of shoes they were wearing. And very sad looking. They made such a bad impression on us that we really, like—uh—if we didn't have what to eat, we lost our appetites completely. The way they looked and—they started telling us stories, what they doing with the people in Auschwitz. We just couldn't believe it.[56]

> Eta B.: And one transport came from Hungaria—from Hungarian women. They brought them. I thought that they delivered a transport with people they came from a insane—from a sanitarium. With shaved heads. With long dresses. I never believed they normal, they didn't look normal![57]

> Esther S.: We tried to give them clothes, from our clothes that we had.[58]

While it is common to find shock at shorn hair and shaved heads in Holocaust testimony, in these particular testimonies the confrontation is not only with a being that appears at odds with gendered reality. As in Esther S.'s telling, in the eyes of the "Polish girls," the unusual appearance of the "Hungarian girls" was interwoven with the extremity of their lived experience. The realization of "what they did to the people" was, as Esther S. remembers, life altering and initially resists representation in language, as Esther S.'s ability to speak breaks down in her initial description. The need to change tapes gives her an opportunity to compose herself. She explains the extreme difference of the arrivals, even placing them outside of time ("from the other century"). Esther S. ends the long anecdote with her memory of an attempt at care and integration ("we tried to give them clothes").

As the extensive scholarship on the Holocaust in Hungary documents, the Nazis had deported these new arrivals to Auschwitz just days or weeks earlier; in a rapid-fire series of events, these "Hungarian girls," who had been living at home until mid-1944, were separated from family, forced to stand naked in front of strangers, shaved completely, deprived of appropriate clothing, and marched or transported to a location utterly foreign to them.[59] Stripped of their hair, their clothing, and the family that had defined and structured their lives, they were unable to assimilate aspects of their Auschwitz-Birkenau experience, although as adults giving testimony they could remember fragments. It is difficult to describe the overwhelming sense of disorientation and fear that those who survived and recorded testimony communicate as they speak about these moments. The description of the Auschwitz selection process is familiar to many who have read memoirs, seen films, or done any scholarly work on the Holocaust. Yet there are aspects of the specific journeys of the girls and young women from Hungary that merit close attention, in part because these journeys—as they recall them—bring to the forefront Auschwitz's function as a source for labor as well as the singularity of the persecution faced by Jews from Hungary.[60]

Almost all of the testimonies of survivors from Hungary highlight the confusion and disorientation of their journeys in a way that contrasts with the experiences of the survivors from Poland. When interviewers ask questions about specific stages, such as the train ride, most of the survivors must make a concerted effort to set apart that stage narratively.

These were, in the main, girls in their early teens whose adult caregivers had given them little inkling about the nature of Hitler's Germany and whose daily lives almost never separated them from their immediate families.

> Aranka T.: You know, we were so naïve. We thought everywhere this can happen, not in Hungary.[61]
>
> Eva H.: I, I knew about Hitler and the Anschluss in, in Vienna. But I remember at the same time my father saying at the dinner table, "Hungary is a democratic country and things like that will never happen here.[62]
>
> Katalin T.: We heard about Poland, you know. That they start the war much earlier. But really, we don't know what's going on. You know, because it was very far from Hungary.[63]

The rapid succession of removal from the home, body searches at the holding center, train journey, separation from family at the Auschwitz-Birkenau ramp, absence of food, water, and toilet, forced nakedness, shaving and beatings, and blunt information about the immediate death of parents and siblings, all with little sense of the larger political context, left many dissociated or with fragmentary memories. Those from Hungary or its provinces had particular difficulty understanding the Polish or Yiddish of the prisoners who were trying to explain the situation to them.

> Frances H.: The moment we arrived [at Auschwitz] the door had been opened and maybe five or ten men in striped uniform and in hat came up to the train and they talked Yiddish to us. But maybe one or two between us came from a different kehillah, I would say, who understand Yiddish. But we didn't, we didn't know what they say.[64]
>
> Magdolna H.: [*crying*] They give so fast the order, we didn't know what is going on![65]
>
> Lili T.: And then everything happened in, in minutes![66]

The separation of families in the minutes after descent from the train is represented in the testimonies of the survivors from the Hungarian territories as the most powerful aspect of the persecutory experience.

It is frequently narrated in halting, fragmented phrases; the interviewee often loses composure multiple times during the telling. The recall and retelling process includes small, vivid details that the survivor has used as grounding material to cope with the memory of the disorientation, and then the return of the disorientation during the interview.

> Alice G.: I was walking with my mother. [*begins to weep*] And, uh, holding on very tight. With my grandmothers and my cousins and everybody. And, uh, then, uh, I guess this Polish guard came and tore me away from her.[67]
>
> Magdolna H.: And beside me was with my mother and two cousins, my age. One has the two-year-old girl. And my cousin, who was a young girl, kept in the hand that child . . . "Give to the mother the child." In that minute he separate from my mother. And they went left. The mother, the child, and my mother. And that young girl, my cousin, we went right.[68]
>
> Rose S.: [born in 1914 in a territory annexed to Hungary, she was married with an infant in 1944] Somebody came to me and took my child and gave it to my grandmother. I didn't know what was happening, you know, we were absolute—we didn't know what happened.[69]
>
> Eva D.: [describing arrival at Auschwitz] It was in a split second that mother already disappeared. She was there, father was already there, everything was so fast.[70]
>
> Elaine G.: I said to a German [guard], when do the people come out? You know, I see where they go. I want to go, too. Everybody wants to go. Nobody wants their family [separated] in a lot of places. So he says to me, "Look up there" . . . Only the smoke.[71]

It may be that the age of the girls when this occurred, their relative shelter from violence prior to this event, and the nature of their connections to the family unit made this moment at the selection point so traumatic. Almost none of the interviewees had spent time outside of the family home, except for school, prior to 1944. However, it is also the case that as adults giving testimony many years later, they have become aware that at the moment of separation they themselves were assigned to labor and in this way given the possibility of survival, while their loved ones were immediately sent to be killed. This awareness may have added an intensity and grief to their memories of these specific moments. Alice G. adds to her previous excerpt, in which she described camp personnel pulling her away from her mother. She was thirteen at the time.

> Alice G.: And I didn't want to go. And my mother kept saying, "Go, go ahead, go." And I said, "No, I want to stay with you." And he pulled me away and took me to the other side. And I ran back. And he pulled me away again.[72]

While Alice G. remembers a moment of kissing her mother goodbye, many did not.

> Ella J.: Once Mengele—who was the selecting officer there, the SS officer—once he chose you, he didn't look at you anymore. We were like cattle anyway . . . so I went with my cousins. We were four cousins, together . . .
> Interviewer: Did your mother give you any instructions before you were separated?
> Ella J.: We were sure that we would see them later. We were just—that we will go home to eat. I'm sure she kissed me. But the rush was such—so sudden, everything went so suddenly, that you—there was no orderliness in the mind. It was a very sudden thing. [*in a muted voice*] I can't remember to say goodbye to my mother. [*pause, silence*][73]

Ella J. allows the lack of "orderliness in the mind" to manifest in her testimony as she returns to the memory of the separation. She pauses frequently, changes her tone, and even changes to the present tense. "I can't remember" now, becomes conflated with "I didn't remember" then. She perhaps cannot bear to say it plainly: she did not say goodbye to her mother.

As is the case with other Auschwitz survivors, the shaving in particular was experienced as an assault on body, mind, and identity. Halbmayr singles out shaving as sexualized violence that simultaneously attacks the gendered personhood of the individual, her bodily privacy, and, socially, her ability to recognize herself and others.[74]

Magda F.: Then came the German. Young Germans. And they start to—[*loses composure, pauses*] shave us. And when that was coming the private part, that was terrible. You know, we were young girls. It was a shame.[75]

Lili T.: Then we were shaved off, everybody crying. And look, and look, and cry, screaming about—"Who is mother?" Nobody recognized nobody![76]

Eva D.: Then they shaved our hair. The underarm. And the pubic area. And then we were given some schmatte, some dress, something to wear ... And then they took us to the barrack. It was Auschwitz-Birkenau. It was C Lager. Barracks C ... There were thousand bald women. So we were simply in shock. Seeing thousand bald faces.[77]

Eva H.: [*crying*] I remember the feeling when they shaved off my head the hair. And I looked at my sister. And I realized that I became a nonentity. I just became a number. I just became nobody...[78]

Magdolna H.: After when we were shaved already we had to go into another room. And there was a glass. On the door. And I looked inside. And I look on the glass. And I say, "Who is that? That is a boy." I didn't believe it, that's me.[79]

Magdolna's memory of calling herself a boy supports the argument of scholar Monika Flaschka that shaving is an erasure of femininity because of the centrality of hair to gender, and thus should be viewed as an altering of gendered identity.[80] However, most of the survivors in this particular group remember that they thought of themselves as female—"a thousand bald women." They remember themselves as people who had lost their identities not because their hair marked them as female, but because hair was a crucial marker for distinguishing *among* people. In fact, the pubic shaving exposed genitalia, heightening the vulnerability associated with femininity "for a young girl." The shock was of an inability to recognize anyone at all, to locate oneself among others.

The survivors from the Hungarian-occupied territories who gave Shoah Foundation testimony and who had found themselves in the camps in the Trautenau region had been picked out for labor within weeks or months of their registration at Auschwitz.[81] According to researcher Kazimierz Smoleń, "The choice of prisoners was carried out by plant representatives. They received a special permit for this purpose, entitling them to enter the camp with the commander of the camp."[82] This process of being looked over also involved nakedness at times, and the male gaze was experienced as objectifying and sexualizing.

> Eva D.: There were these selections. When German places—I don't know, factories or whoever needed free labor, helpers—they came to select us. And they had to see us naked. I don't know what for. So we had to line up again and completely naked.[83]
>
> Magdolna H.: After two months came some, some, uh, came the *Lagerälteste*. That they need three hundred girls. They take two blocks. To the shower. That to my eye, to our eye, was very strange, usually they asking to go to the shower, this means crematorium. And I didn't want to go. But my cousin pushed me. "Don't be crazy, they will send us to work." . . . After the shower came some civilian men and a woman. They said that they are from a factory and they need three hundred girls.[84]
>
> Magdolna H.: They examined the eyes and the hands. They, they separate [us] from the others.[85]
>
> Livia R.: We were selected. And there was [an] official from the factory. We didn't know that—who came to selection. We were selected completely naked. No clothes whatsoever. Our hair was shaved out, off already. And they looked at, and they looked at mostly at our hands.[86]

Once assigned to a work site, the girl or woman would be given a small amount of food and clothing—sometimes a shower—so that their future civilian coworkers would not be as unsettled at the prospect of working alongside them.

> Hedy W.: They just selected young girls. And they put us, those what were selected, to these factories, they took us to another barrack, clothed us for a couple of days and they give us, they dressed us. They gave us a portion of bread and they put us

> again in cattle trucks and shipped us to Reichenbach. [She was transferred to Parschnitz a few months later.]⁸⁷

The transports from Auschwitz arrived in the Trautenau-region camps suddenly and in large groups, shocking those from Zagłębie. Most of the "Polish girls" in the Trautenau-area factories had difficulty in processing the true meaning of what the Hungarian arrivals had been through. They had heard rumors about Auschwitz, or "Auschwitz," a symbol laden with abstracted associations of disappearance, negation, nothingness, "the end of you." These arrivals made this word concrete; there was no mistaking the shaved bodies and the suffering. The specificity was hard to take in.

> Ida G.: They were burned to a crisp. They had scabs on [*gestures to her head*]—first of all, they had shaven, shaven heads. They had the uniforms on. And they were burned from the sun, whatever.⁸⁸

Ida G., who had been transferred for labor from Sosnowiec at seventeen and who was nineteen in 1944 when the Hungarian girls and women arrived, speaks to the impact of their presence:

> Ida G.: We were told that a transport of Hungarian women came from Auschwitz to us . . . The Hungarian women were quarantined on the top level. Where we were but on the other side. And we were in the, in, outside, milling around a little bit and the SS people around us. And, you know, we were afraid. But it was a sunny day. It was a beautiful sunny day . . . We look up, and all of a sudden—these little windows, pane windows, factory pane windows—some of them were broken and some open up, one pane open up. All of a sudden one pane window opened up. And the girl stuck her head out. And she started singing. And she had such a gorgeous operatic voice. She started singing in German opera songs . . . Soon [the SS guards] turned off the radio to listen to her sing. For one infinitesimal moment we felt like victors, not the vanquished.⁸⁹

Testimony-givers remember the presence of this new group jolting the "Polish girls" out of their routines. It reminded them of other worlds, other modes of interacting with their world. It woke them up to some fragments of what was occurring in the rest of Europe. Ida G. was put in the position of using a coat that had belonged to someone who had been processed at Auschwitz.

> Ida G.: With them came a cargo of clothes. From Auschwitz. From these clothes the Hungarians were told to choose for them. To pick out. There was a whole [*gestures*] moundful of clothes that was dropped off . . . I found a coat that I needed badly. And it was a wonderful coat. But I realized that this coat belonged to somebody, to a girl that was my age because it fitted me perfectly. And every time I would put on that coat after they told us what had happened there, I was thinking about that girl. And I was very disturbed and I wrote a poem for her.[90]

Ida G. asks if she can read the poem, but the tape has run out and has to be changed. She begins the story again in the second tape and reads her poem. It is an elegy marking out multiple losses: the life of the coat's owner, the possibilities extinguished by the persecution of Jews, the potential of a future Jewish world, and Ida G.'s own girlhood. An excerpt:

> Ida G.: We long for the music that is not played and the songs that are not sung.[91]

Ida G. remembers that she shared her poem with the others in the camp.

> Ida G.: We all shared it and we all sat and cried and thought about what we inherited from these people who have unfortunately given their life in Auschwitz.[92]

The shock initially created obstacles to integration into the social world that the "Polish girls" had formed. The testimony-givers discuss the language barrier, which was real, but a deeper barrier was that truly identifying with them as Jews would mean accepting what was happening to Jews across Europe and what had likely happened to their own families.

> Rosalie S.: We didn't speak Hungarian. There was very little communication.[93]
>
> Anna W.: When we came back [from the night shift] there were about twenty-five [*pauses*] call it "people." You couldn't distinguish

what they were. They had no hair. They were in those striped uniforms. Just standing there waiting for the ss. And when they were assigned where to sleep, they told us all about Auschwitz. They were Hungarian Jewish women. They had been sent to Auschwitz. Somehow they got out of Auschwitz and got sent to this camp . . . And they told us about what's happening in Auschwitz. That all our people perished. So the camp was— we sat shiva, we cried, everybody cried. Loud. That was the day we knew that nobody was left alive from our families.[94]

After this moving portion of testimony, Anna W. was silent. The interviewer asks her about her emotions at that time. In a contrast to the purposeful, careful narration of the shared grief of those in the camp, she remembers that part of her refused to accept the reality:

Anna W.: I still didn't believe that my father was not alive.[95]

The trauma, physical markers, and information carried by the "Hungarian girls" was undeniable. But at the same time, hope for reunification with family was a sustaining strategy—so both truths were held at the same time.

Helena K.: In my imagination and dreams I followed [them] step by step. [*breaks down crying*][96]

Shoshana G.: If you didn't have hope [about one's family], you could never survive.[97]

Lucy M.: [referring to Auschwitz] We knew all the things that were going on, after a while. I don't know how. But those things got around, from—nowhere! People were picking it out from the air, but they knew what was going on . . . But you never believed that it's going to happen to you, or to your dear ones.[98]

How did the Jewish girls and women from the Hungarian territories view the "Polish girls" in Parschnitz, Ober Altstadt, Bernsdorf/Schatzlar, and Gabersdorf? Their memories, as they presented them, reflect the fact that many of them were slightly older. There were difficulties in communication and more laborers meant less food and less space.

> Rena M.: I think the Hungarian, uh, and the, and the people from, that were not from Hungary, I don't think they liked each other too much.[99]

> Minnie W.: The relationship between the Polish girls and the Hungarian girls was also not the best. Because they [the Hungarian girls] were jealous. They came, like, completely with nothing.[100]

Frances H., born in December 1918, was twenty-five in the summer of 1944 and remembers a very different interaction. This excerpt from her testimony merits quoting at length, because it captures the essence of the situation of the Jewish girls from Zagłębie in the words of a direct witness.

> Frances H.: When we arrived there we found there maybe three hundred or so young girls. Polish girls. Twelve, thirteen, fourteen. Fourteen was the oldest. And they have been all very small, very tiny. They had been taken from their home not to the [Auschwitz] camp—when the Germans entered to Poland from the Silesian little, little cities. They had been taken as very young girls. They could take a pillow with them or from home that, that bedroom whatever they wanted to. And they didn't know anything about Auschwitz. They didn't know what happened to their parents. They came there to work and they didn't see a newspaper, they didn't know about the world.
> Interviewer: They were Jewish children?
> Frances H.: Jewish children! Ya!
> Frances H.: And the oldest was maybe fourteen when I got there. And they have been so happy to see us! Like they have seen their sisters and mothers. And as I told you they could bring from home a few things. They had, they had extra dresses or whatever. So I got from, it was a taller girl—mind you, I don't, he wasn't, she wasn't tall when she got there, that's for sure—anyway, she gave me a dress, a black dress.[101]
> Frances H.: And these children loved us! Oh, had they been loving us. But we at that time, we didn't have too much love in us, really. Because we just went through such a, such a tremendous, awful situation.[102]

Here the interviewer is able to express surprise in a manner that encourages Frances H. to extend and amplify her comments. Frances H. remembers that the "Polish girls" were the source of much-needed clothing (at least a single dress), in contrast to the memory of Ida G., who recalls the Hungarian girls as being accompanied by a shipment of clothes. In either case, these particular testimony-givers remember an exchange of clothing and a warm receptivity to each other, although as Frances H. notes, "we did not have too much love in us."

Among the survivors of these camps are women who arrived from Auschwitz but originated from the Łódź ghetto or from Radom, Poland.[103] As was the case with the Hungarian Jews, ss personnel selected out young people to be leased out for labor at the end of the train ramp, and it was from this group that factory owners selected additional girls and young women, some of whom were assigned to Parschnitz, Ober Altstadt, or other camps and transferred to Parschnitz in early 1945.

> Frieda W.: The second day they put me, they make a selection and put us on a transport. To go to a work camp. So we again went for a shower. And then they gave us, um, they gave us—a dress. I don't know if they—and slip, a long slip and a dress. And they gave us some kind of shoes.[104]
>
> Rose B.: The people from the factory of Siemens came to Auschwitz and they collect us to go to work.[105]

As was the case with the Jewish girls and women from Hungary, the girls and women from Łódź and Radom encountered the "Polish girls" in the Trautenau camps in ways that affected both groups.

> Gucia R.: It was a camp also of girls from Sosnowca and Będzin. They were there from the beginning, as the war started, with their own hair. We looked like out of space, like animals. They looked like normal people, with clothes, shoes, they had the covers [for bed], the quilts, everything from home. We walked in like—like wild people. They looked at us. They said, "Where are you coming from?" And we told them.[106]

The emphasis in Gucia R.'s recollection is on her own sense of strangeness. She remembers feeling alienated from her own sense of self, a person with no context—"out of space." Not only did she notice what they had that she did not, but she also noticed their naïveté and lack of knowledge.

In 1944 the new availability and coordination of Jewish labor at Auschwitz aligned with the increasing desire for labor by private firms. Multiple subcamps appeared as companies expanded their production. For example, Siemens expanded its production of airplane parts into Ober Altstadt, housing Jewish girls and women staff as well as non-Jewish forced laborers (male and female) of different nationalities in Jungbuch (today's Mladé Buky), a short distance from the factory.[107] At the same time, supply and transport flows became difficult. A practice emerged in which companies transferred—or loaned out—groups of Jewish female prisoners for short periods of time to respond to quotas, deadlines, and supply issues. A Jewish girl or young woman might be sent to a number of different factories in Silesia on passenger trains within the space of a few months. The Parschnitz camp, with its huge repurposed factory halls, functioned as a type of way station for these shifting squads already in late 1943, adding to the numbers sequestered in the barracks and complicating any definitive count of the number of prisoners.

> Anna W.: [transferred from Hannsdorf to Parschnitz] The camp was a big, disused factory. Big holes. We were 1,500.[108]
>
> Frieda W.: So one night we had to wait in a station—they took us to one station and then we had to wait all night for another train. And we were sitting in one corner. And the train was busy! The Germans were traveling and they looked at us. "Ooooh." I don't know if they knew. Maybe they did know. And sometimes they threw us a piece of sugar or a piece of bread. They threw like they throw to a dog.[109]
>
> Shoshana L.: It happened one day that a civilian man came to this place and said he needed a few girls for his *Abteilung*. His part. Another place. Where I was working was very cold . . . I was selected. I was so happy because the place was very warm.[110]

Even more movement occurred in mid-1944 when the Allies bombed fuel refineries using coerced labor north of the Trautenau region and in early 1945 when war production began shutting down. The local ss guards were ordered to march the prisoners working at these locations elsewhere, and several new groups of Jewish girls and women arrived at Parschnitz or spent time at Parschnitz before being moved again. Ruth R. had been a prisoner and coerced laborer at the Telefunken plant in Reichenbach and remembers encountering other groups walking in the opposite direction.

> Ruth R.: It was crisscross! Honestly, crisscross.[111]

Mania R.'s testimony is unusual in that she and her sister evaded the Schmelt system summons to work and hid during the 1942 mass deportation in Sosnowiec and Będzin. They were able to find periodic stints in some of the small workshops in Będzin that still operated in 1943 but remained in hiding until the ss captured them when they left in search of food. Mania R. and her sister were transported to Auschwitz, were selected there for entry into the camp, and endured a year of humiliation and physical brutality until they managed to join a group being sent to Reichenbach. In 1945 Mania R., like Ruth R., was also marched to Parschnitz.

> Mania R.: The march was terrible. Through the snow, through the mountains. Marching. The view was gorgeous. But food—no food.[112]
>
> Eva H.: The ss said, "If you sit down, I shoot you." So I grabbed my sister and put her over my shoulder. And I dragged her. And we went kilometer after kilometer after kilometer. How did I do it? To this day I cannot understand.[113]
>
> Lusia B.: It was winter. March. We were freezing. We didn't have anywhere to sleep. We were sleeping just in the snow.[114]

This fluid situation makes identifying the exact number imprisoned at Parschnitz—or at Ober Altstadt, Bernsdorf, Gabersdorf, or Schatzlar—difficult. Parschnitz was frequently used by authorities as a transit camp for groups of Jewish laborers. This could have been because of the huge open floors at the Haase buildings attached to the Parschnitz factories. At times laborers stayed only a week; at other times, for months. The transfers, combined with overcrowding and withholding of hygiene, led to outbreaks of lice and bedbugs, similar to most other sites of detention in the Holocaust.

This chapter was introduced as an exploration of how testimonies revise perpetrator-focused accounts of institutional change within the Nazi concentration camp system, with special attention paid to how violence is received as sexualized but mediated by coping strategies. These strategies differed for the Trautenau-region camps in comparison with those who went through Auschwitz processes of forced nakedness, shaving, and looking. Moreover, the specific situation of the Trautenau-region camps—a long-standing community of Jewish girls and young women from Poland experiencing the arrival of Jewish young women from Hungary (as well as *Łódź* and Radom) at the early stages of their pathway through persecution—allow us to go beyond comparison and hear how the interaction of different prisoner groups was remembered by survivors from each. These narrated memories deliver a complex, multilayered picture of these sites of persecution as spaces in which violence could potentially be redirected, revised, warded off, and even function as a source of insight.

CHAPTER 6

Ethics of Care and Prisoner Society

Shoshana G. was eighteen when she began working at one of the factories in Parschnitz. In her testimony she recalls battling hunger, managing the small amount of food given to her, handling dirty machines, and attempting to stay clean in an environment with little opportunity to do so. She then explains what she believes helped her to survive:

> Shoshana G.: I survived really because I transformed myself. I saw a girl and she had a brooch here. [*gestures*] And I made a little song out of it. And I started to do little poems and little poems. And it felt good. I had to find where to write it. There were little . . . it was a problem . . . I think I asked a German woman. She should bring me some paper. I wrote quite a few poems.[1]

In simple yet evocative language, Shoshana G. remembers the process of developing her own ethic of care. Unlike academic uses of "ethic of care" in which "care" is defined as a womanly giving to others, Shoshana G. remembers caring for herself by noticing what she needed to survive and gradually allowing herself to partake in that activity because of its power to sustain her. Significantly, her testimony about her poetry begins as a relation to another laborer ("I saw a girl") and ends with reference to another relation, a Gentile woman who brings her paper.

This chapter develops the importance of the various "ethics of care" that are expressed in testimonies using an approach in which narratives of remembered experiences that center care for the self are noted for their framing of care as a practice pursued intentionally, consistently, and "relationally," that is, emerging via an awareness of the interdependency of self with others. Many Holocaust scholars as well as memoirists and testimony-givers have demonstrated the importance of relating to others for survival and for retaining one's ability to cope. The conditions of concentration camp and death camp everyday life led to individuals grasping tightly to each other in dyads or small groups, a phenomenon also evident in the Trautenau-region labor camps, or relating to others in terms of national, ethnic, or religious identity. Some scholars have extended the frame of relationships in camp settings to analyze "camp society" or "prisoner society." Scholars of "prisoner society" such as Anna Hájková and Maja Suderland emphasize prewar social categories such as class in the expression of identities in ghettos and camps and trace the positioning of specific identities within social understandings.[2] For example, Michael Becker and Dennis Bock show how the camp identity of *"Muselman"*—a label for prisoners who had become disconnected from an inner drive to survive—functioned to sustain the larger camp social structure.[3]

This chapter works with a notion of "society" that views it as a product of "relationality" rather than "identity," that is, as a practice of developing (and constantly revising) one's sense of self through connection and reference to others, such that ties emerge (and fade) situationally but do so through solidarity rather than status hierarchies.[4] The concept of "relationality" has been taken up in many disciplines, notably theology, sociology, psychology, and the health sciences, but it has been developed in greatest depth by scholars of diasporas such as Édouard Glissant, who contrasts relationality to a fixed attachment to place, and scholars of indigeneity such as Glen Sean Coulthard, who finds relationality to be a necessary challenge to European requirements of hierarchical identification, as it is embedded in a deep and adaptive reciprocity with land, ancestors, and other beings.[5] In the specific historical context of the Holocaust—a very different context from Glissant's and Coulthard's—"relationality" is helpful to our understanding of "camp society" in that it points to moments in which individuals used a perceptual framework for organizing their experience that prioritized ongoing connection beyond one's specific partner in survival (or "camp sister") or specific, fixed friendship group. In these instances, the testimony-giver's prewar identity and connection to a specific place are still powerful but they do not determine her choices.

Because the constant threat of death of oneself or one's loved ones (such as a sister in the camp) made intentional relational ethics of care unreliable, risky, and contingent, such instances do not appear frequently in the testimonies. To develop the "society" characterizing the camps in the Trautenau region, this chapter expands the scope of source material from testimonies to include the objects testimony-givers created, received, and carried, which they later donated to archives as expressions of their experience of persecution and survival. As scholar Leora Auslander notes, objects are potentially "active agents in history" in part because of their "communicative, performative, emotive, and expressive capacities."[6] What immediately comes to mind are the diaries documented by Alexandra Garbarini in *Numbered Days*, which registered events, emotions, and the need to simply write or draw.[7] In settings of extreme persecution the capacities of objects such as diaries, whose material forms were shaped by the context of deprivation and violence, may be the only resort for personal expression.

The surviving objects discussed in this chapter—postcards, poems, and an example of the small autograph albums (also called *Stammbücher* or *pamiętniki*) circulated by adolescent girls in Europe—were intentionally saved by survivors and then curated by Holocaust archivists. Thus, they can be considered in one sense as extensions of the experiences related in testimony, but also items affected by professional and personal curatorial practice, as noted by Laura Levitt in her discussion of objects after violence.[8] The testimony and objects presented in the following paragraphs bring forward how ethics of care in relational modes functioned (when they did) and the pleasures and even beauty they brought to the coerced labor experience in the Trautenau region.

It is important to state that an "ethics of care" is not the same as "ethical behavior." The problematic status of standards of ethical behavior imposed on those targeted in Holocaust settings has been well developed, from Primo Levi to Cynthia Ozick to Claude Lanzmann to Jean Améry. The Holocaust ethics scholar John K. Roth argues that the disintegrative effect of the Nazi project in not just physical but also moral terms rendered any ethical standard fragile.[9] The aim in this chapter is not to create an external standard by which to judge survivor choices. Instead, it offers observations of moments in the testimonies in which transactions made to survive or avoid violence shift into a different mode. They become internalized and regularized as a practice of care, for others but including the self.

Cesia T. remembers being part of a group of ten Jewish girls and women at Bernsdorf who were sent one Saturday to work at a local herring processing factory. She begins the story with reference to the *Lagerführerin* choosing her for her productivity, and initially it appears that her testimony will present her sense of relief, luck, or pride at being singled out. The story takes a confusing turn when she insists on explaining how important it was that she wear her coat, although the weather was quite hot. It becomes clear that Cesia T. only wore this coat to hide fish in the lining to bring back to the barracks and trick the guard conducting a search.

> Cesia T.: And as soon as I brought that in, everybody invaded [her bunk space]. And the whole camp, we shared.[10]

Her joy at this twist in the telling process is apparent. She refrains from centering her own generosity in the testimony but instead formulates the act as "we shared." It was, of course, only Cesia T. who "shared." She revises the act in her narration from an individual (herself) to the collective to extend its pleasure for her.

Estelle C. had a job in the kitchen in Parschnitz, a much sought-after situation in almost all camp settings during the Holocaust. Estelle C. could not only provide herself but also her sister in the camp with extra food. She had no real need to help anyone else. In her testimony, Estelle C. remembers being assigned to monitor a supply wagon of potatoes outdoors. When the *Lagerführerin* stepped away, several campmates approached the wagon to take some of the food.

> Estelle C.: The girls were so hungry! They, they said, "You don't have to see everything." I said, "You're right. So go ahead."[11]

Gerda F. was in the Ober Altstadt camp working for the Etrich factory. She remembers that her facility with repairing the machinery led the factory management to transfer her to the machine shop, where she was the only female (and the only seventeen-year-old). In an extended and carefully delivered narrative, Gerda F. explains that prisoners of war were used to deliver machine parts periodically, and that one prisoner of war in particular began to drop notes on the floor for her asking if the girls and women needed anything that the prisoners of war could give them from the Red Cross packages they were entitled to receive.

Gerda F. responded, also through dropped notes, that they needed tea for diarrhea, medication to address typhus, or, lacking that, cigarettes to trade for the medicine.

> Gerda F.: And so I would have some cigarettes to get medicine. I was able to save the life of my very best friend, who was dying.[12]

Anna O., one of the "Hungarian girls," arrived in Parschnitz with her mother, whom she worried about and spent quite a bit of effort supporting. Her barrack was one of the improvised older buildings and had multiple small rooms that were off-limits to the regular Jewish workers, but that could be accessed by those with special privileges. Anna O.'s bunk was in a corner, next to an adjacent room that had a bathtub. Anna O. remembers that two young Jewish women with privileged positions—one a nurse and the other a kitchen worker with access to heated water—became lovers and periodically took a bath together surreptitiously in this room.

> Anna O.: After we had gone to bed I heard some water splashing. And I thought, tsk, how would it be if I could get this water after they had taken their bath so I could wash up my mom. Because we were really, our skins were broken out and, you know, scabies and all kinds of stuff.[13]

Anna O. remembers planning how to request use of the leftover water in the bathtub, such that she would not offend or interrupt the women in their intimacy.

> Anna O.: I didn't want to come too early, but if I wait too long, they will pour out the water and that's it. I was a little bit afraid that they would scream at me.[14]

She approached the two women and they let her know they were happy to leave the water in the tub; more importantly, they did not report Anna O. for asking or expose her transgression in accessing the tub to anyone. While Anna O. pauses in her testimony to register a moment of slight disgust at the used water, she quickly rationalizes that the gray color "was because of the light which was just one little bulb there hanging."[15] This shift allows her to keep the memory of giving her mother the gift of a bath without compromise.

> Anna O.: And I woke up my mother there. And—[she was] startled! We were always afraid, you know, the news was only bad, you know. You were going on another trip or you were taken who knows where. So I said, "No, don't worry, I found some water and we'll have a bath." [*smiles broadly*] And I, you know, sponged her up a little bit and—I think I must have bathed myself a little bit but I don't remember that. I only remember how grateful she was for water touching her body again.[16]

The testimony then moves from describing the bath as a negotiated transaction that allowed Anna O. to take care of her mother to an acknowledgment of the ongoing consideration that the two lovers gave her.

> Anna O.: And then these girls just were wonderful. Because after that, I don't know how many times—not every time—but here and there they would come to me and say, "You want some water?" And I would wash my mother.[17]

With this practice the care the original pair show each other is extended such that Anna O. can continue to show care to her mother in the same intimate space of the enclosed room, a small enclave of safety and privacy.

As has been presented in an earlier chapter, Czech coworkers at times treated the Jewish girls and women with compassion by leaving food or sharing medicine. However, in the Schatzlar camp the culture among the Gentile Czech coworkers was more complex than what testimony-givers from other camps remember. Fela G. remembers an atmosphere in which some Czech employees surveilled not only the Jewish workers but also each other and reported any infraction. In this context, Czech help was risky. Fela G. remembers developing a protective intervention practice with a coworker that enveloped both of them.

> Fela G.: I have a picture from the Czech woman that—she helped me with a sandwich every day. Because I made some slippers, you know, from the thread and different things I was crocheting.
> Interviewer: And you bartered? Would—it was like an exchange? You gave her something and she—
> Fela G.: No, no. I just made it for her. She used to, I used to go to the bathroom and she used to tell me news, what's going on. And, uh, she used to give me a sandwich and later it got so bad

185

because another Czech were spying on her. So she used to hide the sandwich. She used to come and leave the sandwich on my machine so I have something to eat.[18]

It is interesting that Fela G. rejects the description of a barter for these interactions, which at first glance appear quite transactional. Although she receives sandwiches, she insists that she gave the slippers unmotivated by the food. It appears that Fela G. and her Czech helper developed a practice of moving through the factory to encounter and support each other when the opportunity arose and there is an implication that Fela G. cooperated with the helper to protect the latter from consequences for sharing food. Whether this relationship was "really" transactional or not is less important than Fela G.'s use of her narrative to present it as something else. In other words, for her it was a mutual care practice.

At the end of each Shoah Foundation testimony is a segment reserved for sharing photos. Fela G. not only chose to share a photo of her Czech helper but also gives her a name in her testimony record and notes the date it was taken—May 5, 1945, when the helper likely knew the SS presence was diminished. At this point in the testimony Fela G. calls the photo a "gift" and states that:

Fela G.: She lived close by to the factory where we were working. So I used to see her every day . . .[19]

What Fela G. means is that after liberation, when she and others remained at the camp to improve their health, access food, and organize travel, her helper remained in relationship with her "every day."

Identification with one another, empathy, and solidarity could occur more often in these camps than in others in part because these camps were characterized by a lower level of violence, deprivation, and humiliation. But testimony-givers remember a sense of protective group care practices even when humiliation and the threat of death were at hand. Paula S. was in Parschnitz during the selections in which the girls and women were made to present themselves without clothing to visiting SS. Some, including Paula S., were particularly afraid of the SS officer Mengele, whose reputation as a bringer of death was already circulating, perhaps by the guards. Paula S. remembers a pregnant campmate, Luba, who had been hiding her pregnancy for some months when the SS squad arrived for the selection. Paula S. makes space for the story by noting that she intends to speak of an experience out of chronological order.

> Paula S.: Oh, I want to say something else. [*pause*] That was in the other camp [Parschnitz]. Mengele came. They announce in the camp, now Mengele's coming to the camp.[20]

She explains that one of the Jewish workers was a pregnant woman named Luba, whom Paula S. takes care to say was married and older than most of the others in the camp. She speaks of Luba with sympathy and makes it clear that the other girls and women felt protective of her; they were aware that she would most certainly be sent to Auschwitz during this selection.

> Paula S.: We wanted now to, to protect this—her name was Luba, the one, she was expecting a baby. So how could we do it?[21]

She introduces another campmate who physically substituted herself for Luba in front of the SS.

> Paula S.: We was, well, we were a group of about ten girls in the room. [He] came in. Everybody was shaking. Introduced himself . . . First, we were hiding the Luba. She didn't come in at all. And then Mala Blaustein went twice. And she risked her life. And she changed her makeup. And she went for the Luba. And Luba survived. She had there, the baby in camp.
> Interviewer: Was Luba the one that was pregnant?
> Paula S.: Yes [*smiling*].
> Interviewer: And who was Mala?
> Paula S.: Mala was a girl, what's like me [*smiling*].[22]

Paula S. continues to explain that the clinic hid Luba and the infant and that both survived. She expresses satisfaction that she knows where Luba lives (at the time of her testimony) and that the deception was successful (at the time of persecution). Notable in Paula S.'s narrative is the specificity of depiction not of Luba but of Mala Blaustein, who is given a last name, makeup, and the job of deceiving a feared SS officer on behalf of the other girls and women, in answer to, "How could we do it?" Moreover, Paula S. identifies with Mala Blaustein in response to the interviewer's question: "a girl, what's like me."

Paula S.'s story of a surviving pregnant woman could be interpreted as a wishful projection of the ability of childbearing to subvert Nazi aims. However, other testimony-givers also remember Luba.[23] Bella K. remembers first substituting herself for her ill sister in the same naked selection.[24] She then explains:

> Bella K.: There was a pregnant woman. That the Germans didn't know that she was pregnant . . . She worked in the kitchen. For the Germans. And she had a wide coat. A brown wide coat so nobody could see that she was pregnant . . . Somebody, another girl went in for her, too. And saved her.[25]
>
> Bella K.: This girl was born eight days before the liberation . . . Now she lives in Canada. She has children on her own. Grown children. [*smiling*][26]

Bella K.'s priority was to support her weaker sister, as she makes clear throughout her testimony; Luba's experience is a joyful coincidence. In this light, Paula S.'s memory of a wider, relational effort with multiple participants—all naked and shaking with fear—illustrates the possibilities of care under extreme conditions.

The deprivation and violence of camp life meant that there were many girls and women who could not manage any ethic of care, and the unpredictable nature of access to food or rest made "continuity" something that could not be assumed. But a few testimony-givers remember organizing food to share (a practice common in other camp settings), receiving information from Gentiles, responding to illness and death, and creating or exchanging objects in processes that were intentional, ongoing, and planned. In other words, while previous chapters have documented food sharing by Czech coworkers, for example, this chapter takes note of practices that were justified with reference to the position of oneself in a community with others.

Sustaining oneself in relation to others did not necessarily alleviate suffering in the Schmelt system. Campmates who died had to be mourned and buried. Survivors report no executions in these camps with one exception, the public hanging of two women, sometimes described as mother and daughter, in one of the Parschnitz camps. This event is never described with the specificity found in, for example, descriptions of hangings in Zagłębie. It is always rendered in general terms and no external documentation exists. Most of those who died on site (as opposed to being sent to Auschwitz-Birkenau) did so because of disease, malnutrition, or when a physical punishment caused an infection or other condition that was unsurvivable without medical care.

Neither the factory staff nor the *Lagerführerinnen* had at hand processes or materials for addressing the physicality of a dead body, much less the emotional or spiritual implications. In Parschnitz, the workers were assigned to bury those who had died in an improvised fashion.

> Minnie W.: There were incidents that girls, they died of starvation. A girl got sick—so they took them out by the—who knows where and they dumped them somewhere.[27]

In contrast are instances in which testimony-givers recall a death with specificity and describe it was a trauma for the entire community.

> Irene W.: [Gabersdorf] There was one girl from Zawiercie. Her name was Passerman. She was very tiny, petite. But she was older, much older than I was. I would say she was already in her twenties ... and she got so religious—more so in camp—that she didn't eat nothing but the baked potato.

> Irene W.: So she died in camp. And she was buried—I think in the backyard, in the ground. On the grounds.[28]

Tosia J. also remembers a death in Gabersdorf. It is unclear whether it is the same person as in Irene W.'s testimony. A camp friend developed a digestive illness and died in the barracks.

> Tosia J.: At that time we went to our *Lagerführerin*—that means the camp—she was German, but she was a nice woman. We asked if, because we knew we have to bury her in shrouds—that's what we remembered. So she gave us a sheet. And there was a lady and me and a couple of friends. We did bury her in the sheet. Yeah. We went to a cemetery. It wasn't a Jewish cemetery. But we did bury her ... compared to other camps that was—beautiful.[29]

Here Tosia J. acknowledges the shared expectation that the interviewer and the audience will always have Auschwitz in mind when thinking of "camp." She reminds the listeners that while the sheet was only a modest attempt at reproducing Jewish religious practice, her relationship with the *Lagerführerin* allowed her to achieve what could not be achieved elsewhere. It is her striking use of the word "beautiful" that moves this act into an ethic of care that includes her friends, the dead girl, and herself.

The Jewish girls and women were also deeply concerned for family members at other camps, living in the family home, or relocated to a new district in Zagłębie. The recent increased awareness among archivists that the Schmelt system allowed for correspondence between coerced laborers and family members has also brought attention to this correspondence as a set of historical objects to be archived and curated. Letters, postcards, and small items sent to the girls and women between 1940 and mid-1943 generate meaning not just through the content of the words but also in their material forms, which carry traces of political conditions at home, the physical resources and emotions of the sender, and the attachments of the receiver as she holds and hides these items.

The value of photographs for the girls and women were well known to *Lagerführerinnen*, other campmates, and the Gentile coworkers in the factories. Photos were taken away as punishment, hidden as favors or for money, and shared with other laborers to extend their pleasures. Dora R. tells of downtimes between shifts for the civilian workers at Bernsdorf, during which the Jewish girls and women were assigned odd jobs.

> Dora R.: And one day I worked in a shed and I found—they took away all the photos what we had, just a few only. And I took back—that's why I have my mother—this picture—and another two or three. I found them all on the ground in a heap. So I picked up quickly whatever I could.[30]

Dora R. expresses delight at this chance discovery in her testimony. She does not remark on the violence of the disposal of the cherished items. Furthermore, her discovery is not only for herself but also allows her to "have" her mother, recover her from being discarded as debris. In the testimony process Dora R. gestures off camera to indicate with pleasure the photo on display in her home.

The objects sent in packages loom large in the memories of the survivors. Often clothing, these were remembered as crucial aids to survival, concrete connections to home, and valuable items for transactions. Sala

P., a survivor of the Gabersdorf camp, offers an anecdote about receiving a large package that is atypical, in that most families in Zagłębie did not have the resources to send much, but that offers insights about social relations inside the camp. The anecdote begins at the end of Tape 1 and Sala P. has to begin telling it again on Tape 2:

> Sala P.: Yeah, the package arrived and there were some red shoes in it. We—the lady in charge of the, uh, concentration camp, had the same size I was wearing. And some other shoes, cork shoes. Lovely things, you know! Because before the war my parents used to have for us handmade things. Like even shoes were handmade . . . And, uh, so she liked those red shoes. I gave it to her with a smile. She could have just taken them! She didn't have to ask for it. The whole package she could have—gave—just—but I guess that's how they were acting. At that time. It was—she was happy.[31]

Afterward, in Sala P.'s memory, the *Lagerführerin* allows Sala P. to accompany her on trips to town for bread, meaning that Sala P. was able to access more food for herself and for others as well. The notion that someone in a camp would have access to handmade red shoes challenges the general understanding of camps as places of colorless deprivation. The red shoes would have been items of surprise and delight. In the arrival of the package, the care of the family extends into the camp; Sala P. directly connects the shoes with the care her parents gave her before the war. Yet in her testimony she remembers giving the shoes to the *Lagerführerin* without hesitation, admitting neither a sense of loss nor injustice. The *Lagerführerin* seemed to also be invested in the appearance of an unforced gift. Sala P. did not, of course, turn over the red shoes as an act of caring for the *Lagerführerin*. In her testimony, she understands the exchange as an appropriation in which the coercion is implicit rather than explicit. What she does give the *Lagerführerin* is her participation in the pretense that the exchange was a voluntary gift, allowing the *Lagerführerin* to avoid thinking of herself as a bringer of violence, if just for a short time. This appears to be what she needs, "how they were acting" "at that time." It also creates the prospect of the *Lagerführerin* extending the interaction forward, into trips to a bakery. Ultimately, Sala P.'s family gave her, indirectly, what she really needed: more bread.

This question of how the camp guards fit into either "prisoner society" in a sociological sense or in the networks of care and relationality described here is complex. Each testimony-giver remembers camp guards differently because the *Lagerführerin*, with whom each coerced laborer had the most direct contact, was herself an individual with multiple motivations in the camp setting who treated the Jews she supervised differently. Scholars such as Elissa Mailänder have reconstructed the official perpetrator processes recruiting these guards and the formal and informal expectations shaping their actions.[32] They tended to be recruited by local labor offices (*Arbeitsämter*) or from among the employees at the work sites and were themselves under supervision within a hierarchy.[33] Mailänder and others have also sought to understand female guards as figures that do not only manifest perpetrator intentions but also have their own "material interests and personal subjectivities," which may deepen, lessen, or reshape Nazi violence.[34] In the camps in the Trautenau region, the *Lagerführerinnen* had been employees of the company owners and were thrust into a privileged position, granted the prerogatives of using violence, responding to requests at their discretion, and having access to all of the spaces that the Jewish girls and women used, including their bodies. They were still, like most camp guards in the Nazi system, in need of resources beyond their wages and viewed the Jewish girls and women as sources of these resources. From the testimony it seems clear that it was significant that female guards were not assigned to sites away from their homes. They remained embedded in their local communities. The coerced labor sites were places at which their former Gentile coworkers continued to work. It should not be surprising that they took opportunities to travel to other camps as escorts for transferred laborers or to bring laborers with them on work or personal errands.

These guards were often the only figures prosecuted after the war, as they were locally bound to family while the SS officers fled deeper into Germany as the Soviet army approached. In their trial documents, they not surprisingly identify themselves as former employees who were charged by their supervisors with "maintaining order and cleanliness" in the barracks.[35] When accused of identifying resistant Jewish laborers for transport to Auschwitz, Filomena Amler, a Parschnitz guard, stated that the SS was responsible for such transfers, and she listed the favors she had done for other prisoners in her defense.[36] The details are telling:

Amler was routinely stealing items from packages sent to the girls and women by their families. One Jewish woman, called Regina Herzberger in the postwar trial documents, demanded the return of stolen shoes and when Amler refused, hit her. Amler used this as a pretext to report Herzberger, as well as at least two other prisoners, to the factory manager, leading to Herzberger's (and the other two at a different time) transfer to Auschwitz. The anecdote reveals the position of the guard as part of "prisoner society," in that she had to be taken into account—she was part of the transactional economy of the camp. Yet her presence signified the potential for violence and even death. Testimony-giver Bella C. extends the story of Regina ("Hertzberg" in her testimony) with anger and grief, because she was her sister.[37] In other words, guards were an obstacle to care work. Thus, the development of a relational approach to people in the camp and factory is different from the hierarchy included in "prisoner society." Amler was sentenced by a Trutnov court to five years in prison.

There are survivors from every single work camp that report instances of violence perpetrated by these local *Lagerführerinnen*, either directly observed or directly experienced. The guards at the camps in the Trautenau region withheld food; locked people in closets or cellars; shaved off hair; hit with bare hands or with truncheons, whips, or whatever was at hand; used antisemitic language and other forms of verbal abuse; and confiscated photos, letters, and objects. Survivors from the same camps also report guards saving letters for them, giving out extra food, and intervening to protect the girls and women from other violence or transports to Auschwitz-Birkenau. In either case, testimony-givers position *Lagerführerinnen* as only conditionally inside the ethics of care they developed, even when they remember an action that protected them from harm.

An example that aligns with the testimony of Sala P. is that offered by Berta B., in Bernsdorf.

> Berta B.: She wasn't a bad woman. She pretended. She was shouting and she was doing . . . But she was a good person, actually. You know we used to assemble every Sunday and she would look at the girls and she, if she would see one that, uh, was skinny or measly looking, she would take her. Instead of working the factory she would take her to the kitchen and fatten her up a little bit.[38]

Berta B.'s excerpt here contains within it the experienced and anticipated violence of the camp system, in that assemblies and roll calls were instances in which individuals were singled out to be transported to a killing center when the ss were present. It also contains within it not only an instance of giving a coerced laborer extra food, but a practice of doing so. Put another way, the reason that anyone would need extra food is an implicit grounding of the narrative. The guard both enforces camp violence and mitigates it, all at her discretion.

Berta B. adds material to turn the story into one of mutual care. After a laborer was chosen in this manner, she took the opportunity to secure additional food in the kitchen to share with her campmates later:

> Berta B.: The leftovers they would bring home. Like a pot of soup.[39]

A few moments later Berta B. explains the consequences given to a laborer who stole additional materials from the factory to make clothing for herself, consequences delivered by the guard, who is left undepicted and unmentioned:

> Berta B.: The punishment was to shave her head.[40]

Chaya S. at Schatzlar remembers a *Lagerführerin* who withheld food and forced the Jewish girls and women to eat spoiled food:

> Chaya S.: The *Lagerführer* [sic] in the beginning, she treated us not very bad. I mean, it wasn't good, but not bad. But later on, she went to a school. Like a—they made ss woman out of her. She became very famous. So she had to show that she can do something.[41]

Rosalie S. remembers that the *Lagerführerin* at Parschnitz had the power to expel Jewish girls and women from the labor camp. Her testimony is a reminder that receiving help from Gentile coworkers was grounds for punishment:

> Rosalie S.: In fact, some time, at one time as a matter of fact, she sent three girls to concentration camp in Auschwitz. As a reprisal for being a little too chummy with the, with the civilian people.[42]

Because questions about guards are part of the Shoah Foundation questionnaire, almost every testimony-giver has material to share on this topic. The role of the Jewish *Lagerältesten* does not fit easily into the dichotomy between ss and female guard, on the one hand, and the Jewish laborers, on the other. As Andrea Rudorff has documented, these female participants in camp discipline could at times contribute a sense of stability, intervening to support an ill worker, for example.[43] Testimony-givers from among the Shoah Foundation archives tend to remember these individuals negatively, however, because of their verbal and physical abusiveness.

Postcards to and from the camps in the Trautenau region from 1940 through 1943 were objects that connected the coerced laborer with family in Zagłębie. The content of postcards were almost always repetitive phrases of support and concern, because censors would not permit any real information to be sent. As the survivors remember, the content was secondary to the chance to see a mother's or father's handwriting and in this way be able to imagine the context of the writing, such as a familiar kitchen table, or even the voice. Many of these postcards survived because they were hidden and carried as cherished objects throughout the war.

These postcards can also be read for evidence of the changes in the conditions of Jewish families, and it could be that the girls and women who received them interpreted them that way as well. They mention moving to new residences, family members who have been heard from or not heard from, and finding new work. While eyewitnesses recount the mass deportation in summer 1942 as a horrific event in Zagłębie, having to find a new place to live is the only hint in mail received.[44] The 1942 event was also a selection in which new groups of girls and women were sent to the Trautenau-region camps (as well as elsewhere). These new arrivals explained what had occurred back home. In each of the small towns surrounding Sosnowiec, and in Sosnowiec itself, Jews had been summoned on a specific August day to a large public space, ostensibly to renew their legal documents. In Sosnowiec this was the sports stadium. People were instructed to arrive in entire families, or risk immediate dispossession and deportation.[45] Witness, survivor, and chronicler Natan Szternfinkiel estimates sixty thousand were gathered.[46] After being made to wait for over two days, the Schmelt ss and Gestapo, directed by Friedrich Kuczynski, began to separate out individuals they judged able to be leased out for labor from their families. As families protested, Jewish police and Schmelt ss and Gestapo brutally beat and even shot people in full view of the huge gathering. Approximately thirteen thousand remaining family members were again divided into a group sent in trucks to be murdered at Auschwitz-Birkenau over the course of three days; another group was sent back to their homes.⁴⁷

After this event, the Schmelt organization closed off a number of additional streets to Jews in Sosnowiec and Będzin, forcing those who lived there to relocate to a pair of adjacent suburbs just outside of each city's borders, Środula outside of Sosnowiec and Kamionka outside of Będzin. These were ghettos, not walled-in but patrolled by police. This relocation process took place over the course of several months. Throughout the spring of 1943 the Schmelt ss periodically rounded up groups of approximately a thousand people at a time for deportation. Then, in August 1943, Kuczynski and the Schmelt organization conducted a mass roundup in Środula to expel all Jews from the Eastern Strip.⁴⁸ The decision was made by the Reichssicherheitshauptamt (RHSA) office in Katowice.⁴⁹ As Mary Fulbrook details in her study of Będzin centering the perspective of a local German civil authority, many Jews went into hiding, some finding improvised spaces in the degraded buildings of the ghettos, some passing as Gentiles, some using artfully created bunkers they had prepared long before.⁵⁰

The many authorities in Zagłębie at this time—including members of the Jewish Council of Elders—went house to house to arrest or kill Jews in both the Środula and Kamionka ghetto areas. The degraded condition of the buildings hampered the search and allowed some Jews to survive in hiding; the ss had to recruit help from local police, *Selbstschutz* groups, motor units, police trainees, and the local riding school.⁵¹ Over the course of eight days they killed hundreds and transported approximately ten thousand people from Środula, Kamionka, and Dąbrowa Górnicza to Auschwitz-Birkenau, where another process of selecting out those who staff there judged to be able to be leased out for work occurred.⁵²

Dwojra K. was assigned to the Haase factory in Parschnitz. Among the several postcards she received from her family in Sosnowiec, this one from March 1942, prior to the first mass deportation, is typical:

> I send you loving greetings [*grüsse*] and kiss you the entire family sends you love and all aunts your mother who [illegible] Kaminska [the family name]. My dearest child, I am wondering if everything

FIGURE 3 "View of the Kamionka/Srodula Ghetto." Photograph 19635, United States Holocaust Memorial Museum Archives, Washington, DC. Provenance, Arnold Shay (Abram Szyjewicz).

that I sent by mail, and from you we haven't received anything what are you doing my child, have you received everything we have sent you in good health by us is no [illegible] we are healthy and we wish the same for you. Your brother David sends loving greetings [grüsse] the aunts send you loving greetings [grüsse]. From me, your father, W. L. Kaminski.[53]

The postcard is filled to the very edges of the margins with handwriting, offering Dwojra K. as many words of care as possible. The writing style and content is inexpert but allows for the repetition of *grüsse*, which does not have an exact translation in English ("greetings" alone is inadequate) but which is a term of regard and recognition. Dwojra K.'s father "sees" her over and over, but he does not allow her to see what is happening in Sosnowiec: "we are healthy."

Another example of the correspondence as a reflection of sustained relationality is the series that the Zaks family sent to daughters Mania and

Tola in the Walzel barracks in Trautenau and Rose at the Kluge barracks in Ober Altstadt, archived and curated by the United States Holocaust Memorial Museum. The correspondence began in 1942. In April 1943, Mania's and Tola's older sister writes:

> Dear Tola, I was able to get this paper from Cyla. I am happy that you are together with Mania. I have been in a new place for three weeks now, but I am happy to be living with five girls who work for the organization [Schmelt]. The [family name] also already have a new place to live in Środula, and are living well. Cesia can't write to you, she is in Skarzysko [a camp]. She is doing well. Cyla went with her father into camp. Where? I have no idea yet. Maybe she will be sent to you. Mila Fajmann has also been sent to a camp. The [name] is very quiet. It has to be this way. What are you doing, are you happy? . . . We are all healthy and together. I am not working. . . . I send you kisses and much love.[54]

In June 1943 she writes:

> Dear Tola and Mania! You do not need to wonder why we write so little, one has no time to write anymore . . . What are you both doing? Are you both healthy and working well? . . . I am not yet working but now I will be working soon. . . . By us is nothing new. Lala is healthy and a big girl. With Rose, we will be writing next, very much. Are you doing well? Szulek is working. Where is Cyla? It's too bad she is not with you. I send you kisses and send you loving greetings [*grüsse*], Regina.[55]

The words have a veneer of normalcy that cannot be true for the writer, Regina, in 1943, when the Jews left in Zagłębie were well aware that any new deportations would be to Auschwitz-Birkenau and undertaken with violence. But truthful communication about the fear pervading Sosnowiec and the meaning of finding new places to live is likely not what Tola and Mania need in 1943. The repetitive phrasing listing friends and family, work status, and reassurances that "nothing is new" and that loved ones are "doing well" in labor camps removes the burden of worry from the recipients, at least on one level. It is likely that Tola and Mania knew very well that moving in with five girls in the Środula ghetto meant the difficulties facing Regina were great. They may also have noted the effort

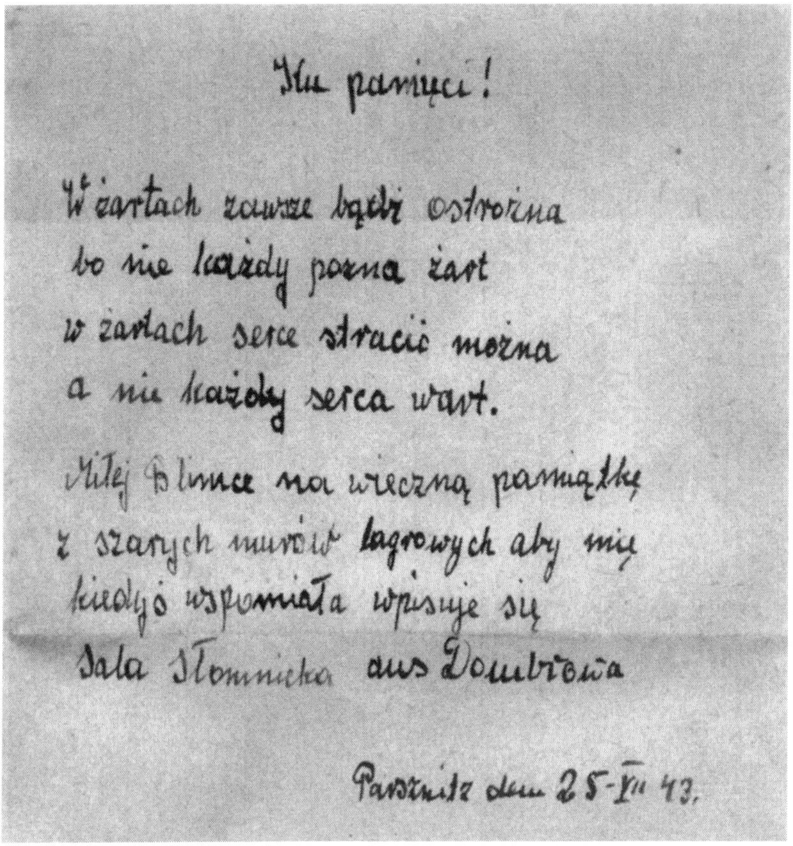
Ku pamięci!

W żartach zawsze bądź ostrożna
bo nie każdy pozna żart
w żartach serce stracić można
a nie każdy serca wart.

Miłej Blimce na wieczną pamiątkę
z szarych murów lagrowych aby mię
kiedyś wspomniała wpisuje się
Sala Słomnicka aus Dombrowa

Parschnitz den 25-VII 43.

FIGURE 4 "A Poem Written in Polish in the Parschnitz Work Camp, by Sala Slomnicki." Photograph 42044, United States Holocaust Memorial Museum Archives, Washington, DC. Provenance, Harry Birnholz.

Regina put into protecting them from this knowledge. The Jewish girls and women stopped receiving any cards or letters after August 1943 but were not certain whether the reason was a change in camp regulations.

In addition to letters from home, the girls and women shared short verses or notes that referenced shared practices of "normal" girlhood and were expressions of support and affection. Sala B. was fourteen when she was forcibly separated from her parents in the 1942 mass selection in Będzin and sent to the Parschnitz camp, and fifteen in 1943, when she wrote this note.

In the middle, Sala B., who is also the testimony-giver Sally B., writes, "Dear Blima, for a forever souvenir from the gray walls of the camp so that one day we will remember, I sign this, Sala Słomnicka from Dombrowa." The act of writing these words to a friend, instead of just speaking them, gave them more permanence and also gave Blima (if she received it) an object to carry with her that promised a future after the war. The assertive, almost legal, sign-off could be interpreted as Sala B. marking her presence and her history, that is, caring for herself as well as Blima.

Sala B.'s note echoes the forms of writing in autograph albums, a phenomenon that began as elite *Stammbücher* in Europe in the 1700s and evolved into a leisure activity for adolescents by the twentieth century. By this time these albums were small bound booklets with empty pages that young people, especially girls, would pass to friends for messages and signatures. Scholar Elżbieta Wichrowska's insight that these albums, which were called "sketchbooks" in nineteenth-century Poland, developed as a practice that was simultaneously private, autobiographical, and shared helps explain why they were important objects in the camps.[56] Other researchers argue that they constitute a genre in which the recorded verses were to be playful, orthographically mischievous, and citational of past shared events.[57] Rina Shapira and Hanna Herzog emphasize the form taken by the signature: a command to remember and an assertion of presence, which connects directly to the example of Sala B.'s poem.[58] While most of the scholars cited here use US and Israeli examples, their observations fit well with the albums donated to archives by survivors of all-female labor camps. The specific setting of the camps in the Trautenau region contributed to these small albums emerging as apt and convenient means for caring for oneself through a relational practice: the girls and women were allowed certain small objects in the barracks; the fact that they could wear their own clothing helped them hide and circulate the books; they had access to small amounts of materials such as paper and thread; and the labor regime dominating their lives was structured such that they had time away from direct surveillance in the evenings (although it was dark) and on Sundays.

Such a *pamiętnik*, or memory book, was created from found fabric scraps for Dwojra K.'s birthday in 1944 in the Parschnitz camp. This object is remarkable in light of the fact that Parschnitz had been changed into a concentration camp in early 1944, with increasingly strict regulations,

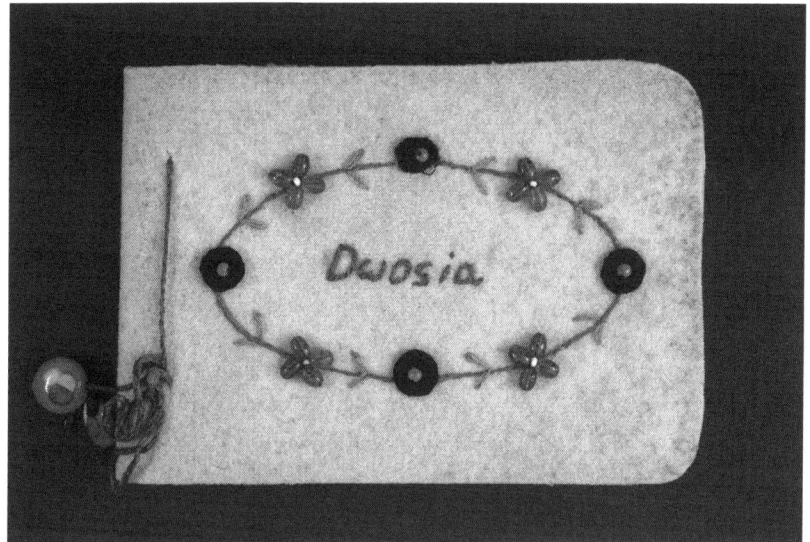

FIGURE 5 From the collection titled, "Postcards Sent to Dwojra Ruchla Kaminski in Parschnitz Camp." Item ID 10781077, Yad Vashem Photo Archive, Jerusalem. O.75/2672.

crowded conditions, and outbreaks of lice and bedbugs. The cover of the memory book was decorated by hand with simple beadwork, carefully spaced to encircle Dwojra K.'s name, evoking the relations among campmates who helped create the object.[59] In a figurative sense, Dwojra K. is depicted in a protective embrace. The different types of beads and the variation in yarn color speak to the efforts made in accumulating the materials. Inside the cover is a poem that is solemn but hopeful. (There may be other writing that is not visible in the digitized images available.) The poem begins with references to the camp as a prison with gray walls and then states that "it will not always be this bad." In careful handwriting centered on the pages, the third verse offers these wishes to Dwojra K.:

> Again you will be hugging your mother's hands, you will be happy and laughing again, you will stop living in such torment, gates will be opened and you will see how beautiful the world is.[60]

The poem continues for more verses and is signed at the end by "Aunt Greta," which could refer to a family member in camp with Dwojra K. or an older friend, and the words "Lager Parschnitz 1944," which makes it unlikely that it was made by a Gentile coworker, who would not have associated herself with the "Lager." In 1944 no mail or packages were arriving because the Jewish Council of Elders, which handled the mail, had been disbanded and most of the Jews of Zagłębie not in camps had been killed or were in hiding. With the memory book, "Aunt Greta" and her campmates provided an object to substitute for the flow of *"grüsse"* from family.

Performances, songs, and poetry were activities that a few survivors remember partaking in or listening to, at times with intentional playfulness and humor. The Yad Vashem World Holocaust Remembrance Center and its archive recently featured the poetry of a survivor of the Gabersdorf camp, Regina H., that is so remarkable it merits special attention.[61] Regina H. kept a diary in Gabersdorf filled with verse and prose, in Polish with some Yiddish and Hebrew elements, which also survived and which she donated to the archive. The poem featured by Yad Vashem is an acrostic, in which the writer uses the first letters of the alphabet as a structuring device, a familiar form with a long history in biblical and popular writing. In 1934, Polish-Jewish poet Julian Tuwim composed verses for children using it, and in 1998 Czesław Miłosz published a literary and social commentary that he called his *"abecadło."* [62] Regina H.'s camp poem immediately begins with transgressive references to sexuality and the body in Polish:

A – ANTEK tracks down blind dates of the girls
B – BARAK (barrack) is the orchestra of the camp
C – CAŁUS (kiss) French kiss tastes good
D – DUPA (ass) is our camp lexicon[63]

The present-day reader does not have access to all of the references (*Antek* likely refers to a male Czech factory employee) but what is apparent is that Regina H. was writing for an audience who was "in" on the camp language and who would have found humor in the verses. The combination of knowing sexuality, childish references, and direct use of an obscenity reflects and extends the preexisting audience that Regina H. was in relation with—these verses are not just for herself. Even just this small portion offers those who are in the camp with Regina H. a tool to ridicule and thus distance camp life and its disciplinary violence.

Additionally, Regina H.'s verses reinsert teasing and transgression—

elements of "normal" girlhood—into the distorted, imposed world of Gabersdorf. Like the postcards, poems, memory books, and even burials, these verses are offerings of beauty, joy, and connection with a prewar social world. Right in the middle of the poem, at "P," is *pieprz*, the Polish word for both "pepper" and "fuck," and the claim that "each of us" is missing one. The full line is "*Pieprz: każdy z nas brakuje*." The Yad Vashem website translates "*pieprz*" as the obscenity. This translation fits with the context—missing pepper does not merit a line in a poem—and with the tone and purpose of the poem as playful. With "*pieprz*" Regina H. continues her wordplay, using the slippage between the two meanings to write the strongly transgressive "fuck" without literally doing so.

Both the word and the assertion that sexual activity is to be taken for granted among the unmarried girls exceed the transgression of the earlier "ass." Its transgressive nature demonstrates Regina H.'s refusal of the personal disintegration brought on by the Nazi camp system. Moreover, this use of another obscenity is renormalizing. Certainly, there were many things the girls and women were missing, among them safety, food, and parents. The idea that there exists a world in which one is only missing a *pieprz* is a hopeful act of inclusive care, relationality, and future-making.

Yet despair is also present. Regina H. offers for her "N" the word "*nysym*," written as NYSYM and translated by Yad Vashem as "(miracles in Yiddish)." She then writes, "We are asking for them." It is noteworthy that Regina H.'s poem is in linguistic motion, traveling among Yiddish, Polish, "camp" terms, and words from home, and between humor and pain. In its complexity, attentiveness to audience, and documentary intentions, one might say it begins to approach the type of wartime literature analyzed by the scholar of Yiddish, David Roskies.[64] Although at the time of her writing Regina H. is not yet aware of the scale of the catastrophe, her poem can be viewed as a literary response to persecution and an attempt to "represent the many," in Roskies's words.[65] The "we" in "we are asking for them" most directly invokes the girls and women who are her campmates, but while the previous references to barracks and *Antek* are quite specific to the Gabersdorf context, this line, with its shift to Yiddish and religious reference point, seems to open the "we" to a wider Jewish community.

This view is supported by the fact that Regina H.'s diary is full of other textual material, including a Passover Haggadah also presented by Yad Vashem curators; her creative capacity to summon and sustain a multidimensional Jewish world goes beyond her *abecadło*. The ability to bring a practice of care from one's pre-detention experience forward into the camp after a series of traumas deepens the understanding of these testimony-givers as women who resisted many of the dimensions of the Nazi project. They insisted on their own survival. They did so, at times, in forms that supported the survival of others, a practice that they found nourishing. Finally, they refused the coerced labor camp's requirement to transform themselves into bodies that responded only to commands for productivity and obedience, a requirement aimed in part at rendering Jewish moral and cultural life inaccessible. With the materials at hand, they created vehicles for their own emotional lives and, tellingly, offered these objects after the war as formations that would continue to provide understanding, generate meaning, and, as the scholar of objects Laura Levitt puts it, "remain vital," that is, life-giving.[66]

CHAPTER 7

Desire and Space in the Coerced Labor Experience

Lola W. was one of the younger prisoners in the Parschnitz concentration camp, born in March 1929. She remembers making sure to forge a tight bond with four "older" girls who were seventeen or so. In Lola W.'s testimony, she offers a story that speaks to the awareness of the girls and women in the Trautenau-region camps of themselves as young people with the potential for physical and sexual intimacy, both desired and desiring. In this portion of her testimony, Lola W. insists that most in the Parschnitz camp were preoccupied with their hunger and their families but admits that other types of interaction also occurred.

> Interviewer: What kind of discussions would you have with other girls when you were—
>
> Lola W.: About boys. Men! I didn't know what [I was] saying. Finally the four [friends], they said, "Let's get her." I think I told you. So they asked me if I'm a virgin. "No." "Excuse me?" First this one [*pointing*], then this one—they were all older than I, a few years older, not much. Three years or so [*shaking her head, reenacting the conversation*] Everybody said, "No." Comes my turn. [*laughs*] If it's good for her, it's good for me, too! I said, "No. No, you know me! No!" [*laughing*] They started laughing![1]

Throughout this section, the interviewer laughs along with Lola W., which seems to allow her to become more expressive than she had been at any other point in the interview. Lola W. not only laughs and uses humorous facial expressions but also invites the immediate audience—interviewer and technical staff—into the story as participants with her body language. The memory of friendships close enough for this type of teasing and of the ability of the older girls to disrupt the boundary between naïveté and sexual knowingness without harming her seems to bring her genuine joy.

Desire is an uncommon topic in Holocaust scholarship, although sexual interaction, including assault, has recently become more frequently researched. As Lola W. herself insists, concern with food and for family members were most on the minds of the girls and women.

There were very few men present in the material world of the Jewish factory workers in the Trautenau region. Perhaps for this reason they played a large role in the imaginations of the girls and women. Indeed, the overwhelmingly female population of the Trautenau sites, combined with the ages of the laborers, led to a social world in which men were the topic of much speculation and, indeed, desire. This chapter pulls from the testimonies to offer three vignettes that indicate the range of responses to men present, past, and future. It notes the function of romantic fantasies, the longing for partnership, and hopes for a future of Jewish family life in the coping strategies of the girls and women. The first vignette addresses the handful of older Czech men who either supervised the factory floor or repaired machinery, whom the girls and women positioned as paternal figures; the second addresses the more sexually charged visits of French and English prisoners of war from nearby camps for periodic heavy-duty machine work; and the third addresses an encounter with a death march of Jewish men in 1945 that was deeply disturbing to the girls and women, who were by that time officially Gross-Rosen prisoners. In each of the three instances, testimony-givers recall how the presence of men brought up deep emotions and losses. At the same time, juxtaposing these vignettes against each other brings forward the inescapable structuring force of the material spaces in which the girls and women lived and worked.

Elderly or disabled Czech-speaking men circulated among the workplaces in Trautenau, mostly to maintain and repair the machinery. Each factory site employed a male floor supervisor. Many of the survivors recalled these men as "kind" (with some exceptions) and looked to them for extra food periodically. Just as important as the gifts of food was the fact that these individuals had information about the outside world and were willing to share encouraging words about the progress of the war. The survivors viewed them as kindly "uncles," deferential to the rules restricting the lives of the Jewish laborers but willing to offer vaguely worded news of the war ending soon or general encouragement.

DESIRE AND SPACE IN THE COERCED LABOR EXPERIENCE

Ida G.: [about a mechanic who gave her war news] He was our ray of hope. We used to call him, we called him "Uncle." He was our "uncle."[2]

Lucy M.: In my situation we had the men that were working in the tool room that were coming and fixing the machines. And they were older men. And a lot of them would tell us what was going on and what's happening. So they were giving us encouragement many a times.[3]

Frymeta F.: He said to the *Judenälteste*, "Listen, listen, in a short time—I think they are getting closer—the war will be finished. And you will all go home." We heard that, we were jumping to the skies.[4]

Mania S.: There was one guy, a mechanic. A German guy. And he was so good to us. He used to come in, and he had mercy. He used to come in and he was pretending that the machine is broken. He specially broke the machine for a few hours and he tried to give us a break. We couldn't work because the machine was broken. He was trying to fix it. For a few hours or maybe a day. And sometimes he brought us a sandwich. A bread, a piece of cheese. We called him "Wujek." "Wujek" means "uncle."[5]

Ida G. remembers one Czech repairman in particular. In Ida G.'s barracks the workers had been given a small metal pot for carrying food (probably soup) and a spoon. But the pots had no covers, making it difficult to transport one's food or protect it from debris.

Ida G.: So that man took it upon himself to clandestinely—in the smithery they had, um, materials there, um, like, whatever. Out of some kind of material he made covers. A gray cover with even a handle on it. And soon—and he didn't care when, he gave it out, you know!—and soon every single girl had pot on their—I mean a cover on the pot.[6]

It is remarkable that the details of this object remain in Ida G.'s memory so many years later. The specificity of the memory and Ida G.'s attentiveness to detail echo the attentiveness of the smith in adding handles and making sure each person received a cover.

Another testimony-giver remembers an "uncle" who was gripped by his realization that some of the girls and women had been through Auschwitz-Birkenau:

> Gucia R.: There I had a man, Volksdeutscher he was. He was nice to us. He was sorry for us. He used to bring us something to eat sometimes. He was really good to us, to all the girls. He was sitting there and he said, "How can it happen? How did you survive? Where were you?" He used to ask me.[7]

Not all the work sites had kindly uncles. Anna W. remembers an engineer at one of the Parschnitz factories becoming angry because she needed to rest for a moment.

> Anna W.: He started to scream and yell. "You are doing sabotage!"[8]

Helena K. also remembered an individual man who was punitive.

> Helena K.: There was a special man, the vice-director of the factory. His, his only duty was to, to think of bad things to do . . . He said [of Helena], "She is proud and arrogant . . . *stolz und eingebildet.*"[9]

Helena K. calls him a "sadist" and added, "He was in trouble with German women, too."[10] Other survivors do not mention him, but this could be because he targeted Helena K. specifically because she was already an adult, *stolz und eingebildet,* in contrast to those in their teenage years. Yetta P. also remembers a cruel "Meister" who intentionally dropped tools onto her feet:

> Yetta P.: He was terrible. He was such a sadist.[11]

The precise depictions of the "uncles"—even the angry ones—can be contrasted with how the women recall their imagining of the factory owners themselves, whom they never encountered. In their testimonies from the 1990s they mostly refrain from criticizing Etrich, Haase, Kluge, or Walzel as individuals or expressing anger at them. Overall, they viewed these men as aloof, unaware of the wretched conditions of the barracks, doing their best in harsh circumstances, and very wealthy and powerful. In their eyes, the owners' status placed them "above" the positions of the factory supervisors, "uncles," female guards, Gentile coworkers, and ultimately the Jewish girls and women themselves.

> Shoshana G.: But they could have sent us to Auschwitz. But Mr. Walzel didn't allow that. He also didn't allow us to go on a march. All the camps around us, all the camps, they were going on a death march . . . He was a human being.[12]
>
> Bella C.: [speaking about Walzel] A millionaire! Everything belonged to him.[13]
>
> Estera S.: The owner of the factory, he paid money to the Germans for the, for the work we had done. And he watched the kitchen, he asked sometimes around. His name was Alois Haase. He was an elderly man. He was like a bourgeois factory owner.[14]
>
> Lola W.: I worked in the garden for the boss. Haase, Haase. His name was Haase. It just came back to me. We actually never saw him. He had nothing to do with us. Because it was all done by the ss [referring to their detention].[15]

The notion that a wealthy elderly male benefactor existed who would help if he only knew of their specific situation likely performed an important function for the survivors both at the time of their imprisonment and at the time of their testimony. It was a safe fantasy in that it could never be ruptured because this old man would never truly appear.

> Shoshana G.: He was the one who went to Berlin and he explained to them why he doesn't want to send his girls to Auschwitz.[16]

But perhaps more importantly, it was a way of coping with the overwhelming burden of being a young person charged with the responsibility for surviving in a setting of hostility, deprivation, and isolation, one in which the gift of a pot cover is considered an act of great generosity. The social setting of the barracks, in which small fragments of information leaked through and were amplified in the absence of any larger context, influenced these coping responses. Dora R. at Bernsdorf reports on the belief that Etrich was Jewish.

> Dora R.: The name of the factory was Etrich. He was a Jew. He had a few factories around all the villages. And the people, they were not allowed to send him away. Because he was so nice to the people. That they didn't allow to send him to Auschwitz or wherever. And the money that came from the factory, they put it in a spare *konto* [account], that's what they did.[17]

The Etrich family was not Jewish, and Igo Etrich made huge profits from his wartime businesses, which he and his family relied on when they fled at the end of the war. Yet Dora R. expands on the elderly benefactor symbol to make him not only Jewish, but a Jewish person who was not sent to Auschwitz. Furthermore, it was his inner personal qualities—"he was so nice to the people"—that convinced these "people" to allow him to remain a member of their community. That a Jewish person could exist in some unseen place and be cherished by "people" simply for his kindness is a notion that retains Jewishness as personal identity and removes racist hatred at the same time. And as for the exploitative nature of coerced labor, the narrative places these profits in a protected place, away from Nazi authorities.

In contrast to the desexualized uncles watching over the workplace, men who were either prisoners of war—or in at least one instance, a Czech civilian—represented intimacy and romance, heightened by the fact such relations were forbidden by Nazi policy, Jewish law, and the norms of Jewish family life. In the Trautenau region, prisoners of war were used as forced labor separately from the Jewish girls and women, but periodically brought into different factories for mechanical work or heavy lifting, as Gerda F. explains in her description of Ober Altstadt. They had access to more food and other goods than the Jewish prisoners.[18] As was the case for liaisons between Gentile German women and prisoners of war in the Reich, as documented by Cornelie Usborne, it was the French in particular who were objects of desire, inciting emotional, romantic, and sexual responses.[19]

> Suzan L.: Once in a great while a French prisoner would, would give me an apple. About this size, you know [*gestures, smiling*]. He would have it in his hand and I was standing next to him and he would put it in my hand. And it was wonderful. It was feast,

> because I took it home in the evening and cut it to five pieces so everybody had a slice.[20]
>
> Ida G.: Not far away was a prisoner—a French prisoner camp for the French soldiers. And they would smuggle in certain material to us. They used to come into our building there to pick up certain things they needed . . . They even carried on some, some love affairs with some of the women who were in, who had some position in there . . . They met in the courtyard.[21]

Much later in her testimony, Ida G. decides to return to the topic but with much more specificity. She remembers the name of the male prisoner of war, but notably does not name or even depict his romantic partner, her campmate.

> Ida G.: There was one in particular. One French prisoner of war who was, who was dispensing the spools in our factory . . . His name was Marcel. And he—actually had an affair with one of the girls in our camp. I don't know why he favored me to, to send some news to his girlfriend. But once in a while he would put a piece of chocolate between the spools and when he put the spools down, he says, "Tell her to be there at six o'clock!"[22]

Remarkable here is the ability to envision the transgressive pleasure of "an affair" in a context of violence, deprivation, and embodied suffering. Nationality—a frequent signifier in Holocaust testimonies—appears here to set these men (or this man) apart from the paternal "Uncle" and the terrifying SS conducting selections. Ida G. adds to the fantasized pleasure by becoming a part of the affair, the person who facilitates it, and thus gets some of the "chocolate." She participated in the romance at the time and in her memory centers her interaction with Marcel over the couple's relationship—"he favored me." In other words, "affairs" were enjoyed not only by those who directly participated but also as symbols of a romantic life beyond reach but still possible.

In this testimony, Olga K. not only remembers a French prisoner of war's "charm" but also takes care to note his name and its spelling.

> Olga K.: We worked at the AEG [factory] in Trautenau with foreign slave laborers. Among them was French people. And one of

> them, by the name of George Alardet—[*spells the name out*] A-l-a-r-d-e-t—told us in his broken—he was so charming! [*smiles and closes her eyes*] I can still hear his voice! When he started telling us, "*Viele Russe in Pol, viele Rus in Pol!*" Meaning, there are many Russians in Poland.[23]

Yetta P., in Ober Altstadt, also recalls an interaction with a French prisoner of war in detail. In her memory, it is the French man who endows the Jewish woman with a name.

> Yetta P.: One French man—he was weighing the, the cotton. And a girl across from him, they, they had a love affair. From just, like—he used to give her sheets of French. And she learned French from that. And he used to write—she taught him Polish. He used to write on—because there were lots of dust from that, uh, from that cotton. Flax, they called it . . . He used to write on the dust, "I love Mila." And in fact, after the war he took her to France. He married her.[24]

Here the factory itself is a player in the romance as the prisoner of war repurposes the dust and perhaps other factory material ("sheets of French") to create a relationship and express love. Yetta P. directly links the affair to a postwar future that seems to promise a family.

Usborne notes that factors specific to German social life in the Reich—such as popular films—contributed to Gentile German women partaking in intimacy with prisoners of war.[25] However, these testimony-givers, from conservative Jewish homes in western Poland, also remember prisoners of war as sexually potent. The theme of romantic intimacy with French and Italian prisoners of war also appears throughout the survivor memoir, *Franci's War*.[26] It appears that these men served an important symbolic function, as reminders of youthfulness, transgression, the generative power of potential intimacy, and the ability of desire to overcome obstacles. Phyllis Y. remembers French prisoners of war in the Walzel factory.

> Interviewer: What kind of contact did you have with them?[27]
> Phyllis Y.: [*a few seconds of smiling and laughing*] You know!
> Interviewer: Young people!
> Phyllis Y.: Young people, right? What can I tell you!

This burst of laughter interrupts the seriousness and solemnity with which Phyllis Y. had been speaking for the two previous hours, such that the interviewer herself joins in the merriment for the moment. The interviewer chooses to pursue the opening in more detail. Phyllis Y. states that she did not know the French language at that time.

> Interviewer: So how did you communicate? What was the interaction?[28]
>
> Phyllis Y.: [*smiles and shrugs*] There was a couple of woman-man interaction, believe it or not!
>
> Interviewer: Sexual contact.
>
> Phyllis Y.: Well, I don't know that it went that far, because there was just no place to, [*laughs*] to do it. But, uh, the feelings! The feelings were there. Absolutely. The feelings were there.

Here Phyllis Y. gently challenges the interviewer's equivalence of desire with a sexual act by continuing to laugh but asserting quite strongly that the atmosphere around these prisoners was sexually charged: "Absolutely."

Not all interactions with prisoners of war were characterized by these elements. Many of the testimony-givers from the Schatzlar camp make special note of a building housing French prisoners of war that the girls and women walked past during the period in 1945 when they were made to work outdoors digging. They recall feeling cheered by the men waving to them out of the windows. This excerpt follows a question from Eva W.'s interviewer regarding how she kept up her morale.

> Eva W.: When we went to work there were French soldiers there. In another camp.
>
> Interviewer: They were prisoners of war.
>
> Eva W.: [*continuing after a break*] They were prisoners, right. And they had the rooms, they lived upstairs—like an upper floor. And when we went by from our camp to work, they looked down the window and they let us know [by their] hands, how the war was coming along. And sometimes they were throwing down little leaflets to us.[29]

The interviewer does not inquire about the content of the leaflets. Eva W. does not identify any specific man, likely because they were at a distance. In Rose K.'s testimony, it is a local Czech who becomes the lover of a girl, Regina, in the factory. Rose K. worked at Kluge in Ober Altstadt, while the previous testimony-givers worked at Walzel and Haase in Parschnitz, which may account for the different details. Rose K., originally from the Hungarian territories, remembers Regina as also from one of these territories and fluent in Czech:

> Rose K.: So this girl, the Hoffmann Regina, made friends with this Christian [Czech] boy. He wasn't a Jewish boy. And the girl was very religious. She came from a very religious house. This was already—must be end of April [1945]. And he took her away from the factory. During the night.[30]

The next morning the entire camp was counted, recounted, and denied food.

> Rose K.: A big German guy came out and he was pointing out with the finger. "Hoffmann Regina had been caught and had been killed." And that's going to happen with us if anybody tries to run away. But we wasn't fooled. Because we knew if she would be caught, she be brought into the camp and punished in front of us. So somehow we knew that's not true.[31]

A few minutes later, Rose K. tells the interviewer that Regina and her "boyfriend" arrived back at the camp on the day of liberation, presenting themselves to the newly freed prisoners. This story is also repeated in other testimony:

> Tola G.: One of the girls, at the end of the war—the very end—through a Bohemian guy got away . . . Her name was Regina Hoffmann . . . And after we were liberated she came to camp.[32]

> Lena M.: We had one girl, two girls, which walked together with one of the mens—men—and there was a little flirtation. Or something. That we heard about it. But uh—and one of them got married after the war![33]

> Aranka T.: One of the Czech who have relatives there, she helped her to escape. And there was a story about that they caught her and they was punished. But it wasn't true. End of the war, we find out that she survived.[34]

Whether truth or rumor, the episode speaks to the forms that desire took in the minds and memories of the survivors. The power of the affair is such that Regina is not only saved, she is depicted as saved by a chosen lover, overturning assertions of her own death, and even returns in freedom, partnered and triumphantly embodying the transgression of intimacy with a Gentile without regret. The notion that such activities could occur in a forced labor space added to their attraction. The discussions over what possible spaces in the factories or on its grounds could have been used for sexualized intimacy seemed to add pleasure to the already pleasurable narrative of the man on the premises.

In fact, local Czechs were not restricted in their movements and even prisoners of war possessed much more mobility and access to resources than other prisoners or coerced laborers.[35] Prisoners of war were in labor camps and required to work, but the German army was officially in charge of the conditions of their imprisonment, not the ss. Because the Wehrmacht, as well as some government elites, were sensitive to the perceptions (and Geneva Convention rules) of the international community as well as the reciprocity issue, West European prisoners of war could receive packages, obtain aid from organizations, and had some ability to barter for more food.[36] Prisoners of war from France, Italy, and Great Britain (including soldiers from New Zealand and Australia) lived near the Trautenau factories. The Nazis treated the prisoners of war from the Soviet Union with utter brutality and sadism in general, and the girls and women never saw them.

Irene W., who survived Bernsdorf, remembers a romance in which both the Jewish laborer and her English prisoner of war partner were morally deserving, ethical, and able to survive together.

> Irene W.: And our *Judenälteste*, that was a Jewish girl, she was one of a darling, she was so nice, so good ... And one English man fell in love with her. His name was Noel. I will never forget it. And he was good to every girl. If he could help, he helped. And she said she's not going to leave the girls alone [at liberation]. Most of us were young girls yet. And he took—he married her! He took her with him, I think Australia, he was an Australian.[37]

One can note here the concreteness (in Pollin-Galay's terminology) of the depiction of the English prisoner of war. Irene W. does not note the name of the Jewish girl but "will never forget" Noel's name and even recalls the country of his citizenship. A postwar interview initiative in Great Britain includes at least one Gabersdorf survivor, Edith S., who married an English prisoner of war who worked in the textile factory.[38]

The sustaining power of fantasies of romance and rescue existed within a larger memory context of reuniting with family, which was a powerful coping strategy for many. The third vignette demonstrates the confrontation of longings for intimacy, family, and the recovery of Jewish community with one of the most brutalizing aspects of the Holocaust, the death march. This incident occurred in the early months of 1945. Testimony-givers describe it as profoundly disillusioning and that it plunged many of the girls and women into despair. However, it also demonstrates the ability of those in the Parschnitz barracks to continue to imagine a Jewish future at this time and to enact their hopes through the material spaces of the buildings in which they were imprisoned.

In April 1944 the Nazi authorities began the evacuations of prisoners from specific camps such as Majdanek near Lublin in response to the westward movement of the Soviet army; evacuations such as these from other locations eventually became death marches.[39] As SS personnel escorted large groups of prisoners out from labor camps, concentration camps, and the killing center, Auschwitz-Birkenau, on foot deeper into Germany, the route westward took them through the Sudetenland and Silesia.[40] The death rate was high because no planning had been made for food or shelter, and SS guards were free to shoot or beat prisoners arbitrarily.[41] The routes of these marches were often improvised, based on poor information, and groups of prisoners crossed paths while going in opposite directions.[42] Because so many died as they were forced to walk through what became postwar Czechoslovakia, Czechoslovakian researchers in particular have traced the specific routes and developed a body of scholarship (and memory practices) regarding death marches. In a definitive early study, Irena Malá and Ludmila Kubátová used perpetrator documents, eyewitness interviews, and United Nations Relief and Rehabilitation Administration (UNRRA) Central Tracing archives to reconstruct many of these marches.[43] UNRRA itself interviewed death march survivors, local municipal authorities such as the mayors of the towns the marches passed through, and local residents, who often had to bury the dead themselves.

DESIRE AND SPACE IN THE COERCED LABOR EXPERIENCE

Václav Sádlo has mapped out the particular death march that proceeded from the main Gross-Rosen concentration camp through Trautenau itself in early 1945, although several passed through the region.[44] The men were housed overnight in the Haase factory, which at this point doubled as barracks for Jewish girls and women. Testimony-givers remember they had no information about the purpose of prisoner movements. They simply awoke in their third-floor barracks to discover that there were hundreds of men entering the barracks yard. The girls and women were instructed to stay inside their barracks and forbidden from looking out of the window. But some did look.

> Rose S.: We heard, like in the evening, at night when we came from work, we heard that they are bringing, like—men are coming. Marching in. And they are chasing them like cattle into the, into the backyard, into the yard from the, from our camp. And we look, we say: men! We saw they had the star. So from other camps! So everybody was looking through the window and wanted to see, if there were some relatives or something.[45]

> Anna W.: I've never seen anything like it in my life. It was a sea of marching people. In those uniforms. The striped uniforms. It was a sea![46]

> Rosalie S.: One transport stopped at our camp overnight. And, uh, we weren't allowed to go to the window. To look.[47]

> Estelle C.: They came and we see so many Jewish people—so everybody was anxious to see if it's not anybody that's a relative. But they forbidded us.[48]

> Frymeta F.: Before the war was going to finish, then they brought a transport of men. To our concern—to our *Lager*. And then everybody was, nu, it's just, maybe a father came, maybe a brother. Let me go look.[49]

> Shoshana G.: There was a transport. Of men. And they put them in one room. They couldn't sit. They couldn't stand. They couldn't lie down. It's—you, forget it—forget about it, to lie down. They couldn't. It was no space.[50]

Lucy M.: Also there were men transported. They were on a death march. And they had [some] five thousand men. And we had to draw the shades. We were not allowed to look down, otherwise they shot . . . The girls were looking anyways.[51]

Phyllis Y.: And I have never seen [*breaks into a sob*]. We looked next to them like we just got back from a resort or something . . . But when we saw them! They were emaciated. They couldn't walk.[52]

These fragments of testimony express the complexity of the emotions incited by the "sea" of Jewish men suddenly appearing combined with the command to not look. In these words, as they are spoken, looking itself becomes laden with assertion and even yearning. Lucy M.'s "looking anyways" can refer either to the taking in of the number of men or the search for a recognizable person—the remainder of her testimony does not clarify which. This glimpse, if they could get it, would tell them Jews still lived, Jewishness still existed, a future family was possible for them, and maybe even their own families somehow still lived.

In parallel with the memories of the French prisoner of war, "looking" is represented as something transgressive yet desired—and perhaps more desired because of its transgression. This desire was not overtly sexualized but remembered as a need and yearning to see Jewish men in particular. Gucia R., originally from Łódź (Lodz in Yiddish), had been brought to the Parschnitz camp in 1944 after the SS deported her to Auschwitz. She worked at a factory making gas masks, likely AEG in Trautenau, and did not live in the same Haase barracks that most testimony-givers did.

Gucia R.: At night we saw them through the windows. Well, it was no windows, it was like a factory, little windows. We could look out. We were not allowed to go out. And we saw people, men, men marching.

Interviewer: Did you know they were Jewish men?

Gucia R.: Yes, because we were calling out to them and they were calling back. Some of them were from Lodz. And we didn't know names, we didn't know who they were. We didn't know where they were going. They didn't know themselves where they were going.[53]

DESIRE AND SPACE IN THE COERCED LABOR EXPERIENCE

Those in the Haase factory also remembered feeling a complex connection to the men.

> Anna W.: We were told not to look out the windows. I was a little bit more curious. So I went to one hall, which I thought nobody was there. And I looked out the windows.[54]

> Phyllis Y.: It was [*begins to weep*] the first time I saw a Jewish man since 1941. They came into our camp.[55]

The men were then housed overnight on the floor below them, which simultaneously brought them into closer proximity but prevented "looking." The testimony repeats, among a number of survivors, a negotiation between a forbidden looking through windows and a secretly snatched looking for "pipe cracks" and other gaps in the structure of the barracks.

> Olga K.: I just had to go to the window and just look, because I, I saw that, I—[*pauses*] I was hoping—I probably wasn't sure—that I saw one of my uncles.[56]

> Ida G.: After we came home and we passed the gate and we were counted and everything, when we approached the building to go upstairs we were told to go—not to look, to go straight, to go upstairs, not to look out the windows. Not to look out the windows . . . We were told that there is a transport of men that passed on the way and they are housed on the bottom, in the bottom, on the bottom floor. At night we stole down, we went down the stairs quietly, and as it was a factory, it had pipes going down from top to bottom. And in between the pipes there was a little place where you could look down.[57]

These barracks were a cleared-out factory floor. There were numerous loose boards and holes in the wood. In this case, pipes carrying water vertically were accommodated by a small circular gap in the floor around them. Because this was not the "forbidden" window, looking through it neither exposed the girls and women to punishment nor officially violated the order of not to look out the windows.

The girls and women did not only look, however. They hoped desperately for some kind of interaction with the mass of men. They wanted a response. To elicit such a response, they dropped notes and bread down through the pipe gaps. In the testimonies it seems as if they had multiple hopes: to get news of male relatives; to document their own names and location with some other Jewish audience; to provide comfort; and to receive recognition, comfort, and some kind of connection in return. They had, of course, been isolated from the facts of what condition these men must have been in—the extent of their deprivation and the breakdown of moral codes and mental faculties. The event unfolded in a process that shocked them.

> Regina G.: They brought in a transport of men. And they used to scream, "Girls! We are so hungry! Please give us something." So we fasted this day and we threw down our piece of bread that we got.[58]
>
> Shoshana G.: And we tried everybody give a piece of bread.[59]
>
> Ida G.: We decided to take together whatever bread we have and stuff it between and throw it down ... [One man] would stuff it in his striped uniform for himself. So we realized he was hoarding it for himself and we went to another pipe.[60]

Ida G. remembers that the girls and women had expected that the men would share the bread among themselves, exactly as they did when they acquired smuggled or stolen food. Even at the time of her testimony, when Ida G. surely knows the condition of the men, she describes the male prisoner's actions as "hoarding."

But then the behavior of the men was utterly shocking. These prisoners clawed for the bread almost without awareness, animal-like, snatching it out of the hands of others.

> Shoshana G.: And we all gave a big plate. All the girls gave. To go down to the men. And guess what. [*pauses*] They were fighting like animals. We couldn't do this. It was [*raises her hands to her head*] unbearable! To understand that! Like animals. They became animals. They were so hungry. They were killing each other. We couldn't do it anymore.[61]

The bread thrown down seemed to cause aggression, anguish, and desperation. The Jewish girls and women had never seen anything like this.

After their withdrawal from the pipe gap there seemed to have been a period of grappling with the reality they had confronted: "We couldn't do this . . . We couldn't do it anymore."

> Phyllis Y.: The prisoners—they were killing each other. To catch a piece of bread.[62]

In this excerpt Lena M. combines her analysis of the war and the death marches, her memory of the event of the men at Parschnitz, and postwar information about her family's pathway through persecution.

> Lena M.: As a matter of fact in 1942 [she means 1945] January, they had brought to us in the back two thousand prisoners from other camps because the Russians were coming close. So they, they, they, you know, they make them march. They went with them wherever. As far as they could go. So they came. And they were at night. We opened the windows and we helped them out. Surprisingly, would you believe it, I had an uncle and Joe [her husband at the time of testimony], Joe's brother was with this transport. And they came closer to the window. And we gave them whatever we had. What was going on, don't ask.[63]

She seems as if she would describe the response of the men to the food-giving and then refuses, marking the extremity of what occurred as unspeakable with "don't ask." Her "don't ask" functions also as a protective phrase that keeps the dehumanizing behavior out of the space of her testimonial practice, possibly because she feels connected to the men personally.

The next morning it appears that the strictures against looking through the windows had been loosened. The testimony-givers spoke of realizing, from what they could see the next day, that the men they had seen the night before had been near death.

> Ida G.: We looked out the window, little, you know, corners we picked up, and we saw there was a cart, a two-wheel cart with big wheels, and they loaded all their dead that died during the night on the cart. And they were lying like broken rags on it. Arms and legs hanging down . . . And then we realized what is happening to our people.[64]

Shoshana G.: And then we saw a wagon. Schlepped by another man. And these men were lying down. I will never forget that. And they wanted to live. They were like half dead. And they were [*gesturing with her arms*], "I'm alive, I'm alive," with their arms.[65]

Estera S.: One night I remember we heard the whole night screaming. "Shema Israel, Shema Israel." Such [*pauses*]— In the morning we woke up and we had seen mountains of dead bodies.[66]

Regina G.: We saw truckloads with bodies. Still moving.[67]

Estelle C.: The people that came to stay overnight—[*pauses*] Every five minutes another died. You saw, uh, wagons and horses and they put them on the wagons when they were half dead, three-quarters dead, or dead. They put them all on the wagon.[68]

Rose S.: When we came down they were sitting like that [*huddles forward*] in the morning. Frozen already.[69]

The grief at the frustrated attempt at connection blended with the grief of seeing Jewish men dead, which in turn became a wider understanding of the nature of the Holocaust—something that the girls and women had been aware of but had not directly witnessed. Even those from the Hungarian territories who had spent days or weeks at Auschwitz, and who had seen its horrors, seem to not have fully integrated the scope of the Nazi project. As Ida G. said, "We realized what is happening to our people." The realization marked the extinguishment, for the time being, of their naïveté and longing. This event marked the end of hopes of connection with specific men, but also altered their understanding of the possibilities of creating new Jewish lives with Jewish men after survival.

Rena M. articulates the poignant conflict of finally seeing males, but then facing the fact that these particular males were near death, and thus not only disempowered, emasculated, but also unable to present themselves as men:

Rena M.: That camp [Parschnitz], they had men coming through —I don't know who would have liberated them—but to tell you, these men could hardly walk. They were dying. They were dying

DESIRE AND SPACE IN THE COERCED LABOR EXPERIENCE

>by the hundreds. And they came overnight to park their bodies in our camp. And in the morning, when we woke up there was like a wagon full with corpses of men lying outside and on the wagon. And they pushed these men further and further to walk because they didn't want them to be liberated. [*The interviewer begins to vocalize "okay" more than once to encourage Rena M. to end this anecdote, but she continues.*] And that was the only time we had men in the ca—hardly men! Because they were more dead than alive—
>
>Interviewer: [*changing the topic and speaking at the same time as Rena M.*] And so all of your guards were also again women.
>
>Rena M.: [*continues to speak about the men while the interviewer is speaking*] It was incredible.[70]

Rena M. communicates the difficulty the girls and women had in assimilating the appearance of "these men," who were "hardly men." They were men, but not men at the same time. "It was incredible," that is, literally not to be believed. The death march could not be fit into the hope that there was a Jewish world outside of Trautenau. In Rena M.'s telling, "that was the only time we had men," meaning specifically Jewish men, a reality that merited not complying with the interviewer.

>Rose S.: We saw the men looked horrible, terrible. Just like dead bodies.[71]
>
>Anna W.: That night a whole lot of men arrived. We could not see them. They were—it was a door behind that hall, so I could hear them. The whole night. I could hear Shema Israel—somebody was dying. In the morning they were driven further. And who didn't survive was put on a cart right in front of kitchen there. Maybe twenty bodies [in a cart]. One hand was still moving. So the German woman which was in the kitchen, she got out and got a cup of hot—coffee? it wasn't coffee—and she gave it to the man with this hand. Then some girls were selected to go and bury the poor people. Another day some other girls were collected to go, selected to go to a railway station, where there were more bodies.[72]

223

Anna W.'s testimony is full of details that speak to how these deaths were received by those living and working in Parschnitz. It is also telling in regard to the continued mobility of the Jewish laborers even in 1945. The gesture of a hot drink given to a Jewish prisoner—a gesture that was certainly illegal—suggests that the Gentile employees were likely disturbed by the extremity of the suffering and death.

Anna W.'s words also remind us that when people die in a residential area they must be removed from sight and they must be buried such that their decomposition does not affect the drinking water. That this task fell to the very same girls and women who had hoped so desperately to see a sign of potency in this group of Jewish men is staggering to consider. Moreover, the memories and insights of the testimony-givers regarding their encounter with the death march reflect their complex, multidimensional, social concept of "survival." Survival was of course experienced on an individual level because hunger was always present. But it was also conceptualized through the frame of their remembered position in their families and in the wider Jewish world, that is, in terms of their future as Jews with the capacity to generate children, connections, intimacy, and families and to enrich the Jewish world they had been born into. Each survivor remembered the function of this moment differently, using it to either extend her despair or hold it at bay.

CHAPTER 8

The Violence and Losses of Liberation

On May 8, 1945, the war ended for the residents of Trautenau.

> Gucia R.: So, I was lying on my bunk and I was crying. I didn't even want to go out. I said, where do I go now? What do I do? Who do I have? Where do I find somebody?[1]

What was "liberation" for the girls and women imprisoned in the Trautenau region's camps? "Liberation" is the formal term used for the moment in time when Allied troops arrived at a specific location and officially ended the imprisonment of individuals there. It occurred at different times in different locations; Trautenau and its surrounding towns were among the last.[2] The testimony conveys the mixture of emotions of the young women who had spent so many of their teenage years as imprisoned laborers, gradually realizing the extent of Nazi murderousness yet hoping that somehow their family—or part of their family—had survived.

In the first months of 1945 the factory owners, staff, and other civilians living in the Trautenau region faced a rapidly changing social and political reality. Before Germany had annexed the Sudetenland in 1938, Trautenau and the towns nearby were ethnically and linguistically mixed, with a highly stratified economic and social life. There may have been tensions between Czech and German speakers, and between Gentiles and Jews, but the fact that the industrialist, German-speaking families of Etrich, Haase, Kluge, and Walzel controlled most of the employment possibilities meant that residents of the region were dependent on them. When these owners, as well as Siemens and AEG, began the process of shutting down their factories in spring 1945, many—but not all—German-speaking civilians began a process of relocating westward, deeper into Germany, leaving their homes vacant.

Himmler required the SS to remain at their posts or, when ordered to do so, march any prisoners westward. The response to his directives varied, in part because officers and civil administrators feared retribution when the Allies arrived, and in part because, as noted previously, specific timetables for these marches were confusing. However, the SS at Parschnitz did not evacuate the prisoners. Instead, guards (borrowed from a nearby men's camp) required the girls and women to dig trenches, unload coal wagons, and do other outdoor work.

> Anna W.: But the factory closed. They shut the factory about maybe a month before the war's end. We were assigned to go to the fields and, um, dig trenches for the soldiers.[3]

> Helena K.: There was times that there was no rail delivery for the yarns. It was not enough work. And we were taken to—when the Russians approached, to dig the, to dig the [trenches].[4]

> Frances H.: At that time it wasn't anymore factory work. It was, we have been digging anti-tank—things. How do you call it? Trenches.[5]

While most testimony-givers make note of the outdoor period of their persecution and emphasize the arduous nature of the work, Regina G. remembers it as fatal for many.

> Regina G.: That period of time was the worst from all the periods. Because we came back—they didn't have nothing for us to give even to eat! People were dying. You should have seen, every morning, every morning they used to have ten, twenty girls lying already to be, to be moved already to the graves. They have a little wagon. They throw the bodies on the wagon. And there were a couple of girls, this was their job. To go every day, every day to go, to the fields. To the—some of them were on one field, the other ones were in a, in the forest. They did dig ditches and to throw them in.[6]

Regina G. points out the extension of labor from the factory into the work of managing the deaths of their campmates. Her description not only lacks precise depictions and names of those who died but represents the process of coping with death as neglectful and careless, using "throw" more than once. This description stands in sharp contrast to the care shown for some who died on site in earlier months. For Regina G. this treatment of those who died is a further condemnation of the perpetrators.

The Soviet army's westward advance in 1945 altered the social dynamics of the Trautenau region. Testimony-givers remember a sense that German speakers living in the Sudetenland who had worked with and benefited from annexation to the Reich were suddenly vulnerable. Local Germans feared that Soviet soldiers would behave brutally toward German factory owners and factory workers alike. The Czech-speaking residents of the area had long harbored resentment toward local German authorities; local Germans were aware that many of their Czech neighbors were ready to "turn the tables" in response to years of exploitation. The smaller camps throughout the Sudetenland were not a priority for the Soviet Union's military. Inside Czechoslovakia, Soviet forces prioritized taking the main city, Prague. The Trautenau region was left in a kind of vacuum, with civilian workers no longer having access to wage income, factory owners hoping to preserve their assets, no Soviet soldiers yet in sight, and barracks full of Jewish prisoners with no work to do and dwindling food supplies.

The outdoor work included climbing a standing railroad car filled with coal and transferring the coal into a truck. In one instance, an arriving train hit the standing coal car, injuring many of those working.

> Magda-Madeleine F.: We were working on a—you know, where the railway, where the rail goes, railway [*gesturing*] . . . Suddenly a train came. The German woman screamed, "Train is coming!" So people jumped out. And I jumped out . . . I started to run like crazy, down. And the girl with whom I worked just jumped out and stayed there. And she had to have her leg amputated.[7]

Bella C. describes being flung from the train car, trapped in debris and severely injured.[8] The rest of the girls and women dug trenches, which many seemed to believe were their own graves, but which others recognized as military defenses. One implication of this outdoor work was that they were exposed to even more local civilians in the area, but also exposed for greater lengths of time to direct SS supervision.

At the same time the practice of transferring small groups of Jewish girls and women in other coerced labor settings either to Parschnitz or through Parschnitz increased. Several survivors only arrived in Trautenau in 1945; some stayed for a few weeks and then were transferred again. Some of these groups were transferred because Allied bombing had damaged their work sites. Some were transferred as companies bought and sold Jewish bodies themselves, as they moved production, closed down, or sought to fill gaps.

The girls and women observed changes in the behavior of ss supervisors and civilian Germans and Czechs by spring 1945.

> Estera S.: Once we walked through Trautenau and we saw people standing on the corners of the street and talking about it and talking and they saw us walking by. And we realized that something happened.⁹

Survivors remember noticing a stark absence of people in general in Trautenau the first week of May. Not only factory staff, but also ss personnel, local government officials, shop owners, and German-speaking residents began to vanish.

> Gucia R.: It became very quiet. We didn't know where the guards disappeared to. And we didn't see anybody. And we were scared to go outside.¹⁰
>
> Shoshana L.: We been left alone. With no money. With no, with no supervision. With no help, with no doctors. With no one, no one cares for us. We been left at the mercy of God again.¹¹
>
> Frieda W.: All of a sudden late in the afternoon, May 9th—it was already, the war was over the 8th but this was a day later—May 9th they [the local Germans] heard that the Russians are coming. They run away and the street was empty. There was not a soul in the whole city. Just us, the prisoners.¹²
>
> Livia R.: It was very, very confusing.¹³

By May 8 the girls and women were left completely alone in their barracks. This was the case not only for the barracks in Trautenau, Parschnitz, and Ober Altstadt, but also for Schatzlar/Bernsdorf and Gabersdorf. There were no *Lagerführerinnen*, no summons for roll call or to walk to work, no food or drink. This aloneness after years of regimentation was experienced as a specific kind of vulnerability rather than an empowering sense of freedom. Almost all survivors articulate a sense of disorientation and confusion—they all waited in their barracks for what was to come. Since these barracks were located in various parts of town, there was no way to coordinate a liberation strategy. Czech partisans arrived at some barracks. These men brought food, news that the war was over, and warned the girls and women to lock the doors when the Soviet army arrived because the soldiers would likely sexually assault them. Other interviewees recall a single Jewish officer (some remember him on a motorcycle) who arrived on May 7 to warn them about the Soviet soldiers. Other interviewees had no notion who would arrive, when, or that those arriving would attempt to rape them. And some girls and women ran out of their barracks to embrace the soldiers and climb onto their vehicles.

> Regina L.: [in Ober Altstadt] But then when the first Russian tank broke the gates and the barbed wire, when they walked in, [*sighs and smiles*] girls went crazy. They really went. They jumped on top of the soldiers. They jumped on the tanks.[14]

Most were concerned with remaining safe in an environment in which the new authorities were also threats.

> Esther K.: I had one, I got one wish what I had. I said, I don't have nothing in my life. But I want to be a girl [*sic*] when I marry. That's what I was wishing. So I was avoiding them . . . [They were] very rough on everybody.[15]

> Lola W.: It wasn't good. Because first of all, like any other soldier, they wanted to rape us. They did.[16]

> Chana B.: It was happy [liberation] but some soldiers were very mean. Because they want to come to the camp. In the daytime they were okay. But at night they want the girls. "We liberated you and you don't want to go with us." We all were young. So we barricaded with tables, with chairs. Because if somebody was in front of the camp watching, so they could go from a different way, through the window. I don't know how they . . . And each night. Until they had more guards not to let them into the camp. They wanted to sleep with the girls.[17]

> Lena M.: It wasn't the easiest . . . [18]

> Magda-Madeleine F.: We came down very happy. They actually put me on a tank [*laughs*] and took me for a while. I was lucky that they didn't do anything. Because they also raped girls.[19]

> Cesia T.: [at Bernsdorf] They came in and new trouble started. At night we had to hide. Girls—twenty, thirty in a room—and block the doors because they were raping girls.[20]

While Cesia T.'s testimony emphasizes blocking men out, Lusia B.'s implies that some entered the barracks.

> Lusia B.: We were happy that they came, but we, we—it was in Parschnitz—but we, at night we were all very much afraid, because they came. They were looking for women. And we ran from one bed to the other. We were very much afraid.[21]

There was no single, shared response to the unexpected threat of rape. As Chana B. and Cesia T. stated, some groups of prisoners stayed in their barracks and reinforced possible entry points. Some survivors chose not to include the practice of sexual assault and the heightened sexualization of the atmosphere at the barracks and in the region in their recorded testimony. They were aware that the interview was also an archive; it would be viewed by family as well as the wider public while the interviewee was still alive. They may have felt unable to control the external judgments of any potential audience member. Yet more survivors discussed it than one might expect, often using indirect methods or strategic silences.

In this example from the testimony of Mania S., the interviewer's response was crucial in shaping the direction of the testimony.

> Mania S.: If they could get a hand of you, you know. They raped you and did all kinds of things.
> Interviewer: Did anything happen to you?
> Mania S.: No, thank God![22]

In this exchange we see the "you" first in "if they could get a hand of you." Taken in isolation from what follows, this "you" is the substitute for "myself and people like me," meaning Mania S. herself. This phrase combines "if they could get a hold of you" with "if they could put a hand on you," to summon both experiences in an apparent syntax error, but one that is revealing. Putting a hand on the body is the same here as restricting the body's movement. This is followed by "they raped you." This collective "you" that includes the speaker is also an invitation for the listener to include themselves. In a certain sense it is an opening for an empathic connection.

The interviewer acknowledges the opening but then separates herself from it by asking directly if Mania S. was raped. "Did anything happen to you" is a revision of the ambiguous, collective "you" into the personal "you": Mania S. only. This movement is illustrative of the circulation of empathy inside testimony practice and an act that scholar Anna Veprinska might call "empathic dissonance."[23] The revision of "you" stops any potential exploration of how vulnerable Mania S. felt, what she may have observed or experienced, and protects the interviewer from being included in the experience via empathy. It transforms a complex narrative strategy that both names and does not name into a legal issue of witnessing: yes or no. Mania S. uses this opening to step out of the common "you" and say emphatically, "no."

Some testimony-givers created distance from the experience by using justificatory language. Speaking years later as adults, they invoked biological maleness, being a soldier, having suffered through the war, the chaos of the situation, and their own naïveté.

> Lena M.: The Russians are not American. They, they went through hell! You understand? They opened our camps. They saw how we looked. But you know, a man is a man.[24]
>
> Shoshana L.: It was a mishmash, you know. Soldiers. It was after the war.[25]
>
> Ida G.: We all ran out into the streets, on top of the tanks and everything. Wild, completely wild. It was bedlam. Little did we know. That those are soldiers, you know. So, uh, we were, we were completely discombobulated, completely wild about it, and happy and crying and singing and doing all the crazy things. But soon enough the Russian soldiers overran our, our camp and they came in [to the barracks] and they started running around . . . We had to protect ourselves.[26]

> Estelle C.: They did nasty things . . . But I would assume that they, that they did this to—the girls weren't that nice. You know? I'm meaning maybe they asked for it. Or, or whatever.²⁷
>
> Regina G.: But a lot of girls done a lot of mistakes, what they done with the Russians, what they shouldn't done and they were later on, you know—[*nodding*] they were in a lot of trouble.²⁸

In the testimony of Regina P., the interviewer's intervention is taken by her as permission to be frank:

> Regina P.: We weren't long with the Russians. We were only a few days with the Russians. They came. And the first day when they came, they were looking, I don't know for who they were looking. [*tilts her head*] We were still in the beds because we don't have to go to work, nothing to do. And a Ger—a Russian came in. Like a soldier, he was a soldier. He came in and was looking, looking. And we, when he came in, we started to run. I don't know why we started to run. And that girl, I don't know what happened. And—[*raises eyebrows*]
> Interviewer: What happened to her?
> Regina P.: He raped her.²⁹

Regina P. initially states that she does not know what the Soviet soldiers intended; she constructs a naïveté that keeps the event narratively at a distance. She then presents a soldier who enters their intimate space ("still in the beds") and will not leave ("looking, looking"). In a shift she makes explicit that there was a person targeted—"that girl'—but reasserts her own not-knowing. When the interviewer gently refuses to accept Regina's evasion, Regina immediately and directly answers with full knowledge of the assault.

Rusia Y.'s testimony combines indirection, ambiguity, justification, and then finally direct acknowledgment of what occurred in plain language. As is the case with some testimony-givers, she blends languages and intersperses her narrative with requests for words or references to previous topics, indicated with ellipses here.

> Rusia Y.: What the girls have done . . . they ran up to the soldiers. There was kissing. There was kissing and they go away with

> them, with the soldiers ... Then, then it was very bad because the soldiers were without women for maybe four years. And the girls gave them a chance, they run, they kissed ... Then the boys come at the night, the Russians. When they catch a girl by the food, they rape her ... how you say? Rape her, yes. The screaming was something terrible.[30]

Indeed, she even asks herself (including the interviewer) if she could state the assault directly with "how you say?" after she has already used the word "rape." And then answers more directly.

Shoshana G. uses frank and direct language.

> Shoshana G.: During the night they went to the camp and they raped the girls.[31]

Shoshana G. stops, pauses, and looks directly at the interviewer (who is off camera) for several seconds. The effect is to create a space for the seriousness of Shoshana G.'s intent to emerge. She then adds:

> Shoshana G.: It was such a terrible thing. They are not human beings. They knew that they are Jewish girls. And that's what they did.[32]

A few of the survivors ventured out into public space, where they negotiated with Russian soldiers, Jewish officers in the Soviet army, or local Czechs for protection. The strategy of identifying a male protector is common in settings of sexualized violence. Atina Grossmann, in her path-breaking study of German women (Jewish and non-Jewish) responding to the sexual assaults of Soviet soldiers, uses the story of Marta Hillers to document the choices women made—or were forced to make—regarding access to their bodies in the postwar years.[33] Hillers wrote her memoir, *A Woman in Berlin*, after the war anonymously to allow for a graphic, frank portrayal of how sexual negotiation emerges as a method of coping with constant rape. Grossmann's work carefully presents the historical reality that women cope with the threat of sexual violence in a range of ways, mediated by the social and cultural context in which they find themselves. They must take into account their resources, what shelter they will or will not have after the assault, their future possibility for making a family, their physical pain and ability to travel or work afterward, how their response positions them for either future assaults or protects them against more, and even their privilege and status.

Early scholarship on sexual violence in wartime interprets sexual assault as an extension of warfare itself. In this material, soldiers are the predators, impelled by revenge, ethnic hatred, male bonding, or the desire to wreak havoc. However, there was no mistaking that the Jewish girls and women in these barracks were prisoners of the Nazi system rather than perpetrators. The sexual assault they faced was a result of an absence of protection rather than a presence of warfare. Their experiences reinforce insights from more recent scholarship that foreground the structural vulnerability created by persecutory systems such as the camps.[34] When there are no consequences for exploiting a person's bodily integrity, rape and other forms of bodily abuse will occur, and this heightened vulnerability shapes choices. In May 1945 it was up to the girls and women themselves to identify a protector or protect themselves, in a few cases bartering access to their bodies.

> Lena M.: Some girls went to town and promised them, if they come back, they will have sex with them, whatever.[35]

Sexual barter is frequent in conflict and post-conflict settings; its function in the Holocaust in particular is being taken up by scholars more systematically since the publication of Anna Hájková's important article on the topic in 2013.[36] Barter itself is not determinative of a coercive relationship or sexualized violence, because physical desire and the need for bartered objects or services can coexist with coercive elements in a sexual interaction. Furthermore, whether the promise is fulfilled, postponed, or evaded must also be taken into account in assessing the degree of coercion at play. And Debórah Dwork has recently offered a rereading of male children's camp lives in light of their own use of their bodies as sexual currency, a barter that included violence but also emotional attachment.[37] As Marion Kaplan has written, if a sexual transaction is indeed a choice, how are we to understand that choice?[38] What conditions matter in such a choice?

Most of the testimony excerpts presented here treat the Soviet soldiers without individual specificity, as an undifferentiated group. Some survivors did make distinctions. The most prevalent was the identification of a Jewish officer or Jewish soldiers who delivered warnings that soldiers would attempt to assault them. At times testimony-givers remember running across a Jewish officer who then protects them from the soldiers. The girls and women identified themselves as Jewish by shouting out some Yiddish words.

> Chana B.: Girls find a few Jewish Russian men. From them we was not so afraid.[39]

In an extended anecdote, Lydia B. develops this theme of a Jewish protector in her story of liberation. Born in a border town in Transylvania, Lydia was sent with her family to Auschwitz in 1944 and then assigned to the Telefunken factory in Reichenbach, Germany. In early 1945 she was transferred first to Parschnitz and then to nearby Kratzau (in Czech, Chrastava), also part of the Gross-Rosen subcamp system. Lydia B.'s story begins in May 1945 when the camp guards have disappeared. The Gentile Czech coworkers informed the Jewish laborers that the Soviet army was approaching to officially liberate the camp, and a group of Jewish young women (Lydia B. was eighteen at this time) decided to wander out beyond the camp. Although Lydia B.'s experience was over sixty miles away from Parschnitz, Ober Altstadt, Gabersdorf, or Schatzlar/Bernsdorf, her testimony is one of the few that lingers on specific interactions with Soviet soldiers. The absence of authority in the days between the departure of German speakers and ss authorities, the lack of a death march, and the interaction with civilians echo conditions at liberation in the Trautenau-region camps.

> Lydia B.: We went out to the road and, uh, Russian army came in . . . It stopped. And one guy said, "I'm Jewish. Are you Jewish?" I said, "Ya!" He said, "What are you doing here?" And in short we told him what has happened to us. He said—and I was there with my two cousins and that other girl, this Lola—and he said, "Come to, we are going to break open to a field where we have to rest the horses. And you will tell us all about it." Stupid us, I mean, we didn't know to be afraid of our liberators or what![40]

She continues, noting the elements of joy and freedom in the setting and seems struck by the casualness with which the soldiers ignore the constrictions of the landscape.

> Lydia B.: We walked along and soon there was a big, beautiful orchard. And they just broke down the fences and went in and let out the horses. For pasture. It was May already.⁴¹

Lydia B. then presents in specific detail the transformation of the Jewish soldiers into protectors.

> Lydia B.: And there was a young officer that—I don't know—he laid an eye on me. I was very thin and very young, whatever. And he came. And I remember he brought a long salami. A thin one. He took his, his foot and broke it over his knee [*smiling*] and started giving us pieces of salami. And then he came and brought a scarf. And we were sitting with those men, telling them our life story and he threw it in my lap. And you know something? There is an instinct that a girl, a woman feels that there is something dangerous going on. And the Jewish man saw that we are getting in trouble. He said, he asked us in Jewish, if there are girls where you can spend the night with. My cousin [protested] ... And he said, "Meydlekh, girls, leave!" And we got up ... Like Lot was told, never look back! We never looked back.⁴²

In this excerpt from Lydia B.'s testimony she allows herself to develop the sense of place and time carefully, bringing forward the picnic-like setting of young people casually sitting in a meadow. She gradually introduces her sense of danger using evocative imagery centering on objects being exchanged. The identification of the men as Jewish comes and goes: a Jewish soldier led her group to the meadow, an unnamed soldier gives her sausage, and then the "Jewish man" intervenes. As she remembers it, her decision to accept the interpretation of the Jewish man, communicated in Yiddish—possibly to avoid provoking the non-Jewish soldiers in the party—allows her group to find a way out.

In contrast to Lydia B.'s story, Tola G. offers a memory in which she crossed language, religious, and gender barriers in an extraordinary act of insight and courage, communicated by her in understated and fragmented language. She also remembers the Soviet soldier as an individual with an emotional inner life, although he goes unnamed. In this anecdote, Tola G. and most of the other young women in her barrack are asleep in their bunk beds during the week of liberation. In the middle of the night, they are awakened by a large drunken Soviet soldier in the middle of the crowded room, standing on an empty lower bunk and demanding access to the bodies of the girls and women. One of Tola G.'s barrack mates used Polish in an attempt to urge her to leave and find help. The Soviet soldier understands the request and is deeply angered.

> Tola G.: And he got down from that, these bunk beds and he pulled out his gun . . . He's going to shoot her! "She's going to report me—your liberator! To the Germans you are giving and to us you don't want to!" You know, they, he wants sex. And he was screaming so that his saliva was coming out. He was so angry. He was maneuvering with his body, with his hands, screaming.[43]

Tola G. then sees that the soldier has a wound on his hand that is bleeding.

> Tola G.: On our little stove, which we hardly used—we were staying—we were getting ready to move on. So we prepared—somehow we had got some gauze. A piece of gauze was laying there and water in the—in jars, because water we drank, you know. And he must have been wounded. When he started to shake his body and his hands moved around I saw that blood is coming through his band-aid. And I don't know what got into me, I swear to you. I know that I was so scared of him, like anything. And I was still on the floor. I had no place to go . . . And I took that band-aid, you know, and I un-band-aided his hand and I wiped his bl—, the blood off and put the fresh band-aid on him. And he screams. He doesn't even know what I am doing. And suddenly he took a look. And he says to me in Russian, "What are you doing?" And I said, "You were bleeding. See?" I showed him that band-aid, the dirty one. It was soaking black with blood. And you know, and he said, "Oh." And he said, "I don't mean to harm you. I really don't. I just want to sleep." So I said, "Come on, I show you where to sleep." And I go to the door and showed him. "See there? The first room is completely empty." . . . I want you to know that soon, he just picked himself up and left the room. And right away we built barricades. Whatever was in our room was against the door.[44]

Tola G.'s fragmented approach to giving testimony in English actually helps capture the instability of the situation she found herself in. It allows her space to fill in details that help us understand how such a thing could occur. The phrase, "And he said, 'Oh,'" works to allow for a shift in mood and tone. In this way Tola G. allows herself to remember a frightening scenario, contain it, and then acknowledge her own ability to recognize a wounded person in spite of that person's monstrous behavior.

Pleasure and desire also coexisted with the fear of rape. Often this "desire" took the form of a generalized wish to appear as feminine, to acquire adornments for the body, or to simply assert oneself in taking things. Several girls and women left the barracks when they realized the guards had fled, to loot or to just look through the empty German-owned shops for items to acquire. Some went into the recently abandoned homes of the German-speaking population, often justified in the survivor's testimony as a search for much-needed food and clothing. As was the case in describing rape, the survivors at times removed themselves from the actions of the others, saying that both "everyone was looting," "the whole *Lager*," but not the speaker. At times this activity was intertwined with sexualized interactions with Soviet soldiers.

> Suzan L.: We looked around and it turned out Agnes and my cousin Theresa didn't have really proper boots. And I said, "Then we have to get boots!" So we walked to the village. This [was] a small town, this Trutnov [Trautenau]. I never figured out how big it is, but it is a small town. And so we were not very far, as it turned out, from the middle of the town where the stores were. And of course, like many places people broke in the windows. And they broke in the front door to the stores. It was, it looked pretty bad.[45]

> Mania S.: And the day they [the Soviet army] came in, they liberated us. So everybody was on the run. Going into the town and looting. All the girls. The stores, you know. Looting.[46]

> Ida G.: Some of them [the townspeople] were afraid. They closed their doors on us. There was a lot of plundering going around, too... And the soldiers and the girls and people all around and other people, were plundering.[47]

Shoshana L.: A lot of girls went to loot. Looting in the city. Because we never went out from the camp. That was the first time we went out.[48]

Elizabet B.: [quoting the Soviets at liberation] "Today in the evening you are free and you can do whatever you want. If you want to go and to rob the German houses, you are free. You can take anything you want from the German houses. You can do everything. But it stops tomorrow. Tomorrow starts the quarantine. And then you can go home." And the whole *Lager*—I told you before, I don't remember the numbers, if there were two hundred, four hundred, a hundred and fifty, I don't remember—went to rob or to visit German houses, I don't know.[49]

Fanny W.: And then we were looting! We broke into stores. We had to have to eat, to drink, clothes.[50]

Rena M.: And then the women who had more strength, or some of them, they went to town, to Trautenau, and I understand they smashed all the windows, storefronts, and were—what do you call it? Taking merchandise.[51]

Hedy W.: In the morning we went to rob the German houses. We went for food. We went for clothes. What was interesting for us, only food and clothes.[52]

Hedy W.: [later in her testimony] We went robbing. For food and clothes.[53]

The experience of breaking into spaces that had previously been forbidden was heady and seemed as pleasurable as the items behind the glass. As Hedy W. puts it, access to food and clothes was significant but the impulse to go "robbing" was powerful. Her words are also a reminder that many of those liberated were still teenagers in 1945. Hedy W. was eighteen at the time and remembers one episode vividly:

Hedy W.: There was an elderly woman in one house where we were especially. She was very upset that we took everything. She said to me, "Leave something for us for when my family comes back."

I said, "I go home. I don't know where is my family. You killed my family. Why should I leave you [anything]?" I was very nasty to her. I said, "You don't deserve to live! I go home, I have nobody. And I won't have food at home. Do I care what you have to eat?" We were so nasty. We were nasty! She deserved it.[54]

Phyllis Y.'s testimony attests to the different ways that the time of liberation was experienced and remembered. In her narrative, she reconfigures the priorities of fear of rape and desire, in that she remembers first and foremost the celebratory atmosphere. She recalls the joyfulness of the social interaction and recalls the camp being transformed into a space of sociability. She is challenged, however, by an interviewer who seeks to redirect her answers away from pleasure. The interviewer herself seems to realize she is being overly directive and rephrases her first question.

> Phyllis Y.: The Russians brought in a lot of food and booze, you know. They were known for that. And the girls were having a ball. A party![55]
> Interviewer: Did they mistreat the prisoners in any way? Or, how did they treat the prisoners?
> Phyllis Y.: Which prisoners?
> Interviewer: Well, the former prisoners.
> Phyllis Y.: Oh, you mean us girls? Oh no, they were very good to us.
> Interviewer: Were you afraid of them?
> Phyllis Y.: Yeah. Because they had a reputation. Of rape.
> Interviewer: Did they—
> Phyllis Y.: Yeah. A couple of, there were a couple of incidents.

Even with the interviewer's guidance, Phyllis Y. resists allowing the assaults to displace the pleasure she remembers.

Yetta P. remembers intentionally enjoying the transformation of a space of persecution into a space for enjoyment.

> Yetta P.: In the camp where we were liberated by the Russians, we were afraid to go out. But then we heard the Russians are playing on—what do you call this, you know—they had an orchestra playing. And singing and dancing. And this was the hall where the Germans used to have their meetings. We used to look there

[during their internment], you know, they have food and beer and drinking . . . And we went there to hear the music . . .⁵⁶

She then speaks of being followed by soldiers carrying rifles and her fears of sexual assault.

> Shoshana L.: [speaking about the Soviet soldiers] They start to sing songs, you know, and they start to share with us whatever they had—vodka.⁵⁷

These short excerpts indicate that not all Soviet soldiers committed rape and that rape was not the only thing they did. The extensive scholarship on rape in wartime continues to grow as historians and social scientists research the function of sexualized violence in the context of political goals, social expectations of wartime entitlement, and categories of civilians constructed to justify such violence.⁵⁸ With regard to the Soviet army in 1945 in particular, Oleg Budnitskii presents the varying reactions of Soviet Jewish officers who wrote about their wartime experiences of the sexual assaults they observed and the sexual interactions they engaged in.⁵⁹ His work documents the interwoven landscape of civilian survivors and wartime strategies of occupation, such that German women specifically "were beings of a lower order, the spoils of war."⁶⁰

Vojin Majstorović also uses individual experiences as well as official documents to explore how the impact of encountering the Holocaust on the ground challenged Soviet Jewish soldiers to reconsider their ethnic identities (and worry for their families), but did not necessarily change their view of who they were entitled to assault sexually or otherwise.⁶¹ Regina Mühlhäuser's research on German military commanders' understanding of the likelihood of rape by regular soldiers in their approach to the war is particularly helpful, in that she points out that their explicit removal of consequences for sexual assault in effect permitted it.⁶² In her words, rape occurs when a space and practice of "impunity" is created.⁶³ It is precisely this absence of consequences and authority that the testimony-givers recall most sharply:

> Shoshana L.: We been left alone. . . . been left at the mercy of God again.⁶⁴

Testimony-givers remember having to decide whether to stay in the barracks, the local area, or to travel. The Soviet authorities announced a quarantine in most of the Trautenau-region camps to contain typhus but looked the other way as some survivors ignored the rules. Some stayed at the barracks for quite some time, especially if they had a sister or friend who could not travel because of illness. Some left immediately, on foot or improvising transport. Soviet army officials, Czech individuals, and even the factory owners created new systems to provide food and medical care, but only some survivors remember being positioned to access these systems. None remembers the type of postwar Jewish communal aid organizations prevalent in Poland in the immediate postwar period.

> Shoshana L.: We were left alone. With no money. With no supervision. With no help. With no doctors. No one, no one cares for us. We just said, we want to get out.[65]
>
> Anna O.: We didn't know what to do! Nobody was there to look after us.[66]
>
> Gerda F.: We are free. Free to do what? To go where? And with whom? No education, no parents, no family, no home, no money. No country that wants us. What do we do?[67]

The journeys to either their prewar homes, to nearby camps where sisters or brothers had been imprisoned, or to displaced persons camps were also precarious and insecure. Esther L. and her sisters made the most of the sexual interest of soldiers by hitching rides with one Soviet military vehicle, jumping off, and then finding another:

> Esther L.: And there were the Russians. We were occupied by Russia. And the military Russians were very, very bad to the young girls. They wanted to make love to us. They wanted us, to take us on their bus . . . They were always pointing at me . . . So we have to jumping from one bus to the other one.[68]
>
> Anna O.: [speaking of her journey home] Every day was taken up trying to find a place where we felt safe to go to sleep because of the Russian soldiers.[69]

Berta P. has a different story because she escaped her imprisonment in spring 1945. Berta P. was part of a group of Jewish girls and women who were shunted from work site to work site in the wider region. After assignment to Ober Altstadt, she was transferred to a camp that was evacuated westward on foot. During one long march through a village she saw others escaping, running through the forest nearby. She also fled, encountered Gentile German local residents evacuating (for fear of Soviet soldiers), and "mixed in between" them.[70] She recalls several days of improvisation, pretending, and simply being uncertain and disoriented. Then Berta P. encountered a Gentile Pole riding a horse and she presented herself as a Gentile Polish escapee from a camp. He helped her by identifying a German family nearby who would give her refuge. When the family fled as the Soviet army approached, Berta P. had to hide until the soldiers passed through for fear of being taken for a German civilian. In her view, "I would say that I liberated myself."[71]

Almost all of the testimony-givers remember that period as one in which they still held onto their dreams of finding family members and "going home."

> Minnie W.: So now I knew that I left my, my home. My parents, my mother, my father, meyn, meyn everybody, my brothers, my sisters. I have to go home. Probably everybody's at home . . . They're probably waiting for me.[72]
>
> Shoshana I.: We thought there would be someone waiting for us, waiting for us. Well, we hoped so.[73]

For the "Polish girls," the attachment to this hope pushed most to undertake the arduous journeys back to the Zagłębie region. The "Hungarian girls" knew that the Nazi officials at Auschwitz had murdered their immediate families; still, some did hope that relatives who had not been traveling with their family group on the deportation trains may have survived, and so also undertook journeys to their small towns or to Budapest. Helen F. had spent her years in the Ober Altstadt work camp "praying" that she would see her family again. Born in Radom in 1921, she was one of the workers who ended up in the Trautenau region after first being sent to Auschwitz. She returned to Radom, went to her home, and knocked. "I was ready to greet my family!"[74] The Gentile Polish man who had taken the house slammed the door.[75]

> Ida G.: And we all came in and got off the train and, and the first thing I remember is, I say to myself, I was, I wanted to shout, I say, "Look! I made it! I came home! I'm here!" I looked around the people and I just wanted to shout. But immediately we started, a lot of, with tears in our eyes, we came off the train and we started walking. Home . . . [The occupant of her apartment told her] "You don't belong here!" I said, "You are in my apartment." She says, "It's not your apartment."[76]

> Rose K.: [when returning to her family home] I was told to get away.[77]

> Esther L.: And we came to Poland. We don't find nothing. In our homes. Nothing was left. There were, other people were living there.[78]

> Yetta P.: We went home. And we came to the town where we lived. We came to the apartment house where we lived. Every window was broken. And our bakery, all the bricks were taken out because the Poles thought we hid money there.[79]

> Eva K.: It wasn't a happy ending. Not to find anyone alive.[80]

There is growing scholarly literature on the phenomenon of Jewish encounters with Gentiles living in their homes or with Gentile neighbors after the war.[81] Anna Cichopek-Gajraj calls the encounter "no home," stating that there "was nothing familiar in the physical or social landscape of postwar Eastern Europe."[82] However, for the specific case of the testimony-givers from Zagłębie, the journey homeward was significant in their remembered processes of dismantling the fantasies of family survival that they had relied on throughout their persecution. In the testimonies, the trip to the childhood apartment or house takes on a ritualistic tone, almost as if it is necessary to finally address grief.

> Rose K.: When I came [to Sosnowiec] I was hoping—that I go home. That my parents—I couldn't think that they are no more there. And I got very sick, emotionally sick.[83]

VIOLENCE AND LOSSES OF LIBERATION

The confrontation with the non-Jews who had taken their childhood homes brought sustaining hopes to an abrupt end. First, the association of the home itself with parents was powerful. To see others—sometimes strangers, sometimes former neighbors—in the intimate rooms of so many holiday gatherings and family interactions felt like a violation. Second, as Ida G. communicates, the arrival at the threshold was a statement in itself: "I made it!" There was a desire to have that survival and all the losses that it entailed acknowledged. Many survivors remembered the exact interactions and words of refusal. Finally, the rejection represented by the shutting doors and being "told to get away" was the final rupture of the fantasy that something from their childhood could be recuperated—if not a parent, then the furniture, carpets, pictures, and objects associated with the parent.

Fay B.'s memory of her journey back to Sosnowiec in 1945 reminds us that these girls and young women lost their parents at the specific time in their lives when they were still financially and emotionally dependent but old enough to have had experiences of going to the store or traveling to a relative's home on their own. They held on to the imagery and associations of this moment of separation. As Fay B. recalls her experience, the disillusionment and fragmentation created by the confrontation with what had actually occurred is palpable:

> Fay B.: After liberation I thought my parents would be waiting for me.[84]

She traveled with friends from the camp back to Sosnowiec. Fay B. remembers that she had it firmly fixed in her mind that not only would her parents be alive, but that they would be at the Sosnowiec train station when she arrived, a belief that speaks to how powerfully it was needed. The platform was empty.

> Fay B.: I screamed. I screamed and I looked and I screamed. "Where is everybody?!!"[85]

Her travel mates temporarily calmed her. But as the group rushed down the city streets to see their homes, they were shocked at the emptiness of the cityscape.

> Fay B.: Slowly, the people came out. I go into my own house.
> I look at the people. "Your mother said you would come back."

245

> They have hate-filled faces. I go to my mother's room. The pictures are still on the wall. "Let the ground open and let me go in. Everybody is dead. Everybody is burnt."[86]

The response documented in this particular Shoah Foundation collection of testimonies was overwhelmingly to travel to one of the displaced persons camps the United States had established inside Germany near the prewar border with Poland, because testimony-gathering practices of the Shoah Foundation were strongest in the United States, Israel, Canada, and Australia. In other words, the survivors who chose to stay in Poland or Germany or even in the Trautenau region are not well represented in these sources. The displaced persons camps offered shelter, food, medical care, job training, and a system for finding possible family members who may have survived. Many survivors quickly identified a life partner, married, and started the process of migration, although, as many historians have shown, this process was itself complicated by the difficult processes of reestablishing one's social identity without access to familiar lifeways of home, school, and family.[87] Once in a new country, they sustained contact with their previous "camp sisters" and even had reunions, a phenomenon especially prevalent in Israel. Giving testimony to the Shoah Foundation or in other settings was for many the first time they revisited their coerced labor experience in all of its dimensions.

In sum, engagement with the testimony of survivors from the Trautenau region's camps available in the Shoah Foundation collection supports a view of "liberation" that is contextually bounded by increased vulnerability to sexual assault once the SS and local Sudeten Germans fled, new possibilities for pleasure in the vacuum of lawlessness, and the need to travel to one's childhood home as part of the process of grieving, a process that cannot be said to have been completed at the time of the testimony-giving. As survivors explained their journeys homeward, the importance of the belief that one's compliance was sustaining family is put into sharp relief. The glimpses of family furniture, the empty roads, and the doors slammed shut were experienced not as a strange new landscape but as the loss of any remaining continuity with the prewar Jewish world.

> Ann F.: We were happy and we were sad. We didn't know where we were going, what our home will be, and really, what to do. We were stripped.[88]

CHAPTER 9

Conclusion and Coda

Interviewer: Tell me, does, does the past ever interfere with your life today?
Fryda F.: Every single minute.

After the first week of May 1945, a few of the young women stayed on in Trautenau, now called Trutnov, part of postwar Czechoslovakia. Some were waiting for sisters or friends to gain enough strength for the journey home. There was no organized transportation for the survivors; although they could board trains at no cost, train schedules were erratic and many rail facilities had been damaged. The factories resumed operation for the summer months of 1945. The barracks in Ober Altstadt became a detention center for German speakers suspected of collaboration with the Nazi regime.[1] In mid-May the Czechoslovakian National Committee took over local government in Trutnov and created laws to compel all "Reich Germans" to leave. Sudeten Germans did not have to emigrate, but the Czechoslovakian government refused to protect them from violence and they were subject to local court proceedings.[2] Many German-speaking Trutnov residents were physically attacked and compelled to perform forced labor for some months after the end of the war.[3] Early scholarship on this period focused either on the ethnic German flight from the Soviet zone of occupation generally and Czechoslovakia specifically, or on the abuses suffered by German speakers, and the impact of these "expellees" on politics in West Germany or Austria.[4] The general understanding was that Czech partisans, the new government, and unruly mobs simply ethnically cleansed the Sudetenland region of Germans.

Recent work has documented a more nuanced, mixed picture. Stefan Wolff notes that "for Poland and Czechoslovakia [the continued presence of local Germans] was essential to guarantee the continued functioning of their economies. Germans had not only owned a number of factories, mines, etc., but they were also needed as specialists to oversee the proper running of these enterprises."[5] The need to restart industrial production and employment was complicated by the Czechoslovakian government's own nationalization priorities.[6] This need explains the Haase account books that continued to record incoming and outgoing sums, but in Czech rather than German beginning in June 1945.[7] The continuing presence of the German owners and the ongoing activity of the factories add another dimension to our understanding of the specific local context of Northern Bohemia or what some scholars call "the borderlands" in the 1940s.[8]

What of the factory owners themselves? Haase and his family relocated to West Germany or Austria. A son became a well-known photographer and activist for the Sudeten German cause. Kluge's family also became activists for the Sudeten Germans in West Germany. Etrich's company had diversified into airplane parts before the war; Igo Etrich was an amateur aviator and innovator in flying and continued this vocation in postwar Austria. The Trutnov city museum celebrated the Etrich family's contributions to local history in the 2000s with only passing mention of the family's coerced labor camps.[9] It is unclear where the Walzel brothers and their families migrated to.[10] The larger companies that purchased Jewish labor in Trautenau such as Siemens and AEG garnered much more attention after the war. Today in the Trutnov region are several small monuments to the coerced labor and concentration camp victims, increasing academic and public interest in the topic, and periodic exhibitions by local museums addressing this local history.[11]

Many of the Jewish girls and women whose work had enriched Haase, Kluge, Etrich, and Walzel found their way to displaced persons camps in the American zone. More accurately, the Shoah Foundation Visual History collection is overrepresented by survivors who traveled first to displaced persons camps in the US zone and then chose to emigrate to Israel, Canada, Australia, or the United States. These émigrés are the voices heard in this book. The number who stayed in Trutnov (Trautenau), Zagłębie, or Budapest after the war or migrated to Great Britain are not notably present in this particular archive (with some exceptions), although their experiences were captured by Jewish historical commissions who sought them out in the early postwar years and then again by the renewed efforts by German prosecutors to bring legal action against perpetrators in the 1960s and 1970s. Their written testimonies are plentiful in the Yad Vashem archives and the Wiener Library, along with do-

CONCLUSION AND CODA

nated objects, photos, and diaries, some of which were used in this book. Several married local Gentile Czech men after the war and remained in Trutnov.[12] Their stories are still waiting to be told.

One example of a survivor who did not partake in the Shoah Foundation archive is Edith S., the nineteen-year-old mentioned in chapter 7 who was assigned to work for the Barthel firm (owned by Kluge) in Gabersdorf and who married a prisoner of war she met during the period she was in coerced labor. She was interviewed in England in 1955 through a British-Jewish initiative.[13] Her words are available in a typed transcript rather than a video. The documentation she offers parallels that of the Shoah Foundation testimony-givers in many ways, in that she explains the amount of food given, the conditions of the barracks, the nature of the work she was forced to perform, and the help given by the prisoners of war. She explains that she began a romantic relationship with the prisoner of war she would marry after the war, furtively meeting and exchanging letters. Edith S. also offers a compelling anecdote in which she describes the discovery by the ss of her letters in her future husband's belongings. The camp guards locked her in a cellar without access to food. It was only when the prisoner of war was able to arrange a bribe that she was released. Because of the skillful notetaking by the interviewing staff—the techniques of testimony-giving practice—the reader is able to receive this story of survival and intimacy in the camp in its detailed and vivid imagery.

Similarly, the Jewish Historical Institute in Poland collected a self-authored witness document from Nache B. in Poland in 1945, which she had developed as part of a prosecution of guards and other perpetrators at the Parschnitz camp.[14] Also hand-typed, in this document Nache B. lists twenty-eight staff members and thirty-two Gentile coworkers, accusing the former of cruelty and the latter of "disloyalty." Among the accused are the familiar names of Ritterbusch and Hawlik, but also of two foremen and a number of workplace supervisors. While Edith S.'s 1955 interview transcript aligns with the shared experience of the camp survivors giving testimony through the Shoah Foundation, Nache B.'s is quite different. The document gives no indication of relationships or even transactions with coworkers, foremen, or *Lagerführerinnen*; instead, in her 1945 recollection, Gentile coworkers positioned the Jewish laborers as individuals to be degraded and intentionally overworked. Supervisors placed the girls and women at machines that they could not master to expose them to punishment. Regarding Haase himself, who the Shoah testimony-givers placed at a distance from the persecution, Bochenek writes:

> We charge the boss of the Aloys [sic] Haase company to have taken advantage of us to the last. He watched indifferently as the Jewish forced laborers had to work barefoot and in extremely poor clothing without work aprons in the hot fine-spinning room on stone tiles. The result of this is 50 percent TB. Even the smallest investment in the camp was too much for him.

Nache B. was able to convey details that precisely document violations on the factory floor but also deliver a structural critique of the owner's approach to his own factors of production.

The juxtaposition of this 1945 witness account prepared for a legal process with the Shoah Foundation materials prepared to create a record for family as well as the public highlights the mediated nature of testimony-giving. Both can be constructed to incite evidence of atrocities or instances of compassion; both are forms of truth-telling. In terms of this book's reconstruction of the coerced labor experience for the Jewish girls and women of Zagłębie, the juxtaposition also creates an opening to note that no single person's testimony is exemplary, a standard-bearer of clarity, authenticity, and completeness. This book did not seek out the definitive survivor story of the Schmelt organization and the Gross-Rosen subcamp system. Instead, it highlighted how a coerced labor circuit embedded in a specific local context generated a specific range of coping strategies and responses among the Jews it targeted, and that these responses were deeply inflected by the gender and age of the participants. In doing so, it presented coerced labor sites (and the concentration camps into which they evolved) as characterized by a social life, in which relations among Jewish girls and women were distorted by the actions of perpetrators but in which Jews could also carve out space for pride, exchange, care, longing, desire, and humor.

Relatedly, this book has not highlighted instances of what might be called "human failing" on the part of survivors, an absence that may also be a result of the nature of the testimony practices of the Shoah Foundation, curated for family and the wider public. Scholars of the Holocaust know well that there were individuals who abandoned loved ones, collaborated with perpetrators, betrayed campmates for the smallest piece of food, and committed murder themselves. These actions must have existed among the Jewish girls and women of Zagłębie. In fact, survivors discuss observing this behavior in others. But as Felicja Karay has shown in her analysis of the Skarżysko-Kamienna camp, individual choices and patterns of behavior during the Holocaust were deeply affected by the conditions of food scarcity and prevalence of arbitrary violence, even at a so-called coerced labor camp with a strong civilian presence.[15] What the Shoah Foundation interviews provide is the opportunity for testimony-givers to explore the perpetrator-designed context of difficult choices at length and with nuance.

For example, Gerda F., working for Etrich at Ober Altstadt, remembers an incident that occurred after a young Jewish woman escaped (possibly Regina Hoffmann), likely in cooperation with one or more Gentile Czechs in the region. Gerda F. offers no specifics in her testimony regarding the identity or circumstances of the escapee. As was the case in other sites of detention under the Nazis, escapes were treated as one of the most serious offenses. At the time of this event, an ss officer at Ober Altstadt assembled all of the Jewish girls and women and told them that he would shoot, one by one, a select group of ten of them until someone shared information about this escape. Gerda F. was among the ten. She remembers her extreme fear and awareness that death was near. Eventually the *Lagerführerin* arrived and spoke with the officer. He released the hundreds of assembled girls and women back to their barracks with the exception of the ten selected. Once the yard was empty, he wielded his weapon and told the ten that they had only a few moments to run into their barracks before he would start shooting.

> Gerda F.: And we start running on that ice and on that snow and trying to get on the stairs on that barrack. And pushing in through that narrow door. You only think of yourself. I want to live. Not my friend [*begins to cry*], not the girl behind me or in front of me. I want to be through that door and save my life. Something you'd never do in normal circumstances. What I'm trying to say is, this is the way they dehumanized us. That we didn't care about our fellow prisoners.[16]

Gerda F. had remembered previously developing a friendship with a prisoner of war and risking her life to smuggle cigarettes he left her to barter for medicine, saving her friend. Yet in this fragment she remembers an altogether different response. The imagery of the girls pushing through the door communicates that more is going on than "you only think of yourself." Instead, the camp inmates push others out of the way. As Gerda F. puts it, "We didn't care about our fellow prisoners."

Gerda F. is distressed throughout the telling of the anecdote. The SS officer's act was intended to disrupt her sense of self in relation to others, and she seems to still feel this disruption, palpably, at the time of testimony-giving. At the same time, through her testimony she assertively locates the source of her behavior in factors outside of herself. These actions were the result of Nazi tactics of dehumanization, driving individuals to do things they would "never do in normal circumstances." The SS officer drew on the precise combination of predictable regulation and violent impulsivity to throw the camp's social world off-balance. This sense of how disorienting, traumatizing, and confusing the coerced labor experience was for Jewish girls and women is something we can only get by listening to (and watching) these survivors; they are the ones who show us how camp systems could be so multidimensionally exploitive and yet how people trapped in them could create spaces of care, connection, pride, and small moments of recovery from terror.

In his introduction to a collected volume on the Holocaust in the annexed territories, Peter Longerich writes that a focus on the peripheral, atypical territories of Nazi domination—meaning areas such as Zagłębie and the Eastern Strip—demonstrates the complex interplay among the strategies of local perpetrators such as Schmelt, the pragmatics of labor policy, and ideological antisemitism.[17] For Longerich, any one of these factors cannot be viewed in isolation from the other. The Nazi goals of destroying Jewish life and of crushing any capacity for sustaining a continuity with the Jewish past were ever-present, even if they appeared to be at arm's length in the rational, technical world of the textile factory in which producing for the war effort was seemingly the highest value. Indeed, this interplay is exactly what was at work in Gerda's anecdote: the ability of the *Lagerführerin* to negotiate with the SS officer, technically her superior, which speaks to the importance of informal relationships and local context; the constant push to work, such that even the infraction of a campmate's escape is not allowed to interfere with the bodies needed for the next shift; and the prerogative of the ss officer to terrorize the assembled girls and women, simply because they were Jewish.

The testimony-givers centered in this book have also given us the crucial insight that the Nazi project affected the young, unmarried girls and women trapped in coerced labor in very specific ways. From the first days of the occupation, their understanding of family and authority, and their reference points for their own identities and futures, were challenged. In their testimonies, these survivors refused to participate in any illusion that their coping strategies, while often innovative and life-giving, were enough to repair the deep ruptures of family separation, suffering, and death created by the Nazi regime. A hidden diary, a furtive prayer, a collection of photographs saved by a Gentile coworker—these practices, while remarkable and nourishing, did not add up to a reconstituted Jewish world. Thus, the testimonies here offer a window into significant aspects of the coerced labor experience in the Holocaust, but the speakers do not promise a full accounting. In the words of Sala K., discussing how much detail to share after describing being beaten by the *Lagerführerin*:

> Sala K.: I could go on like that for a whole year. If I would go into every little thing that happened. But so much I can't talk about. There's some things I won't talk about. It's very difficult. Too—even more difficult than that [the beating]. And there's no, there's no other way I can do it. Really, no other way.[18]

LIST OF TESTIMONY-GIVERS

Testimony references include archival information, place of interview, and date of the author's first access. The Shoah Foundation testimonies were digitally accessed at the United States Holocaust Memorial Museum and the Sheridan Library of the Johns Hopkins University.

Bart, Berta. Interviewed by Jan Smith, Sydney, Australia, 1995. Interview 1911. Visual History Archive, USC Shoah Foundation, Los Angeles, CA. Accessed July 3, 2021.

Batalion, Eta. Interviewed by Lorrie Fein, Brooklyn, New York, United States, 1996. Interview 12241. Visual History Archive, USC Shoah Foundation, Los Angeles, CA. Accessed June 2, 2021.

Baumgarten, Lusia. Interviewed by Mary Ziegler, Sydney, Australia, 1995. Interview 4606. Visual History Archive, USC Shoah Foundation, Los Angeles, CA. Accessed January 24, 2017.

Baumgold, Rose. Interviewed by Sidney Burke, Los Angeles, California, United States , 1995. Interview 469. Visual History Archive, USC Shoah Foundation, Los Angeles, CA. Accessed April 10, 2017.

Benedek, Elizabet. Interviewed by Nina Elazar-Wolff, Tel Aviv, Israel, 1997. Interview 37905. Visual History Archive, USC Shoah Foundation, Los Angeles, CA. Accessed October 3, 2016.

B., Fay. Interviewed by author. Hackensack, New Jersey, United States. February 10, 2018.

Bigayer, Regina. Interviewed by Susan Peirez, Bayside, New York, United States, 1998. Interview 43967. Visual History Archive, USC Shoah Foundation, Los Angeles, CA. Accessed June 27, 2021.

Birnholz, Sally. Interviewed by Maximilian Lerner, Brooklyn, New York, United States, 1995. Interview 1556. Visual History Archive, USC Shoah Foundation, Los Angeles, CA. Accessed October 3, 2016.

Bloch, Zuzi. Interviewed by Sally Alsher, Philadelphia, Pennsylvania, United States, 1997. Interview 33619. Visual History Archive, USC Shoah Foundation, Los Angeles, CA. Accessed July 3, 2021.

Brandys, Chana. Interviewed by Phyllis Dreazen, Skokie, Illinois, United States, 1996. Interview 14459. Visual History Archive, USC Shoah Foundation, Los Angeles, CA. Accessed October 5, 2016.

Brown, Lydia. Interviewed by Lenore Weinstein, North Miami Beach, Florida, United States, 1995. Interview 6335. Visual History Archive, USC Shoah Foundation, Los Angeles, CA. Accessed July 9, 2019.

Cecemski, Bella. Interviewed by Naomi Rappaport, Passaic, New Jersey, United States, 1996. Interview 13823. Visual History Archive, USC Shoah Foundation, Los Angeles, CA. Accessed October 3, 2016.

LIST OF TESTIMONY-GIVERS

Charman, Estelle. Interviewed by Dan Gelford, Buffalo Grove, Illinois, United States, 1998. Interview 42464. Visual History Archive, USC Shoah Foundation, Los Angeles, CA Accessed December 28, 2016.
Danziger, Ala. Interviewed by Roberta Berger, Dallas, Texas, United States, 1995. Interview 10606. Visual History Archive, USC Shoah Foundation, Los Angeles, CA. Accessed December 19, 2017.
David, Eva. Interviewed by Renée Firestone, Beverly Hills, California, United States, 1998. Interview 43340. Visual History Archive, USC Shoah Foundation, Los Angeles, CA. Accessed December 30, 2016.
Elerat, Erna. RG-50.120.0035. Oral History Interview with Erna Elerat by Nathan Beyrak, Israel, 1993. Jeff and Toby Herr Oral History Archive. United States Holocaust Memorial Museum Archives, Washington, DC. Accessed September 22, 2016.
Federman, Ann. Interviewed by Milton Katz and Sharon Hamil, Kansas City, Missouri, 1999. Midwest Center for Holocaust Education, Overland Park, KS. Accessed March 16, 2019.
Feldman, Frymeta. Interviewed by Burton Leiser, White Plains, New York, United States, 1997. Interview 29000. Visual History Archive, USC Shoah Foundation, Los Angeles, CA. Accessed May 2, 2017.
Fischer, Magda. Interviewed by Gay Wendy Belfer, Sydney, Australia, 1995. Interview 2468. Visual History Archive, USC Shoah Foundation, Los Angeles, CA. Accessed January 30, 2018.
Flancbaum, Yetta. Interviewed by Lenore Weinstein, North Miami Beach, Florida, United States, 1996. Interview 14940. Visual History Archive, USC Shoah Foundation, Los Angeles, CA. Accessed August 23, 2017.
Fleish, Fryda. Interviewed by Robert Feldman, Farmington Hills, Michigan, United States, 2008. Interview 55639. Visual History Archive, USC Shoah Foundation, Los Angeles, CA. Originally recorded by the Holocaust Memorial Center, Zekelman Family Campus, Farmington Hills, Michigan. Accessed July 3, 2021.
Fleischmann, Magda-Madeleine. Interviewed by Shelly Javasky, Toronto, Ontario, Canada, 1996. Interview 11359. Visual History Archive, USC Shoah Foundation, Los Angeles, CA. Accessed May 3, 2017.
Frank, Betti. RG-50.462.0059. Oral History Interview with Betti Frank by Sylvia Brockmon, Haifa, Israel, 1991. Jeff and Toby Herr Oral History Archive. United States Holocaust Memorial Museum Archives, Washington, DC. Accessed May 23, 2016.
Freeman, Helen. Interviewed by Mary Rothschild, Pasadena, California, United States, 1995. Interview 593. Visual History Archive, USC Shoah Foundation, Los Angeles, CA. Accessed March 9, 2022.
Frieberg, Gerda. Interviewed by Linda Ruth Davidson, Toronto, Ontario, Canada, 1996. Interview 13395. Visual History Archive, USC Shoah Foundation, Los Angeles, CA. Accessed January 24, 2017.
Gelbart, Ida. Interviewer and location unavailable, 1993. Interview 52326. Visual

LIST OF TESTIMONY-GIVERS

History Archive, USC Shoah Foundation, Los Angeles, CA. Originally recorded by the JFCS Holocaust Center, San Francisco, California. Accessed December 19, 2016.

Gilbert, Tola. Interviewed by Donna Miller, West Bloomfield, Michigan, United States, 1983. University of Michigan-Dearborn, Holocaust Survivor Oral History Archive, West Bloomfield, Michigan. Accessed August 7, 2017.

Ginsberg, Alice. Interviewed by Louise Bobrow, Brooklyn, New York, United States, 2000. Interview 51263. Visual History Archive, USC Shoah Foundation, Los Angeles, CA. Accessed January 3, 2016.

Gipsman, Fela. Interviewed by Merle Goldberg, Los Angeles, California, United States, 1994. Interview 159. Visual History Archive, USC Shoah Foundation, Los Angeles, CA. Accessed June 26, 2021.

Gitler, Regina. Interviewed by Chaim Rosov, Boca Raton, Florida, United States, 1995. Interview 8351. Visual History Archive, USC Shoah Foundation, Los Angeles, CA. Accessed January 5, 2016.

Gliksman, Regina. Interviewed by Caroline Kohn, Toronto, Ontario, Canada, 1994. Interview 169. Visual History Archive, USC Shoah Foundation, Los Angeles, CA. Accessed August 23, 2017. See also Silverstein, Regina, Interview 54317.

Goodman, Ann. Interviewed by Yana Katzap, Tarzana, California, United States, 1998. Interview 42187. Visual History Archive, USC Shoah Foundation, Los Angeles, CA. Accessed January 9, 2017.

Greenbaum, Shoshana. Interviewed by Ferne Hassan, Linden, New Jersey, United States, 1998. Interview 45508. Visual History Archive, USC Shoah Foundation, Los Angeles, CA. Accessed April 12, 2017.

Gross, Elaine. Interviewed by Janie Brown, Philadelphia, Pennsylvania, United States, 1996. Interview 18971. Visual History Archive, USC Shoah Foundation, Los Angeles, CA. Accessed August 23, 2017.

Haftarczyk, Helen. Interviewed by Michael Kuelker, Universal City, Missouri, United States, 1996. Interview 19227. Visual History Archive, USC Shoah Foundation, Los Angeles, CA. Accessed October 13, 2016.

Harari, Bracha. Interviewed by Lenore Weinstein, North Miami Beach, Florida, United States, 1997. Interview 29347. Visual History Archive, USC Shoah Foundation, Los Angeles, CA. Accessed January 6, 2017.

Hart, Eva. Interviewed by Gretta Rusanow, Sydney, Australia, 1995. Interview 4530. Visual History Archive, USC Shoah Foundation, Los Angeles, CA. Accessed January 5, 2017.

Hercz, Magdolna. Interviewed by Edie Kalb, Toronto, Ontario, Canada, 1995. Interview 2228. Visual History Archive, USC Shoah Foundation, Los Angeles, CA. Accessed December 20, 2016.

Hoyd, Frances. Interviewed by Allen Charney, Toronto, Ontario, Canada, 1996. Interview 13971. Visual History Archive, USC Shoah Foundation, Los Angeles, CA. Accessed October 13, 2016.

Jakubowitz, Ella. Interviewed by Rickey Halperin, Brooklyn, New York, United

States, 1995. Interview 8689. Visual History Archive, USC Shoah Foundation, Los Angeles, CA. Accessed January 12, 2017.

Jakubs-Schwartzbaum, Tosia. Interviewed by Arlene Adler, Boca Raton, Florida, United States, 1996. Interview 12418. Visual History Archive, USC Shoah Foundation, Los Angeles, CA. Accessed June 23, 2021.

Jankielewitz, Mina. Interviewed by Ann Page, Hallandale, Florida, United States, 1996. Interview 13325. Visual History Archive, USC Shoah Foundation, Los Angeles, CA. Accessed June 15, 2021.

Keen, Helena. Interviewed by Rona Arato, Toronto, Ontario, Canada, 1995. Interview 8516. Visual History Archive, USC Shoah Foundation, Los Angeles, CA. Accessed December 21, 2016.

Kirschner, Sala. Interviewed by Susie Grama, Monsey, New York, United States, 1997. Interview 33589. Visual History Archive, USC Shoah Foundation, Los Angeles, CA. Accessed July 3, 2021.

Klein, Esther. Interviewed by Naomi Rappaport, New York, New York, United States, 1996. Interview 13949. Visual History Archive, USC Shoah Foundation, Los Angeles, CA. Accessed August 22, 2016.

Klein, Rose. Interviewed by Risa Hochbaum Miron, Deerfield Beach, Florida, United States, 1996. Interview 12381. Visual History Archive, USC Shoah Foundation, Los Angeles, CA. Accessed August 22, 2016.

Koplowicz, Eva. Interviewer and location unavailable, 2007. Interview 55311. Visual History Archive, USC Shoah Foundation, Los Angeles, CA. Originally recorded by Jahsena: The Jewish Archives and Historical Society of Edmonton and Northern Alberta, Edmonton, Alberta, Canada. Accessed March 9, 2022.

Korn, Bella. Interviewed by Donna Puccini, Skokie, Illinois, United States, 1995. Interview 4153. Visual History Archive, USC Shoah Foundation, Los Angeles, CA. Accessed December 19, 2016.

Kovacs, Olga. Interviewed by Dorothy Shiloff Hughes, New York, New York, United States, 1995. Interview 3012. Visual History Archive, USC Shoah Foundation, Los Angeles, CA. Accessed January 5, 2017.

Kozlovsky, Rose. Interviewed by Lucy Samorodin, Baltimore, Maryland, United States, 1997. Interview 28182. Visual History Archive, USC Shoah Foundation, Los Angeles, CA. Accessed December 19, 2016.

Kutscher, Hela. Interviewed by Mona Clayman, Montréal, Québec, Canada, 1997. Interview 34330. Visual History Archive, USC Shoah Foundation, Los Angeles, CA. Accessed January 12, 2017.

Laufer, Suzan. Interviewed by Miriam Rutiz, Altadena, California, United States, 1995. Interview 1847. Visual History Archive, USC Shoah Foundation, Los Angeles, CA. Accessed January 14, 2017.

Leichter, Rose. Interviewed by Claudette Feier, San Diego, California, United States, 1996. Interview 11673. Visual History Archive, USC Shoah Foundation, Los Angeles, CA. Accessed March 2, 2022.

Lewin, Regina. Interviewed by Deborah Kattler-Kupetz, Los Angeles, California,

LIST OF TESTIMONY-GIVERS

United States, 1995. Interview 719. Visual History Archive, USC Shoah Foundation, Los Angeles, CA. Accessed December 5, 2016.

Lijek, Esther. Interviewed by Joanne Silberstein, Silver Spring, Maryland, United States, 1996. Interview 20470. Visual History Archive, USC Shoah Foundation, Los Angeles, CA. Accessed January 9, 2017.

London, Margaret. Interviewed by Edie Kalb, Toronto, Ontario, United States, 1995. Interview 10008. Visual History Archive, USC Shoah Foundation, Los Angeles, CA. Accessed January 11, 2017.

Loven, Shoshana. Interviewed by Hana Morris, Melbourne, Australia, 1996. Interview 20492. Visual History Archive, USC Shoah Foundation, Los Angeles, CA. Accessed January 9, 2017.

Lowbeer, Edith. Interviewed by Anita Fisher, Sydney, Australia, 1995. Interview 1916. Visual History Archive, USC Shoah Foundation, Los Angeles, CA. Accessed March 20, 2018.

Luner, Gerda. Interviewed by Marcia Blitstein, Downers Grove, Illinois, United States, 1995. Interview 3768. Visual History Archive, USC Shoah Foundation, Los Angeles, CA. Accessed December 15, 2016.

Mandelbaum, Lena. Interviewed by Marilyn Simon, Monroe Township, New Jersey, United States, 2000. Interview 50791. Visual History Archive, USC Shoah Foundation, Los Angeles, CA. Accessed January 10, 2018.

Mann, Renate. RG-50.106.022. Interviewed by Julie Kopel, location not available, 2013. Oral History Interview with Renate Mann. Jeff and Toby Herr Oral History Archive. United States Holocaust Memorial Museum, Washington, DC. Accessed December 15, 2016.

Matzner, Lucy. Interviewed by Leora Saposnik, Sheboygan, Wisconsin, United States, 1995. Interview 7461. Visual History Archive, USC Shoah Foundation, Los Angeles, CA. Accessed December 15, 2016.

Nesselroth, Anna. Interviewed by Sylvia Ben Simon, Israel, 1998. Interview 46995. Visual History Archive, USC Shoah Foundation, Los Angeles, CA. Accessed December 16, 2016. In German, translation by author.

Ornstein, Anna. Interviewed by Helene Elkus, Cincinnati, Ohio, United States, 1996. Interview 12481. Visual History Archive, USC Shoah Foundation, Los Angeles, CA. Accessed November 22, 2018.

Paryzer, Fay. Interviewed by Louise Bobrow, Tucson, Arizona, United States, 1997. Interview 30681. Visual History Archive, USC Shoah Foundation, Los Angeles, CA. Accessed June 18, 2018.

Posesorski, Yetta. Interviewed by Shainey Silver, Toronto, Ontario, Canada, 1988. Interview 54245. Visual History Archive, USC Shoah Foundation, Los Angeles, CA. Originally recorded by the Sarah and Chaim Neuberger Holocaust Education Centre, Toronto, Canada. Accessed April 3, 2022.

Potash, Berta. Interviewed by Saerina Tauritz, Delray Beach, Florida, United States, 1997. Interview 24481. Visual History Archive, USC Shoah Foundation, Los Angeles, CA. Accessed July 27, 2016.

Poziniaz, Regina. Interviewed by Myrna Riback, Toronto, Ontario, Canada, 1998. Interview 43438. Visual History Archive, USC Shoah Foundation, Los Angeles, CA. Accessed July 27, 2016.

Price, Sala. Interviewed by Pamela Travis, Naples, Florida, United States, 1996. Interview 15292. Visual History Archive, USC Shoah Foundation, Los Angeles, CA. Accessed June 25, 2021.

Prince, Helen. Interviewed by Masha Loen, Los Angeles, California, United States, 1996. Interview 11152. Visual History Archive, USC Shoah Foundation, Los Angeles, CA. Accessed March 27, 2017.

Radford, Livia. Interviewed by Gary Lubell, Denver, Colorado, United States, 1995. Interview 6244. Visual History Archive, USC Shoah Foundation, Los Angeles, CA. Accessed July 27, 2016.

Redlitz, Esther. Interviewed by Joseph Huttler, Brooklyn, New York, United States, 2000. Interview 50927. Visual History Archive, USC Shoah Foundation, Los Angeles, CA. Accessed July 3, 2021.

Reiss, Brenda. Interviewed by Marilyn Feingold, West Bloomfield, Michigan, United States, 1996. Interview 14637. Visual History Archive, USC Shoah Foundation, Los Angeles, CA. Accessed July 28, 2016.

Reti, Edith. Interviewed by Christian Froelicher, Surfer's Paradise, Australia, 1997. Interview 38279. Visual History Archive, USC Shoah Foundation, Los Angeles, CA. Accessed July 28, 2016.

Retman, Dora. Interviewed by Rita Lubitz, Melbourne, Australia, 1997. Interview 30450. Visual History Archive, USC Shoah Foundation, Los Angeles, CA. Accessed June 23, 2021.

Richman, Mania. Interviewed by Kathy Strochlic, New York, New York, United States, 1995. Interview 730. Visual History Archive, USC Shoah Foundation, Los Angeles, CA. Accessed June 19, 2018.

Riedler, Rita. Interviewed by Sherry Amatenstein, Forest Hills, New York, United States, 1996. Interview 22917. Visual History Archive, USC Shoah Foundation, Los Angeles, CA. Accessed January 12, 2018.

Rittenberg, Dasha. Interviewed by Janice Englehart and Piotr Kadlcik, New York, New York, United States, 1995. Interview 2441. Visual History Archive, USC Shoah Foundation, Los Angeles, CA. Accessed June 30, 2021.

Roman, Ruth. Interviewed by Stella Eliezrie, Anaheim, California, United States, 1995. Interview 10082. Visual History Archive, USC Shoah Foundation, Los Angeles, CA. Accessed August 2, 2016.

Rosen, Gucia. Interviewed by Dina Brustman, Melbourne, Australia, 1996. Interview 24384. Visual History Archive, USC Shoah Foundation, Los Angeles, CA. Accessed August 2, 2016.

Rotenstein, Ester. Interviewed by Chana Gotlieb, Jerusalem, Israel, 1998. Interview 47236. Visual History Archive, USC Shoah Foundation, Los Angeles, CA. Accessed January 9, 2018.

Rubner, Eda. Interviewed by Rosanne Krusner, Toronto, Ontario, Canada, 1995. Interview 7868. Visual History Archive, USC Shoah Foundation, Los Angeles, CA. Accessed July 3, 2021.

Salzberg, Jack. RG-50.005.0048. Interviewer and location not available, 1984. Oral History Interview with Jack Salzberg. Jeff and Toby Herr Oral History Archive. United States Holocaust Memorial Museum Archives, Washington, DC. Accessed July 9, 2021.

Sarna, Mania. Interviewed by Ruth Meyer, Englewood Cliffs, New Jersey, United States, 1997. Interview 25887. Visual History Archive, USC Shoah Foundation, Los Angeles, CA. Accessed January 14, 2017.

Schenkler, Nettie. Interviewed by Cheryl Lynn Conway, Dover, New Jersey, United States, 1997. Interview 25774. Visual History Archive, USC Shoah Foundation, Los Angeles, CA. Accessed January 10, 2017.

Schlussel, Esther. Interviewed by Elise Arden, Coconut Creek, Florida, United States, 1995. Interview 7210. Visual History Archive, USC Shoah Foundation, Los Angeles, CA. Accessed January 11, 2017.

Scholder, Rose. Interviewed by Joseph Cohn, Fort Lauderdale, Florida, United States, 1995. Interview 2799. Visual History Archive, USC Shoah Foundation, Los Angeles, CA. Accessed January 11, 2017.

Schulman, Rose. Interviewed by E. Tina Tito, Monticello, New York, United States, 1996. Interview 18420. Visual History Archive, USC Shoah Foundation, Los Angeles, CA. Accessed August 3, 2016.

Schwarzberg, Rosa. Interviewed by Robert Clary, Laguna Hills, California, United States, 1995. Interview 9645. Visual History Archive, USC Shoah Foundation, Los Angeles, CA. Accessed July 3, 2021.

Schweitzer, Masha. Interviewed by Deborah Tellerman Berkowitz, Hollywood, Florida, United States, 1995. Interview 9634. Visual History Archive, USC Shoah Foundation, Los Angeles, CA. Accessed August 3, 2016.

Sharp, Chana. Interviewed by Lara Singal, Melbourne, Australia, 1997. Interview 26373. Visual History Archive, USC Shoah Foundation, Los Angeles, CA. Accessed July 25, 2016.

Shelonko, Bluma. Interviewed by Hilary Adah Helstein, Los Angeles, California, United States, 1997. Interview 24886. Visual History Archive, USC Shoah Foundation Institute, Los Angeles, CA. Accessed January 23, 2021.

Silberberg, Chaya. Interviewed by Ann Lieb, Monticello, New York, United States, 1996. Interview 18783. Visual History Archive, USC Shoah Foundation, Los Angeles, CA. Accessed June 29, 2021.

Silberberg, Estera. Interviewed by Rhoda F. Daum-Kenner, Rego Park, New York, United States, 1995. Interview 9049. Visual History Archive, USC Shoah Foundation, Los Angeles, CA. Accessed August 3, 2016.

Silverstein, Regina. Interviewed by Agi Hecht, Toronto, Ontario, Canada, 1990. Interview 54317. Visual History Archive, USC Shoah Foundation, Los Angeles,

CA. Originally recorded by the Sarah and Chaim Neuberger Holocaust Education Centre, Toronto, Ontario, Canada. Accessed August 4, 2016. See also Gliksman, Regina, Interview 169.

Singer, Augusta. Interviewed by Penelope Ann Toltz, Sydney, Australia, 1995. Interview 3469. Visual History Archive, USC Shoah Foundation, Los Angeles, CA. Accessed August 4, 2016.

Sontag, Rose. Interviewed by Ann Lieb, Brooklyn, New York, United States, 1996. Interview 21902. Visual History Archive, USC Shoah Foundation, Los Angeles, CA. Accessed July 25, 2016.

Stach, Rose. Interviewed by Jason Walker, Melbourne, Australia, 1997. Interview 30911. Visual History Archive, USC Shoah Foundation, Los Angeles, CA. Accessed January 10, 2017.

Steinweis, Rosalie. Interviewed by Steve Greenberg, Miami Beach, Florida, United States, 1996. Interview 10835. Visual History Archive. USC Shoah Foundation, Los Angeles, CA. Accessed December 5, 2016.

Steinweis, Rosalie. Interviewed by author. Miami Beach, Florida, United States. Conducted by phone, June 4, 2021.

Szczygielski, Sonia. Interviewed by Shirley Small, Montréal, Québec, Canada, 1996. Interview 17956. Visual History Archive, USC Shoah Foundation, Los Angeles, CA. Accessed April 12, 2017.

Szentivanyi, Judith. Interviewed by Claudia Steckler, Lutz, Florida, United States, 1997. Interview 30379. Visual History Archive, USC Shoah Foundation, Los Angeles, CA. Accessed December 28, 2016.

Szmulewitz, Paula. Interviewed by Elise Arden, Delray Beach, Florida, United States, 1995. Interview 5362. Visual History Archive, USC Shoah Foundation, Los Angeles, CA. Accessed December 28, 2016.

Tau, Cesia. Interviewed by Phyllis Hochberg, Hewlett, New York, United States, 1996. Interview 14979. Visual History Archive, USC Shoah Foundation, Los Angeles, CA. Accessed June 15, 2021.

Tenenbaum, Gitla. Interviewed by Stanley Asher, Montréal, Québec, Canada, 1994. Interview 53879. Visual History Archive, USC Shoah Foundation, Los Angeles, CA. Originally recorded by the Montreal Holocaust Museum, Montréal, Québec, Canada. Accessed December 28, 2016.

Trepper, Lili. Interviewed by Deborah Joselson, Melbourne, Australia, 1997. Interview 34765. Visual History Archive, USC Shoah Foundation, Los Angeles, CA. Accessed September 19, 2016.

Tusak, Aranka. Interviewed by Myer Bloom, Melbourne, Australia, 1997. Interview 36847. Visual History Archive, USC Shoah Foundation, Los Angeles, CA. Accessed September 21, 2016.

Tyler, Katalin. Interviewed by Kaye Fink, Melbourne, Australia, 1996. Interview 18673. Visual History Archive, USC Shoah Foundation, Los Angeles, CA. Accessed September 19, 2016.

Wald, Fanny. Interviewed by Janice Englehart, Seattle, Washington, United States, 1996. Interview 16491. Visual History Archive, USC Shoah Foundation, Los Angeles, CA. Accessed June 2, 2021.

Weinreich, Frieda. Interviewed by Jenifer Joyce, Fairlawn, New Jersey, United States, 1995. Interview 9814. Visual History Archive, USC Shoah Foundation, Los Angeles, CA. Accessed September 22, 2016.

Weiss, Anna. Interviewed by Sharon Savdie, Sydney, Australia, 1995. Interview 7132. Visual History Archive, USC Shoah Foundation, Los Angeles, CA. Accessed September 23, 2016.

Wellner, Eva. Interviewed by Robert Clary, Laguna Hills, California, United States, 1995. Interview 9342. Visual History Archive, USC Shoah Foundation, Los Angeles, CA. Accessed June 26, 2021.

Wieder, Hedy. Interviewed by Barbara Sharon Linz, Sydney, Australia, 1996. Interview 15262. Visual History Archive, USC Shoah Foundation, Los Angeles, CA. Accessed September 23, 2016.

Wolgelernter, Minnie. Interviewed by Mary Rothschild, Los Angeles, California, United States, 1995. Interview 2115. Visual History Archive, USC Shoah Foundation, Los Angeles, CA. Accessed September 22, 2016.

Wolinsky, Roza. Interviewed by Steven Cohen, Montréal, Québec, Canada, 1996. Interview 54711. Visual History Archive, USC Shoah Foundation, Los Angeles, CA. Originally recorded by the Montreal Holocaust Museum, Montréal, Québec, Canada. Accessed June 22, 2021.

Wolnerman, Irene. Interviewed by Judy M. Shiffman, Milwaukee, Wisconsin, United States, 1996. Interview 21416. Visual History Archive, USC Shoah Foundation, Los Angeles, CA. Accessed June 23, 2021.

Wolpert, Lola. Interviewed by Rachel Alkallay, Montréal, Québec, Canada 1998. Interview 39042. Visual History Archive, USC Shoah Foundation, Los Angeles, CA. Accessed January 18, 2018.

York, Rusia. Interviewed by Mary Ziegler, Sydney, Australia, 1995. Interview 5213. Visual History Archive, USC Shoah Foundation, Los Angeles, CA. Accessed September 23, 2016.

Young, Phyllis. Interviewed by Helen Desman, Sunrise, Florida, United States, 1995. Interview 8359. Visual History Archive, USC Shoah Foundation, Los Angeles, CA. Accessed January 9, 2017.

Zimmerman, Rose. Interviewed by Rona Arato, Toronto, Ontario, Canada, 1995. Interview 2169. Visual History Archive, USC Shoah Foundation, Los Angeles, CA. Accessed September 26, 2016.

ARCHIVES CONSULTED

Archiwum Gross-Rosen (AGR)
Archiwum Państwowe w Katowicach (APK)
Bundesarchiv Lichterfelde (BL)
International Tracing Service (ITS)
Joint Distribution Committee Archives (JDCA)
Muzeum Podkrkonoší v Trutnově (MPT)
New York Public Library (NYPL)
Státní Oblastní Archiv Liberec (SOAL)
Státní Oblastní Archiv v Zámrsk (SOAZ)
Státní Okresní Archiv Trutnov (SOAT)
United States Holocaust Memorial Museum (USHMM)
Visual History Archive, USC Shoah Foundation (VHA)
Wiener Library (WL)
Yad Vashem Archives (YVA)

NOTES

INTRODUCTION

Epigraph: Nettie Schenkler, interview by Cheryl Lynn Conway, Dover, New Jersey, United States, 1997, Interview 25774, Visual History Archive, USC Shoah Foundation, Los Angeles, CA. Accessed January 10, 2017. Tape 2, 21:29.

1. In 1938, 58,300 Jews lived in the region. Wojciech Jaworski, "Żydowskie Gminy Wyznaniowe w Zagłębiu Dąbrowskim," *Biuletyn Żydowskiego Instytutu Historycznego w Polsce* 1–2 (1988): 144.

2. Bogdan Cybulski, "Żydzi Polscy w Prowincji Górnośląskiej w Okresie II Wojny Światowej," *Śląski Kwartalnik Historyczny Sobótka* 44, no. 1 (1989): 140.

3. Cybulski, "Żydzi Polscy w Prowincji Górnośląskiej," 140.

4. Wacław Długoborski, "Die Juden aus den eingegliederten Gebieten im Vernichtungslager Auschwitz-Birkenau," in *Der Judenmord in den eingegliederten polnischen Gebieten 1939–1945*, eds. Jacek Andrzej Młynarczyk and Jochen Böhler, 226 (Osnabrück: Fibre Verlag, 2010); Mark Mazower, *Hitler's Empire: How the Nazis Ruled Europe* (New York: Penguin, 2008), 198. Hugo Service points out that Jews were expelled from the western portions of Upper Silesia but were resettled in the Eastern Strip. Hugo Service, "The Imagined Ethno-Racial Border and the Expulsion of Jews from Western Poland, 1939–41," *German History* 38, no. 3 (2020): 419.

5. Bella Gutterman, *A Narrow Bridge to Life: Jewish Forced Labor and Survival in the Gross-Rosen Camp System, 1940–1945* (New York: Berghahn Books, 2008), 44, 48.

6. Sybille Steinbacher, *"Musterstadt" Auschwitz: Germanisierungspolitik und Judenmord in Ostoberschlesien* (München: K. G. Saur, 2000), 138–39, 144; Alfred Sulik, "Volkstumspolitik und Arbeitseinsatz Zwangsarbeiter in der Großindustrie Oberschlesiens," in *Europa und der "Reichseinsatz": Ausländische Zivilarbeiter, Kriegsgefangene und KZ-Häftlinge in Deutschland 1938–1945*, ed. Ulrich Herbert, 110 (Essen: Klartext Verlag, 1991).

7. Alfred Konieczny, *KL Gross-Rosen: Hitlerowski Obóz Koncentracyjny na Dolnym Śląsku 1940–1945* (Wałbrzych: Muzeum Gross-Rosen, 2012), 24.

8. Steinbacher, *"Musterstadt" Auschwitz*, 293.

9. Phyllis Young, interview by Helen Desman, Sunrise, Florida, United States, 1995, Interview 8359, Visual History Archive, USC Shoah Foundation, Los Angeles, CA. Accessed January 9, 2017. Tape 2, 3:04.

10. Rita Riedler, interview by Sherry Amatenstein, Forest Hills, New York, United States, 1996, Interview 22917, Visual History Archive, USC Shoah Foundation, Los Angeles, CA. Accessed January 12, 2018. Tape 1, 21:47.

11. Shoshana Greenbaum, interview by Ferne Hassan, Linden, New Jersey, United States, 1998, Interview 45508, Visual History Archive, USC Shoah Foundation, Los Angeles, CA. Accessed April 12, 2017. Tape 1, 28:14.

NOTES TO INTRODUCTION

12. Lena Mandelbaum, interview by Marilyn Simon, Monroe Township, New Jersey, United States, 2000, Interview 50791, Visual History Archive, USC Shoah Foundation, Los Angeles, CA. Accessed January 10, 2018. Tape 3, 8:19.

13. Lawrence L. Langer, *Holocaust Testimonies: The Ruins of Memory* (New Haven, CT: Yale University Press, 1991); Annette Wieviorka, *The Era of the Witness* (Ithaca, NY: Cornell University Press, 2006); Shoshana Felman and Dori Laub, *Testimony: Crises of Witnessing in Literature, Psychoanalysis, and History* (New York: Routledge, 1991); Geoffrey Hartman, "Learning from Survivors: The Yale Testimony Project," *Holocaust and Genocide Studies* 9, no. 2 (1995): 192–207.

14. Friedländer has many works in this mode. A prime example is Saul Friedländer, *The Years of Extermination: Nazi Germany and the Jews, 1939–1945* (New York: HarperCollins, 2007).

15. Christopher Browning, *Remembering Survival: Inside a Nazi Slave-Labor Camp* (New York: Norton, 2010).

16. Zoë Waxman, *Writing the Holocaust: Identity, Testimony, Representation* (New York: Oxford University Press, 2006).

17. Waxman, *Writing the Holocaust*, 158.

18. Anna Hájková, *Menschen ohne Geschichte sind Staub: Homophobie und Holocaust* (Göttingen: Wallstein Verlag, 2021).

19. Alexandra Garbarini, *Numbered Days: Diaries and the Holocaust* (New Haven, CT: Yale University Press, 2006), 3–4.

20. Garbarini, *Numbered Days*, 4.

21. Noah Shenker, *Reframing Holocaust Testimony* (Bloomington: Indiana University Press, 2015).

22. Shenker, *Reframing Holocaust Testimony*, 1.

23. USC Shoah Foundation, *Testimony: The Legacy of Schindler's List and the USC Shoah Foundation* (New York: NewMarket Press for It Books/HarperCollins, 2014), 186, 189–97.

24. Examples include Anna Reading, "Clicking on Hitler: The Virtual Holocaust @Home," in *Visual Culture and the Holocaust*, ed. Barbie Zelizer, 323–39 (New Brunswick, NJ: Rutgers University Press, 2001), and Oren Baruch Stier, "The Place of Holocaust Survivor Videotestimony: Navigating the Landmarks of First-Person Audio-Visual Representation," in *The Palgrave Handbook of Holocaust Literature and Culture*, eds. Victoria Aarons and Phyllis Lassner, 669–86 (Cham: Palgrave Macmillan, 2020).

25. Jeffrey Shandler, *Holocaust Memory in the Digital Age: Survivors' Stories and New Media Practices* (Stanford, CA: Stanford University Press, 2017).

26. Hannah Pollin-Galay, *Ecologies of Witnessing: Language, Place, and Holocaust Testimony* (New Haven, CT: Yale University Press, 2018).

27. Pollin-Galay, *Ecologies of Witnessing*, 1–2, 123.

28. Pollin-Galay, *Ecologies of Witnessing*, 17.

29. Lawrence Langer, *Holocaust Testimonies: The Ruins of Memory* (New Haven, CT: Yale University Press, 1991).

30. "Pre-interview Questionnaire," USC Shoah Foundation, Institute for Visual History and Education, https://sfi.usc.edu/content/pre-interview-questionnaire.

31. Nettie Schenkler, interview by Cheryl Lynn Conway, 1997. Tape 5, 4:38.

32. Dori Laub, "Bearing Witness or the Vicissitudes of Listening," in *Testimony*, eds. Felman and Laub, 57–74; Geoffrey Hartman, "A Note on the Testimony Event," in *The Power of Witnessing: Reflections, Reverberations, and Traces of the Holocaust*, eds. Nancy R. Goodman and Marilyn B. Meyers, 83 (New York: Routledge, 2012).

33. In his study of David Boder's approach, Alan Rosen notes Boder's handling of "perplexity." *The Wonder of Their Voices: The 1946 Interviews of David Boder* (New York: Oxford University Press, 2010), 7.

34. USC Shoah Foundation, *Testimony*, 189–97.

35. The USC guidelines for videographers are revealing on these restrictions. See "Videographer Guidelines," USC Shoah Foundation, Institute for Visual History and Education, https://sfi.usc.edu/content/videographer-guidelines.

36. This issue is carefully elaborated by Xine Yao, *Disaffected: The Cultural Politics of Unfeeling in Nineteenth-Century America* (Durham, NC: Duke University Press, 2021), 7.

37. Yao, *Disaffected*, 209.

38. Joel Fineman, "The History of the Anecdote: Fiction and Friction," in *The New Historicism*, ed. H. Aram Veeser, 65–92 (New York: Routledge, 1989); Jane Gallop, *Anecdotal Theory* (Durham, NC: Duke University Press, 2002); Florian Sedlmeier and MaryAnn Snyder-Körber, "Introduction," in *Anecdotal Modernity: Making and Unmaking History*, eds. James Dorson, Florian Sedlmeier, MaryAnn Snyder-Körber, and Birte Wege, 2–5 (Berlin: De Gruyter, 2020).

39. The Visual History Archive does not mark these as the same person. See Regina Silverstein, interview by Agi Hecht, 1990, originally recorded by the Sarah and Chaim Neuberger Holocaust Education Centre in Toronto, Ontario, Canada, and Regina Gliksman, interview by Caroline Kohn, 1994.

40. Berta Potash, interview by Saerina Tauritz, Delray Beach, Florida, United States, 1997, Interview 24481, Visual History Archive, USC Shoah Foundation, Los Angeles, CA. Accessed July 27, 2016. Tape 2, 20:01.

41. Ann Federman, interview by Milton Katz and Sharon Hamil, Kansas City, Missouri, United States, 1999, Midwest Center for Holocaust Education, Overland Park, Kansas. 10:41.

42. Dasha Rittenberg, interview by Janice Englehart and Piotr Kadlcik, New York, New York, United States, 1995, Interview 2441, Visual History Archive, USC Shoah Foundation, Los Angeles, CA. Accessed June 30, 2021. Tape 3, 27:41.

43. Many historians admit that it is difficult to distinguish between the cultural category of "childhood" and the people who speak, write, and act from the position of "children." Tara Zahra offers more than one case of wartime survivors who were considered by postwar relief agencies as children but who insisted on their own autonomy regarding postwar citizenship or nationality. Tara Zahra, *The Lost*

NOTES TO INTRODUCTION

Children: Reconstructing Europe's Families After World War II (Cambridge, MA: Harvard University Press, 2011), 136, 143, 203.

44. Gabriel N. Finder, "Child Survivors in Polish Jewish Collective Memory after the Holocaust: The Case of *Undzere kinder*," in *Displaced Children in Russia and Eastern Europe, 1915–1953*, ed. Nick Baron, 219 and ff. (Leiden: Brill, 2016). See also the memoir of child survivor Helen Sendyk, *New Dawn: A Triumph of Life after the Holocaust* (Syracuse, NY: Syracuse University Press, 2002), and Zahra, *The Lost Children*, 132–38.

45. Debórah Dwork, *Children with a Star: Jewish Youth in Nazi Europe* (New Haven, CT: Yale University Press, 1991).

46. Joanna Beata Michlic, ed., *Jewish Families in Europe, 1939–Present: History, Representation, and Memory* (Waltham, MA: Brandeis University Press, 2017), xvi.

47. See, for example, the narratives in Joanna Sliwa, "Clandestine Activities and Concealed Presence: A Case Study of Children Concealed in the Kraków Ghetto," in *Jewish Families in Europe*, ed. Michlic, 26–45; Joanna Sliwa, *Jewish Childhood in Kraków: A Microhistory of the Holocaust* (New Brunswick: Rutgers University Press, 2021); and Boaz Cohen, "The Children's Voice: Postwar Collection of Testimonies from Child Survivors of the Holocaust," *Holocaust and Genocide Studies* 21, no. 1 (2007): 73–95.

48. Rebecca Clifford, *Survivors: Children's Lives After the Holocaust* (New Haven, CT: Yale University Press, 2020).

49. Johannes-Dieter Steinert, *Deportation und Zwangsarbeit: Polnische und sowjetische Kinder im nationalsozialistischen Deutschland und im besetzten Osteuropa, 1939–1945* (Essen: Klartext Verlag, 2013) and *Holocaust und Zwangsarbeit: Erinnerungen jüdischer Kinder 1938–1945* (Essen: Klartext Verlag, 2018).

50. Sonia Szczygielski, interview by Shirley Small, Montréal, Québec, Canada, 1996, Interview 17956, Visual History Archive, USC Shoah Foundation, Los Angeles, CA. Accessed April 12, 2017. Tape 2, 27:07.

51. Helena Keen, interview by Rona Arato, Toronto, Ontario, Canada, 1995, Interview 8516, Visual History Archive, USC Shoah Foundation, Los Angeles, CA. Accessed December 21, 2016. Tape 2, 22:49.

52. Helena Keen, interview by Rona Arato, 1995. Tape 2, 23:48.

53. Nettie Schenkler, interview by Cheryl Lynn Conway, 1997. Tape 2, 3:20.

54. Gitla Tenenbaum, interview by Stanley Asher, Montréal, Québec, Canada, 1994, Interview 53879, Visual History Archive, USC Shoah Foundation, Los Angeles, CA. Accessed December 28, 2016. Tape 1, 12:36. For "Silesia" she does not use the Yiddish "*shlezye*" but the Polish pronunciation.

55. Minnie Wolgelernter, interview by Mary Rothschild, Los Angeles, California, United States, 1995, Interview 2115, Visual History Archive, USC Shoah Foundation, Los Angeles, CA. Accessed September 22, 2016. Tape 1, 20:24.

56. Yetta Posesorski, interview by Shainey Silver, Toronto, Ontario, Canada, 1988, Interview 54245, Visual History Archive, USC Shoah Foundation, Los Angeles, CA. Accessed April 3, 2022. Tape 2, 2:05.

57. Donald Bloxham and Tony Kushner's *The Holocaust: Critical Historical Approaches* (Manchester: Manchester University Press, 2005), 29–32, emphasizes the evidentiary purposes to which testimonies were put; Laura Jockusch documents the extraordinary efforts to create an historical record of the Holocaust in *Collect and Record! Jewish Holocaust Documentation in Early Postwar Europe* (New York: Oxford University Press, 2012), 18–45. David Boder's approach was to allow survivors to control the narrative. See Alan Rosen, *The Wonder of Their Voices: The 1946 Holocaust Interviews of David Boder* (New York: Oxford University Press, 2010). More directly addressing trauma is Lawrence Langer's 1991 volume, *Holocaust Testimonies: The Ruins of Memory*. Also important in this regard are Felman and Laub, eds., *Testimony*, and Cathy Caruth, *Unclaimed Experience: Trauma, Narrative and History* (Baltimore: Johns Hopkins University Press, 1996).

58. Marc Buggeln, *Slave Labor in Nazi Concentration Camps* (Oxford: Oxford University Press, 2014), 142–43; Felicja Karay, *Death Comes in Yellow: Skarżysko-Kamienna Slave Labor Camp* (Amsterdam: Harwood Academic, 1996), 179–96.

59. One example among many is Halina Birenbaum, *Hope Is the Last to Die: A Personal Documentation of Nazi Terror* (New York: Twayne Publishers, 1971) [reissued by M. E. Sharpe in 1996 and Routledge in 2015].

60. Terrence Des Pres, *The Survivor: An Anatomy of Life in the Death Camps* (New York: Oxford University Press, 1980), 102–41.

61. Maja Suderland, *Inside Concentration Camps* (Malden, MA: Polity Press, 2013).

62. Anna Hájková, *The Last Ghetto: An Everyday History of Theresienstadt* (New York: Oxford University Press, 2020), 98.

63. Marcia Pally, *Commonwealth and Covenant: Economics, Politics and Theologies of Relationality* (Grand Rapids, MI: Wm. B. Eerdmans, 2016), 133.

64. Édouard Glissant, *Poetics of Relation* (Ann Arbor: University of Michigan Press, 1997 [orig. 1990]), 11, 171.

65. Hájková, *The Last Ghetto*, 1.

66. Gerda Frieberg, interview by Linda Ruth Davidson, Toronto, Ontario, Canada, 1996, Interview 13395, Visual History Archive, USC Shoah Foundation, Los Angeles, CA. Accessed January 24, 2017. Tape 6, 16:50.

67. Lena Mandelbaum, interview by Marilyn Simon, 2000. Tape 3, 11:59.

68. Alan Rosen, *The Holocaust's Jewish Calendars: Keeping Time Sacred, Making Time Holy* (Bloomington: Indiana University Press, 2019), 50.

69. Rosen, *The Holocaust's Jewish Calendars*, 103.

70. Marc Buggeln and Michael Wildt, "Einleitung," in *Arbeit in Nationalsozialismus*, eds. Marc Buggeln and Michael Wildt, xxiv–xxv (München: De Gruyter Oldenbourg, 2014).

71. Adam Tooze, *The Wages of Destruction: The Making and Breaking of the Nazi Economy* (New York: Viking, 2006), 59–66, 513–22, 528.

72. Marc Buggeln, *Arbeit & Gewalt: Das Außenlagersystem des KZ Neuengamme* (Göttingen: Wallstein, 2009); Wolfgang Kirstein, *Das Konzentrationslager als*

Institution totalen Terrors: Das Beispiel Natzweiler (Pfaffenweiler: Centaurus-Verlagsgesellschaft, 1992); Karin Orth, *Das System der Nationalsozialistischen Konzentrationslager: Eine Politische Organisationsgeschichte* (Hamburg: Hamburger Edition, 1999), 162–97; Karay, *Death Comes in Yellow*; Debórah Dwork and Robert Van Pelt, *Auschwitz: 1270 to the Present* (New York: Norton, 1996).

73. Wolf Gruner, *Jewish Forced Labor under the Nazis: Economic Needs and Racial Aims, 1938–1944* (New York: Cambridge University Press and the United States Holocaust Memorial Museum, 2006); Wolf Gruner and Jörg Osterloh, eds., *The Greater German Reich and the Jews: Nazi Persecution Policies in the Annexed Territories 1935–1945* (New York: Berghahn Books, 2015); Markus Nesselrodt, *Dem Holocaust entkommen: Polnische Juden in der Sowjetunion, 1939–1946* (Berlin: De Gruyter, 2019).

74. Browning, *Remembering Survival*.

75. Christopher Browning, *Nazi Policy, Jewish Workers, German Killers* (Cambridge: Cambridge University Press, 2000), 147–48.

76. Stephan Lehnstaedt, "Coercion and Incentive: Jewish Ghetto Labor in East Upper Silesia," *Holocaust and Genocide Studies* 24, no. 3 (2010): 409.

77. Wolf Gruner, *Jewish Forced Labor under the Nazis*, 221–23.

78. Jacek Andrzej Młynarczyk and Jochen Böhler, "Vorwort," in *Der Judenmord in den eingegliederten polnischen Gebieten, 1939–1945*, eds. Jacek Andrzej Młynarczyk and Jochen Böhler, 9–10 (Osnabrück: Fibre Verlag, 2010).

79. Volker Zimmermann, *Die Sudetendeutschen im NS-Staat: Politik und Stimmung der Bevölkerung im Reichsgau Sudentenland (1938–1945)* (Essen: Klartext Verlag, 1999), 196.

80. See the testimony of Rose Scholder, interview by Joseph Cohn, Fort Lauderdale, Florida, United States, 1995, Interview 2799, Visual History Archive, USC Shoah Foundation, Los Angeles, CA. Accessed January 11, 2017.

81. Evgeny Finkel, *Ordinary Jews: Choice and Survival during the Holocaust* (Princeton, NJ: Princeton University Press, 2017).

82. Elissa Bemporad, "Questions of Choice: The Soviet Case and the Absence of Gender Identity in *Ordinary Jews*," *Shofar* 36, no. 1 (2018): 209–13.

83. Natalia Aleksiun, "Social Networks of Support: Trajectories of Escape, Rescue and Survival," in *A Companion to the Holocaust*, eds. Simone Gigliotti and Hilary Earl, 279–93 (Hoboken, NJ: Wiley, 2020).

84. Aleksandra Namysło, *Zagłada Żydów zagłębiowskich* (Będzin: Instytut Pamięci Narodowej, 2004) and *Zagłada Żydów na polskich terenach wcielonych do Rzeszy* (Warszawa: Instytut Pamięci Narodowej, 2008); Andrzej Strzelecki, *Zagłada Żydów z Zagłębia Dąbrowskiego w KL Auschwitz: Opracowanie i wybór źródeł* (Oświęcim: Wydawnictwo Państwowego Muzeum Auschwitz-Birkenau, 2014); Steinbacher, *"Musterstadt" Auschwitz*, 138–57.

85. Bernard Robinson, "Zbrodnie popełnione w obozach 'Organizacji Schmelt' w świetle wspomnień więźniarek," in *Wykorzystanie Niewolniczej Pracy Więźniów KL Gross-Rosen przez III Rzeszę*, ed. Aleksandra Kobielec, 105–38 (Wałbrzych: Museum

Gross-Rosen, 2004). These included the well-known "Rossner" (or "Rosner") shops. See Robinson, p. 106.

86. Lehnstaedt, "Coercion and Incentive," 402–05, 410.

87. See Benjamin B. Ferencz, *Less Than Slaves: Jewish Forced Labor and the Quest for Compensation* (Cambridge, MA: Harvard University Press, 1979).

88. Dietrich Eichholtz, "Zwangsarbeit in der deutschen Kriegswirtschaft," in *Stiften gehen: NS-Zwangsarbeit und Entschädigungsdebatte*, ed. Ulrike Winkler, 26 (Köln: PapyRossa Verlag, 2000).

89. Andrea Rudorff, "Arbeit und Vernichtung *Reconsidered*: Die Lager der Organisation Schmelt für Polnische Jüdinnen und Juden aus dem Annektierten Teil Oberschlesiens," *Sozial Geschichte Online* 7 (2012): 24. Klaus-Peter Friedrich calls the Schmelt system a labor camp netting ("*Lagernetz*"), that is, an all-encompassing grid. *Die Verfolgung und Ermordung der Europäischen Juden durch das Nationalsozialistische Deutschland 1933–1945* (München: R. Oldenbourg Verlag, 2011), 45.

90. Miroslav Kryl and Ludmila Chládková, *Pobočky koncentračního tábora Gross-Rosen ve lnářských závodech Trutnovska na nacistické okupace* (Trutnov: Generalní Ředitelství VHJ Lnářský Průmysl, 1981).

91. "Filie obozu Gross-Rosen," Muzeum Gross-Rozen w Rogoźnicy, www.gross-rosen.eu.

92. Rosalie Steinweis, interview by author, Miami Beach, Florida, United States, conducted by phone, June 4, 2021.

93. Bella Gutterman, *A Narrow Bridge to Life*, 114.

94. "Subcamps of KL Gross-Rosen," Muzeum Gross-Rozen w Rogoźnicy, https://en.gross-rosen.eu/historia-kl-gross-rosen/filie-obozu-gross-rosen/#.

JEWISH GIRLHOOD AND JEWISH SURVIVAL IN ZAGŁĘBIE

1. Marion A Kaplan, *Between Dignity and Despair: Jewish Life in Nazi Germany* (New York: Oxford, 1998).

2. Kaplan, *Between Dignity and Despair*, p. 5. Kaplan's work develops the concept of "social death" in depth in the context of antisemitism in Germany. It was first used by Orlando Patterson to analyze the dehumanization attempted by enslavement in the Americas. See Orlando Patterson, *Slavery and Social Death: A Comparative Study* (Cambridge, MA: Harvard University Press, 1982). Christopher Browning briefly distinguished "social death" from "civic death" and "economic death" in an early essay. See Christopher Browning, "The German Bureaucracy and the Holocaust," in *Genocide: Critical Issues of the Holocaust*, eds. Alex Grobman, Daniel Landes, and Sybil Milton, 145 (Chappaqua, NY: Rossel Books, 1983). Claudia Card has used "social death" to theorize "evil" across historical contexts. Claudia Card, *Confronting Evils: Terrorism, Torture, Genocide* (Cambridge: Cambridge University Press, 2010).

3. Kaplan, *Between Dignity and Despair*.

4. Jerzy Tomaszewski, *Auftakt zur Vernichtung: Die Vertreibung Polnischer Juden aus Deutschland im Jahre 1938* (Osnabrück: Verlag Fibre, 2002), 114–17; Uta Larkey,

"Fear and Terror: The Expulsion of Polish Jews from Saxony/Germany in October 1938," *Dapim: Studies on the Holocaust* 31, no. 3 (2017): 243–60; Marcel Reich-Ranicki, *The Author of Himself: The Life of Marcel Reich-Ranicki* (Princeton, NJ: Princeton University Press, 2001), 106–08.

5. Wacław Długoborski, "Die Juden aus den eingegliederten Gebieten im Vernichtungslager Auschwitz-Birkenau," in *Der Judenmord in den Eingegliederten Polnischen Gebieten 1939-1945*, eds. Jacek Andrzej Młynarczyk and Jochen Böhler, 221 (Osnabrück: Fibre Verlag, 2010).

6. Joanna B. Michlic, *Poland's Threatening Other: The Image of the Jew from 1880 to the Present* (Lincoln: University of Nebraska Press, 2006); Celia Stopnicka Heller, *On the Edge of Destruction: Jews of Poland Between the Two World Wars* (New York: Columbia University Press, 1977), 77–114.

7. Kenneth B. Moss, *An Unchosen People: Jewish Political Reckoning in Interwar Poland* (Cambridge, MA: Harvard University Press, 2021), 317.

8. Sonia Szczygielski, interview by Shirley Small, 1996. Tape 1, 9:09; John Ranz, *Inhumanity: Death March to Buchenwald and the Last Jews of Bendzin* (Bloomington, IN: AuthorHouse 2007), 95–96; Jaff Schatz, *The Generation: The Rise and Fall of the Jewish Communists of Poland* (Berkeley: University of California Press, 1991), 104–07.

9. Sonia Szczygielski, interview by Shirley Small, 1996. Tape 1, 12:22.

10. Berta Potash, interview by Saerina Tauritz, 1997. Tape 1, 5:12.

11. Brenda Reiss, interview by Marilyn Feingold, West Bloomfield, Michigan, United States, 1996, Interview 14637, Visual History Archive, USC Shoah Foundation, Los Angeles, CA. Accessed July 28, 2016. Tape 1, 3:30.

12. Masha Schweitzer, interview by Deborah Tellerman Berkowitz, Hollywood, Florida, United States, 1995, Interview 9634, Visual History Archive, USC Shoah Foundation, Los Angeles, CA. Accessed August 3, 2016. Tape 1, 22:20.

13. Rosalie Steinweis, interview by Steve Greenberg, Miami Beach, Florida, United States, 1996, Interview 10835, Visual History Archive, USC Shoah Foundation, Los Angeles, CA. Accessed December 5, 2016. Tape 1, 4:11.

14. Masha Schweitzer, interview by Deborah Tellerman Berkowitz, 1995. Tape 1, 23:12.

15. Shoshana Loven, interview by Hana Morris, Melbourne, Austrialia, 1996, Interview 20492, Visual History Archive, USC Shoah Foundation, Los Angeles, CA. Accessed January 9, 2017. Tape 1, 4:06.

16. Mary Fulbrook, *A Small Town Near Auschwitz: Ordinary Nazis and the Holocaust* (Oxford: Oxford University Press, 2012), 48–49; Ryszard Kaczmarek, *Górny Śląsk podczas II wojny światowej: Między niemieckiej wspólnoty narodowej i rzeczywistością okupacji na terenach wcielonych do Trzeciej Rzeszy* (Katowice: Wydawnictwo Uniwersytetu Śląskiego, 2006), 47–63.

17. Rose Baumgold, interview by Sidney Burke, Los Angeles, California, United States, 1995, Interview 469, Visual History Archive, USC Shoah Foundation, Los Angeles, CA. Accessed April 10, 2017. Tape 1, 1:00.

18. Berta Potash, interview by Saerina Tauritz, 1997. Tape 1, 3:54.

19. Esther Lijek, interview by Joanne Silberstein, Silver Spring, Maryland, United States, 1996, Interview 20470, Visual History Archive, USC Shoah Foundation, Los Angeles, CA. Accessed January 9, 2017. Tape 1, 5:43.

20. Esther Schlussel, interview by Elise Arden, Coconut Creek, Florida, United States, 1995, Interview 7210, Visual History Archive, USC Shoah Foundation, Los Angeles, CA. Accessed January 11, 2017. Tape 1, 3:39.

21. Ann Goodman, interview by Yana Katzap, Tarzana, California, United States, 1998, Interview 42187, Visual History Archive, USC Shoah Foundation, Los Angeles, CA. Accessed January 9, 2017. Tape 1, 20:08.

22. Ann Goodman, interview by Yana Katzap, 1998. Tape 1, 8:33.

23. Frymeta Feldman, interview by Burton Leiser, White Plains, New York, United States, 1997, Interview 29000, Visual History Archive, USC Shoah Foundation, Los Angeles, CA. Accessed May 2, 2017. Tape 2, 0:20.

24. Frymeta Feldman, interview by Burton Leiser, 1997. Tape 2, 2:03.

25. Eta Batalion, interview by Lorrie Fein, Brooklyn, New York, United States, 1996, Interview 12241, Visual History Archive, USC Shoah Foundation, Los Angeles, CA. Accessed June 2, 2021. Tape 1, 18:35.

26. Shoshana Loven, interview by Hana Morris, 1996. Tape 1, 14:58.

27. Rita Riedler, interview by Sherry Amatenstein, 1996. Tape 1, 13:39.

28. Eliyana R. Adler and Natalia Aleksiun, "Seeking Relative Safety: The Flight of Polish Jews to the East in the Autumn of 1939," *Yad Vashem Studies* 46, no. 1 (2018): 41–71; Eliyana R. Adler, *Survival on the Margins: Polish Jewish Refugees in the Wartime Soviet Union* (Cambridge, MA: Harvard University Press, 2020), 22–27.

29. Adler, *Survival on the Margins*, 23.

30. Sonia Szczygielski, interview by Shirley Small, 1996. Tape 1, 15:59.

31. Yetta Flancbaum, interview by Lenore Weinstein, North Miami Beach, Florida, United States, 1996, Interview 14940, Visual History Archive, USC Shoah Foundation, Los Angeles, CA. Accessed August 23, 2017. Tape 1, 19:42.

32. Esther Schlussel, interview by Elise Arden, 1995. Tape 1, 18:21.

33. Mania Richman, interview by Kathy Strochlic, New York, New York, United States, 1995, Interview 730, Visual History Archive, USC Shoah Foundation, Los Angeles, CA. Accessed June 19, 2018. Tape 1, 17:25.

34. Sonia Szczygielski, interview by Shirley Small, 1996. Tape 1, 22:27.

35. Paweł Wiederman, *Płowa Bestia* (München: Monachium, 1948). Some sources cite the author as "Paweł Wiedermann."

36. See Aleksandra Namysło, "Kim Jestem—Polakiem, Niemcem, Żydem? Stosunki Żydowsko- Żydowskie na Dawnym Górnym Śląsku," *Biuletyn Instytutu Pamięci Narodowej* 11, no. 120 (2010): 52–56. Fay B., a survivor, shared a copy with me and insisted on its accuracy, in her experience. She knew of Wiederman in Sosnowiec. The European Holocaust Research Infrastructure (EHRI) includes it in its "Guide to Sources on the Holocaust in Occupied Poland," edited by Alina Skibińska, 2014, https://jri-poland.org/help/Sources-on-the-Holocaust-in-Occupied-Poland.pdf.

37. Wiederman, *Płowa Bestia*, 42. Author's translation.

38. Helen Prince, interview by Masha Loen, Los Angeles, California, United States, 1996, Interview 11152, Visual History Archive, USC Shoah Foundation, Los Angeles, CA. Accessed March 27, 2017. Tape 1, 12:48.

39. Alexander B. Rossino, "Nazi Anti-Jewish Policy During the Polish Campaign: The Case of Einsatzgruppe von Woyrsch," *German Studies Review* 24, no. 1 (2001): 35–53. Rossino argues that one goal of the von Woyrsch squad was to expel Jews; however, neither the *Einsatzgruppe* nor any other agency of the occupation allowed Jews the mobility to relocate, 37.

40. Klaus-Peter Friedrich, *Die Verfolgung und Ermordung der europäischen Juden durch das nationalsozialistische Deutschland 1933-1945: Polen September 1939–Juli 1941* (München: R. Oldenbourg Verlag, 2011), 32; Christian Jansen and Arno Weckbecker, *Der "Volksdeutsche Selbstschutz" in Polen 1939/40* (München: R. Oldenbourg Verlag, 1992), 46.

41. Regina Poziniaz, interview by Myrna Riback, Toronto, Ontario, Canada, 1998, Interview 43438, Visual History Archive, USC Shoah Foundation, Los Angeles, CA. Accessed July 27, 2016. Tape 1, 14:28.

42. Esther Schlussel, interview by Elise Arden, 1995. Tape 1, 19:57.

43. Fanny Wald, interview by Janice Englehart, Seattle, Washington, United States, 1996, Interview 16491, Visual History Archive, USC Shoah Foundation, Los Angeles, CA. Accessed June 2, 2021. Tape 1, 22:46.

44. Maddy Carey, *Jewish Masculinity in the Holocaust: Between Destruction and Construction* (London: Bloomsbury Publishing, 2017), 54, 59, 63, 66–68.

45. Eta Batalion, interview by Lorrie Fein, 1996. Tape 1, 20:02.

46. Regina Silverstein, interview by Agi Hecht, Toronto, Ontario, Canada, 1990, Interview 54317, Visual History Archive, USC Shoah Foundation, Los Angeles, CA. Accessed August 4, 2016. Tape 1, 16:03.

47. Regina Gliksman, interview by Caroline Kohn, Toronto, Ontario, Canada, 1994, Interview 169, Visual History Archive, USC Shoah Foundation, Los Angeles, CA. Accessed August 23, 2017. Tape 1, 21:53.

48. Sonia Szczygielski, interview by Shirley Small, 1996. Tape 2, 2:25.

49. While some scholars such as Klaus-Peter Friedrich find evidence for mass registration as Germans to take advantage of new policies allowing the appropriation of Jewish property and for joining the *Selbstschutz*, Ryszard Kaczmarek notes that the interest in signing Volksdeutsche lists vacillated over time, especially as individuals quickly realized that becoming officially "German" meant being drafted into the Wehrmacht and leaving their property unprotected. Klaus-Peter Friedrich, "Collaboration in a 'Land without a Quisling': Patterns of Cooperation with the Nazi German Occupation Regime in Poland During World War II," *Slavic Review* 64, no. 4 (2005): 711–46; Kaczmarek, *Górny Śląsk podczas II wojny światowej*.

50. Berta Potash, interview by Saerina Tauritz, 1997. Tape 1, 24:18.

51. Berta Potash, interview by Saerina Tauritz, 1997. Tape 2, 0:30.

52. Birgit Beck, *Wehrmacht und sexuelle Gewalt: Sexualverbrechen vor deutschen Militärgerichten, 1939-1945* (Paderborn: Ferdinand Schöningh, 2004); Regina

Mühlhäuser, *Eroberungen: Sexuelle Gewalttaten und intime Beziehungen deutscher Soldaten in der Sowjetunion, 1941–1945* (Hamburg: Hamburger Edition HIS, 2010), 102–03, 109, 372–73. The issues raised by rape and sexual interactions in wartime settings are explored in many texts, but one of the best is Gaby Zipfel, Regina Mühlhäuser, and Kirsten Campbell, eds., *In Plain Sight: Sexual Violence in Armed Conflict* (New Delhi: Zubaan Academic, 2019).

53. Doris L. Bergen, "Tenuousness and Tenacity: The Volksdeutschen of Eastern Europe, World War II, and the Holocaust," in *The Heimat Abroad: The Boundaries of Germaness*, eds. K. Molly O'Donnell, Renate Bridenthal, and Nancy Reagin, 271 (Ann Arbor: University of Michigan Press, 2005); Edward B. Westermann, "'Friend and Helper': German Uniformed Police Operations in Poland and the General Government, 1939–1941," *The Journal of Military History* 58, no. 4 (1994): 649–50.

54. Alexander B. Rossino, "Destructive Impulses: German Soldiers and the Conquest of Poland," *Holocaust and Genocide Studies* 11, no. 3 (1997): 351–65.

55. Phyllis Young, interview by Helen Desman, 1995. Tape 1, 24:26.

56. Anna Weiss, interview by Sharon Savdie, Sydney, Australia, 1995, Interview 7132, Visual History Archive, USC Shoah Foundation, Los Angeles, CA. Accessed September 23, 2016. Tape 2, 7:17.

57. Dagmar Herzog, "Sexuality, Memory, Morality," *History & Memory* 17, no. 1 (2005): 238–66.

58. Nettie Schenkler, interview by Cheryl Lynn Conway, 1997. Tape 1, 19:07.

59. Esther Schlussel, interview by Elise Arden, 1995. Tape 1, 25:30.

60. Mania Richman, interview by Kathy Strochlic, 1995. Tape 1, 23:55.

61. Shoshana Loven, interview by Hana Morris, 1996. Tape 1, 21:38.

62. Shoshana Loven, interview by Hana Morris, 1996. Tape 1, 24:06.

63. Esther Schlussel, interview by Elise Arden, 1995. Tape 2, 3:21.

64. Esther Schlussel, interview by Elise Arden, 1995. Tape 2, 3:38.

65. Elizabeth Harvey, *Women and the Nazi East: Agents and Witnesses of Germanization* (New Haven, CT: Yale University Press, 2003), 56, 206.

66. See the documentation of the experience of the Oświęcim Jewish community in the online exhibit by the Jewish Museum in Oświęcim, titled "Oshpitzin: The Town Known as Auschwitz," https://artsandculture.google.com/exhibit/oshpitzin-the-auschwitz-jewish-center/_wJSImdgJOFkKg?hl=en.

67. Lola Wolpert, interview by Rachel Alkallay, Montréal, Québec, Canada, 1998, Interview 39042, Visual History Archive, USC Shoah Foundation, Los Angeles, CA. Accessed January 18, 2018. Tape 2, 25:11.

68. Lola Wolpert, interview by Rachel Alkallay, 1998. Tape 2, 28:15.

69. Berta Potash, interview by Saerina Tauritz, 1997. Tape 1, 6:50.

70. Sonia Szczygielski, interview by Shirley Small, 1996. Tape 1, 19:15.

71. For an example of how Schmelt communicated with Merin, see Document 198, "The Special Representative from the SS for Forced Labor Requires the Jewish Council to Seize Jews," issued on November 15, 1940, reprinted in Friedrich, *Verfolgung und Ermordung der Juden 1939–1945*, 446–47.

NOTES TO CHAPTER 1

72. Aleksandra Namysło, "Der Einfluss der Zentrale der Jüdischen Ältestenräte in Ostoberschlesien auf das Verhalten der Juden," in *Der Judenmord in den eingegliederten polnischen Gebieten 1939-1945*, eds. Jacek Andrzej Młynarczyk and Jochen Böhler, 311-14 (Osnabrück: Fibre Verlag, 2010).

73. Philip Friedman, "Two 'Saviors' Who Failed: Moses Merin of Sosnowiec and Jacob Gens of Vilna," in *The Nazi Holocaust, Part 6: The Victims of the Holocaust*, ed. Michael Marrus, 489 (Westport, CT: Meckler, 2011).

74. Report on the Activities of the Olkusz Jewish Community, 12/24/1940, Item ID 2635947, Warsaw Collection 1939-1941, Joint Distribution Committee Archives (JDCA).

75. Letter from M. Merin to "American Joint Distribution Committee" Warschau, 9/28/1940, Item ID 2627127, Warsaw Collection 1939-1941, JDCA; "In Memoriam: Isaac Bornstein," Joint Distribution Committee Archives website, https://archives.jdc.org/exhibits/in-memoriam/isaac-bornstein; Bericht über unsere Wohlfahrt, 1/9/1940, Item ID 2636266, Warsaw Collection 1939-1941, JDCA.

76. Dan Porat, *Bitter Reckoning: Israel Tries Holocaust Survivors as Nazi Collaborators* (Cambridge, MA: Harvard University Press, 2019), 187-212.

77. Sonia Szczygielski, interview by Shirley Small, 1996. Tape 1, 22:40.

78. Helen Prince, interview by Masha Loen, 1996. Tape 1, 20:08.

79. Ester Rotenstein, interview by Chana Gotlieb, Jerusalem, Israel, 1998, Interview 47236, Visual History Archive, USC Shoah Foundation, Los Angeles, CA. Accessed January 9, 2018. Tape 2, 17:16.

80. Nettie Schenkler, interview by Cheryl Lynn Conway, 1997. Tape 2, 4:00.

81. Esther Schlussel, interview by Elise Arden, 1995. Tape 2, 11:34.

82. Dan Michman, *The Emergence of Jewish Ghettos During the Holocaust* (Cambridge: Cambridge University Press, 2011), 152-53.

83. Sonia Szczygielski, interview by Shirley Small, 1996. Tape 1, 23:26.

84. Lucy Matzner, interview by Leora Saposnik, Sheboygan, Wisconsin, United States, 1995, Interview 7461, Visual History Archive, USC Shoah Foundation, Los Angeles, CA. Accessed December 15, 2016. Tape 3, 5:34.

85. Phyllis Young, interview by Helen Desman, 1995. Tape 1, 28:03.

86. Phyllis Young, interview by Helen Desman, 1995. Tape 1, 28:10.

87. Shoshana Loven, interview by Hana Morris, 1996. Tape 2, 0:28.

88. Shoshana Loven, interview by Hana Morris, 1996. Tape 2, 1:57.

89. Ida Gelbart, interviewer unavailable, 1993, Interview 52326, Visual History Archive, USC Shoah Foundation, Los Angeles, CA. Accessed December 19, 2016. Tape 1, 33:46.

90. Ester Rotenstein, interview by Chana Gotlieb, 1998. Tape 2, 20:00.

91. Regina Poziniaz, interview by Myrna Riback, 1998. Tape 1, 25:07.

92. Rusia York, interview by Mary Ziegler, Sydney, Australia, 1995, Interview 5213, Visual History Archive, USC Shoah Foundation, Los Angeles, CA. Accessed September 23, 2016. Tape 2, 11:16.

NOTES TO CHAPTER 1

93. Berta Potash, interview by Saerina Tauritz, 1997. Tape 1, 10:09.

94. Berta Potash, interview by Saerina Tauritz, 1997. Tape 1, 13:49.

95. Nettie Schenkler, interview by Cheryl Lynn Conway, 1997. Tape 2, 4:44.

96. Krzysztof Kocjan, *Zagłada olkuskich Żydów* (Olkusz: O. S. K. "Brama," 2002), 14–15.

97. For the official postwar description of the Schmelt organization, including the practice of allowing forced laborers to live in their homes, see the 1978 legal proceedings against the Sosnowitz Gestapo officer Alfred Ludwig (who served under Lindner), Bayern Landeskriminalamt, report 534, October 31, 1978, B.162/3.596, 1946–1950, USHMM.

98. Herman Weiss, "Reichsautobahnlager Geppersdorf (Rzędziwojowice k. Niemodlina), 1940–1942," *Śląski Kwartalnik Historyczny Sobótka* 1, no. 67 (2012): 49–66.

99. Regina Silverstein, interview by Agi Hecht, 1990. Tape 1, 22:30.

100. The Shoah Foundation acquires those interviews in which the structure of chronological questioning and the role of rapport between interviewer and interviewee are similar to its own approach. Author correspondence with Shoah Foundation staff, 2022.

101. Regina Gliksman, interview by Caroline Kohn, 1994. Tape 1, 16:50.

102. Regina Gliksman, interview by Caroline Kohn, 1994. Tape 1, 16:50.

103. Sonia Szczygielski, interview by Shirley Small, 1996. Tape 2, 7:19.

104. Sonia Szczygielski, interview by Shirley Small, 1996. Tape 2, 7:30.

105. This new border was a jurisdictional change that allowed Nazi authorities to more easily assign and transfer Jewish, non-Jewish Polish, and later, prisoner-of-war labor. Sulik, "Volkstumspolitik und Arbeitseinsatz Zwangsarbeiter in der Großindustrie Oberschlesiens," 110 and ff.

106. Sonia Szczygielski, interview by Shirley Small, 1996. Tape 2, 12:08.

107. Helen Prince, interview by Masha Loen, 1996. Tape 1, 22:04.

108. Helen Prince, interview by Masha Loen, 1996. Tape 1, 23:59.

109. Helen Prince, interview by Masha Loen, 1996. Tape 2, 2:20.

110. Maren Röger, *Wartime Relations: Intimacy, Violence, and Prostitution in Occupied Poland, 1939–1945* (New York: Oxford University Press, 2021), 100.

111. Mark Spoerer, "The Nazi War Economy, the Forced Labor System, and the Murder of Jewish and Non-Jewish Workers," in *A Companion to the Holocaust*, eds. Simone Gigliotti and Hilary Earl, 141 (Hoboken, NJ: Wiley, 2020).

112. Stephan Lehnstaedt calls the Schmelt system a mix of "coercion and incentive." Lehnstaedt, "Coercion and Incentive," 400.

113. A-7928 Texlen 16 110/5, AGR.

114. Yetta Flancbaum, interview by Lenore Weinstein, 1996. Tape 1, 24:10.

115. Chana Brandys, interview by Phyllis Dreazen, Skokie, Illinois, United States, 1996, Interview 14459, Visual History Archive, USC Shoah Foundation, Los Angeles, CA. Accessed October 5, 2016. Tape 1, 7:49.

116. Rose Schulman, interview by E. Tina Tito, Monticello, New York, United States, 1996, Interview 18420, Visual History Archive, USC Shoah Foundation, Los Angeles, CA. Accessed August 3, 2016. Tape 1, 24:26.

117. Estera Silberberg, interview by Rhoda F. Daum-Kenner, Rego Park, New York, United States, 1995, Interview 9049, Visual History Archive, USC Shoah Foundation, Los Angeles, CA. Accessed August 3, 2016. Tape 1, 27:30.

118. Anna Weiss, interview by Sharon Savdie, 1995. Tape 2, 5:31.

119. Rose Schulman, interview by E. Tina Tito, 1996. Tape 1, 24:36.

120. Masha Schweitzer, interview by Deborah Tellerman Berkowitz, 1995. Tape 2, 22:55.

121. Aleksandra Namysło, *Zagłada Żydów zagłębiowskich* (Będzin: Instytut Pamięci Narodowej, 2004); Fulbrook, *A Small Town Near Auschwitz*, 218, 224, 241–43; "Yizkor Book for Chrzanow," JewishGen, 99, www.jewishgen.org/yizkor/Chrazanow/Chrzanow.html.

122. Natan Szternfinkiel, *Zagłada Żydów Sosnowca* (Katowice: Centralna Żydowska Komisja Historyczna, 1946 [reissued 2017]).

123. Berta Potash, interview by Saerina Tauritz, 1997. Tape 1, 15:05.

124. Estera Silberberg, interview by Rhoda F. Daum-Kenner, 1995. Tape 2, 3:06.

125. Lucy Matzner, interview by Leora Saposnik, 1995. Tape 3, 3:10.

126. Anna Weiss, interview by Sharon Savdie, 1995. Tape 2, 16:10.

127. Rose Sontag, interview by Ann Lieb, Brooklyn, New York, United States, 1996, Interview 21902, Visual History Archive, USC Shoah Foundation, Los Angeles, CA. Accessed July 25, 2016. Tape 3, 12:41.

128. Esther Schlussel, interview by Elise Arden, 1995. Tape 2, 22:26.

129. Estera Silberberg, interview by Rhoda F. Daum-Kenner, 1995. Tape 2, 2:39.

130. Lucy Matzner, interview by Leora Saposnik, 1995. Tape 3, 6:55.

131. Yetta Flancbaum, interview by Lenore Weinstein, 1996. Tape 1, 21:18.

132. Regina Silverstein, interview by Agi Hecht, 1990. Tape 1, 26:40.

133. Mania Sarna, interview by Ruth Meyer, Englewood Cliffs, New Jersey, United States, 1997, Interview 25887, Visual History Archive, USC Shoah Foundation, Los Angeles, CA. Accessed January 14, 2017. Tape 2, 2:52.

134. Chana Brandys, interview by Phyllis Dreazen, 1996. Tape 2, 8:17.

135. Anna Weiss, interview by Sharon Savdie, 1995. Tape 2, 14:29.

136. Shoshana Loven, interview by Hana Morris, 1996. Tape 3, 0:52.

137. Shoshana Loven, interview by Hana Morris, 1996. Tape 3, 1:20.

138. Rusia York, interview by Mary Ziegler, 1995. Tape 2, 13:22.

139. Szternfinkiel, *Zagłada Żydów Sosnowca*, 37.

140. Rita Riedler, interview by Sherry Amatenstein, 1996. Tape 1, 21:47. According to her birth date given to the Shoah Foundation, Rita R. was thirteen years old in February 1941.

141. Rose Sontag, interview by Ann Lieb, 1996. Tape 2, 18:02.

142. Regina Silverstein, interview by Agi Hecht, 1990. Tape 1, 24:30.

143. Fay B., interview by author, February 10, 2018. Fay B. and her family requested that her last name not be published.

144. Frank Bajohr, "The Holocaust and Corruption," in *Networks of Nazi Persecution: Bureaucracy, Business, and the Organization of the Holocaust*, eds. Gerald Feldman and Wolfgang Seibel, 118–39 (New York: Berghahn Books, 2005).

145. Fay B., interview by author, February 10, 2018.

146. These existed prior to the more well-known Auschwitz subcamps, Gleiwitz I, II, III, and IV.

147. Fay B., interview by author, February 10, 2018.

148. Namysło, *Zagłada Żydów zagłębiowskich*.

149. Eta Batalion, interview by Lorrie Fein, 1996. Tape 2, 7:59.

150. Regina Poziniaz, interview by Myrna Riback, 1998. Tape 2, 0:12.

151. Rosalie Steinweis, interview by Steve Greenberg, 1996. Tape 2, 10:43.

152. Shoshana Loven, interview by Hana Morris, 1996. Tape 2, 13:04.

153. Tola Gilbert, interview by Donna Miller, West Bloomfield, Michigan, United States, 1983, University of Michigan-Dearborn, Holocaust Survivor Oral History Archive, West Bloomfield, MI. "Being Separated from Family," 4:28.

154. Lola Wolpert, interview by Rachel Alkallay, 1998. Tape 3, 1:43.

155. The 1943 raids and relocation to the ghettos are detailed in contemporary accounts available in 2001.71, Testimonies of Zaglembia [*sic*] Survivors, USHMM. See also Browning, *Nazi Policy, Jewish Workers*, 147.

156. Tola Gilbert, interview by Donna Miller, 1983. 0:36.

157. Kaplan, *Between Dignity and Despair*, 8, 17. Writing about 1933–34, Kaplan observes, "In their public tirades and actions, the Nazis focused on Jewish males . . . women took on new roles—interceding for their men with the police, the tax offices, and the landlord—while continuing older patterns of mediating for their families in the neighborhood, at the grocery, or in schools," 17.

158. Finkel, *Ordinary Jews*, 197; Hájková, in *The Last Ghetto*, writes that "Terezín produced a complex society in which ethnicity, social networks, age, gender, and other factors created diverse yet interconnected groups," 59, which she later shows were consequential in negotiating and even at times facilitating processes such as transports to the east.

THE LOCAL LOGICS OF COERCED LABOR

1. Gruner, *Jewish Forced Labor under the Nazis*.

2. Sulik, "Volkstumspolitik und Arbeitseinsatz Zwangsarbeiter in der Großindustrie Oberschlesiens," 108. Sulik finds this labor office network to have been instituted immediately in 1939. The new regulations covered non-Jewish Poles and Germans as well as Jews and were also the means by which the authorities identified and moved Poles for mining and other extractive work. See also Eichholtz, "Zwangsarbeit in der deutschen Kriegswirtschaft," 26.

3. Gutterman, *A Narrow Bridge to Life*, 48; Friedrich, *Die Verfolgung und Ermordung der Europäischen Juden*, 45.

NOTES TO CHAPTER 2

4. Hermann F. Weiss, "Reichsautobahnlager Geppersdorf (Rzędziwojowice k. Niemodlina), 1940–1942," *Śląski Kwartalnik Historyczny* 67, no. 1 (2012): 49–65.

5. RG-10.233, Testimonies of Zaglembia [sic] Survivors, Protokół zeznania świadka Katarzyna Mincer (Witness statement by Katarzyna Mincer), taken on May 27, 1947, by the Jewish Historical Commission in Poland. 2001.71, USHMM.

6. Browning, *Nazi Policy, Jewish Workers*, 62, 88, 148.

7. Peter Hayes, *Industry and Ideology: IG Farben in the Nazi Era* (New York: Cambridge University Press, 1987).

8. Gutterman, *A Narrow Bridge to Life*, 21.

9. See Elissa Mailänder, *Female SS Guards and Workaday Violence: The Majdanek Concentration Camp, 1942–1944* (East Lansing: Michigan State University, 2015); Johannes Schwartz, *"Weibliche Angelegenheiten": Handlungsräume von KZ-Aufseherinnen in Ravensbrück und Neubrandenburg* (Hamburg: Hamburger Edition, 2018).

10. Andrea Rudorff, "Die Strafverfolgung von KZ-Aufseherinnen in Polen," *Zeitschrift für Geschichtswissenschaft* 61, no. 4 (2013): 332.

11. Rose Leichter, interview by Claudette Feier, San Diego, California, United States, 1996, Interview 11673, Visual History Archive, USC Shoah Foundation, Los Angeles, CA. Accessed March 2, 2022. Tape 2, 16:16.

12. Fay B., interview by author, February 10, 2018.

13. International Tracing Service, *Vorläufiges Verzeichnis der Konzentrationslager und deren Außenkommandos sowie anderer Haftstätten unter dem Reichsführer SS, 1933–1945* (Arolsen: International Committee of the Red Cross, 1969), xxix, 1.

14. Alfons Adam, *"Die Arbeiterfrage soll mit Hilfe von KZ-Häftlingen gelöst werden": Zwangsarbeit in KZ-Außenlagern auf dem Gebiet der heutigen Tschechischen Republik* (Berlin: Metropol Verlag, 2013), 14–17.

15. "Verzeichnis der KZ-ähnlichen Lager und Haftstätten sowie von Institutionen und Betrieben . . . ," Zwangsarbeit im NS-Staat, EVZ [Erinnerung Verantwortung Zukunft], 2010, www.bundesarchiv.de/zwangsarbeit/haftstaetten.

16. Meister at Etrich to the head of the Trautenau Arbeitsamt, July 4, 1942, Texlen 16 89/ 5, Státní Okresní Archiv Trutnov (SOAT). The writer is likely referring to the Reichenbach textile cooperative, established in 1942 to coordinate production in private firms so that war needs could be met, when he writes "demanded by the highest places."

17. Constantin Goschler, ed., *Compensation in Practice: The Foundation "Remembrance, Responsibility and Future" and the Legacy of Forced Labour During the Third Reich* (New York: Berghahn Books, 2017); Ferencz, *Less Than Slaves*.

18. The EVZ portal is available at https://www.stiftung-evz.de.

19. Caitlin Murdock, *Changing Places: Society, Culture, and Territory in the Saxon-Bohemian Borderlands, 1870–1946* (Ann Arbor: University of Michigan Press, 2010), 4–5.

20. Klaus J. Bade, *Migration in European History*, trans. Allison Brown (Malden, MA: Blackwell, 2003), 34.

21. Lex Heerma van Voss, Els Hiemstra-Kuperus, and Elise van Nederveen Meerkerk, eds., *The Ashgate Companion to the History of Textile Workers, 1650–2000* (Farnham, Surrey: Ashgate, 2010).

22. The best resource is Bohumír Smutný, *Šest studií k dějinám lnářství na Trutnovsku* (Trutnov: Texlen, 1983).

23. Bohumír Smutný, "Firma Alois Haase—Trutnov," *Lnársky Průmysl: Prsipevky k dejinám* 4 (1981): 165–83, 169. SOAT.

24. Artur Feist, *Die Ostböhmische Leinenindustrie von Trautenau* (Leipzig: Buchdruckerei Helm & Torton, 1927), 72; Claire Morelon, "Respectable Citizens: Civic Militias, Local Patriotism, and Social Order in Late Habsburg Austria (1890–1920)," *Austrian History Yearbook* 51 (2020): 193–219, 204.

25. Bohumír Smutný, "Firma Bratri Walzelove v Poříčí u Trutnova," *Lnársky Průmysl: Prsipevky k dejinám* 3 (1980): 187–210, 203. SOAT.

26. Bohumir Smutný, *České lnářské textilní závody* (Trutnov: Texlen, 1987), 101.

27. Bohumír Smutný, "Firma Bratri Walzelove v Poříčí u Trutnova," *Lnársky Prumysl: Prsipevky k dejinám* 3 (1980): 204–05. SOAT; Harold James, *The Deutsche Bank and the Nazi Economic War against the Jews: The Expropriation of Jewish-owned Property* (Oxford: Cambridge University Press, 2001), 50, 150.

28. Smutný, *České lnářské textilní závody*, 100; Adam, "Die Arbeiterfrage," 84.

29. Ferencz, *Less Than Slaves*, 122–23. Siemens used labor at many concentration camps throughout the Reich and the areas Germany occupied, including non-Jewish forced labor.

30. *Compaß: Kommerzielles Jahrbuch, 1943: Sudetenland*, no publisher information available. This series was an annual guidebook of businesses throughout Germany and Austria. Available from the Zedhia database, https://zedhia.at. For example, Ignaz Etrich owned the Ober Altstadt factory as well as a factory in Bausnitz; Johann Etrich owned the factories in Trautenau and Bernsdorf as well as one each in Jungbuch and Arnau, Julian Etrich owned another concern in the region. Nine Haase family members had businesses in the area.

31. Zimmermann, *Die Sudetendeutschen im NS-Staat*; Jörg Osterloh, *Nationalsozialistische Judenverfolgung im Reichsgau Sudetenland 1938–1945* (München: R. Oldenbourg Verlag, 2006); Murdock, *Changing Places*, 60, 153, 184.

32. Murdock, *Changing Places*, 14, 104; Karl F. Bahm, "The Inconveniences of Nationality: German Bohemians, the Disintegration of the Habsburg Monarchy, and the Attempt to Create a 'Sudeten German' Identity," *Nationalities Papers* 27, no. 3 (1999): 375–405.

33. Ronald M. Smelser, "The Betrayal of a Myth: National Socialism and the Financing of Middle- Class Socialism in the Sudetenland," *Central European History* 5, no. 3 (1972): 256–77.

34. Werner Röhr, "Das Sudetendeutsche Freikorps—Diversionsinstrument der Hitler-Regierung bei der Zerschlagung der Tschechoslowakei," *Militärgeschichtliche Mitteilungen* 52 (1993): 35–66.

35. Citing Ronald Smelser, *Das Sudetenproblem und das Dritte Reich (1933–1938)*,

Peter Longerich writes: "Himmler had already gained experience in the field of ethnic policy after the SD had begun to take an interest in the Sudeten Germans in 1934. Himmler's intelligence agency ran the so-called Sudeten German Control Centre, which Hitler's deputy, Hess, had set up in December 1933 with the help of a Gestapo functionary from Dresden in order to identify any Czech spies among Sudeten German refugees." Peter Longerich, *Heinrich Himmler* (New York: Oxford University Press), 386.

36. Murdock, *Changing Places*, 184.

37. Jörg Osterloh, "Sudetenland," in *The Greater German Reich and the Jews: Nazi Persecution Policies in the Annexed Territories 1935–1945*, eds. Wolf Gruner and Jörg Osterloh, 72 (New York: Berghahn Books, 2015). See also his *Nationalsozialistische Judenverfolgung im Reichsgau Sudetenland 1938–1945* (München: Oldenbourg Verlag, 2006).

38. Mark Cornwall, *The Devil's Wall: The Nationalist Youth Mission of Heinz Rutha* (Cambridge, MA: Harvard University Press, 2012).

39. Eagle Glassheim, *Cleansing the Czechoslovak Borderlands: Migration, Environment, and Health in the Former Sudetenland* (Pittsburgh, PA: University of Pittsburgh Press, 2016); Tara Zahra, *Kidnapped Souls: National Indifference and the Battle for Children in the Bohemian Lands, 1900–1948* (Ithaca, NY: Cornell University Press, 2008).

40. Osterloh, *Nationalsozialistische Judenverfolgung im Reichsgau Sudetenland*.

41. Reinhard Lamer, *Trautenau: Geschichte einer deutschen Stadt* (Wien: Volkstum Verlag, 1971).

42. Zimmermann, *Die Sudetendeutschen im NS-Staat*, 195–96.

43. Osterloh, *Nationalsozialistische Judenverfolgung*, 142; Zimmermann, *Die Sudetendeutschen im NS-Staat*, 209.

44. Smutný, *České lnářské textilní závody*, 98.

45. Götz Aly and Susanne Heim explain that on Kristallnacht "the antisemitism of the street and the mob" became "a coordinated government policy." Götz Aly and Susanne Heim, *Architects of Annihilation: Auschwitz and the Logic of Destruction* (Princeton, NJ: Princeton University Press, 2002), 10.

46. Zimmermann, *Die Sudetendeutschen im NS-Staat*, 387; Osterloh, *Nationalsozialistische Judenverfolgung*, 158–61.

47. Hermann Beck, "State and Society in Pre-March Prussia: The Weavers' Uprising, the Bureaucracy, and the Association for the Welfare of Workers," *Central European History* 25, no. 3 (1992): 303–31; Christina von Hodenberg, *Aufstand der Weber: Die Revolte von 1844 und ihr Aufstieg zum Mythos* (Bonn: Verlag J. H. W. Dietz Nachfolger, 1997), 137–40; Tomasz Kamusella, *Silesia and Central European Nationalisms: The Emergence of Nationalist and Ethnic Groups in Prussian Silesia and Austrian Silesia, 1848–1918* (West Lafayette, IN: Purdue University Press, 2007), 24.

48. Hayes, *Industry and Ideology*; Michael Thad Allen, *The Business of Genocide: The SS, Slave Labor, and the Concentration Camps* (Chapel Hill: University of North Carolina Press, 2002), 63, 71, 76, 127–33.

49. Bernard R. Kroener, Rolf-Dieter Müller, and Hans Umbreit, *Germany and the Second World War*, vol. V (New York: Oxford University Press, 2000), 668. Peter Hayes's case study of IG Farben executives is unparalleled in its picture of how industry adapted and resisted the Nazi program. Hayes, *Industry and Ideology*.

50. Kroener, Müller, and Umbreit, *Germany and the Second World War*, 618; Ulrich Herbert, *Hitler's Foreign Workers: Enforced Foreign Labor in Germany under the Third Reich* (New York: Cambridge University Press, 1997), 61; RG-10.233, Protokół zeznania świadka Katarzyna Mincer (Witness statement by Katarzyna Mincer), taken on May 27, 1947, by the Jewish Historical Commission in Poland, USHMM.

51. Kazimierz Popiołek, *Historia Śląska od pradziejów do 1945 roku* (Katowice: Śląski Instytut Naukowy, 1972). In English, see T. Hunt Tooley, *National Identity and Weimar Germany: Upper Silesia and the Eastern Border, 1918–1922* (Lincoln: University of Nebraska Press, 1997); James Bjork, *Neither German nor Pole: Catholicism and National Indifference in a Central European Borderland* (Ann Arbor: University of Michigan Press, 2009).

52. The significance of the Eastern Strip and the importance of the annexation to the development of Schmelt's labor circuit is expertly researched and presented by Sybille Steinbacher. Sybille Steinbacher, "East Upper Silesia," in *The Greater German Reich and the Jews: Nazi Persecution Policies in the Annexed Territories, 1935–1945*, eds. Wolf Gruner and Jörg Osterloh, 239–66 (New York: Berghahn Books, 2015). See also her more extensive treatment in her *"Musterstadt" Auschwitz*.

53. Gutterman, *A Narrow Bridge to Life*, 32.

54. Sulik, "Volkstumspolitik und Arbeitseinsatz Zwangsarbeiter in der Großindustrie Oberschlesiens."

55. Steinbacher, *"Musterstadt" Auschwitz*, 140–41.

56. Długoborski, "Die Juden aus den eingegliederten Gebieten im Vernichtungslager Auschwitz-Birkenau," 222; "Oshpitzin Exihibition," Jewish Museum in Oświęcim.

57. Friedrich, *Die Verfolgung und Ermordung der europäischen Juden durch das nationalsozialistische Deutschland*, 45.

58. Jansen and Weckbecker, *Der "Volksdeutsche Selbstschutz" in Polen 1939/40*; Ryszard Kaczmarek, "Zwischen Altreich und Besatzungsgebiet: Der Gau Oberschlesien 1939/41–1945," in *Die NS-Gaue: Regionale Mittelinstanzen im Zentralischen "Führerstaat*," eds. Jürgen John, Horst Möller, and Thomas Schaarschmidt, 348–60 (München: R. Oldenbourg Verlag, 2007).

59. Schmelt would, from October 1940, have sole authority over "the entire exploitation of the Jewish labor force." Document ID 82192734, International Tracing Service Archive (ITS), USHMM.

60. Deposition of Else Herta Seidelmann, secretary to Albrecht Schmelt, taken by the Bayerisches Landeskriminalamt, October 31, 1978. She discusses the transfer by Schmelt of Heinrich Lindner and another officer from Breslau to Sosnowiec, as well as Himmler's directive to Schmelt. B 162/ 3.596, Bundesarchiv Lichterfelde (BL).

NOTES TO CHAPTER 2

61. The importance of the coordination of Schmelt and Bracht is mentioned by Rudolf Höss in his memoir. Document ID 82346827, ITS, USHMM.

62. Kaczmarek, "Zwischen Altreich und Besatzungsgebiet," 351.

63. See the Jewish Council receipt for received funds for the wages of Jewish skilled labor employed by the Sosnowiec city administration, noting the Breslau bank account 72583 for the "Reichsführer SS und Chef der Deutschen Polizei für fremdvölkischen Arbeitseinsatz in Oberschlesien," that is, Schmelt, dated October 24, 1941. This is one of many receipts in this file. RG-15.132M, file 0004, document 00025, USHMM.

64. Rudorff, "Arbeit and Vernichtung Reconsidered," 14.

65. Memo informing Himmler that Schmelt and Bracht were using "the surplus of funds from the employment of Jewish labor" for a villa in Parzymiechy. This villa also functioned as a so-called "model farm" and had its own forced labor squad. Document ID 82474558, ITS, USHMM. For Schmelt's transfer to Góra świętej Anny/ St. Annaberg, see Hermann F. Weiss, "Johannsdorf: A Forgotten Forced Labor Camp for Jews in Western Upper Silesia, 1940–1943," *Śląski Kwartalnik Historyczny Sobótka* 75 (2020): 93–121.

66. For the official postwar description of the Schmelt organization, including the practice of allowing Jewish forced laborers to live in their homes, see the 1978 legal proceedings against the Sosnowitz Gestapo officer Alfred Ludwig (who served under Lindner), Bayern Landeskriminalamt, report 534, October 31, 1978, B.162/3.596, 1946–1950, USHMM.

67. Witness and survivor Dov Zalmanovich calls this "a secret partnership with Jewish business owners." In *Spring in the Dark: The Loss of Youth in Bedzin and the Camps* (online resource), https://benyehuda.org/read/6975, n.p., author's translation.

68. RG-50.005.0048, oral history interview with Jack Salzberg, interviewer not available, 1983. 18:22.

69. Hadassah Rosensaft, *Yesterday: My Story* (Washington, DC: The United States Holocaust Memorial Museum, 2004), 20.

70. See Mary Fulbrook, "'Unschuldig schuldig werden'? Systematische Gewalt und die Verfolgung der Juden von Będzin," in *Alltag im Holocaust: Jüdisches Leben im Großdeutschen Reich 1941–1945*, eds. Andrea Löw, Doris L. Bergen, and Anna Hájková, 117–36 (München: R. Oldenbourg Verlag, 2013).

71. Chana Sharp, interview by Lara Singal, Melbourne, Australia, 1997, Interview 26373, Visual History Archive, USC Shoah Foundation, Los Angeles, CA. Accessed July 25, 2016. Tape 1, 20:13.

72. Roza Wolinsky, interview by Steven Cohen, Montréal, Québec, Canada, 1996, Interview 54711, Visual History Archive, USC Shoah Foundation, Los Angeles, CA. Accessed June 22, 2021. Tape 1, 15:53.

73. Fanny Wald, interview by Janice Englehart, 1996. Tape 1, 29:19.

74. Lehnstaedt, "Coercion and Incentive," 410.

75. Susanne Barth, "Revisiting the 'Cosel Period': A Fresh Perspective on the Stopping of Western Deportation Trains En Route to Auschwitz, 1942–1943,"

Shofar 39, no. 2 (2021): 58–60; Herman van Rens and Annelies Wilms, *Tussenstation Cosel: Joodse Mannen uit West Europa naar Dwangarbeiderskampen in Silezië, 1942–1945* (Hilversum: Verloren, 2020).

76. Rudolf Höß, *Kommandant in Auschwitz: Autobiographische Aufzeichnungen des Rudolf Höß*, ed. Martin Broszat (München: Deutscher Taschenbuch Verlag, 2006 [orig. 1963]). See also his immediate postwar testimony, B 162/19.683, pp. 19–20, BL.

77. The policy required employers to submit documentation on "the total of German [Volksdeutsch], Polish and German workers," "the wages paid to Jews up to now," and to answer questions about wage taxes and whether German or Polish labor was available. October 1940. Document ID 82192734, ITS, USHMM.

78. Wochenbericht 54, June 1–7, 1942, Document ID 82348827, ITS.

79. Gutterman, *A Narrow Bridge to Life*, 52.

80. Gutterman, *A Narrow Bridge to Life*, 44–45; Andrea Rudorff, "Arbeit und Vernichtung Reconsidered," 14.

81. Günter Morsch and Agnes Ohm, eds., *The Administrative Centre of the Concentration Camp Terror: The Concentration Camps Inspectorate 1934–1945* (Berlin: Metropol Verlag, 2015), 98–99, 142, 147–52, 267. Morsch and Ohm offer sample requests from firms. Michael Thad Allen argues that Maurer's Inspectorate of the Concentration Camps evaded Pohl's attempts to control it, in part because Pohl's WVHA really did not want to take over the management of prisoner labor from private companies. Allen, *The Business of Genocide*, 201.

82. Christian Gerlach, *The Extermination of the European Jews* (Cambridge: Cambridge University Press, 2016), 199.

83. Gutterman, *A Narrow Bridge to Life*, 27.

84. This person appears to have been Ritterbusch, meaning that Maurer had the Gross-Rosen commandant assign the local inspectors; Ritterbusch's correspondence in 1944 indicates that he was carrying out directives from Department DII. It appears that Maurer's system was to have Gross-Rosen assign SS as inspectors to its subcamps but that DII would decide on specific policies. See MGR-A-7928, circular from *Kommando* Trautenau (Ritterbusch) to the *Arbeitslagern* Parschnitz, Ober Altstadt, Gabersdorf, Bernsdorf, Liebau, and Hohenelbe, Archiwum Gross-Rosen (AGR); MGR-A-7928, from *Konzentrationslager* Gross-Rosen, Haasebroeck (the commandant), to Ritterbusch, AGR.

85. Parschnitz was officially a subcamp of Gross-Rosen by late 1943 but it is unclear exactly when Ritterbusch arrived. The archives contain correspondence only beginning in 1944. See the Office of the Chief of Counsel for War Crimes, Translation of "Instructions to Concentration Camp Commandants' Labor Offices," June 1944, Nuremburg Military Tribunal, vol. 4. See also Allen, *The Business of Genocide*.

86. Adam, *"Die Arbeiterfrage,"* 119.

87. Karay, *Death Comes in Yellow*.

88. Karay, *Death Comes in Yellow*, 125.

NOTES TO CHAPTER 3

THE SOCIAL WORLD OF COERCED LABOR

1. Chana Brandys, interview by Phyllis Dreazen, 1996. Tape 2, 7:40.
2. Helena Keen, interview by Rona Arato, 1995. Tape 2, 22:03.
3. Tola Gilbert, "Life in a Concentration Camp," 5:52. University of Michigan-Dearborn, Holocaust Survivor Oral History Archive, 1983.
4. Chana Brandys, interview by Phyllis Dreazen, 1996. Tape 2, 10:38.
5. Ann Federman, interview by Milton Katz and Sharon Hamil, 1999. 12:03.
6. Shoshana Greenbaum, interview by Ferne Hassan, 1998. Tape 1, 28:24.
7. Berta Potash, interview by Saerina Tauritz, 1997. Tape 1, 16:15.
8. Lucy Matzner, interview by Leora Saposnik, 1995. Tape 3, 9:28.
9. Masha Schweitzer, interview by Deborah Tellerman Berkowitz, 1995. Tape 3, 15:51.
10. Regina Gliksman, interview by Caroline Kohn, 1994. Tape 2, 14:33.
11. Suzan Laufer, interview by Miriam Rutiz, 1995. Tape 3, 14:11.
12. Elizabet Benedek, interview by Nina Elazar-Wolff, Tel Aviv, Israel, 1997, Interview 37905, Visual History Archive, USC Shoah Foundation, Los Angeles, CA. Accessed October 3, 2016. Tape 4, 8:30.
13. Bracha Harari, interview by Lenore Weinstein, North Miami Beach, Florida, United States, 1997, Interview 29347, Visual History Archive, USC Shoah Foundation, Los Angeles, CA. Accessed January 6, 2017. Tape 3, 23:16.
14. Rose Schulman, interview by E. Tina Tito, 1996. Tape 2, 10:36.
15. Rose Kozlovsky, interview by Lucy Samorodin, Baltimore, Maryland, United States, 1997, Interview 28182, Visual History Archive, USC Shoah Foundation, Los Angeles, CA. Accessed December 19, 2016. Tape 2, 5:09.
16. Regina Silverstein, interview by Agi Hecht, 1990. Tape 1, 48:30.
17. Anna Nesselroth, interview by Sylvia Ben Simon, Israel, 1998, Interview 46995, Visual History Archive, USC Shoah Foundation, Los Angeles, CA. Accessed December 16, 2016. Translated from German by the author.
18. RG-50.106.022, oral history interview with Renate Mann, interview by Julie Kopel, location not available, 2013. Jeff and Toby Herr Oral History Archive, United States Holocaust Memorial Museum, Washington, DC, 40:29. This testimony is audio only and was conducted by phone.
19. Rita Riedler, interview by Sherry Amatenstein, 1996. Tape 2, 3:53.
20. Frymeta Feldman, interview by Burton Leiser, 1997. Tape 3, 1:20.
21. Lucy Matzner, interview by Leora Saposnik, 1995. Tape 3, 10:47.
22. Ann Federman, interview by Milton Katz and Sharon Hamil, 1999. 25:40.
23. Kathleen Canning, *Languages of Labor and Gender: Female Factory Work in Germany, 1850–1914* (Ann Arbor: University of Michigan, 1996).
24. Nettie Schenkler, interview by Cheryl Lynn Conway, 1997. Tape 2, 14:48. This interaction occurred in Hannsdorf, a camp outside of the Trautenau region. However, the interaction with the stage of textile processing in which bands must be repaired, the help of Gentiles, and the reaction of the Jewish girls was similar to Parschnitz, where Nettie was transferred soon after.

25. Anna Weiss, interview by Sharon Savdie, 1995. Tape 2, 18:31.

26. Franciszek Piper, "Slave Labour by the Prisoners," in *Selected Problems from the History of KL Auschwitz*, ed. Kazimierz Smoleń, 66 (Oświęcim: Państwowe Muzeum w Oświęcimiu, 1979).

27. Chana Brandys, interview by Phyllis Dreazen, 1996. Tape 2, 13:12.

28. Ann Federman, interview by Milton Katz and Sharon Hamil, 1999. 24:58. Ann F. could be using a technical term that sounds like "barrel," such as "burl."

29. Rosalie Steinweis, interview by Steve Greenberg, 1996. Tape 2, 23:10.

30. Phyllis Young, interview by Helen Desman, 1995. Tape 1, 10:04.

31. Lili Trepper, interview by Deborah Joselson, Melbourne, Australia, 1997, Interview 34765, Visual History Archive, USC Shoah Foundation, Los Angeles, CA. Accessed September 19, 2016. Tape 2, 22:18.

32. AEG, or Allgemeine Elektricitäts-Gesellschaft AG, had been founded in the early 1900s and was a major industrial concern. It worked together with Siemens to create Telefunken, which also used Jewish labor from the Schmelt system and from Auschwitz. Siemens was forced to create a compensation fund through the Jewish Claims Conference after the war and has a statement of apology on its website: https://www.siemens.com/global/en/company/about/history/company/1933-1945.html. On the coerced labor experience at Telefunken, see Lydia Brown, interview by Lenore Weinstein, North Miami Beach, Florida, United States, 1995, Interview 6335, Visual History Archive, USC Shoah Foundation, Los Angeles, CA. Accessed July 9, 2019.

33. Augusta Singer, interview by Penelope Ann Toltz, Sydney, Australia, 1995, Interview 3469, Visual History Archive, USC Shoah Foundation, Los Angeles, CA. Accessed August 4, 2016. Tape 3, 9:17.

34. Yetta Flancbaum, interview by Lenore Weinstein, 1996. Tape 2, 4:24.

35. Frymeta Feldman, interview by Burton Leiser, 1997. Tape 3, 5:52.

36. Ida Gelbart, interviewer unavailable, 1993. Tape 1, 1.04:06.

37. Shoshana Loven, interview by Hana Morris, 1996. Tape 3, 11:06. Here Shoshana L. is referring to her time in the small camp, Gräben, located at some distance from Trautenau. She was transferred to Parschnitz later in the war. Gräben was also part of the Schmelt system, and the dynamic between Gentile and Jewish female workers there was similar to that in the Trautenau-region camps.

38. Helena Keen, interview by Rona Arato, 1995. Tape 3, 13:40.

39. RG-14.101M.2909, B 162/15900, "Zentrale Stelle der Landesjustizverwaltungen Ludwigsburg," Protokoll of Anna Hrda, October 2, 1969, USHMM.

40. Estera Silberberg, interview by Rhoda F. Daum-Kenner, 1995. Tape 2, 13:16.

41. Elizabet Benedek, interview by Nina Elazar-Wolff, 1997. Tape 4, 6:08.

42. Frymeta Feldman, interview by Burton Leiser, 1997. Tape 4, 19:50.

43. Fay B., interview by author, February 10, 2018.

44. Aranka Tusak, interview by Myer Bloom, Melbourne, Australia, 1997, Interview 36847, Visual History Archive, USC Shoah Foundation, Los Angeles, CA. Accessed September 21, 2016. Tape 2, 6:53.

45. Lucy Matzner, interview by Leora Saposnik, 1995. Tape 3, 25:16.

46. Frieda Weinreich, interview by Jenifer Joyce, Fairlawn, New Jersey, United States, 1995, Interview 9814, Visual History Archive, USC Shoah Foundation, Los Angeles, CA. Accessed September 22, 2016. Tape 4, 20:35.

47. Anna Weiss, interview by Sharon Savdie, 1995. Tape 3, 11:03.

48. Magda-Madeleine Fleischmann, interview by Shelly Javasky, Toronto, Ontario, Canada, 1996, Interview 11359, Visual History Archive, USC Shoah Foundation, Los Angeles, CA. Accessed May 3, 2017. Tape 1, 27:59.

49. Yetta Flancbaum, interview by Lenore Weinstein, 1996. Tape 2, 3:42.

50. Paula Szmulewitz, interview by Elise Arden, Delray Beach, Florida, United States, 1995, Interview 5362, Visual History Archive, USC Shoah Foundation, Los Angeles, CA. Accessed December 28, 2016. Tape 3, 1:05.

51. Nettie Schenkler, interview by Cheryl Lynn Conway, 1997. Tape 3, 10:45.

52. Nettie Schenkler, interview by Cheryl Lynn Conway, 1997. Tape 3, 11:57.

53. Karay, *Death Comes in Yellow*, 80–81, 115.

54. Frances Hoyd, interview by Allen Charney, Toronto, Ontario, Canada, 1996, Interview 13971, Visual History Archive, USC Shoah Foundation, Los Angeles, CA. Accessed October 13, 2016. Tape 5, 13:59.

55. Pollin-Galay, *Ecologies of Witnessing*, 123.

56. Regina Gliksman, interview by Caroline Kohn, 1994. Tape 2, 13:38.

57. Bella Cecemski, interview by Naomi Rappaport, Passaic, New Jersey, United States, 1996, Interview 13823, Visual History Archive, USC Shoah Foundation, Los Angeles, CA. Accessed October 3, 2016. Tape 2, 7:12. Tape 2, 7:12.

58. Sonia Szczygielski, interview by Shirley Small, 1996. Tape 3, 10:32.

59. Edith Reti, interview by Christian Froelicher, Surfer's Paradise, Australia, 1997, Interview 38279, Visual History Archive, USC Shoah Foundation, Los Angeles, CA. Accessed July 28, 2016. Tape 3, 21:26.

60. Lucy Matzner, interview by Leora Saposnik, 1995. Tape 3, 14:19.

61. Masha Schweitzer, interview by Deborah Tellerman Berkowitz, 1995. Tape 2, 28:51.

62. Lena Mandelbaum, interview by Marilyn Simon, 2000. Tape 3, 5:15.

63. Hela Kutscher, interview by Mona Clayman, Montréal, Québec, Canada, 1997, Interview 34330, Visual History Archive, USC Shoah Foundation, Los Angeles, CA. Accessed January 12, 2017. Tape 2, 29:31.

64. Rosalie Steinweis, interview by Steve Greenberg, 1996. Tape 2, 27:14.

65. Ann Federman, interview by Milton Katz and Sharon Hamil, 1999. 18:55.

66. Tola Gilbert, "Living Conditions in Camp II," 3:34. University of Michigan-Dearborn, Holocaust Survivor Oral History Archive, 1983.

67. Yetta Posesorski, interview by Shainey Silver, 1988. Tape 1, 34:08.

68. Hájková, *The Last Ghetto*, 132–67.

69. Anna Ziółkowska, "Medycyna obozowa. O tym jak chorowali, cierpieli i umierali żydowscy robotnicy w obozach pracy przymusowej w Poznaniu (1941–1943)," *Zagłada Żydów* 8 (2012): 119–44.

70. Ann Federman, interview by Milton Katz and Sharon Hamil, 1999. 20:32.
71. Ann Federman, interview by Milton Katz and Sharon Hamil, 1999. 26:35.
72. Zimmermann, *Die Sudetendeutschen im NS-Staat*.
73. Helena Keen, interview by Rona Arato, 1995. Tape 2, 24:21.
74. Nettie Schenkler, interview by Cheryl Lynn Conway, 1997. Tape 3, 1:58.
75. Fay B., interview by author, February 10, 2018.
76. Berta Potash, interview by Saerina Tauritz, 1997. Tape 1, 19:01.
77. Nettie Schenkler, interview by Cheryl Lynn Conway, 1997. Tape 2, 19:50.
78. Yetta Posesorski, interview by Shainey Silver, 1988. Tape 1, 24:05.
79. Ester Rotenstein, interview by Chana Gotlieb, 1998. Tape 3, 23:27.
80. Estelle Charman, interview by Dan Gelford, Buffalo Grove, Illinois, 1998, Interview 42464, Visual History Archive, USC Shoah Foundation, Los Angeles, CA. Accessed December 28, 2016. Tape 3, 20:13.
81. Shoshana Loven, interview by Hana Morris, 1996. Tape 3, 26:27.
82. Shoshana Greenbaum, interview by Ferne Hassan, 1998. Tape 2, 8:38.
83. Shoshana Greenbaum, interview by Ferne Hassan, 1998. Tape 2, 9:40.
84. Shoshana Greenbaum, interview by Ferne Hassan, 1998. Tape 2, 12:02.
85. Shoshana Greenbaum, interview by Ferne Hassan, 1998. Tape 3, 6:22.
86. Shoshana Greenbaum, interview by Ferne Hassan, 1998. Tape 3, 7:56.
87. Lucy Matzner, interview by Leora Saposnik, 1995. Tape 4, 2:05.
88. Shoshana Greenbaum, interview by Ferne Hassan, 1998. Tape 2, 22:33.
89. Berta Potash, interview by Saerina Tauritz, 1997. Tape 1, 17:10.
90. Sonia Szczygielski, interview by Shirley Small, 1996. Tape 3, 11:09.
91. Regina Gliksman, interview by Caroline Kohn, 1994. Tape 3, 9:43.
92. Ida Gelbart, interviewer unavailable, 1993. Tape 1, 1.35:56.
93. Magda-Madeleine Fleischmann, interview by Shelly Javasky, 1996. Tape 2, 21:15.
94. Suzan Laufer, interview by Miriam Rutiz, 1995. Tape 3, 10:40.
95. Magda-Madeleine Fleischmann, interview by Shelly Javasky, 1996. Tape 2, 21:35.
96. Regina Gliksman, interview by Caroline Kohn, 1994. Tape 2, 17:57.
97. Estera Silberberg, interview by Rhoda F. Daum-Kenner, 1995. Tape 2, 5:11.
98. Rosalie Steinweis, interview by Steve Greenberg, 1996. Tape 2, 21:47.
99. Gitla Tenenbaum, interview by Stanley Asher, 1994. Tape 1, 10:43.
100. Minnie Wolgelernter, interview by Mary Rothschild, 1995. Tape 2, 18:45.
101. Ann Kirschner, *Sala's Gift: My Mother's Holocaust Story* (New York: Free Press, 2006).
102. Gitla Tenenbaum, interview by Stanley Asher, 1994. Tape 1, 21:17.
103. Israel Gutman and Michael Berenbaum, *Anatomy of the Auschwitz Death Camp* (Bloomington: Indiana University Press, 1994), 21. For an example of the socially embedded approach, see Susana Narotzky and Paz Moreno, "Reciprocity's Dark Side: Negative Reciprocity, Morality and Social Reproduction," *Anthropological Theory* 2, no. 3 (2002): 281–305.
104. Magda Hollander-Lafon, *Four Scraps of Bread* (Notre Dame, IN: University of Notre Dame Press, 2016); Noah Benninga, "The Bricolage of Death: Jewish

Possessions and the Fashioning of the Prisoner Elite in Auschwitz-Birkenau, 1942–1945," in *Objects of War: The Material Culture of Conflict and Displacement*, eds. Leora Auslander and Tara Zahra, 204 (Ithaca, NY: Cornell University Press, 2018).

105. Frymeta Feldman, interview by Burton Leiser, 1997. Tape 3, 5:50.

106. Ann Federman, interview by Milton Katz and Sharon Hamil, 1999. 16:50.

107. Chana Brandys, interview by Phyllis Dreazen, 1996. Tape 2, 27:31.

108. Minnie Wolgelernter, interview by Mary Rothschild, 1995. Tape 1, 28:16.

109. Minnie Wolgelernter, interview by Mary Rothschild, 1995. Tape 2, 3:07.

110. Rita Riedler, interview by Sherry Amatenstein, 1996. Tape 2, 10:47.

111. Helen Freeman, interview by Mary Rothschild, Pasadena, California, United States, 1995, Interview 593, Visual History Archive, USC Shoah Foundation, Los Angeles, CA. Accessed March 9, 2022. Tape 2, 7:12.

112. Phyllis Young, interview by Helen Desman, 1995. Tape 2, 9:07.

113. Frieda Weinreich, interview by Jenifer Joyce, 1995. Tape 4, 17:06.

114. Fay B., interview by author, February 10, 2018.

115. Lola Wolpert, interview by Rachel Alkallay, 1998. Tape 3, 22:27.

116. Item ID 4415506, Sig. 7633/8, "Parschim, Poland [sic], Bela Kaftori's (on the right) photo," Yad Vashem Photo Archives. Used by permission, courtesy of Ze'ev Kaftori. Author's note: This photo is mislabeled in the Yad Vashem Photo Archives as a photo of Bela Kaftori herself. It is instead a photo of a Czech Gentile woman who befriended Kaftori, and who is standing with a guard. The Czech woman gave Kaftori this photo at liberation as a memento. Interview by author with Bela Kaftori's son, Ze'ev Kaftori, July 25, 2021.

117. Yetta Flancbaum, interview by Lenore Weinstein, 1996. Tape 2, 2:33.

118. "Krankenrevier des Bezirkes VII, Verflegung [sic] d. eingeladen Jüdinnen," 16 112/5, Texlen, AGR.

119. Rose Schulman, interview by E. Tina Tito, 1996. Tape 2, 12:06.

120. Regina Gliksman, interview by Caroline Kohn, 1994. Tape 2, 15:25.

121. Sala Kirschner, interview by Susie Grama, Monsey, New York, United States, 1997, Interview 33589, Visual History Archive, USC Shoah Foundation, Los Angeles, CA. Accessed July 3, 2021. Tape 3, 9:15.

122. Masha Schweitzer, interview by Deborah Tellerman Berkowitz, 1995. Tape 2, 30:43.

123. Rose Sontag, interview by Ann Lieb, 1996. Tape 4, 1:20.

124. Lola Wolpert, interview by Rachel Alkallay, 1998. Tape 3, 14:45.

125. RG-50.120.0035, oral history interview with Erna Elerat, interview by Nathan Beyrak, Israel, 1993, Jeff and Toby Herr Oral History Archive, United States Holocaust Memorial Museum Archives, Washington, DC, 1993.

126. RG-50.120.0035, oral history interview with Erna Elerat, interview by Nathan Beyrak, 1993.

127. RG-14.101M.2909, B 162/15900, Zentrale Stelle der Landesjustizverwaltungen Ludwigsburg, Document 622. "Vernehmungsniederschrift, Herr Dr. Wolf Laitner," February 13, 1970. USHMM. Author's translation.

128. Danuta Czech, *Auschwitz Chronicle, 1939–1945* (New York: Henry Holt, 1990), 525–26.

129. Lucy Matzner, interview by Leora Saposnik, 1995. Tape 4, 10:04.

130. Andrea Rudorff, *Frauen in den Außenlagern des Konzentrationslagers Groß-Rosen* (Berlin: Metropol-Verlag, 2014), 224–26.

131. See Regina Gliksman, interview by Caroline Kohn, 1994. Tape 3, 4:40.

132. Helena Keen, interview by Rona Arato, 1995. Tape 2, 28:15.

133. Helena Keen, interview by Rona Arato, 1995. Tape 3, 0:13.

THE CONFLICTED PATHWAY TO SURVIVAL:
A STUDY OF THREE PERIPHERAL CAMPS

1. Rudorff, *Frauen in den Außenlagern*; Gutterman, *A Narrow Bridge to Life*; Isabell Sprenger, *Gross-Rosen: Ein Konzentrationslager in Schlesien* (Köln: Böhlau, 1996).

2. Kryl and Chládková, *Pobočky koncentračního tábora Gross-Rosen*.

3. Miroslav Kryl, "Gabersdorf," United States Holocaust Memorial Museum, *Encyclopedia of Camps and Ghettos 1933–1945*, vol. 1, ed. Geoffrey P. Megargee (Bloomington: Indiana University Press, 2009), 731.

4. Muzeum Gross-Rosen, *Filie Obozu Konzentracyjnego Gross-Rosen* (Wałbrzych: Muzeum Gross-Rosen, 2008), 29–30, AGR; Response to International Tracing Service query by survivor Machela Drapichrust, March 1950, Document ID 1.1.0.7.-87764676, ITS.

5. Response to International Tracing Service query by survivor Sara Helfgott, March 1950, Document ID 1.1.0.7.-87764677 and 87764678, ITS.

6. Miroslav Kryl, "Bernsdorf," United States Holocaust Memorial Museum, *Encyclopedia of Camps and Ghettos 1933–1945*, vol. 1, ed. Geoffrey P. Megargee (Bloomington: Indiana University Press), 706–07.

7. Muzeum Gross-Rosen, *Filie Obozu Konzentracyjnego Gross-Rosen* (Wałbrzych: Muzeum Gross-Rosen, 2008), 10–11, AGR.

8. Response to International Tracing Service query by survivor Simona Hoerburger, March 1950, Document ID 1.1.0.7.-87764836, ITS; Response to International Tracing Service query by survivor Ester Stopnitzer, March 1950, Document ID 1.1.0.7.-87764837, ITS.

9. Muzeum Gross-Rosen, *Filie Obozu Konzentracyjnego Gross-Rosen* (Wałbrzych: Muzeum Gross-Rosen, 2008), 77–78, AGR. Alternative spellings in the sources include "Bühl u. Sohn" or "Buhl und Sohne."

10. Hermann F. Weiss, "Reichsautobahnlager Geppersdorf (Rzędziwojowice k. Niemodlina), 1940–1942," *Śląski Kwartalnik Historyczny Sobótka* 1, no. 67 (2012): 49–66; Materials in the trial of Alfred Ludwig, B 162/3.596, p. 106, BL.

11. Fela Gipsman, interview by Merle Goldberg, Los Angeles, California, United States, 1994, Interview 159, Visual History Archive, USC Shoah Foundation, Los Angeles, CA. Accessed June 26, 2021. Tape 1, 9:20; Edward Gastfriend, *My Father's Testament: Memoir of a Jewish Teenager, 1938–1945* (Philadelphia: Temple University

Press, 2000); Alter Wiener, *64735: From a Name to a Number: A Holocaust Survivor's Autobiography* (Bloomington, IN: AuthorHouse, 2007).

12. Adam, *"Die Arbeiterfrage,"* 119.

13. Kirschner, *Sala's Gift*.

14. Ann Kirschner, Debórah Dwork, and Robert Jan van Pelt, *Letters to Sala: A Young Woman's Life in Nazi Labor Camps* (New York: New York Public Library, 2006).

15. RG-50.431.0448, oral history interview with Sala Kirschner. Jeff and Toby Herr Oral History Archive, United States Holocaust Memorial Museum, Washington, DC; Sala Kirschner, interview by Susie Grama, 1997. The USHMM interview is not excerpted in this book.

16. Dasha Rittenberg, interview by Janice Englehart and Piotr Kadlcik, 1995.

17. Dasha Rittenberg, interview by Janice Englehart and Piotr Kadlcik, 1995. Tape 3, 26:41.

18. Fela Gipsman, interview by Merle Goldberg, 1994. Tape 1, 7:33.

19. Regina Bigayer, interview by Susan Peirez, Bayside, New York, United States, 1998, Interview 43967, Visual History Archive, USC Shoah Foundation, Los Angeles, CA. Accessed June 27, 2021. Tape 3, 7:30.

20. Fryda Fleish, interview by Robert Feldman, Farmington Hills, Michigan, 2008, Interview 55639, Visual History Archive, USC Shoah Foundation, Los Angeles, CA. Accessed July 3, 2021. Tape 1, 29:31.

21. Eda Rubner, interview by Rosanne Krusner, Toronto, Ontario, Canada, 1995, Interview 7868, Visual History Archive, USC Shoah Foundation, Los Angeles, CA. Accessed July 3, 2021. Tape 2, 15:49.

22. Esther Redlitz, interview by Joseph Huttler, Brooklyn, New York, United States, 2000, Interview 50927, Visual History Archive, USC Shoah Foundation, Los Angeles, CA. Accessed July 3, 2021. Tape 2, 12:06.

23. Rosa Schwarzberg, interview by Robert Clary, Laguna Hills, California, United States, 1995, Interview 9645, Visual History Archive, USC Shoah Foundation, Los Angeles, CA. Accessed July 3, 2021. Tape 1, 26:30.

24. Sala Kirschner, interview by Susie Grama, 1997. Tape 2, 11:45.

25. Lehnstaedt, "Coercion and Incentive," 406, 408–09.

26. Sala Kirschner, interview by Susie Grama, 1997. Tape 2, 17:52.

27. Sala Kirschner, interview by Susie Grama, 1997. Tape 2, 16:37.

28. Sala Kirschner, interview by Susie Grama, 1997. Tape 4, 26:43.

29. Regina Bigayer, interview by Susan Peirez, 1998. Tape 3, 24:53.

30. Chaya Silberberg, interview by Ann Lieb, Monticello, New York, United States, 1996, Interview 18783, Visual History Archive, USC Shoah Foundation, Los Angeles, CA. Accessed June 29, 2021. Tape 3, 1:38.

31. Chaya Silberberg, interview by Ann Lieb, 1996. Tape 3, 2:02.

32. Irene Wolnerman, interview by Judy M. Shiffman, Milwaukee, Wisconsin, United States, 1996, Interview 21416, Visual History Archive, USC Shoah Foundation, Los Angeles, CA. Accessed June 23, 2021. Tape 3, 0:24.

33. Bluma Shelonko, interview by Hilary Adah Helstein, Los Angeles, California, United States, 1997, Interview 24886, Visual History Archive, USC Shoah Foundation, Los Angeles, CA. Accessed January 23, 2021. Tape 2, 20:00.

34. Tosia Jakubs-Schwartzbaum, interview by Arlene Adler, Boca Raton, Florida, United States, 1996, Interview 12418, Visual History Archive, USC Shoah Foundation, Los Angeles, CA. Accessed June 23, 2021.

35. Tosia Jakubs-Schwartzbaum, interview by Arlene Adler, 1996. Tape 1, 2:38.

36. Bluma Shelonko, interview by Hilary Adah Helstein, 1997. Tape 2, 8:35.

37. Irene Wolnerman, interview by Judy M. Shiffman, 1996. Tape 3, 15:44.

38. Dora Retman, interview by Rita Lubitz, Melbourne, Australia, 1997, Interview 30450, Visual History Archive, USC Shoah Foundation, Los Angeles, CA. Accessed June 23, 2021. Tape 3, 7:11.

39. Roza Wolinsky, interview by Steven Cohen, 1996. Tape 2, 9:25.

40. Cesia Tau, interview by Phyllis Hochberg, Hewlett, New York, United States, 1996, Interview 14979, Visual History Archive, USC Shoah Foundation, Los Angeles, CA. Accessed June 15, 2021. Tape 2, 12:15.

41. Cesia Tau, interview by Phyllis Hochberg, 1996. Tape 2, 12:58.

42. Cesia Tau, interview by Phyllis Hochberg, 1996. Tape 3, 2:25.

43. Cesia Tau, interview by Phyllis Hochberg, 1996. Tape 3, 22:54.

44. Mina Jankielewitz, interview by Ann Page, Hallandale, Florida, United States, Interview 13325, Visual History Archive, USC Shoah Foundation, Los Angeles, CA. Accessed June 15, 2021. Tape 1, 26:48.

45. Mina Jankielewitz, interview by Ann Page, 1996. Tape 1, 28:16.

46. Mina Jankielewitz, interview by Ann Page, 1996. Tape 3, 7:52.

AUSCHWITZ ARRIVES IN TRAUTENAU

1. Brigid Halbmayr, "Sexualized Violence Against Women during Nazi 'Racial' Persecution," in *Sexual Violence Against Jewish Women During the Holocaust*, eds. Sonja M. Hedgepeth and Rochelle G. Saidel, 29–30 (Waltham, MA: Brandeis University Press, 2010).

2. Daniel Blatman, *The Death Marches: The Final Phase of Nazi Genocide* (Cambridge, MA: Belknap/Harvard University Press, 2011).

3. Halbmayr, "Sexualized Violence Against Women," 29–30.

4. Standortbefehl Nr. 53/43, p. 3, dated November 22, 1943, NS-4/11/F.1, BL. The exact wording requires businesses using prisoner labor to be accountable to the commandant of camp in their region.

5. Nikolaus Wachsmann, *KL: A History of the Nazi Concentration Camps* (New York: Farrar, Straus, and Giroux, 2015).

6. Herbert, *Hitler's Foreign Workers*.

7. Blatman, *The Death Marches*, 40.

8. Longerich, *Heinrich Himmler*, 665.

9. Estera Silberberg, interview by Rhoda F. Daum-Kenner, 1995. Tape 2, 23:43.

10. Regina Gitler, interview by Chaim Rosov, 1995. Tape 1, 20:34.

11. Sally Birnholz, interview by Maximilian Lerner, Brooklyn, New York, United States, 1995, Interview 1556, Visual History Archive, USC Shoah Foundation, Los Angeles, CA. Accessed October 3, 2016. Tape 1, 15:19.

12. Phyllis Young, interview by Helen Desman, 1995. Tape 2, 21:31.

13. Phyllis Young, interview by Helen Desman, 1995. Tape 2, 23:02.

14. Phyllis Young, interview by Helen Desman, 1995. Tape 2, 23:27.

15. Mieczysław Mołdawa, *Gross-Rosen: Obóz Koncentracyjny na Śląsku* (Warszawa: Wydawnictwo Polonia, Warsaw, 1967), 94–95; Alfred Konieczny, *Frauen im Konzentrationslager Groß-Rosen in den Jahren 1944–1945* (Wałbrzych: Państwowe Muzeum Gross-Rosen, 1994).

16. Aleksandra Kobielec, *Więźniowie Żydzi w KL Gross-Rosen: Stan Badań* (Wałbrzych: Państwowe Muzeum Gross-Rosen, 1993).

17. Gutterman, *A Narrow Bridge to Life*, 112.

18. Food allowance receipts for 1944 submitted to the Gross-Rosen Supply Department, MGR-A7928 Texlen 16/110 karton 5, AGR.

19. Three German women working for Haase were rejected from training in Ravensbruck because they were "unfit" to be SS officers. The subject line of this memo is "attitude." MGR-A7928 Texlen 16/110 karton 5, AGR.

20. Ida Gelbart, interviewer unavailable, 1993. Tape 1, 1.43:16.

21. Nettie Schenkler, interview by Cheryl Lynn Conway, 1997. Tape 3, 6:17.

22. Fay B., interview by author, February 10, 2018.

23. Alfred Konieczny, "Das Konzentrationslager Groß-Rosen," in *Dachauer Heft* 5, *Die vergessenen Lager*, eds. Wolfgang Benz and Barbara Distel, 22 (Dachau: Verlag Dachauer Hefte, 1989); Kobielec, *Więźniowie Żydzi w KL Gross-Rosen*; Roman Olszyna, *KL Gross-Rosen: Wybór artykułów* (Wałbrzych: Państwowe Muzeum Gross-Rosen, 2005); Sprenger, *Gross-Rosen: Ein Konzentrationslager in Schlesien*; Kryl and Chládková, *Pobočky koncentračního tábora Gross-Rosen*.

24. Letter from Ritterbusch to the firm Alois Haase dated April 14, 1944. MGR-A7928 Texlen 16/110 karton 5, AGR.

25. Nettie Schenkler, interview by Cheryl Lynn Conway, 1997. Tape 3, 0:29.

26. Robert Sommer, in his research on brothels, offers a full discussion of the development of the coupon system because it was used there extensively. Sommer, "Sexual Exploitation of Women in Nazi Concentration Camp Brothels," in *Sexual Violence against Jewish Women during the Holocaust*, eds. Hedgepeth and Saidel, 46–47. See also Nikolaus Wachsmann's discussion in *KL: A History of the Nazi Concentration Camps*, 412–13. For coupons in Trautenau, see the correspondence between the Haase firm and the Gross-Rosen Supplies Department, MGR-A7928 Texlen 16/110 karton 5, AGR.

27. RG 14-101, B 162/8211, USHMM. His evaluation letter from Gross-Rosen noted that "as a camp commandant and a man he could be harder. He puts too much faith in his fellow man."

28. In a postwar deposition given by former *Lagerführerin* Maria Mühl (Weiß

at the time of the deposition), Mühl remembers Ritterbusch as an "aged, gaunt person." RG-14.101M.2909, B 162/15902, Zentrale Stelle der Landesjustizverwaltungen Ludwigsburg, Document 1120, Protokoll of Maria Weiß, June 25, 1975, USHMM.

29. Anna Weiss, interview by Sharon Savdie, 1995. Tape 3, 24:10.
30. Lola Wolpert, interview by Rachel Alkallay, 1998. Tape 4, 1:44.
31. Estelle Charman, interview by Dan Gelford, 1998. Tape 4, 1:58.
32. RG-14.101M.2909, B 162/15900, Zentrale Stelle der Landesjustizverwaltungen Ludwigsburg, Document 696, Protokoll of Helen Šrámková, September 10, 1970, USHMM.
33. Fay B., interview by author, February 10, 2018.
34. Suzan Laufer, interview by Miriam Rutiz, 1995. Tape 3, 26:27.
35. Ester Rotenstein, interview by Chana Gotlieb, 1998. Tape 3, 26:54.
36. Lucy Matzner, interview by Leora Saposnik, 1995. Tape 3, 22:23.
37. Regina Gliksman, interview by Caroline Kohn, 1994. Tape 2, 19:10.
38. Sonia Szczygielski, interview by Shirley Small, 1996. Tape 3, 24:15.
39. Phyllis Young, interview by Helen Desman, 1995. Tape 2, 14:08.
40. Ann Federman, interview by Milton Katz and Sharon Hamil, 1999. 23:45.
41. Bella Cecemski, interview by Naomi Rappaport, 1996. Tape 2, 9:39.
42. Sonia Szczygielski, interview by Shirley Small, 1996. Tape 3, 25:13.
43. Regina Gliksman, interview by Caroline Kohn, 1994. Tape 2, 19:35.
44. Halbmayr, "Sexualized Violence Against Women," 30.
45. Correspondence from KL Gross-Rosen to the firm Alois Haase in Trautenau, April 14, 1944, MGR-A 7928, AGR.
46. From Ritterbusch to "Lagerführer Trautenau," April 26, 1944, MGR-A-7928, AGR.
47. From Konzentrationslager Gross-Rosen, Kommandantur, to firm Alois Haase, November 14, 1944, MGR-A-7928, AGR.
48. From Konzentrationslager Gross-Rosen, Kommandantur, to firm Alois Haase, November 14, 1944, MGR-A-7928, AGR.
49. Regina Silverstein, interview by Agi Hecht, 1990. Tape 1, 53:26.
50. Regina Silverstein, interview by Agi Hecht, 1990. Tape 1, 53:55.
51. Minnie Wolgelernter, interview by Mary Rothschild, 1995. Tape 2, 23:44.
52. Ida Gelbart, interviewer unavailable, 1993. Tape 2, 1.03:30.
53. Referenced by Ritterbusch in correspondence with factory owners, dated April 26, 1944, Texlen 16 113/5. SOAT.
54. Finkel, *Ordinary Jews*.
55. Esther Schlussel, interview by Elise Arden, 1995. Tape 2, 26:48.
56. Esther Schlussel, interview by Elise Arden, 1995. Tape 3, 0:17.
57. Eta Batalion, interview by Lorrie Fein, 1996. Tape 3, 8:29.
58. Esther Schlussel, interview by Elise Arden, 1995. Tape 3, 1:06.
59. Randolph L. Braham, *The Politics of Genocide: The Holocaust in Hungary* (New York: Columbia University Press, 1981) and *The Nazi's Last Victims: The*

NOTES TO CHAPTER 5

Holocaust in Hungary (Detroit: Wayne State University Press, 1998); Tim J. Cole, "Constructing the 'Jew,' Writing the Holocaust: Hungary 1920–45," *Patterns of Prejudice* 33, no. 3 (1999): 19–27. For a focus on the territories granted in the 1930s, see Raz Segal, "Beyond Holocaust Studies: Rethinking the Holocaust in Hungary," *Journal of Genocide Research* 16, no. 1 (2014): 1–23. For a selection of detailed studies that include social responses to persecution, see Zoltán Vági, László Csősz, and Gábor Kádár, *The Holocaust in Hungary: Evolution of a Genocide* (Lanham, MD: AltaMira Press, 2013). A specific account touching on the themes in this chapter is Franciszek Piper, "Fragmenty Relacji Sándorní Földes," *Głosy Pamięci* 9 (2015): 150.

60. The Jewish communities living within the borders of Hungary at the time of their deportation (1944) were not necessarily ethnically "Hungarian." Hungary was a multiethnic state. In addition, Germany granted Hungary the right to annex border territories with significant populations that had lived under Czechoslovakian or Ukrainian rule. A Jewish family living in 1940 Hungary, for example, could have any number of ethnic self-identifications. Because the girls and women transferred to Trautenau for labor in 1944 were from territories governed by Hungary at the time, they were called "Hungarian Jews" by those already working at the sites.

61. Aranka Tusak, interview by Myer Bloom, 1997. Tape 1, 18:38.

62. Eva Hart, interview by Gretta Rusanow, Sydney, Australia, 1995, Interview 4530, Visual History Archive, USC Shoah Foundation, Los Angeles, CA. Accessed January 5, 2017. Tape 1, 24:08.

63. Katalin Tyler, interview by Kaye Fink, Melbourne, Australia, 1996, Interview 18673, Visual History Archive, USC Shoah Foundation, Los Angeles, CA. Accessed September 19, 2016. Tape 1, 10:00.

64. Frances Hoyd, interview by Allen Charney, 1996. Tape 4, 3:02.

65. Magdolna Hercz, interview by Edie Kalb, Toronto, Ontario, Canada, 1995, Interview 2228, Visual History Archive, USC Shoah Foundation, Los Angeles, CA. Accessed December 20, 2016. Tape 2, 10:57.

66. Lili Trepper, interview by Deborah Joselson, 1997. Tape 2, 11:39.

67. Alice Ginsberg, interview by Louise Bobrow, Brooklyn, New York, United States, 2000, Interview 51263, Visual History Archive, USC Shoah Foundation, Los Angeles, CA. Accessed August 7, 2017. Tape 2, 9:09.

68. Magdolna Hercz, interview by Edie Kalb, 1995. Tape 2, 11:23.

69. Rose Stach, interview by Jason Walker, Melbourne, Australia, 1997, Interview 30911, Visual History Archive, USC Shoah Foundation, Los Angeles, CA. Accessed January 10, 2017. Tape 1, 16:40.

70. Eva David, interview by Renée Firestone, Beverly Hills, California, United States, 1998, Interview 43340, Visual History Archive, USC Shoah Foundation, Los Angeles, CA. Accessed December 30, 2016. Tape 3, 10:26.

71. Elaine Gross, interview by Janie Brown, Philadelphia, Pennsylvania, United States, 1996, Interview 18971, Visual History Archive, USC Shoah Foundation, Los Angeles, CA. Accessed August 23, 2017. Tape 1, 28:35.

72. Alice Ginsberg, interview by Louise Bobrow, 2000. Tape 2, 9:48.

73. Ella Jakubowitz, interview by Rickey Halperin, Brooklyn, New York, United States, 1995, Interview 8689, Visual History Archive, USC Shoah Foundation, Los Angeles, CA. Accessed January 12, 2017. Tape 2, 12:59.

74. Halbmayr, "Sexualized Violence Against Women," 36–37.

75. Magda Fischer, interview by Gay Wendy Belfer, Sydney, Australia, 1995, Interview 2468, Visual History Archive, USC Shoah Foundation, Los Angeles, CA. Accessed January 30, 2018 . Tape 1, 18:23.

76. Lili Trepper, interview by Deborah Joselson, 1997. Tape Tape 2, 12:36.

77. Eva David, interview by Renée Firestone, 1998. Tape 3, 13:03.

78. Eva Hart, interview by Gretta Rusanow, 1995. Tape 2, 13:42.

79. Magdolna Hercz, interview by Edie Kalb, 1995. Tape 2, 16:35.

80. Monika J. Flaschka, "'Only the Pretty Women Were Raped': The Effect of Sexual Violence on Gendered Identities in Concentration Camps," in *Sexual Violence Against Jewish Women During the Holocaust*, eds. Hedgepeth and Saidel, 77–93.

81. Kazimierz Smoleń, citing the postwar testimony of Gerhard Maurer, in *From the History of KL-Auschwitz*, vol. 2 (Oświęcim: Państwowe Muzeum w Oświęcimiu, 1976), 44–45. Peter Hayes documents the frequent visits of IG Farben executives in *Industry and Ideology*, 361–62.

82. Smoleń, citing the postwar testimony of Gerhard Maurer, *From the History of KL-Auschwitz*, 44–45. See also the testimony of Karl Sommer, presented in Bernhard Strebel, *Das KZ Ravensbrück: Geschichte eines Lagerkomplexes* (Paderborn: Schoeningh Ferdinand, 2003), 439.

83. Eva David, interview by Renée Firestone, 1998. Tape 3, 28:22.

84. Magdolna Hercz, interview by Edie Kalb, 1995. Tape 2, 28:36.

85. Magdolna Hercz, interview by Edie Kalb, 1995. Tape 3, 1:01.

86. Livia Radford, interview by Gary Lubell, Denver, Colorado, United States, 1995, Interview 6244, Visual History Archive, USC Shoah Foundation, Los Angeles, CA. Accessed July 27, 2016. Tape 3, 21:11.

87. Hedy Wieder, interview by Barbara Sharon Linz, Sydney, Australia, 1996, Interview 15262, Visual History Archive, USC Shoah Foundation, Los Angeles, CA. Accessed September 23, 2016. Tape 2, 24:17.

88. Ida Gelbart, interviewer unavailable, 1993. Tape 1, 2.01:17.

89. Ida Gelbart, interviewer unavailable, 1993. Tape 1, 1.58:16.

90. Ida Gelbart, interviewer unavailable, 1993. Tape 1, 2.02:24.

91. Ida Gelbart, interviewer unavailable, 1993. Tape 2, 3:21.

92. Ida Gelbart, interviewer unavailable, 1993. Tape 2, 4:27.

93. Rosalie Steinweis, interview by Steve Greenberg, 1996. Tape 3, 5:35.

94. Anna Weiss, interview by Sharon Savdie, 1995. Tape 3, 14:47.

95. Anna Weiss, interview by Sharon Savdie, 1995. Tape 3, 16:11.

96. Helena Keen, interview by Rona Arato, 1995. Tape 3, 16:01.

97. Shoshana Greenbaum, interview by Ferne Hassan, 1998. Tape 3, 9:50.

98. Lucy Matzner, interview by Leora Saposnik, 1995. Tape 3, 23:31.
99. RG-50.106.022, oral history interview with Renate Mann, interview by Julie Kopel, 2013. 1:14:13.
100. Minnie Wolgelernter, interview by Mary Rothschild, 1995. Tape 2, 8:39.
101. Frances Hoyd, interview by Allen Charney, 1996. Tape 5, 4:56.
102. Frances Hoyd, interview by Allen Charney, 1996. Tape 5, 7:00.
103. For Łódź the foundational source is Isaiah Trunk, *Łódź Ghetto: A History*, ed. Robert Moses Shapiro (Bloomington: Indiana University Press, 2006 [originally published in Yiddish in 1962]). See also Andrea Löw, *Juden im Getto Litzmannstadt: Lebensbedingungen, Selbstwahrnehmung, Verhalten* (Göttingen: Wallstein Verlag, 2013). For Radom, see Idit Gil, "The Value of Labor for Jewish Women in Radom," *Nashim: A Journal of Women's Studies and Gender Issues* 27 (2014): 14–37; Sara Bender, "'Here you must work impeccably, otherwise you will be beaten and sent for selection': Jewish Laborers in the City of Radom, Poland 1942–1944," *Kwartalnik Historii Żydów* 252, no. 4 (2014): 749–73.
104. Frieda Weinreich, interview by Jenifer Joyce, 1995. Tape 4, 6:23.
105. Rose Baumgold, interview by Sidney Burke, 1995. Tape 1, 18:38.
106. Gucia Rosen, interview by Dina Brustman, Melbourne, Australia, 1996, Interview 24384, Visual History Archive, USC Shoah Foundation, Los Angeles, CA. Accessed August 2, 2016. Tape 3, 7:17.
107. Ferencz, *Less Than Slaves*, 122–23.
108. Anna Weiss, interview by Sharon Savdie, 1995. Tape 3, 11:28.
109. Frieda Weinreich, interview by Jenifer Joyce, 1995. Tape 4, 15:41.
110. Shoshana Loven, interview by Hana Morris, 1996. Tape 3, 8:17.
111. Ruth Roman, interview by Stella Eliezrie, Anaheim, California, United States, 1995, Interview 10082, Visual History Archive, USC Shoah Foundation, Los Angeles, CA. Accessed August 2, 2016. Tape 3, 16:06.
112. Mania Richman, interview by Kathy Strochlic, 1995. Tape 3, 23:44.
113. Eva Hart, interview by Gretta Rusanow, 1995. Tape 2, 34:18.
114. Lusia Baumgarten, interview by Mary Ziegler, Sydney, Australia, 1995, Interview 4606, Visual History Archive, USC Shoah Foundation, Los Angeles, CA. Accessed January 24, 2017. Tape 3, 11:19.

ETHICS OF CARE AND PRISONER SOCIETY

1. Shoshana Greenbaum, interview by Ferne Hassan, 1998. Tape 2, 7:06.
2. Hájková, *The Last Ghetto*; Suderland, *Inside Concentration Camps*.
3. Michael Becker and Dennis Bock, "Muselmänner and Prisoner Societies: Toward a Sociohistorical Understanding," *The Journal of Holocaust Research* 34, no. 3 (2020): 158–74.
4. Sarah Lucia Hoagland, "Denying Relationality: Epistemology and Ethics and Ignorance," in *Racism and Epistemologies of Ignorance*, eds. Shannon Sullivan and Nancy Tuana, 97 (Albany: State University of New York Press, 2007).
5. Édouard Glissant, *Poetics of Relation* (Ann Arbor: University of Michigan

Press, 1997 [orig. 1990]); Glen Sean Coulthard, *Red Skin, White Masks: Rejecting the Colonial Politics of Recognition* (Minneapolis: University of Minnesota Press, 2014).

    6. Leora Auslander, "Beyond Words," *The American Historical Review* 110, no. 4 (2005): 1017.

    7. Garbarini, *Numbered Days*.

    8. Laura Levitt, *The Objects That Remain* (University Park: Pennsylvania State University Press, 2020).

    9. John K. Roth, *The Failures of Ethics: Confronting the Holocaust, Genocide, and Other Mass Atrocities* (New York: Oxford University Press, 2015).

    10. Cesia Tau, interview by Phyllis Hochberg, 1996. Tape 2, 12:58.

    11. Estelle Charman, interview by Dan Gelford, 1998. Tape 5, 2:13.

    12. Gerda Frieberg, interview by Linda Ruth Davidson, 1996. Tape 6, 8:50.

    13. Anna Ornstein, interview by Helene Elkus, Cincinnati, Ohio, United States, 1996, Interview 12481, Visual History Archive, USC Shoah Foundation, Los Angeles, CA. Accessed November 22, 2018. Tape 4, 3:41. Edith L. also mentions a sexual relationship between a Polish Jewish kitchen worker and a nurse. See Edith Lowbeer, interview by Anita Fisher, Sydney, Australia, 1995, Interview 1916, Visual History Archive, USC Shoah Foundation, Los Angeles, CA. Accessed March 20, 2018. Tape 4, 21:17.

    14. Anna Ornstein, interview by Helene Elkus, 1996. Tape 4, 4:16.

    15. Anna Ornstein, interview by Helene Elkus, 1996. Tape 4, 4:54.

    16. Anna Ornstein, interview by Helene Elkus, 1996. Tape 4, 4:59.

    17. Anna Ornstein, interview by Helene Elkus, 1996. Tape 4, 5:32.

    18. Fela Gipsman, interview by Merle Goldberg, 1994. Tape 1, 11:45.

    19. Fela Gipsman, interview by Merle Goldberg, 1994. Tape 3, 16:31.

    20. Paula Szmulewitz, interview by Elise Arden, 1995. Tape 3, 3:00.

    21. Paula Szmulewitz, interview by Elise Arden, 1995. Tape 3, 3:51.

    22. Paula Szmulewitz, interview by Elise Arden, 1995. Tape 3, 4:06.

    23. Brenda Reiss, interview by Marilyn Feingold, 1996. Tape 1, 19:50. Brenda Reiss remembers her as Luba Frankel.

    24. Bella Korn, interview by Donna Puccini, Skokie, Illinois, United States, Interview 4153, Visual History Archive, USC Shoah Foundation, Los Angeles, CA. Accessed December 19, 2016. Tape 3, 18:33.

    25. Bella Korn, interview by Donna Puccini, 1995. Tape 3, 20:40.

    26. Bella Korn, interview by Donna Puccini, 1995. Tape 3, 21:16.

    27. Minnie Wolgelernter, interview by Mary Rothschild, 1995. Tape 2, 9:07.

    28. Irene Wolnerman, interview by Judy M. Shiffman, 1996. Tape 3, 10:19.

    29. Tosia Jakubs-Schwartzbaum, interview by Arlene Adler, 1996. Tape 2, 14:50.

    30. Dora Retman, interview by Rita Lubitz, 1997. Tape 3, 9:06.

    31. Sala Price, interview by Pamela Travis, Naples, Florida, United States, 1996, Interview 15292, Visual History Archive, USC Shoah Foundation, Los Angeles, CA. Accessed June 25, 2021. Tape 2, 0:25.

32. Mailänder, *Female SS Guards and Workaday Violence*; Schwartz, "Weibliche Angelegenheiten," 92–96.

33. Mailänder, *Female SS Guards and Workaday Violence*, 57, 77–78.

34. Mailänder, *Female SS Guards and Workaday Violence*, 3.

35. Deposition of Filomena Amler, April 25, 1946, ref. 8637/DP, AGR.

36. Deposition of Filomena Amler, April 25, 1946, ref. 8637/DP, AGR.

37. Bella Cecemski, interview by Naomi Rappaport, 1996. Tape 2, 7:49.

38. Berta Bart, interview by Jan Smith, Sydney, Australia, 1995, Interview 1911, Visual History Archive, USC Shoah Foundation, Los Angeles, CA. Accessed July 3, 2021. Tape 1, 27:56.

39. Berta Bart, interview by Jan Smith, 1995. Tape 1, 28:46.

40. Berta Bart, interview by Jan Smith, 1995. Tape 1, 29:27.

41. Chaya Silberberg, interview by Ann Lieb, 1996. Tape 3, 5:35.

42. Rosalie Steinweis, interview by Steve Greenberg, 1996. Tape 2, 24:12.

43. Andrea Rudorff, "Reimagining the 'Gray Zone': Female Prisoner Functionaries in the Gross-Rosen Sub Camp System, 1944–1945," in *Lessons and Legacies XIV*, eds. Tim Cole and Simone Gigliotti, 21–37 (Evanston, IL: Northwestern University Press, 2020).

44. Gastfriend, *My Father's Testament*, 63–67; Dąbrowa Górnicza, "Pinkas Hakehillot Polin," Encyclopedia of Jewish Communities in Poland [yitzkor buch], JewGen, https://www.jewishgen.org/yizkor/pinkas_poland/pol7_00131.html; Wolfgang Curilla, *Der Judenmord in Polen und die Deutsche Ordnungspolizei, 1939–1945* (Paderborn: Verlag Ferdinand Schöningh, 2011), 149–50.

45. Witness and survivor John Ranz, born Jochanan Goldkranz, in his self-published memoir, *Inhumanity: Death March to Buchenwald and the Last Jews of Bendzin* (Bloomington. IN: AuthorHouse 2007), 127. Ranz was a member of the underground Jewish youth organization in Zagłębie. See also the testimony of witness and survivor Jack Salzberg. RG-50.005.0048, oral history interview with Jack Salzberg, interviewer and location not available, 1983, Jeff and Toby Herr Oral History Archive, United States Holocaust Memorial Museum, Washington, DC, 1983. 18:22.

46. Szternfinkiel, *Zagłada Żydów Sosnowca*, 36.

47. This number is cited in Ryszard Kaczmarek, "Antyżydowska polityka władz niemieckich w rejencji katowickiej," in *Zagłada Żydów zagłębiowskich*, ed. Aleksandra Namysło, 30 (Będzin: Instytut Pamięci Narodowej, 2003). See also "Uzasadnienie wroku w sprawie przeciwko Friedrichowi Kuczyńskiemu wydane przez Sad Okręgowy w Sosnowcu" [Justification of the grounds for the matter against Friedrich Kuczynski, delivered by the District Court of Sosnowiec], reprinted in Namysło, ed., *Zagłada Żydów zagłębiowskich*, 144–54.

48. Kaczmarek, "Antyżydowska politika władz niemieckich w rejencji katowickiej," 13–27, 26–27.

49. Kaczmarek, "Antyżydowska politika władz niemieckich w rejencji katowickiej," 13–27, 26, 29.

50. Fulbrook, *A Small Town Near Auschwitz*, 295–99.

51. Curilla, *Der Judenmord in Polen und die Deutsche Ordnungspolizei*, 153.

52. RG-10.223, postwar testimony of Izrael Rosen, May 24, 1945, Testimonies of Zaglembia [*sic*] Survivors, USHMM; Szternfinkiel, *Zagłada Żydów Sosnowca*, 59; Curilla, *Der Judenmord in Polen und die Deutsche Ordnungspolizei*, 153.

53. "Postcards sent to Dwojra Ruchla Kaminski in Parschnitz camp," Item ID 10781077, Record Group 0.75, File 2672, Yad Vashem Digital Collections (YV).

54. "Letters to Mania Zaks," Rose Kaplovitz Collection, USHMM.

55. "Letters to Mania Zaks," Rose Kaplovitz Collection, USHMM.

56. Elżbieta Wichrowska, "Szkicownik jako document autobiograficzy," *Teksty Drugie* 6 (2018): 54–76.

57. Lisa Reid Ricker, "(De)Constructing the Praxis of Memory-Keeping: Late Nineteenth-Century Autograph Albums as Sites of Rhetorical Invention," *Rhetoric Review* 29, no. 3 (2010): 239–56; Thomas A. Green and Lisa Devaney, "Linguistic Play in Autograph Book Inscriptions," *Western Folklore* 48, no. 1 (1989): 51–58.

58. Rina Shapira and Hanna Herzog, "Understanding Youth Culture Through Autograph Books: The Israeli Case," *Journal of American Folklore* 97, no. 386 (1984): 442–60.

59. "Postcards sent to Dwojra Ruchla Kaminski in Parschnitz camp," Item ID 10781077, Record Group 0.75, File 2672, YV.

60. "Postcards sent to Dwojra Ruchla Kaminski in Parschnitz camp," Item ID 10781077, Record Group 0.75, File 2672, YV.

61. "Spots of Light: Women in the Holocaust," Regina Honigman. Yad Vashem World Holocaust Remembrance Center. https://www.yadvashem.org/yv/en/exhibitions/women-in-the-holocaust/everyday-life/regina-honigman.asp. The translation from Polish is by Yad Vashem.

62. Janusz Stradecki, *Julian Tuwim: Bibliografia* (Warszawa: Państwowe Instytut Wydawniczy, 1959), 255; Czesław Miłosz, *Abecadło Miłosza* (Kraków: Wydawnictwo Literackie, 1997)

63. "Spots of Light: Women in the Holocaust," Regina Honigman.

64. David G. Roskies, "Wartime Victim Writing in Eastern Europe," in *Literature of the Holocaust*, ed. Alan Rosen, 15–32 (Cambridge: Cambridge University Press, 2013).

65. Roskies, "Wartime Victim Writing in Eastern Europe," 24.

66. Levitt, *The Objects That Remain*, 136.

DESIRE AND SPACE IN THE COERCED LABOR EXPERIENCE

1. Lola Wolpert, interview by Rachel Alkallay, 1998. Tape 4, 16:07.
2. Ida Gelbart, interviewer unavailable, 1993. Tape 1, 1.08:40.
3. Lucy Matzner, interview by Leora Saposnik, 1995. Tape 3, 13:29.
4. Frymeta Feldman, interview by Burton Leiser, 1997. Tape 3, 10:35.
5. Mania Sarna, interview by Ruth Meyer, 1997. Tape 2, 27:43.
6. Ida Gelbart, interviewer unavailable, 1993. Tape 1, 1.09:36.
7. Gucia Rosen, interview by Dina Brustman, 1996. Tape 3, 9:22.

8. Anna Weiss, interview by Sharon Savdie, 1995. Tape 3, 18:10.
9. Helena Keen, interview by Rona Arato, 1995. Tape 3, 3:00.
10. Helena Keen, interview by Rona Arato, 1995. Tape 3, 6:56.
11. Yetta Posesorski, interview by Shainey Silver, 1988. Tape 1, 35:26.
12. Shoshana Greenbaum, interview by Ferne Hassan, 1998. Tape 3, 11:03.
13. Bella Cecemski, interview by Naomi Rappaport, 1996. Tape 1, 27:20.
14. Estera Silberberg, interview by Rhoda F. Daum-Kenner, 1995. Tape 2, 21:31.
15. Lola Wolpert, interview by Rachel Alkallay, 1998. Tape 4, 0:31.
16. Shoshana Greenbaum, interview by Ferne Hassan, 1998. Tape 3, 11:04.
17. Dora Retman, interview by Rita Lubitz, 1997. Tape 3, 14:07.
18. Herbert, *Hitler's Foreign Workers*.
19. Cornelie Usborne, "Female Sexual Desire and Male Honor: German Women's Illicit Love Affairs with Prisoners of War During the Second World War," *Journal of the History of Sexuality* 26, no. 3 (2017): 485. Raffael Scheck also emphasizes factors specific to the situation of non-Jewish German women in the Reich in *Love Between Enemies: Western Prisoners of War and German Women in World War II* (Cambridge: Cambridge University Press, 2021).
20. Suzan Laufer, interview by Miriam Rutiz, 1995. Tape 3, 11:42.
21. Ida Gelbart, interviewer unavailable, 1993. Tape 1, 1.38:06.
22. Ida Gelbart, interviewer unavailable, 1993. Tape 2, 57:00.
23. Olga Kovacs, interview by Dorothy Shiloff Hughes, New York, New York, United States, 1995, Interview 3012, Visual History Archive, USC Shoah Foundation, Los Angeles, CA. Accessed January 5, 2017. Tape 4, 27:56.
24. Yetta Posesorski, interview by Shainey Silver, 1988. Tape 1, 27:42.
25. Usborne, "Female Sexual Desire and Male Honor," 477.
26. Franci Rabinek Epstein, *Franci's War: A Woman's Story of Survival* (New York: Penguin, 2020).
27. Phyllis Young, interview by Helen Desman, 1995. Tape 3, 0:33.
28. Phyllis Young, interview by Helen Desman, 1995. Tape 3, 0:49.
29. Eva Wellner, interview by Robert Clary, Laguna Hills, California, United States, 1995, Interview 9342, Visual History Archive, USC Shoah Foundation, Los Angeles, CA. Accessed June 26, 2021. Tape 2, 2:58.
30. Rose Klein, interview by Risa Hochbaum Miron, Deerfield Beach, Florida, United States, 1996, Interview 12381, Visual History Archive, USC Shoah Foundation, Los Angeles, CA. Accessed August 22, 2016. Tape 3, 18:00.
31. Rose Klein, interview by Risa Hochbaum Miron, 1996. Tape 3, 19:53.
32. Tola Gilbert, "Dealing with the SS," 0:15. University of Michigan-Dearborn, Holocaust Survivor Oral History Archive, 1983.
33. Lena Mandelbaum, interview by Marilyn Simon, 2000. Tape 3, 16:50.
34. Aranka Tusak, interview by Myer Bloom, 1997. Tape 2, 13:19.
35. Volker Zimmermann notes that Sudetengau authorities wanted all Czechs resettled, but in practice this did not happen; ethnic policies on the ground were "improvised," allowing local municipalities to avoid any type of anti-Czech ethnic

cleansing. Zimmermann, *Die Sudetendeutschen im NS-Staat*, 287. For prisoners of war, see Usborne, "Female Sexual Desire and Male Honor," 459–60.

36. Simon P. MacKenzie, "The Treatment of Prisoners of War in World War II," *Journal of Modern History* 66, no. 3 (1994): 487–520, 496.

37. Irene Wolnerman, interview by Judy M. Shiffman, 1996. Tape 3, 22:07.

38. Postwar testimony and summary sheet for Edith Stuart, Ref. 1656/3/8/73, Catalog ID 105701, Wiener Library (WL).

39. Blatman, *The Death Marches*, 79–93.

40. Roman Olszyna, *KL Gross-Rosen: Wybór Artykułów* (Wałbrzych: Państwowe Muzeum Gross-Rosen, 2005), 163–64; Osterloh, *Nationalsozialistische Judenverfolgung im Reichsgau Sudetenland*, 551.

41. Ranz describes a death march he was on as a prisoner that passed by Blechhammer. Ranz, *Inhumanity: Death March to Buchenwald and the Last Jews of Bendzin*, 2007.

42. Bohdan Cybulski, *Ewakuacja Więźniów AL Riese do Trautenau: Próba Rekonstrukcji Wydarzeń* (Wałbrzych: Państwowe Muzeum Gross-Rosen, 1989).

43. Irena Malá and Ludmila Kubátová, *Pochody Smrti* (Praha: Nakladatelství Politické Literatury, 1965); Jirí Nenutil, *Pochody Smrti: Česky Príspevek k Otevrené Otázce* (Plzeň: Vydavatelství Západočeské Univerzity v Plzni, 2011).

44. Václav Sádlo, *Gross-Rosen: Historie, Která se nás tyká*, brochure published by the municipal government of Králove Hradecky, Czech Republic.

45. Rose Sontag, interview by Ann Lieb, 1996. Tape 4, 6:26.

46. Anna Weiss, interview by Sharon Savdie, 1995. Tape 3, 22:28.

47. Rosalie Steinweis, interview by Steve Greenberg, 1996. Tape 3, 8:10.

48. Estelle Charman, interview by Dan Gelford, 1998. Tape 4, 14:27.

49. Frymeta Feldman, interview by Burton Leiser, 1997. Tape 2, 22:08.

50. Shoshana Greenbaum, interview by Ferne Hassan, 1998. Tape 3, 12:51.

51. Lucy Matzner, interview by Leora Saposnik, 1995. Tape 4, 7:38.

52. Phyllis Young, interview by Helen Desman, 1995. Tape 3, 14:04.

53. Gucia Rosen, interview by Dina Brustman, 1996. Tape 3, 10:27.

54. Anna Weiss, interview by Sharon Savdie, 1995. Tape 3, 22:10.

55. Phyllis Young, interview by Helen Desman, 1995. Tape 3, 13:42.

56. Olga Kovacs, interview by Dorothy Shiloff Hughes, 1995. Tape 4, 29:32.

57. Ida Gelbart, interviewer unavailable, 1993. Tape 1, 1:52.

58. Regina Gliksman, interview by Caroline Kohn, 1994. Tape 2, 20:38.

59. Shoshana Greenbaum, interview by Ferne Hassan, 1998. Tape 3, 13:14.

60. Ida Gelbart, interviewer unavailable, 1993. Tape 1, 1:54.

61. Shoshana Greenbaum, interview by Ferne Hassan, 1998. Tape 3, 13:25.

62. Phyllis Young, interview by Helen Desman, 1995. Tape 3, 14:59.

63. Lena Mandelbaum, interview by Marilyn Simon, 2000. Tape 3, 18:01.

64. Ida Gelbart, interviewer unavailable, 1993. Tape 1, 1.55:54.

65. Shoshana Greenbaum, interview by Ferne Hassan, 1998. Tape 3, 13:56.

66. Estera Silberberg, interview by Rhoda F. Daum-Kenner, 1995. Tape 3, 5:07.

NOTES TO CHAPTER 8

67. Regina Gliksman, interview by Caroline Kohn, 1994. Tape 2, 21:30.
68. Estelle Charman, interview by Dan Gelford, 1998. Tape 4, 16:15.
69. Rose Schulman, interview by E. Tina Tito, 1996. Tape 2, 19:50.
70. RG-50.106.022, oral history interview with Renate Mann, interview by Julie Kopel, 2013. 1:12:48.
71. Rose Sontag, interview by Ann Lieb, 1996. Tape 4, 7:27.
72. Anna Weiss, interview by Sharon Savdie, 1995. Tape 3, 20:08.

THE VIOLENCE AND LOSSES OF LIBERATION

1. Gucia Rosen, interview by Dina Brustman, 1996. Tape 3, 11:54.
2. For an approach to liberation that addresses ambivalence, see Yehudit Kleiman and Nina Springer-Aharoni, *The Anguish of Liberation: Testimonies from 1945* (Jerusalem: Yad Vashem, 1995).
3. Anna Weiss, interview by Sharon Savdie, 1995. Tape 3, 18:35.
4. Helena Keen, interview by Rona Arato, 1995. Tape 3, 17:01.
5. Frances Hoyd, interview by Allen Charney, 1996. Tape 5, 21:46.
6. Regina Gitler, interview by Chaim Rosov, 1995. Tape 1, 2:29.
7. Magda-Madeleine Fleischmann, interview by Shelly Javasky, 1996. Tape 2, 14:17.
8. Bella Cecemski, interview by Naomi Rappaport, 1996. Tape 1, 20:00.
9. Estera Silberberg, interview by Rhoda F. Daum-Kenner, 1995. Tape 3, 2:58.
10. Gucia Rosen, interview by Dina Brustman, 1996. Tape 3, 8:42.
11. Shoshana Loven, interview by Hana Morris, 1996. Tape 4, 11:56.
12. Frieda Weinreich, interview by Jenifer Joyce, 1995. Tape 4, 21:05.
13. Livia Radford, interview by Gary Lubell, 1995. Tape 4, 21:13.
14. Regina Lewin, interview by Deborah Kattler-Kupetz, Los Angeles, California, United States, Interview 719, Visual History Archive, USC Shoah Foundation, Los Angeles, CA. Accessed December 5, 2016. Tape 3, 23:14.
15. Esther Klein, interview by Naomi Rappaport, New York, New York, United States, 1996, Interview 13949, Visual History Archive, USC Shoah Foundation, Los Angeles, CA. Accessed August 22, 2016. Tape 5, 16:52.
16. Lola Wolpert, interview by Rachel Alkallay, 1998. Tape 4, 23:01.
17. Chana Brandys, interview by Phyllis Dreazen, 1996. Tape 3, 4:49.
18. Lena Mandelbaum, interview by Marilyn Simon, 2000. Tape 3, 23:12. The testimony-giver is referring to the general atmosphere of Soviet soldiers' presence and not to a specific sexual assault.
19. Magda-Madeleine Fleischmann, interview by Shelly Javasky, 1996. Tape 2, 17:31.
20. Cesia Tau, interview by Phyllis Hochberg, 1996. Tape 3, 24.20.
21. Lusia Baumgarten, interview by Mary Ziegler, 1995. Tape 3, 11:19.
22. Mania Sarna, interview by Ruth Meyer, 1997. Tape 2, 28:16.
23. Anna Veprinska, *Empathy in Contemporary Poetry After Crisis* (Cham: Palgrave Macmillan, 2020), 3–4, 48–49.
24. Lena Mandelbaum, interview by Marilyn Simon, 2000. Tape 3, 23:24.

25. Shoshana Loven, interview by Hana Morris, 1996. Tape 4, 12:27.
26. Ida Gelbart, interviewer unavailable, 1993. Tape 2, 11:35.
27. Estelle Charman, interview by Dan Gelford, 1998. Tape 5, 13:29.
28. Regina Gitler, interview by Chaim Rosov, 1995. Tape 2, 5:22.
29. Regina Poziniaz, interview by Myrna Riback, 1998. Tape 3, 0:15.
30. Rusia York, interview by Mary Ziegler, 1995. Tape 4, 1:41.
31. Shoshana Greenbaum, interview by Ferne Hassan, 1998. Tape 3, 21:50.
32. Shoshana Greenbaum, interview by Ferne Hassan, 1998. Tape 3, 22:04.
33. Atina Grossmann, *Jews, Germans, and Allies: Close Encounters in Occupied Germany* (Princeton, NJ: Princeton University Press, 2007).
34. This scholarship includes Sarah M. Cushman, "Sexuality, Sexual Violence, and Sexual Barter in the Auschwitz-Birkenau Women's Camp," in *Agency and the Holocaust: Essays in Honor of Debórah Dwork*, eds. Thomas Kühne and Mary Jane Rein, 105–22 (Cham: Palgrave Macmillan, 2020); Maren Röger, "The Sexual Policies and Sexual Realities of the German Occupiers in Poland in the Second World War," *Contemporary European History* 23, no. 1 (2014): 1–21; Dorota Glowacka, "Sexual Violence Among Men and Boys During the Holocaust: A Genealogy of (Not-So-Silent) Silence," *German History* 39, no. 1 (2021): 78–99.
35. Lena Mandelbaum, interview by Marilyn Simon, 2000. Tape 3, 23:37.
36. Anna Hájková, "Sexual Barter in Times of Genocide: Negotiating the Sexual Economy of the Theresienstadt Ghetto," *Signs* 38, no. 3 (2013): 503–33. Hájková's focus is inmate-to-inmate relations, but her work can be productively placed in conversation with Atina Grossman's to foreground the importance of detailing the specific settings of vulnerability and inequality. See also Katya Gusarov, "Sexual Barter and Jewish Women's Efforts to Save Their Lives: Accounts from the Righteous Among the Nations Archives," *German History* 39, no. 1 (2021): 100–11.
37. Debórah Dwork, "Sexual Abuse, Sexual Barter, and Silence," *Holocaust Studies* 27, no. 4 (2021): 495–500.
38. Marion Kaplan, "Did Gender Matter During the Holocaust?" *Jewish Social Studies* 24, no. 2 (2019): 37–56, 44.
39. Chana Brandys, interview by Phyllis Dreazen, 1996. Tape 3, 6:40.
40. Lydia Brown, interview by Lenore Weinstein, 1995. Tape 5, 4:33.
41. Lydia Brown, interview by Lenore Weinstein, 1995. Tape 5, 5:50.
42. Lydia Brown, interview by Lenore Weinstein, 1995. Tape 5, 6:07.
43. Tola Gilbert, "Dealing with the Russians," 2:42. University of Michigan-Dearborn, Holocaust Survivor Oral History Archive, 1983.
44. Tola Gilbert, "Dealing with the Russians," 3:20.
45. Suzan Laufer, interview by Miriam Rutiz, 1995. Tape 4, 0:36.
46. Mania Sarna, interview by Ruth Meyer, 1997. Tape 2, 28:29.
47. Ida Gelbart, interviewer unavailable, 1993. Tape 2, 16:31.
48. Shoshana Loven, interview by Hana Morris, 1996. Tape 4, 11:47.
49. Elizabet Benedek, interview by Nina Elazar-Wolff, 1997. Tape 4, 18:56.

NOTES TO CHAPTER 8

50. Fanny Wald, interview by Janice Englehart, 1996. Tape 2, 27:57. V

51. RG-50.106.022, oral history interview with Renate Mann, interview by Julie Kopel, 2013. 1:20:11.

52. Hedy Wieder, interview by Barbara Sharon Linz, 1996. Tape 3, 16:11.

53. Hedy Wieder, interview by Barbara Sharon Linz, 1996. Tape 3, 19:49.

54. Hedy Wieder, interview by Barbara Sharon Linz, 1996. Tape 3, 21:07.

55. Phyllis Young, interview by Helen Desman, 1995. Tape 3, 22:44.

56. Yetta Posesorski, interview by Shainey Silver, 1988. Tape 2, 6:41.

57. Shoshana Loven, interview by Hana Morris, 1996. Tape 4, 11:18.

58. Elisabeth Jean Wood, "Armed Groups and Sexual Violence: When Is Wartime Rape Rare?" *Politics & Society* 37, no. 1 (2009): 131–61; Dara Kay Cohen, *Rape During Civil War* (Ithaca, NY: Cornell University Press, 2016); Jeffrey Burds, "Sexual Violence in Europe in World War II, 1939–1945," *Politics & Society* 37, no. 1 (2009): 35–73.

59. Oleg Budnitskii, "The Intelligentsia Meets the Enemy: Educated Soviet Officers in Defeated Germany, 1945," *Kritika* 10, no. 3 (2009): 629–82.

60. Budnitskii, "The Intelligentsia Meets the Enemy," 665.

61. Vojin Majstorović, "Red Army Troops Encounter the Holocaust: Transnistria, Moldavia, Romania, Bulgaria, Yugoslavia, Hungary, and Austria, 1944–1945," *Holocaust and Genocide Studies* 32, no. 2 (2018): 255–56.

62. Regina Mühlhäuser, "Reframing Sexual Violence as a Weapon and Strategy of War: The Case of the German Wehrmacht During the War and Genocide in the Soviet Union, 1941–1944," *Journal of the History of Sexuality* 26, no. 3 (2017): 393–95.

63. Mühlhäuser, "Reframing Sexual Violence as a Weapon and Strategy of War," 400.

64. Shoshana Loven, interview by Hana Morris, 1996. Tape 4, 11:56.

65. Shoshana Loven, interview by Hana Morris, 1996. Tape 4, 11:57.

66. Anna Ornstein, interview by Helene Elkus, 1996. Tape 4, 8:35.

67. Gerda Frieberg, interview by Linda Ruth Davidson, 1996. Tape 7, 5:56.

68. Esther Lijek, interview by Joanne Silberstein, 1996. Tape 2, 20:03.

69. Anna Ornstein, interview by Helene Elkus, 1996. Tape 4, 13:06.

70. Berta Potash, interview by Saerina Tauritz, 1997. Tape 2, 11:41.

71. Berta Potash, interview by Saerina Tauritz, 1997. Tape 2, 16:30.

72. Minnie Wolgelernter, interview by Mary Rothschild, 1995. Tape 3, 0:20.

73. Shoshana Loven, interview by Hana Morris, 1996. Tape 4, 13:42.

74. Helen Freeman, interview by Mary Rothschild, 1995. Tape 2, 10:57. For systematic treatments of the return to home, see Lukasz Krzyzanowski, *Ghost Citizens: Jewish Return to a Postwar City* (Cambridge, MA: Harvard University Press, 2020); Monika Rice, *"What! Still Alive?!" Jewish Survivors in Poland and Israel Remember Homecoming* (Syracuse, NY: Syracuse University Press, 2017).

75. Helen Freeman, interview by Mary Rothschild, 1995. Tape 2, 11:07. During the occupation, Gentile Poles living in Sosnowiec sent letters to the civil administration requesting to be given Jewish homes. RG-132M, Files 007 and 008, USHMM.

76. Ida Gelbart, interviewer unavailable, 1993. Tape 2, 23:59.

77. Rose Kozlovsky, interview by Lucy Samorodin, 1997. Tape 2, 20:04.

78. Esther Lijek, interview by Joanne Silberstein, 1996. Tape 2, 21:11.

79. Yetta Posesorski, interview by Shainey Silver, 1988. Tape 1, 50:58.

80. Eva Koplowicz, interviewer and location not available, 2007, Interview 55311, Visual History Archive, USC Shoah Foundation, Los Angeles, CA. Accessed March 9, 2022. Tape 2, 12:09.

81. The literature includes Jan Gross, *Fear: Anti-Semitism in Poland after Auschwitz* (New York: Random House, 2007); Rice, "What! Still Alive?!"; Laura Quercioli-Mincer, "'Nie będziemy się więcej bać ludzi?' Powrót po Zagładzie w literaturze polsko-żydowskiej," *Kwartalnik Historii Żydów* 222, no. 2 (2007): 199–225; Elizabeth Anthony, *The Compromise of Return: Viennese Jews After the Holocaust* (Detroit: Wayne State University Press, 2021).

82. Anna Cichopek-Gajraj, *Beyond Violence: Jewish Survivors in Poland and Slovakia, 1944–1948* (New York: Cambridge University Press, 2014), 30.

83. Rose Kozlovsky, interview by Lucy Samorodin, 1997. Tape 2, 20:20.

84. Fay B., interview by author, February 10, 2018.

85. Fay B., interview by author, February 10, 2018.

86. Fay B., interview by author, February 10, 2018.

87. Katarzyna Person, "'I Am a Jewish DP. A Jew from the Eternal Nowhere,'" *Kwartalnik Historii Żydów* 246, no. 2 (2013): 312–18; Boaz Cohen, "The Jewish DP Experience," in *The Routledge History of the Holocaust*, ed. Jonathan C. Friedman, 432–42 (New York: Routledge, 2010); Avinoam J. Patt and Michael Berkowitz, eds., *'We Are Here': New Approaches to Jewish Displaced Persons in Postwar Germany* (Detroit: Wayne State University Press, 2010).

88. Ann Federman, interview by Milton Katz and Sharon Hamil, 1999. 30:19.

CONCLUSION AND CODA

Epigraph: Fryda Fleish, interview by Robert Feldman, 2008. Tape 1, 23:34.

1. Lamer, *Trautenau: Geschichte einer deutschen Stadt*.

2. Lamer, *Trautenau: Geschichte einer deutschen Stadt*; Benjamin Frommer, *National Cleansing: Retribution against Nazi Collaborators in Postwar Czechoslovakia* (Cambridge: Cambridge University Press, 2005).

3. Lamer, *Trautenau: Geschichte einer deutschen Stadt*, 194–97.

4. Frommer, *National Cleansing*; Ray Douglas, *Orderly and Humane: The Expulsion of the Germans after the Second World War* (New Haven, CT: Yale University Press, 2012). Douglas analyzes the emergence of detention centers that removed Sudeten German families from their homes and resources, rendering them vulnerable to predation.

5. Stefan Wolff, "Introduction," in *Coming Home to Germany? The Integration of Ethnic Germans from Central and Eastern Europe in the Federal Republic*, eds. David Rock and Stefan Wolff, 10 (New York: Berghahn Books, 2002).

6. David Gerlach, *The Economy of Ethnic Cleansing: The Transformation of the German-Czech Borderlands after World War II* (Cambridge: Cambridge University Press, 2017), 157, 196.

7. Haase Hauptbuchabschluss, Karton 10, Cislo 152, Fond 16, Texlen. SOAT.

8. Glassheim, *Cleansing the Czechoslovak Borderlands*.

9. "Igo Etrich," Trutnov, https://www.ictrutnov.cz/igo-etrich. Etrich invented a new type of air glider and is featured in many technical and aviation museums throughout the world.

10. The Walzel brothers were not related to Oskar Walzel, an Austrian scholar.

11. See the description of the Žaclér exhibit on Sala's Gift at http://www.veselyvylet.cz/cz/pdf/veselyvylet_30_cz.pdf, pp. 24–25.

12. RG-14.101M.2909, B 162/15900, Zentrale Stelle der Landesjustizverwaltungen Ludwigsburg, Document 699, USHMM. The last page of the deposition of Helena Šrámková (born Helena Felczer in Chrzanów) lists four witnesses to events inside the Parschnitz camp with Czech last names; additional depositions were given by women born in Zagłębie but living in the Trutnov region with Czech names.

13. "Eyewitness Account by Edith Stuart," Eva Reichman Collection, 1656/3/8/73, Catalogue ID 105701, Index number P.III.h. Gabersdorf, no. 73, WL.

14. "Eyewitness account by Nache Bochenek," Eva Reichman Collection, 1656/3/8/852
Catalogue ID 105974, Index number P.III.h. Sosnowiec, no. 852, WL.

15. Karay, *Death Comes in Yellow*.

16. Gerda Frieberg, interview by Linda Ruth Davidson, 1996. Tape 6, 20:53.

17. Peter Longerich, "Der Beginn des Holocaust in den Eingegliederten Polnischen Gebieten," in *Der Judenmord in den eingegliederten polnischen Gebieten, 1939–1945*, eds. Jacek Andrzej Młynarczyk and Jochen Böhler, 22 (Osnabrück: Fibre Verlag, 2010).

18. Sala Kirschner, interview by Susie Grama, 1997. Tape 5, 12:28.

BIBLIOGRAPHY

SCHOLARLY AND SECONDARY SOURCES

Adam, Alfons. *"Die Arbeiterfrage soll mit Hilfe von KZ-Häftlingen gelöst werden": Zwangsarbeit in KZ-Außenlagern auf dem Gebiet der heutigen Tschechischen Republik.* Berlin: Metropol Verlag, 2013.

Adler, Eliyana R. *Survival on the Margins: Polish Jewish Refugees in the Wartime Soviet Union.* Cambridge, MA: Harvard University Press, 2020.

Adler, Eliyana R., and Natalia Aleksiun. "Seeking Relative Safety: The Flight of Polish Jews to the East in the Autumn of 1939." *Yad Vashem Studies* 46, no. 1 (2018): 41–71.

Aleksiun, Natalia. "Social Networks of Support: Trajectories of Escape, Rescue and Survival." In *A Companion to the Holocaust*, edited by Simone Gigliotti and Hilary Earl, 279–93. Hoboken, NJ: Wiley, 2020.

Allen, Michael Thad. *The Business of Genocide: The SS, Slave Labor, and the Concentration Camps.* Chapel Hill: University of North Carolina Press, 2002.

Aly, Götz, and Susanne Heim. *Architects of Annihilation: Auschwitz and the Logic of Destruction.* Princeton, NJ: Princeton University Press, 2002.

Anthony, Elizabeth. *The Compromise of Return: Viennese Jews After the Holocaust.* Detroit: Wayne State University Press, 2021.

Auslander, Leora. "Beyond Words." *The American Historical Review* 110, no. 4 (2005): 1015–45.

Bade, Klaus J. *Migration in European History.* Translated by Allison Brown. Malden, MA: Blackwell, 2003.

Bahm, Karl F. "The Inconveniences of Nationality: German Bohemians, the Disintegration of the Habsburg Monarchy, and the Attempt to Create a 'Sudeten German' Identity." *Nationalities Papers* 27, no. 3 (1999): 375–405.

Bajohr, Frank. "The Holocaust and Corruption." In *Networks of Nazi Persecution: Bureaucracy, Business, and the Organization of the Holocaust*, edited by Gerald Feldman and Wolfgang Seibel, 118–39. New York: Berghahn Books, 2005.

Barth, Susanne. "Revisiting the 'Cosel Period': A Fresh Perspective on the Stopping of Western Deportation Trains En Route to Auschwitz, 1942–1943." *Shofar* 39, no. 2 (2021): 32–61.

Beck, Birgit. *Wehrmacht und sexuelle Gewalt: Sexualverbrechen vor deutschen Militärgerichten, 1939–1945.* Paderborn: Ferdinand Schöningh, 2004.

Beck, Hermann. "State and Society in Pre-March Prussia: The Weavers' Uprising, the Bureaucracy, and the Association for the Welfare of Workers." *Central European History* 25, no. 3 (1992): 303–31.

Becker, Michael, and Dennis Bock. "Muselmänner and Prisoner Societies: Toward a Sociohistorical Understanding." *The Journal of Holocaust Research* 34, no. 3 (2020): 158–74.

Bemporad, Elissa. "Questions of Choice: The Soviet Case and the Absence of Gender Identity in *Ordinary Jews*." *Shofar* 36, no. 1 (2018): 209–13.

Bender, Sara. "'Here you must work impeccably, otherwise you will be beaten and sent for selection': Jewish Laborers in the City of Radom, Poland 1942–1944." *Kwartalnik Historii Żydów* 252, no. 4 (2014): 749–73.

Benninga, Noah. "The Bricolage of Death: Jewish Possessions and the Fashioning of the Prisoner Elite in Auschwitz-Birkenau, 1942–1945." In *Objects of War: The Material Culture of Conflict and Displacement*, edited by Leora Auslander and Tara Zahra, 189–220. Ithaca, NY: Cornell University Press, 2018.

Bergen, Doris L. "Tenuousness and Tenacity: The Volksdeutschen of Eastern Europe, World War II, and the Holocaust." In *The Heimat Abroad: The Boundaries of Germanness*, edited by K. Molly O'Donnell, Renate Bridenthal, and Nancy Reagin, 267–86. Ann Arbor: University of Michigan Press, 2005.

Birenbaum, Halina. *Hope Is the Last to Die: A Personal Documentation of Nazi Terror*. New York: Twayne Publishers, 1971.

Bjork, James. *Neither German nor Pole: Catholicism and National Indifference in a Central European Borderland*. Ann Arbor: University of Michigan Press, 2009.

Blatman, Daniel. *The Death Marches: The Final Phase of Nazi Genocide*. Cambridge, MA: Belknap/Harvard University Press, 2011.

Bloxham, Donald, and Tony Kushner. *The Holocaust: Critical Historical Approaches*. Manchester, UK: Manchester University Press, 2005.

Braham, Randolph L. *The Nazis' Last Victims: The Holocaust in Hungary*. Detroit: Wayne State University Press, 1998.

Braham, Randolph L. *The Politics of Genocide: The Holocaust in Hungary*. New York: Columbia University Press, 1981.

Browning, Christopher R. "The German Bureaucracy and the Holocaust." In *Genocide: Critical Issues of the Holocaust*, edited by Alex Grobman, Daniel Landes, and Sybil Milton, 145–49. Chappaqua, NY: Rossel Books, 1983.

Browning, Christopher R. *Nazi Policy, Jewish Workers, German Killers*. Cambridge: Cambridge University Press, 2000.

Browning, Christopher R. *Remembering Survival: Inside a Nazi Slave-Labor Camp*. New York: W. W. Norton, 2010.

Budnitskii, Oleg. "The Intelligentsia Meets the Enemy: Educated Soviet Officers in Defeated Germany, 1945." *Kritika* 10, no. 3 (2009): 629–82.

Buggeln, Marc. *Arbeit & Gewalt: Das Außenlagersystem des KZ Neuengamme*. Göttingen: Wallstein, 2009.

Buggeln, Marc. *Slave Labor in Nazi Concentration Camps*. Oxford: Oxford University Press, 2014.

Buggeln, Marc, and Michael Wildt. "Einleitung." In *Arbeit im Nationalsozialismus*, edited by Marc Buggeln and Michael Wildt, ix–xxxvii. München: De Gruyter Oldenbourg, 2014.

Burds, Jeffrey. "Sexual Violence in Europe in World War II, 1939–1945." *Politics & Society* 37, no. 1 (2009): 35–73.

Canning, Kathleen. *Languages of Labor and Gender: Female Factory Work in Germany, 1850–1914*. Ann Arbor: University of Michigan, 1996.

Card, Claudia. *Confronting Evils: Terrorism, Torture, Genocide*. Cambridge: Cambridge University Press, 2010.

Carey, Maddy. *Jewish Masculinity in the Holocaust: Between Destruction and Construction*. London: Bloomsbury Publishing, 2017.

Caruth, Cathy. *Unclaimed Experience: Trauma, Narrative and History*. Baltimore: Johns Hopkins University Press, 1996 [reissued in 2016].

Cichopek-Gajraj, Anna. *Beyond Violence: Jewish Survivors in Poland and Slovakia, 1944–1948*. New York: Cambridge University Press, 2014.

Clifford, Rebecca. *Survivors: Children's Lives After the Holocaust*. New Haven, CT: Yale University Press, 2020.

Cohen, Boaz. "The Children's Voice: Postwar Collection of Testimonies from Child Survivors of the Holocaust." *Holocaust and Genocide Studies* 21, no. 1 (2007): 73–95.

Cohen, Boaz. "The Jewish DP Experience." In *The Routledge History of the Holocaust*, edited by Jonathan C. Friedman, 414–24. New York: Routledge, 2011.

Cohen, Dara Kay. *Rape During Civil War*. Ithaca, NY: Cornell University Press, 2016.

Cole, Tim J. "Constructing the 'Jew,' Writing the Holocaust: Hungary 1920–45." *Patterns of Prejudice* 33, no. 3 (1999): 19–27.

Cornwall, Mark. *The Devil's Wall: The Nationalist Youth Mission of Heinz Rutha*. Cambridge, MA: Harvard University Press, 2012.

Coulthard, Glen Sean. *Red Skin, White Masks: Rejecting the Colonial Politics of Recognition*. Minneapolis: University of Minnesota Press, 2014.

Curilla, Wolfgang. *Der Judenmord in Polen und die Deutsche Ordnungspolizei, 1939 1945*. Paderborn: Verlag Ferdinand Schöningh, 2011.

Cushman, Sarah M. "Sexuality, Sexual Violence, and Sexual Barter in the Auschwitz-Birkenau Women's Camp." In *Agency and the Holocaust: Essays in Honor of Debórah Dwork*, edited by Thomas Kühne and Mary Jane Rein, 105–22. Cham: Palgrave Macmillan, 2020.

Cybulski, Bohdan. *Ewakuacja Więźniów AL Riese do Trautenau: Próba Rekonstrukcji Wydarzeń*. Wałbrzych: Państwowe Muzeum Gross-Rosen, 1989.

Cybulski, Bogdan. "Żydzi Polscy w Prowincji Górnośląskiej w Okresie II Wojny Światowy." *Śląski Kwartalnik Historyczny Sobótka* 44, no. 1 (1989): 137–49.

Czech, Danuta. *Auschwitz Chronicle, 1939–1945*. New York: Henry Holt, 1990.

Des Pres, Terrence. *The Survivor: An Anatomy of Life in the Death Camps*. New York: Oxford University Press, 1980.

Długoborski, Wacław. "Die Juden aus den eingegliederten Gebieten im Vernichtungslager Auschwitz-Birkenau." In *Der Judenmord in den Eingegliederten Polnischen Gebieten 1939–1945*, edited by Jacek Andrzej Młynarczyk and Jochen Böhler, 219–50. Osnabrück: Fibre Verlag, 2010.

BIBLIOGRAPHY

Douglas, Raymond M. *Orderly and Humane: The Expulsion of the Germans after the Second World War*. New Haven, CT: Yale University Press, 2012.

Dwork, Debórah. *Children with a Star: Jewish Youth in Nazi Europe*. New Haven, CT: Yale University Press, 1991.

Dwork, Debórah. "Sexual Abuse, Sexual Barter, and Silence." *Holocaust Studies* 27, no. 4 (2021): 495–500.

Dwork, Debórah, and Robert J. Van Pelt *Auschwitz: 1270 to the Present*. New York: Norton, 1996.

Eichholtz, Dietrich. "Zwangsarbeit in der deutschen Kriegswirtschaft." In *Stiften gehen: NS-Zwangsarbeit und Entschädigungsdebatte*, edited by Ulrike Winkler, 10–40. Köln: PapyRossa Verlag, 2000.

Epstein, Franci Rabinek. *Franci's War: A Woman's Story of Survival*. New York: Penguin, 2020.

Feist, Artur. *Die Ostböhmische Leinenindustrie von Trautenau*. Leipzig: Buchdruckerei Helm & Torton, 1927.

Felman, Shoshana, and Dori Laub. *Testimony: Crises of Witnessing in Literature, Psychoanalysis, and History*. New York: Routledge Press, 1991.

Ferencz, Benjamin. *Less Than Slaves: Jewish Forced Labor and the Quest for Compensation*. Cambridge, MA: Harvard University Press, 1979.

Finder, Gabriel N. "Child Survivors in Polish Jewish Collective Memory after the Holocaust: The Case of *Undzere kinder*." In *Displaced Children in Russia and Eastern Europe, 1915–1953: Ideologies, Identities, Experiences*, edited by Nick Baron, 218–47. Leiden: Brill, 2016.

Fineman, Joel. "The History of the Anecdote: Fiction and Friction." In *The New Historicism*, edited by H. Aram Veeser, 49–76. New York: Routledge, 1989.

Finkel, Evgeny. *Ordinary Jews: Choice and Survival during the Holocaust*. Princeton, NJ: Princeton University Press, 2017.

Flaschka, Monika J. "'Only the Pretty Women Were Raped': The Effect of Sexual Violence on Gendered Identities in Concentration Camps." In *Sexual Violence Against Jewish Women During the Holocaust*, edited by Sonja M. Hedgepeth and Rochelle G. Saidel, 77–89. Waltham, MA: Brandeis University Press, 2010.

Friedländer, Saul. *The Years of Extermination: Nazi Germany and the Jews, 1939–1945*. New York: HarperCollins, 2007.

Friedman, Philip. "Two 'Saviors' Who Failed: Moses Merin of Sosnowiec and Jacob Gens of Vilna." In *The Nazi Holocaust, Part 6: The Victims of the Holocaust*, edited by Michael Marrus, 488–500. Westport, CT: Meckler, 2011.

Friedrich, Klaus-Peter. "Collaboration in a 'Land without a Quisling': Patterns of Cooperation with the Nazi German Occupation Regime in Poland During World War II." *Slavic Review* 64, no. 4 (2005): 711–46.

Friedrich, Klaus-Peter. *Die Verfolgung und Ermordung der europäischen Juden durch das nationalsozialistische Deutschland 1933–1945: Polen September 1939–Juli 1941, Band 4*. München: R. Oldenbourg Verlag, 2011.

Frommer, Benjamin. *National Cleansing: Retribution against Nazi Collaborators in Postwar Czechoslovakia*. Cambridge: Cambridge University Press, 2005.

Fulbrook, Mary. *A Small Town Near Auschwitz: Ordinary Nazis and the Holocaust*. Oxford: Oxford University Press, 2012.

Fulbrook, Mary. "'Unschuldig schuldig werden'? Systematische Gewalt und die Verfolgung der Juden von Będzin." In *Alltag im Holocaust: Jüdisches Leben im Großdeutschen Reich 1941–1945*, edited by Andrea Löw, Doris L. Bergen, and Anna Hájková, 117–36. München: R. Oldenbourg Verlag, 2013.

Gallop, Jane. *Anecdotal Theory*. Durham, NC: Duke University Press, 2002.

Garbarini, Alexandra. *Numbered Days: Diaries and the Holocaust*. New Haven, CT: Yale University Press, 2006.

Gerlach, Christian. *The Extermination of the European Jews*. Cambridge: Cambridge University Press, 2016.

Gerlach, David. *The Economy of Ethnic Cleansing: The Transformation of the German-Czech Borderlands after World War II*. Cambridge: Cambridge University Press, 2017.

Gil, Idit. "The Value of Labor for Jewish Women in Radom." *Nashim: A Journal of Women's Studies and Gender Issues* 27 (2014): 14–37.

Glassheim, Eagle. *Cleansing the Czechoslovak Borderlands: Migration, Environment, and Health in the Former Sudetenland*. Pittsburgh, PA: University of Pittsburgh Press, 2016.

Glissant, Édouard. *Poetics of Relation*. Ann Arbor: University of Michigan Press, 1997.

Glowacka, Dorota. "Sexual Violence Among Men and Boys During the Holocaust: A Genealogy of (Not-So-Silent) Silence." *German History* 39, no. 1 (2021): 78–99.

Goschler, Constantin, ed. *Compensation in Practice: The Foundation "Remembrance, Responsibility and Future" and the Legacy of Forced Labour During the Third Reich*. New York: Berghahn Books, 2017.

Green, Thomas A., and Lisa Devaney. "Linguistic Play in Autograph Book Inscriptions." *Western Folklore* 48, no. 1 (1989): 51–58.

Gross, Jan. *Fear: Anti-Semitism in Poland after Auschwitz*. New York: Random House, 2006.

Gross, Jan Tomasz, and Irena Grudzińska-Gross. *Golden Harvest: Events at the Periphery of the Holocaust*. New York: Oxford University Press, 2016.

Grossmann, Atina. *Jews, Germans, and Allies: Close Encounters in Occupied Germany*. Princeton, NJ: Princeton University Press, 2007.

Gruner, Wolf. *Jewish Forced Labor under the Nazis: Economic Needs and Racial Aims, 1938–1944*. New York: Cambridge University Press and the United States Holocaust Memorial Museum, 2006.

Gruner, Wolf, and Jörg Osterloh, eds. *The Greater German Reich and the Jews: Nazi Persecution Policies in the Annexed Territories 1935–1945*. New York: Berghahn Books, 2015.

Gusarov, Katya. "Sexual Barter and Jewish Women's Efforts to Save Their Lives:

Accounts from the Righteous Among the Nations Archives." *German History* 39, no. 1 (2021): 100–11.

Gutman, Israel, and Michael Berenbaum. *Anatomy of the Auschwitz Death Camp*. Bloomington: Indiana University Press, 1994.

Gutterman, Bella. *A Narrow Bridge to Life: Jewish Forced Labor and Survival in the Gross-Rosen Camp System, 1940–1945*. New York: Berghahn Books, 2008.

Hájková, Anna. *The Last Ghetto: An Everyday History of Theresienstadt*. New York: Oxford University Press, 2020.

Hájková, Anna. *Menschen ohne Geschichte sind Staub: Homophobie und Holocaust*. Göttingen: Wallstein Verlag, 2021.

Hájková, Anna. "Sexual Barter in Times of Genocide: Negotiating the Sexual Economy of the Theresienstadt Ghetto." *Signs* 38, no. 3 (2013): 503–33.

Halbmayr, Brigid. "Sexualized Violence Against Women during Nazi 'Racial' Persecution." In *Sexual Violence Against Jewish Women During the Holocaust*, edited by Sonja M. Hedgepeth and Rochelle G. Saidel, 29–44. Waltham, MA: Brandeis University Press, 2010.

Hartman, Geoffrey. "A Note on the Testimony Event." In *The Power of Witnessing: Reflections, Reverberations, and Traces of the Holocaust*, edited by Nancy Goodman and Marilyn Meyers, 81–86. New York: Routledge, 2012.

Hartman, Geoffrey H. "Learning from Survivors: The Yale Testimony Project." *Holocaust and Genocide Studies* 9, no. 2 (1995): 192–207.

Harvey, Elizabeth. *Women and the Nazi East: Agents and Witnesses of Germanization*. New Haven, CT: Yale University Press, 2003.

Hayes, Peter. *Industry and Ideology: IG Farben in the Nazi Era*. New York: Cambridge University Press, 1987.

Heerma van Voss, Lex, Els Hiemstra-Kuperus, and Elise van Nederveen Meerkerk, eds. *The Ashgate Companion to the History of Textile Workers, 1650–2000*. Farnham, Surrey: Ashgate, 2010.

Heller, Celia Stopnicka. *On the Edge of Destruction: Jews of Poland Between the Two World Wars*. New York: Columbia University Press, 1977.

Herbert, Ulrich. *Hitler's Foreign Workers: Enforced Foreign Labor in Germany under the Third Reich*. New York: Cambridge University Press, 1997.

Herzog, Dagmar. "Sexuality, Memory, Morality." *History & Memory* 17, no. 1 (2005): 238–66.

Hoagland, Sarah Lucia. "Denying Relationality: Epistemology and Ethics and Ignorance." In *Racism and Epistemologies of Ignorance*, edited by Shannon Sullivan and Nancy Tuana, 95–118. Albany: State University of New York Press, 2007.

von Hodenberg, Christina. *Aufstand der Weber: Die Revolte von 1844 und ihr Aufstieg zum Mythos*. Bonn: Verlag J. H. W. Dietz Nachfolger, 1997.

Hollander-Lafon, Magda. *Four Scraps of Bread*. Notre Dame, IN: University of Notre Dame Press, 2016.

James, Harold. *The Deutsche Bank and the Nazi Economic War against the Jews: The Expropriation of Jewish-owned Property*. Oxford: Cambridge University Press, 2001.

Jansen, Christian, and Arno Weckbecker. *Der 'Volksdeutsche Selbstschutz' in Polen 1939/40*. München: R. Oldenbourg Verlag, 1992.

Jaworski, Wojciech. "Żydowskie Gminy Wyznaniowe w Zagłębiu Dąbrowskim." *Biuletyn Żydowskiego Instytutu Historycznego w Polsce* 1–2 (1988): 131–44.

Jockusch, Laura. *Collect and Record! Jewish Holocaust Documentation in Early Postwar Europe*. New York: Oxford University Press, 2012.

Kaczmarek, Ryszard. "Antyżydowska polityka władz niemieckich w rejencji katowickiej." In *Zagłada Żydów zagłębiowskich*, edited by Aleksandra Namysło, 13–31. Będzin: Instytut Pamięci Narodowej, 2003.

Kaczmarek, Ryszard. *Górny Śląsk podczas II wojny światowej: Między niemieckiej wspólnoty narodowej i rzeczywistością okupacji na terenach wcielonych do Trzeciej Rzeszy*. Katowice: Wydawnictwo Uniwersytetu Śląskiego, 2006.

Kaczmarek, Ryszard. "Zwischen Altreich und Besatzungsgebiet: Der Gau Oberschlesien 1939/41–1945." In *Die NS-Gaue: Regionale Mittelinstanzen im Zentralischen "Führerstaat,"* edited by Jürgen John, Horst Möller, and Thomas Schaarschmidt, 348–60. München: R. Oldenbourg Verlag, 2007.

Kamusella, Tomasz. *Silesia and Central European Nationalisms: The Emergence of Nationalist and Ethnic Groups in Prussian Silesia and Austrian Silesia, 1848–1918*. West Lafayette, IN: Purdue University Press, 2007.

Kaplan, Marion A. *Between Dignity and Despair: Jewish Life in Nazi Germany*. New York: Oxford University Press, 1998.

Kaplan, Marion. "Did Gender Matter During the Holocaust?" *Jewish Social Studies* 24, no. 2 (2019): 37–56.

Karay, Felicja. *Death Comes in Yellow: Skarżysko-Kamienna Slave Labor Camp*. Amsterdam: Harwood Academic, 1996.

Kirschner, Ann, Debórah Dwork, and Robert Jan van Pelt. *Letters to Sala: A Young Woman's Life in Nazi Labor Camps*. New York: New York Public Library, 2006.

Kirstein, Wolfgang. *Das Konzentrationslager als Institution totalen Terrors: Das Beispiel Natzweiler*. Pfaffenweiler: Centaurus-Verlagsgesellschaft, 1992.

Kleiman, Yehudit, and Nina Springer-Aharoni. *The Anguish of Liberation: Testimonies from 1945*. Jerusalem: Yad Vashem, 1995.

Kobielec, Aleksandra. *Więźniowie Żydzi w KL Gross-Rosen: Stan Badań*. Wałbrzych: Państwowe Muzeum Gross-Rosen, 1993.

Kocjan, Krzysztof. *Zagłada olkuskich Żydów*. Olkusz: O. S. K. "Brama," 2002.

Konieczny, Alfred. "Das Konzentrationslager Groß-Rosen." In *Dachauer Heft* 5, *Die vergessenen Lager*, edited by Wolfgang Benz and Barbara Distel, 15–27. Dachau: Verlag Dachauer Hefte, 1989.

Konieczny, Alfred. *Frauen im Konzentrationslager Groß-Rosen in den Jahren 1944–1945*. Wałbrzych: Panstwowe Muzeum Gross-Rosen, 1994.

Kroener, Bernard R., Rolf-Dieter Müller, and Hans Umbreit. *Germany and the Second World War*. Vol. V. New York: Oxford University Press, 2000.

Kryl, Miroslav, and Ludmila Chládková. *Pobočky koncentračního tábora Gross-Rosen* ve lnářských závodech Trutnovska na nacistické okupace. Trutnov: Generalní Ředitelství VHJ Lnářský Průmysl, 1981.

Krzyzanowski, Lukasz. *Ghost Citizens: Jewish Return to a Postwar City*. Cambridge, MA: Harvard University Press. 2020.

Lamer, Reinhard. *Trautenau: Geschichte einer deutschen Stadt*. Wien: Volkstum Verlag, 1971.

Langer, Lawrence L. *Holocaust Testimonies: The Ruins of Memory*. New Haven, CT: Yale University Press, 1991.

Larkey, Uta. "Fear and Terror: The Expulsion of Polish Jews from Saxony/Germany in October 1938." *Dapim: Studies on the Holocaust* 31, no. 3 (2017): 243–60.

Laub, Dori. "Bearing Witness or the Vicissitudes of Listening." In *Testimony: Crises of Witnessing in Literature, Psychoanalysis and History*, edited by Shoshana Felman and Dori Laub, 57–74. New York: Routledge, 1992.

Lehnstaedt, Stephan. "Coercion and Incentive: Jewish Ghetto Labor in East Upper Silesia." *Holocaust and Genocide Studies* 24, no. 3 (2010): 400–30.

Levitt, Laura. *The Objects That Remain*. University Park: Pennsylvania State University Press, 2020.

Longerich, Peter. "Der Beginn des Holocaust in den Eingegliederten Polnischen Gebieten." In *Der Judenmord in den eingegliederten polnischen Gebieten, 1939–1945*, edited by Jacek Andrzej Młynarczyk and Jochen Böhler, 15–25. Osnabrück: Fibre Verlag, 2010.

Longerich, Peter. *Heinrich Himmler*. New York: Oxford University Press, 2012.

Löw, Andrea. *Juden im Getto Litzmannstadt: Lebensbedingungen, Selbstwahrnehmung, Verhalten*. Göttingen: Wallstein Verlag, 2013.

MacKenzie, Simon P. "The Treatment of Prisoners of War in World War II." *Journal of Modern History* 66, no. 3 (1994): 487–520.

Madajczyk, Czesław. *Polityka III Rzeszy w Okupowanej Polsce*. Tom 1. Warszawa: Państwowe Wydawnictwo Naukowe, 1970.

Mailänder, Elissa. *Female SS Guards and Workaday Violence: The Majdanek Concentration Camp, 1942–1944*. East Lansing: Michigan State University Press, 2015.

Majstorović, Vojin. "Red Army Troops Encounter the Holocaust: Transnistria, Moldavia, Romania, Bulgaria, Yugoslavia, Hungary, and Austria, 1944–1945." *Holocaust and Genocide Studies* 32, no. 2 (2018): 249–71.

Malá, Irena, and Ludmila Kubátová. *Pochody Smrti*. Praha: Nakladatelství Politické Literatury, 1965.

Mazower, Mark. *Hitler's Empire: How the Nazis Ruled Europe*. New York: Penguin, 2008.

Michlic, Joanna Beata, ed. *Jewish Families in Europe, 1939–Present: History, Representation, and Memory*. Waltham, MA: Brandeis University Press, 2017.

Michlic, Joanna Beata. *Poland's Threatening Other: The Image of the Jew from 1880 to the Present*. Lincoln: University of Nebraska Press, 2006.

Michman, Dan. *The Emergence of Jewish Ghettos During the Holocaust*. Cambridge: Cambridge University Press, 2011.

Miłosz, Czesław. *Abecadło Miłosza*. Kraków: Wydawnictwo Literackie, 1997.

Młynarczyk, Jacek Andrzej, and Jochen Böhler, "Vorwort." In *Der Judenmord in den eingegliederten polnischen Gebieten, 1939–1945*, edited by Jacek Andrzej Młynarczyk and Jochen Böhler, 9–12. Osnabrück: Fibre Verlag, 2010.

Mołdawa, Mieczysław. *Gross-Rosen: Obóz Koncentracyjny na Śląsku*. Warszawa: Wydawnictwo Polonia, 1967.

Morelon, Claire. "Respectable Citizens: Civic Militias, Local Patriotism, and Social Order in Late Habsburg Austria (1890–1920)." *Austrian History Yearbook* 51 (2020): 193–219.

Morsch, Günter, and Agnes Ohm, eds. *The Administrative Centre of the Concentration Camp Terror: The Concentration Camps Inspectorate 1934–1945*. Berlin: Metropol Verlag, 2015.

Moss, Kenneth B. *An Unchosen People: Jewish Political Reckoning in Interwar Poland*. Cambridge, MA: Harvard University Press, 2021.

Mühlhäuser, Regina. *Eroberungen: Sexuelle Gewalttaten und intime Beziehungen deutscher Soldaten in der Sowjetunion, 1941–1945*. Hamburg: Hamburger Edition HIS, 2010.

Mühlhäuser, Regina. "Reframing Sexual Violence as a Weapon and Strategy of War: The Case of the German Wehrmacht During the War and Genocide in the Soviet Union, 1941–1944." *Journal of the History of Sexuality* 26, no. 3 (2017): 366–401.

Murdock, Caitlin E. *Changing Places: Society, Culture, and Territory in the Saxon-Bohemian Borderlands, 1870–1946*. Ann Arbor: University of Michigan Press, 2010.

Namysło, Aleksandra. "Der Einfluss der Zentrale der Jüdischen Ältestenräte in Ostoberschlesien auf das Verhalten der Juden." In *Der Judenmord in den eingegliederten polnischen Gebieten 1939–1945*, edited by Jacek Andrzej Młynarczyk and Jochen Böhler, 311–28. Osnabrück: Fibre Verlag, 2010.

Namysło, Aleksandra. "Kim Jestem—Polakiem, Niemcem, Zydem? Stosunki Żydowsko-Żydowskie na Dawnym Górnym Śląsku." *Biuletyn Instytutu Pamięci Narodowej* 11, no. 120 (2010): 52–56.

Namysło, Aleksandra. *Zagłada Żydów na polskich terenach wcielonych do Rzeszy*. Warszawa: Instytut Pamięci Narodowej, 2008.

Namysło, Aleksandra, ed. *Zagłada Żydów zagłębiowskich*. Będzin: Instytut Pamięci Narodowej, 2004.

Narotzky, Susana, and Paz Moreno. "Reciprocity's Dark Side: Negative Reciprocity, Morality and Social Reproduction." *Anthropological Theory* 2, no. 3 (2002): 281–305.

Nenutil, Jiří. *Pochody Smrti: Český příspěvek k otevřené otázce*. Plzeň: Vydavatelství Západočeské Univerzity v Plzni, 2011.

Nesselrodt, Markus. *Dem Holocaust entkommen: Polnische Juden in der Sowjetunion, 1939–1946*. Berlin: De Gruyter, 2019.

BIBLIOGRAPHY

Olszyna, Roman. *KL Gross-Rosen: Wybór artykułów*. Wałbrzych: Państwowe Muzeum Gross-Rosen, 2005.

Orth, Karin. *Das System der Nationalsozialistischen Konzentrationslager: Eine Politische Organisationsgeschichte*. Hamburg: Hamburger Edition, 1999.

Osterloh, Jörg. *Nationalsozialistische Judenverfolgung im Reichsgau Sudetenland 1938–1945*. München: R. Oldenbourg Verlag, 2006.

Osterloh, Jörg. "Sudetenland." In *The Greater German Reich and the Jews: Nazi Persecution Policies in the Annexed Territories 1935–1945*, edited by Wolf Gruner and Jörg Osterloh, 68–98. New York: Berghahn Books, 2015.

Pally, Marcia. *Commonwealth and Covenant: Economics, Politics, and Theologies of Relationality*. Grand Rapids, MI: William B. Eerdmans, 2016.

Patt, Avinoam J., and Michael Berkowitz, eds. *"We Are Here": New Approaches to Jewish Displaced Persons in Postwar Germany*. Detroit: Wayne State University Press, 2010.

Patterson, Orlando. *Slavery and Social Death: A Comparative Study*. Cambridge, MA: Harvard University Press, 1982.

Person, Katarzyna. "'I Am a Jewish DP. A Jew from the Eternal Nowhere.'" *Kwartalnik Historii Żydów* 246, no. 2 (2013): 312–18.

Piper, Franciszek. "Fragmenty Relacji Sándorní Földes." *Głosy Pamięci* 9 (2015): 150.

Piper, Franciszek. "Slave Labour by the Prisoners." In *Selected Problems from the History of KL Auschwitz*, edited by Kazimierz Smoleń, 51–68. Oświęcim: Państwowe Muzeum w Oświęcimiu, 1979.

Pollin-Galay, Hannah. *Ecologies of Witnessing: Language, Place, and Holocaust Testimony*. New Haven, CT: Yale University Press, 2018.

Popiołek, Kazimierz. *Historia Śląska od pradziejów do 1945 roku*. Katowice: Śląski Instytut Naukowy, 1972.

Porat, Dan. *Bitter Reckoning: Israel Tries Holocaust Survivors as Nazi Collaborators*. Cambridge, MA: Harvard University Press, 2019.

Quercioli-Mincer, Laura. "'Nie będziemy się więcej bać ludzi?' Powrót po Zagładzie w literaturze polsko-żydowskiej." *Kwartalnik Historii Żydów* 222, no. 2 (2007): 199–225.

Reading, Anna. "Clicking on Hitler: The Virtual Holocaust @Home." In *Visual Culture and the Holocaust*, edited by Barbie Zelizer, 323–39. New Brunswick, NJ: Rutgers University Press, 2001.

Reich-Ranicki, Marcel. *The Author of Himself: The Life of Marcel Reich-Ranicki*. Princeton, NJ: Princeton University Press, 2001.

Reid Ricker, Lisa. "(De)Constructing the Praxis of Memory-Keeping: Late Nineteenth-Century Autograph Albums as Sites of Rhetorical Invention." *Rhetoric Review* 29, no. 3 (2010): 239–56.

van Rens, Herman, and Annelies Wilms. *Tussenstation Cosel: Joodse Mannen uit West Europa naar Dwangarbeiderskampen in Silezië, 1942–1945*. Hilversum: Verloren, 2020.

Rice, Monika. *"What! Still Alive?!" Jewish Survivors in Poland and Israel Remember Homecoming*. Syracuse, NY: Syracuse University Press, 2017.

Robinson, Bernard. "Zbrodnie popełnione w obozach 'Organizacji Schmelt' w świetle wspomnień więźniarek." In *Wykorzystanie Niewolniczej Pracy Więźniów KL Gross-Rosen przez III Rzeszę*, edited by Aleksandra Kobielec, 105–38. Wałbrzych: Muzeum Gross-Rosen, 2004.

Röger, Maren. "The Sexual Policies and Sexual Realities of the German Occupiers in Poland in the Second World War." *Contemporary European History* 23, no. 1 (2014): 1–21.

Röger, Maren. *Wartime Relations: Intimacy, Violence, and Prostitution in Occupied Poland, 1939–1945*. New York: Oxford University Press, 2021.

Röhr, Werner. "Das Sudetendeutsche Freikorps—Diversionsinstrument der Hitler-Regierung bei der Zerschlagung der Tschechoslowakei." *Militärgeschichtliche Mitteilungen* 52 (1993): 35–66.

Rosen, Alan. *The Holocaust's Jewish Calendars: Keeping Time Sacred, Making Time Holy*. Bloomington: Indiana University Press, 2019.

Rosen, Alan. *The Wonder of Their Voices: The 1946 Holocaust Interviews of David Boder*. New York: Oxford University Press, 2010.

Roskies, David G. "Wartime Victim Writing in Eastern Europe." In *Literature of the Holocaust*, edited by Alan Rosen, 15–32. Cambridge: Cambridge University Press, 2013.

Rossino, Alexander B. "Destructive Impulses: German Soldiers and the Conquest of Poland." *Holocaust and Genocide Studies* 11, no. 3 (1997): 351–65.

Rossino, Alexander B. "Nazi Anti-Jewish Policy During the Polish Campaign: The Case of Einsatzgruppe von Woyrsch." *German Studies Review* 24, no. 1 (2001): 35–53.

Roth, John K. *The Failures of Ethics: Confronting the Holocaust, Genocide, and Other Mass Atrocities*. New York: Oxford University Press, 2015.

Rudorff, Andrea. "Arbeit und Vernichtung *Reconsidered*: Die Lager der Organisation Schmelt für Polnische Jüdinnen und Juden aus dem Annektierten Teil Oberschlesiens." *Sozial Geschichte Online* 7 (2012): 10–39.

Rudorff, Andrea. "Die Strafverfolgung von KZ-Aufseherinnen in Polen." *Zeitschrift für Geschichtswissenschaft* 61, no. 4 (2013): 329–50.

Rudorff, Andrea. *Frauen in den Außenlagern des Konzentrationslagers Groß-Rosen*. Berlin: Metropol Verlag, 2014.

Rudorff, Andrea. "Reimagining the 'Gray Zone': Female Prisoner Functionaries in the Gross-Rosen Subcamp System, 1944–1945." In *Lessons and Legacies XIV*, edited by Tim Cole and Simone Gigliotti, 21–37. Evanston, IL: Northwestern University Press, 2020.

Schatz, Jaff. *The Generation: The Rise and Fall of the Jewish Communists of Poland*. Berkeley: University of California Press, 1991.

Scheck, Raffael. *Love Between Enemies: Western Prisoners of War and German Women in World War II*. Cambridge: Cambridge University Press, 2021.

Schwartz, Johannes. *"Weibliche Angelegenheiten": Handlungsräume von KZ-Aufseherinnen in Ravensbrück und Neubrandenburg*. Hamburg: Hamburger Edition, 2018.

Sedlmeier, Florian, and MaryAnn Snyder-Körber. "Introduction." In *Anecdotal Modernity: Making and Unmaking History*, edited by James Dorson, Florian Sedlmeier, MaryAnn Snyder-Körber, and Birte Wege, 1–32. Berlin: DeGruyter, 2020.

Segal, Raz. "Beyond Holocaust Studies: Rethinking the Holocaust in Hungary." *Journal of Genocide Research* 16, no. 1 (2014): 1–23.

Sendyk, Helen. *New Dawn: A Triumph of Life after the Holocaust*. Syracuse, NY: Syracuse University Press, 2002.

Service, Hugo. "The Imagined Ethno-Racial Border and the Expulsion of Jews from Western Poland, 1939–41." *German History* 38, no. 3 (2020): 414–39.

Shandler, Jeffrey. *Holocaust Memory in the Digital Age: Survivors' Stories and New Media Practices*. Stanford, CA: Stanford University Press, 2017.

Shapira, Rina, and Hanna Herzog. "Understanding Youth Culture Through Autograph Books: The Israeli Case." *The Journal of American Folklore* 97, no. 386 (1984): 442–60.

Shenker, Noah. *Reframing Holocaust Testimony*. Bloomington: Indiana University Press, 2015.

Sliwa, Joanna. "Clandestine Activities and Concealed Presence: A Case Study of Children Concealed in the Kraków Ghetto." In *Jewish Families in Europe, 1939–Present: History, Representation, and Memory*, edited by Joanna Beata Michlic, 26–45. Waltham, MA: Brandeis University Press, 2017.

Sliwa, Joanna. *Jewish Childhood in Kraków: A Microhistory of the Holocaust*. New Brunswick, NJ: Rutgers University Press, 2021.

Smelser, Ronald M. "The Betrayal of a Myth: National Socialism and the Financing of Middle-Class Socialism in the Sudetenland." *Central European History* 5, no. 3 (1972): 256–77.

Smoleń, Kazimierz. *From the History of KL-Auschwitz*. Vol. 2. Oświęcim: Państwowe Muzeum w Oświęcimiu, 1976.

Smutný, Bohumír. *České lnářské textilní závody*. Trutnov: Texlen, 1987.

Smutný, Bohumír. *Šest studií k dějinám lnářství na Trutnovsku*. Trutnov: Texlen, 1983.

Sommer, Robert. "Sexual Exploitation of Women in Nazi Concentration Camp Brothels." In *Sexual Violence against Jewish Women during the Holocaust*, edited by Sonja Maria Hedgepeth and Rochelle G. Saidel, 45–60. Waltham, MA: Brandeis University Press, 2010.

Spoerer, Mark. "The Nazi War Economy, the Forced Labor System, and the Murder of Jewish and Non-Jewish Workers." In *A Companion to the Holocaust*, edited by Simone Gigliotti and Hilary Earl, 135–52. Hoboken, NJ: Wiley, 2020.

Sprenger, Isabell. *Gross-Rosen: Ein Konzentrationslager in Schlesien*. Köln: Böhlau, 1996.

Steinbacher, Sybille. "East Upper Silesia." In *The Greater German Reich and the Jews: Nazi Persecution Policies in the Annexed Territories, 1935–1945*, edited by Wolf Gruner and Jörg Osterloh, 239–66. New York: Berghahn Books, 2015.

Steinbacher, Sybille. *"Musterstadt" Auschwitz: Germanisierungspolitik und Judenmord in Ostoberschlesien*. München: K. G. Saur, 2000.

Steinert, Johannes-Dieter. *Deportation und Zwangsarbeit: Polnische und sowjetische Kinder im nationalsozialistischen Deutschland und im besetzten Osteuropa, 1939–1945*. Essen: Klartext Verlag, 2013.

Steinert, Johannes-Dieter. *Holocaust und Zwangsarbeit: Erinnerungen jüdischer Kinder 1938–1945*. Essen: Klartext Verlag, 2018.

Stier, Oren Baruch. "The Place of Holocaust Survivor Videotestimony: Navigating the Landmarks of First-Person Audio-Visual Representation." In *The Palgrave Handbook of Holocaust Literature and Culture*, edited by Victoria Aarons and Phyllis Lassner, 669–86. Cham: Palgrave Macmillan, 2020.

Stradecki, Janusz. *Julian Tuwim: Bibliografia*. Warszawa: Państwowe Instytut Wydawniczy, 1959.

Strebel, Bernhard. *Das KZ Ravensbrück: Geschichte eines Lagerkomplexes*. Paderborn: Schoeningh Ferdinand, 2003.

Strzelecki, Andrzej. *Zagłada Żydów z Zagłębia Dąbrowskiego w KL Auschwitz: Opracowane i wybór źródeł*. Oświęcim: Wydawnictwo Państwowego Muzeum Auschwitz-Birkenau, 2014.

Suderland, Maja. *Inside Concentration Camps: Social Life at the Extremes*. Malden, MA: Polity Press, 2013.

Sulik, Alfred. "Volkstumspolitik und Arbeitseinsatz Zwangsarbeiter in der Großindustrie Oberschlesiens." In *Europa und der "Reichseinsatz": Ausländische Zivilarbeiter, Kriegsgefangene und KZ-Häftlinge in Deutschland 1938–1945*, edited by Ulrich Herbert, 106–26. Essen: Klartext Verlag, 1991.

Szternfinkiel, Natan. *Zagłada Żydów Sosnowca*. Katowice: Centralna Żydowska Komisja Historyczna, 1946.

Tomaszewski, Jerzy. *Auftakt zur Vernichtung: Die Vertreibung Polnischer Juden aus Deutschland im Jahre 1938*. Osnabrück: Verlag Fibre, 2002.

Tooley, T. Hunt. *National Identity and Weimar Germany: Upper Silesia and the Eastern Border, 1918–1922*. Lincoln: University of Nebraska Press, 1997.

Tooze, Adam. *The Wages of Destruction: The Making and Breaking of the Nazi Economy*. New York: Viking, 2006.

Trunk, Isaiah. *Łódź Ghetto: A History*. Translated and edited by Robert Moses Shapiro. Bloomington: Indiana University Press, 2006.

Usborne, Cornelie. "Female Sexual Desire and Male Honor: German Women's Illicit Love Affairs with Prisoners of War During the Second World War." *Journal of the History of Sexuality* 26, no. 3 (2017): 454–88.

USC Shoah Foundation. *Testimony: The Legacy of Schindler's List and the USC Shoah Foundation*. New York: NewMarket Press for It Books/HarperCollins, 2014.

Vági, Zoltán, László Csősz, and Gábor Kádár. *The Holocaust in Hungary: Evolution of a Genocide*. Lanham, MD: AltaMira Press, 2013.

Veprinska, Anna. *Empathy in Contemporary Poetry After Crisis*. Cham: Palgrave Macmillan, 2020.

Wachsmann, Nikolaus. *KL: A History of the Nazi Concentration Camps*. New York: Farrar, Straus and Giroux, 2015.

Waxman, Zoë Vania. *Writing the Holocaust: Identity, Testimony, Representation*. New York: Oxford University Press, 2006.

Weiss, Hermann F. "Johannsdorf: A Forgotten Forced Labor Camp for Jews in Western Upper Silesia, 1940–1943." *Śląski Kwartalnik Historyczny Sobótka* 75 (2020): 93–121.

Weiss, Hermann F. "Reichsautobahnlager Geppersdorf (Rzędziwojowice k. Niemodlina), 1940–1942." *Śląski Kwartalnik Historyczny Sobótka* 67 (2012): 49–66.

Westermann, Edward B. "'Friend and Helper': German Uniformed Police Operations in Poland and the General Government, 1939–1941." *The Journal of Military History* 58, no. 4 (1994): 643–61.

Wichrowska, Elżbieta. "Szkicownik jako document autobiograficzy." *Teksty Drugie* 6 (2018): 54–76.

Wieviorka, Annette. *The Era of the Witness*. Ithaca, NY: Cornell University Press, 2006.

Wolff, Stefan. "Introduction." In *Coming Home to Germany? The Integration of Ethnic Germans from Central and Eastern Europe in the Federal Republic*, edited by David Rock and Stefan Wolff, 1–16. New York: Berghahn Books, 2002.

Wood, Elisabeth Jean. "Armed Groups and Sexual Violence: When Is Wartime Rape Rare?" *Politics & Society* 37, no. 1 (2009): 131–61.

Yao, Xine. *Disaffected: The Cultural Politics of Unfeeling in Nineteenth Century America*. Durham, NC: Duke University Press, 2021.

Zahra, Tara. *Kidnapped Souls: National Indifference and the Battle for Children in the Bohemian Lands, 1900–1948*. Ithaca, NY: Cornell University Press, 2008.

Zahra, Tara. *The Lost Children: Reconstructing Europe's Families After World War II*. Cambridge, MA: Harvard University Press, 2011.

Zimmermann, Volker. *Die Sudetendeutschen im NS-Staat: Politik und Stimmung der Bevölkerung im Reichsgau Sudetenland (1938–1945)*. Essen: Klartext Verlag, 1999.

Ziółkowska, Anna. "Medycyna obozowa. O tym jak chorowali, cierpieli i umierali żydowscy robotnicy w obozach pracy przymusowej w Poznaniu (1941–1943)." *Zagłada Żydów* 8 (2012): 119–44.

Zipfel, Gaby, Regina Mühlhäuser, and Kirsten Campbell, eds. *In Plain Sight: Sexual Violence in Armed Conflict*. New Delhi: Zubaan Academic, 2019.

MEMOIRS AND CONTEMPORARY EYEWITNESS ACCOUNTS

Gastfriend, Edward. *My Father's Testament: Memoir of a Jewish Teenager, 1938–1945*. Philadelphia: Temple University Press, 2000.

Górnicza, Dabrowa. "Pinkas Hakehillot Polin." In *Encyclopedia of Jewish Communities in Poland* [yitzkor buch]. https://www.jewishgen.org/yizkor/pinkas_poland/pol7_00131.html.

Höß, Rudolf. *Kommandant in Auschwitz: Autobiographische Aufzeichnungen des Rudolf Höß*, edited by Martin Broszat. München: Deutscher Taschenbuch Verlag, 2006 [orig. 1963].

Kirschner, Ann. *Sala's Gift: My Mother's Holocaust Story*. New York: Free Press, 2006.

Ranz, John. *Inhumanity: Death March to Buchenwald and the Last Jews of Bendzin*. Bloomington, IN: AuthorHouse, 2007.

Rosensaft, Hadassah. *Yesterday: My Story*. Washington, DC: The United States Holocaust Memorial Museum, 2004.

Wiederman, Paweł. *Płowa Bestia*. München: Monachium, 1948.

Wiener, Alter. *64735: From a Name to a Number: A Holocaust Survivor's Autobiography*. Bloomington, IN: AuthorHouse, 2007.

Zalmanovich, Dov. *Spring in the Dark: The Loss of Youth in Bedzin and the Camps*. https://benyehuda.org/read/6975. Accessed November 3, 2021.

INDEX

Page numbers in *italics* indicate illustrations.

abortions, 133
acrostics, 202–4
Adam, Alfons, 84
Adler, Eliyana, 46
age of testimony-givers. *See* youth of testimony-givers
Aktionen, 40, 63
Alardet, George, 212
Aleksiun, Natalia, 30, 46
Alice G., 168, 169
Allen, Michael Thad, 287n81
Allgemeine Elektricitäts-Gesellschaft (AEG) plant, 104, 112, 218, 225, 248, 289n32
Aly, Götz, 284n45
Améry, Jean, 182
Amler, Filomena, 192–93
Ann F., 16–17, 98, 101, 104, 114, 115, 116, 124–25, 162, 246
Ann G., 44
Anna N., 100
Anna O., 184–85, 242
Anna W., 53, 71, 72, 73, 103, 110, 159, 173–74, 177, 208, 217, 219, 223–24, 226
antisemitism and anti-Jewishness: Kristallnacht (1938), 89, 284n45; *Lagerführerinnen* expressing, 157, 193; prewar experience of, in Zagłębie region, 40–42; in Sudetenland, 87–88
apples, 109, 111, 125–26, 210
Aranka T., 109, 167, 214
Arbeitsämter (labor registration offices), 81, 84, 90, 91, 192
Aufseherinnen, 83, 107, 113, 157
Augusta S., 104–5

Auschwitz-Birkenau: acquiring, making, and exchanging objects at, 5; awareness of forced laborers about circumstances at, 172–74; coat from, 173; death marches from, 216; factory owners and, beliefs of laborers about, 209–10; forced labor at, 28, 94, 177; Gabersdorf as "heaven" in context of, 145; gas chambers at, 131–32; Gentile co-workers, laborers sent to Auschwitz for receiving help from, 194; Hungarian Jews sent to (1944), 94, 95, 152; ill, pregnant, or resistant laborers sent to, 33, 83, 115, 129–34, 192–93; Łódź Jews sent to, 95, 152, 176–77; mass deportations from Zagłębie to, 59, 77–79, 94, 122, 195–96; ritualized humiliations at, 83; roll calls at, 156; singing girl on Hungarian transport from, 172; SS and Gestapo associated with, 161; threat of being sent to, 3. *See also* "Hungarian girls" from Auschwitz
Auschwitz Chronicle (Czech), 132
Auslander, Leora, 182
Austria: forced labor system, annexation and expansion of, 81; textile industry in, 86
autograph albums (*Stammbücher/pamiętniki*), 38, 188, 200–202, *201*

Bad Kudowa, 99
Barenblat, Hirsch, 59
barracks. *See* work camps
Barthel, K. H., and Barthel firm (Jewish textile firm), Gabersdorf, 87, 137, 249

327

INDEX

bathwater, improvised access to, 184–85
Beck, Birgit, 53
Becker, Michael, 181
bedbugs and lice, 95, 178, 201
Bednarczuk, Bartosz, 34
Będzin: Gabersdorf, transport to, 144; ghetto, creation of (1942), 79, 91, 196, *197*; Jewish population of, 2; Jews in hiding in, 178, 196; mass deportation from (1942), 19, 77–79, 178, 195–96; mobility of Jews in, 31; Oświęcim Jews forced to move to, 56; prewar Jewish political organizations in, 41; workshops of, forced labor in, 30–31, 77, 93, 178
behavioral ethics: differentiated from ethics of care, 182; human failings, lack of documentation of, 250–52
Bela K., *128*, 292n116
Bella C., 112, 162, 193, 209, 227
Bella K., 188
Bemporad, Elissa, 30
Benninga, Noah, 124
Berenbaum, Michael, 123
Bernsdorf: description of site, 138, 148; discovery of confiscated photos at, 190; infirmary for, 129; *Lagerführerin* at, 193–94; liberation of, 230; male workers and staff at, abuses by, 148; number of female forced laborers at, 33, 138, 178; prisoner society and ethics of care at, 183; Schatzlar girls and women moved to, 139, 155; selection and transport of laborers to, 140–43; Shoah Foundation archive of survivor testimonies from, 10; as work camp, 32, 37; work engaged in, at, 147–48; as *Zwangsarbeitslager*, 152
Berta B., 193–94
Berta P., 16, 41, 43–44, 51–52, 57, 63, 72, 98, 116, 120, 243
Between Dignity and Despair (Kaplan), 40
Białystok, 30, 164

Blatman, Daniel, 152–53, 154
Blaustein, Mala, 187
Blechhammer, 132, 139, 141–42, 305n41
Bloxham, Donald, 271n57
Bluma S., 145, 147
Bock, Dennis, 181
Boder, David, 24, 269n33, 271n57
Bornstein, Isaac, 59
Bracha H., 99
Bracht, Fritz, 91, 286n65
Brenda R., 41
Browning, Christopher, 7, 29, 273n2
Buchenwald, 132
Budnitskii, Oleg, 241
Buggeln, Marc, 24, 28
Buhl, Gustav Adolph, and Buhl & Sohne, 139, 158, 293n9
Buna, 132
Bund Deutscher Mädel (League of German Girls), 56–57

"camp time" phenomenon, 27, 121
Canning, Kathleen, 101–2
Card, Claudia, 273n2
care, ethics of. *See* prisoner society and ethics of care
Central Committee of Polish Jews, 18
Cesia T., 148–49, 182–83, 230
Chana B., 70, 73, 97, 98, 104, 125–26, 229, 230, 235
Chana S., 92
Chaya S., 144, 194
children and childhood: as contested category, 17–18, 269–70n43; multidimensional wartime experience of, 18–19; self-identification of testimony-givers as children, 15, 19, 21–23. *See also* youth of testimony-givers
Chládková, Ludmila, 32, 33, 136
Chrzanów, 2, 34, 48, 68, 72, 141, 310n12
Cichopek-Gajraj, Anna, 244
cigarettes, as barter, 184, 252
Clifford, Rebecca, 18–19

328

INDEX

clothing, circulation and exchange of, 97, 126, 173, 176, 190, 194
coerced labor. *See* forced labor at Trautenau; forced labor system
Compaß: Kommerzielles Jahrbuch, 283n30
concentration camps: conversion of work camps into, 2, 32, 36, 37, 84, 152–55, 157–58, 200 (*See also* prisoners, formalization of laborers as); factory work sites supposed to partner with, 82; historical development of, 154; Inspectorate of the Concentration Camps (Department D-II), 36, 93–95, 287n81; SS terror campaign, role in, 154. *See also specific camps*
Coulthard, Glen Sean, 181
coupon system, 158, 296n26
co-workers. *See* Gentile co-workers
crowding, 95, 154–55, 201
Czarna, Fania, 60
Czech, Danuta, 132
Czechoslovakian National Committee, 247
Czeladź, 34, 78

Dąbrowa, 2, 19, 34, 78, 99
Dąbrowa Górnicza, 196
Dasha R., 17, 140, 145
death: death marchers, deaths of, 216, 221–24; gas chambers at Auschwitz-Birkenau, 131–32; laborers, management of deaths of, 188–90; outdoor work of laborers after Allied advance and, 226, 227; public hangings, 50–51, 83, 188–89; threat of, 24, 162, 181, 186
Death Comes in Yellow (Karay), 95
death marches: deaths of men on, 216, 221–24; escape of Berta P. from, 243; laborers witnessing, 83, 216–24; march of forced laborers from other sites to Trautenau, 177–78; Parschnitz, shooting of laborer observing death march in, 83; Trautenau laborers not forced into, 4–5, 209, 226, 235
Des Pres, Terrence, 25
detention centers for suspected collaborators, postwar, 247, 309n4
displaced persons camps, 246, 248
Dora R., 148, 190, 209–10
Douglas, Raymond, 309n4
Dreier, Hans, 58
Dulag (*Durchgangslager*), Sosnowitz, 34, 35, 70–77, 93, 98, 140, 143, 149–51, 163
Dwojra K., 196–97, 200–202, *201*
Dwork, Debórah, 18, 28, 139, 234
dysentery and diarrhea, 132, 184

Eastern Strip, 66, 90–91, 196, 252, 267n4, 285n52
East Upper Silesia: forced labor in, in context of general Nazi forced labor policy, 31; forced labor system, annexation and expansion of, 81; importation of Jewish girls and women as forced labor to Trautenau from, 1–6; Jewish population of, 2, 267n1; map, *vi*; Nazi plans for, 2; US Joint Distribution Committee in, 59. *See also* German ethnicity in East Upper Silesia/Zagłębie; *specific towns and cities*
Ecologies of Witnessing (Pollin-Galay), 9
Eda R., 141
Edith L., 301n13
Edith R., 112
Edith S., 216, 249
Einsatzgruppe, 49, 276n39
Elaine G., 168
Elizabet B., 99, 108, 239
Ella J., 169
emigration, postwar, 246, 248
Erinnerung, Verantwortung, Zukunft (EVZ) foundation, 84, 85
Erna E., 131–32
ersatzes, 75

329

INDEX

escapes, 83, 163–65, 214–15, 243, 251–53
Estelle C., 118, 159, 183, 217, 222, 232
Estera S., 71, 72, 73, 107, 121, 155, 209, 222, 228
Ester R., 60, 62, 117–18, 160–61
Esther K., 229
Esther L., 44, 242, 244
Esther R., 141
Esther S., 44, 47, 49–50, 54, 55–56, 60, 72, 165–66
Eta B., 45, 50, 78, 165
ethics, behavioral. *See* behavioral ethics
ethics of care. *See* prisoner society and ethics of care
ethnic Germans. *See* German ethnicity in East Upper Silesia/Zagłębie
Etrich, Ignaz, and Etrich textile plants, 26, 33; Allied advance and closure of, 225; in forced labor system, 84–87, 89, 94–95, 283n30; Jew, Etrich believed by laborers to be, 209–10; postwar experiences, 248, 310n9; prisoners, formalization of laborers as, 157, 158; smaller work camps and, 137, 138; social relations and ethics of care, 127, 183; testimony-givers' view of factory owners, 208–10
Etrich, Johann, 283n30
Etrich, Julian, 283n30
European Holocaust Research Infrastructure (EHRI), 275n36
Eva D., 168, 170, 171
Eva H., 167, 170, 178
Eva K., 244
Eva W., 213

factory camps. *See* work camps
factory managers: elderly males, as "uncle" figures, 206–10; men working as, 97, 112; Sala K. on significance of, 143–44
factory owners: Allied advance and liberation of Trautenau, 225–27; food and supplies, provision of, 116–17; party affiliations of, 21; postwar experiences, 248; postwar outcomes for, 85; prisoners, formalization of laborers as, 155–56, 157, 158, 162–63; at Sosnowitz *Durchgangslager* (*Dulag*), 72; testimony-givers' view of, 32–33, 208–10; young females, preference for, 4 20, 23. *See also specific owners by name*
factory work sites: all-female labor staff at, 97, 101–2; Allied advance, closing of factories due to, 225–27; camps, not originally regarded as, 30–31; concentration camps, supposed to partner with, 82; as family-owned companies, 82, 86–89; marching back and forth from, 109–11; postwar resumption of operations at, 247; strategies of labor exploitation at, 84–89; subleasing of laborers between, 95; treatment of forced laborers at, 95–96; work engaged in, at, 32–33, 97, 99–103, 128, 144–45, 147–48. *See also specific factories by name*
families: Holocaust destruction of, knowledge of Trautenau survivors about, 15–16, 38, 132–33, 147, 174; "Hungarian girls" on separation from, at Auschwitz-Birkenau, 166–69; ill, pregnant, or resistant laborers sent home to, 33, 83, 94, 99, 115, 129, 133; liberation, returning home after, 16, 39, 242–46; mail/packages from, 11, 38, 68, 74, 121–23, 155, 190–91; prewar family life, 43–45; prisoner society, ethics of care for family members in, 183, 184–85, 190; relatives in work camps, visiting/transferring to same camp, 98–99, 114, 115, 117–20, 156; reunification, hopes for, 3, 15–16, 147, 174, 243–46; separation of forced laborers from, 71, 73–74, 76, 78–79,

330

141–42, 146–47; sole family survivors, forced laborers as, 146–47, 150–51; Sosnowitz *Durchgangslager* (*Dulag*), visiting girls taken for forced labor at, 71, 72–76; volunteering for labor duty to save/protect, 71, 83, 92–93, 142–43, 145–47, 149, 163–64

Fanny W., 50, 93, 239

Fay B., 76, 77, 81, 108, 116, 127, 157, 160, 245–46, 275n36

Fela G., 140–41, 185–86

Finder, Gabriel, 18

Fineman, Joel, 13

Finkel, Evgeny, 30, 36, 80, 164

fish taken from herring processing factory, 183

Flaschka, Monika, 170

food and supplies: Allied advance, shortages due to, 226, 227, 228; apples, 109, 111, 125–26, 210; bread, as symbol, 123–24; clothing, circulation and exchange of, 97, 126, 173, 176, 190, 194; death marches fighting over bread given by laborers, 220–21; elderly male "uncles" providing, 206, 207; factory owners' provision of, 116–17; Gentile co-workers, sympathetic gestures by, 7–8, 33, 37, 104–7, 185–86; hunger, pervasiveness of, 26, 38, 110–11, 123, 141, 180, 183, 205, 220–21, 224; *Lagerführerinnen*, extra food supplied by, 193–94; *Lagerführerinnen*, thefts by, 21, 123, 191, 193; looting, after liberation, 238–40; potatoes, 124–25, 183, 189; prisoners of war providing, 210–11; support groups sharing, 183–84, 188, 194; transactional relationships and access to, 191; young Jewish females in Zagłębie sent out to obtain, 54–57, 65–66

forced labor at Trautenau, 1–39; contextualization within Nazi forced labor program, 6, 28–33; documentation and sources, 33–35; "Hungarian girls" from Auschwitz as, 37–38, 152 (See also "Hungarian girls" from Auschwitz); letters soliciting, 70; mobility of laborers, 37, 91, 117–20, 224; naming and terminology, 35; prisoner numbers, 128, 156; purpose and concept of, 2; selection of girls and women for, 61–63, 70–72; social relations in spaces of persecution and, 6, 24–28 (See also prisoner society and ethics of care; social relations); substituting or switching siblings, 74–76; testimony of survivors of, 2–5 (See also testimony of survivors); Trautenau, importation of Jewish girls and women from Zagłębie region to, 1–6 (See also Jewish girlhood in Zagłębie); youth of testimony-givers, effects of, 6, 14–24 (See also youth of testimony-givers). See also forced labor system; liberation of Trautenau; postwar experiences; prisoners, formalization of laborers as; Schmelt system; work camps; *specific camps*

forced labor system, 36, 81–96; as alternative to harsher outcomes, viewed by Jews as, 76, 79, 82, 83, 92–93, 130–31, 144, 209–10; brother sent into, Helen P. smuggling message to, 67–70; concentration camp system and, 154; contextualization of Trautenau within Nazi forced labor program, 6, 28–33; escapes from, 83, 163–65, 214–15, 243, 251–53; German approach to wartime economy and, 89–90; Inspectorate of the Concentration Camps (Department D-II), takeover by, 93–95; labor supply/transport flows in late war and, 177–78; in local workshops, 30–31, 77, 81–82, 91–93, 178; prewar origins of, 81; prisoners of war in, 28, 81, 87,

331

215; spaces of, 84; strategies of labor exploitation, 84–89; subleasing of laborers between factories, 95; threat of illness and death within, 83, 114–16, 129; treatment of forced laborers within, 82, 83, 95–96; work, priority given to, 252–53. *See also* factory owners; factory work sites; Schmelt system; work camps

Four Scraps of Bread (Hollander-Lafon), 124

Frances H., 111–12, 167, 175–76, 226

Franci's War, 212

Freikorps, 87, 89

French prisoners of war, romantic liaisons with, 210–13

Frieda W., 109, 127, 176, 177, 228

Friedländer, Saul, 7, 268n14

Friedman, Philip, 58–59

Friedrich, Klaus-Peter, 273n89, 276n49

Fryda F., 141, 247

Frymeta F., 44–45, 101, 106, 108, 124, 207, 217

Fulbrook, Mary, 196

Gabersdorf: Barthel (Jewish textile firm), 87, 137, 249; deaths of laborers at, 189; description of site, 137–38, *138*; diary and poetry of Regina H. at, 202–4; family separation and survival at, 145–47; as "heaven," 145; infirmary for, 129; number of female forced laborers at, 33, 137, 178; selection and transport of laborers to, 140–43; Shoah Foundation archive of survivor testimonies from, 10; as work camp, 32, 37; work engaged in, at, 144–45; as *Zwangsarbeitslager*, 152

Garbarini, Alexandra, 8, 182

gas chambers at Auschwitz-Birkenau, 131–32

Gauleiter, 90–91

gender: girls and women taking on male roles, 79–80, 101–2; girls passing as men, 64–65; "Hungarian girls," laborers' reactions to appearance of, 165–66; shaving experienced as erasure of, 169–70; social relations, gendered nature of, 135. *See also* men and maleness; sex and sexuality

Generalgouvernement, 29, 31, 61, 95

Geneva Convention, 215

Gentile co-workers: Allied advance and liberation of Trautenau, 225, 227, 235; economic and social positions of, 107–8; elderly males, as "uncle" figures, 206–10; ethnic identification of, 103–4, 107; giving photos of themselves to Jewish laborers, *128*, 186; hiding Jewish laborers' family photos from authorities, 109, 123, 190; postwar testimony against, 249–50; prisoners, formalization of laborers as, 157, 163; prisoners of war, relationships with, 210, 212; punishment of laborers for receiving help from, 194; at smaller camps, 148–49; sympathetic gestures by, 7–8, 33, 37, 104–7, 148–49, 180, 185–86, 188; work engaged in by, 32, 104; working alongside Jewish forced laborers, 6, 33, 36–37, 102–9, *128*

Gentile guards, 82–83, 112–14, 120, 127–28, *128*, 163, 191–95, 228, 235. See also *Aufseherinnen*; *Lagerführerinnen*

Gentile population in Trautenau: errands done by laborers and interactions with, 109; escapes from work camps and ease of interaction with, 83; laborers passing in, after liberation, 243; looting of, after liberation, 238–40; marching back and forth from work sites, 109–11; postwar Czechoslovakia/Sudetenland, 247–48; sexual predation by, 111–12

Gentile population in Zagłębie region:

332

antisemitism and anti-Jewishness, prewar, 40–42; ban on relations between Jews and non-Jews, 53, 54; brother sent into forced labor, Helen P. smuggling message to, 67–70; food and supplies, young Jewish females sent out to obtain, 54, 55, 66; German ethnicity, claiming, 51, 276n49; under German occupation, 51–52, 66–67; girls passing as, 54–57, 66; inhabiting former homes of returning laborers, 244–46, 308n75; prewar relations with Jews, 42; at Sosnowitz *Durchgangslager* (*Dulag*), 76–77; sympathetic gestures by, 57, 66–67

Geppersdorf, 139, 143

Gerda F., 26–27, 28, 183–84, 210, 242, 251–52

Gerlach, Christian, 94

German ethnicity in East Upper Silesia/Zagłębie: at beginning of war, 51, 276n49; politicization of, 87–88; postwar treatment of, 247–48

German invasion and occupation of Poland, 42–48

Gestapo: Auschwitz, association with, 161; forced laborers, selection/movement of, 2, 33, 61, 62, 155; Gross-Rosen concentration camp and, 156; Jewish Council of Elders and, 2, 58, 59, 61; at mass deportations, 195–96; occupation of Poland and, 49; roundups by, 149; Schmelt system staffed by, 2; sexual bribery of, 21; Sosnowitz *Durchgangslager* (*Dulag*) and, 77; survivor perception of, 21

Gitla T., 22, 23, 122, 123

Glassheim, Eagle, 88

Gleiwitz (Gliwice) labor camps, 77, 81

Glissant, Édouard, 26, 181

Glücks, Richard, 94

Gogolin, 118

Gräben, 289n37

Greiser, Arthur, 91

Grossmann, Atina, 233–34, 307n36

Gross-Rosen Archive, 32, 33, 34

Gross-Rosen concentration camp, 156, 217

Gross-Rosen subcamp system: coupons, 158; ritualized humiliations at, 83; SS inspectors, assignment of, 287n84; transformation of Schmelt system into, 29, 32, 34, 37, 86, 136, 139, 152, 156, 157

Gruner, Wolf, 28, 29, 81

Grząślewicz, Tomasz, 34

guards. See *Aufseherinnen*; Gentile guards; *Judenältesten*; *Lagerältesten*; *Lagerführerinnen*

Gucia R., 176–77, 208, 218, 225, 228

Gutman, Israel, 123

Gutterman, Bella, 33, 93, 94, 136

Haase, Alois, and Haase textile factories, 16, 33, 70; Allied advance and closure of, 225; death marchers housed at, 217, 218, 219; in forced labor system, 85–87, 89, 94–95, 283n30; postwar experiences, 248; postwar testimony against, 250; prisoners, formalization of laborers as, 155–56, 157, 158, 162–63, 296n19; prisoners of war and other men working at, 214; smaller work camps and, 137; social relations, prisoner society, and ethics of care at, 127, 128, 196; testimony-givers' view of factory owners, 208–9; transit camp, Parschnitz's use as, 178

hair: facial hair of Jewish men, Nazis' public cutting of, 50; "Hungarian girls," forced laborers' reactions to shaved heads of, 165–66, 172, 174; "Hungarian girls," shaving experienced by, 169–70; punitive head-shaving of forced laborers, 83, 124, 194

Hájková, Anna, 7, 25, 26, 80, 115, 181, 234, 281n158, 307n36

INDEX

Halbmayr, Brigid, 152, 153, 160, 162, 169
hangings, public, 50–51, 83, 188–89
Hannsdorf, 21, 177, 288n24
Hartman, Geoffrey, 7, 11–12
HASAG camps, 95, 111
Hassebroek, Johannes, 158
Hawlik[owa], Elsa, 118, 126, 127, 131, 132, 156–57, 249
Hayes, Peter, 285n49, 299n81
head-shaving. *See* hair
Hedy W., 171–72, 239–40
Heim, Susanne, 284n45
Heine's "The Weavers of Silesia," 89
Hela (sister of Shoshana G.), 118–20
Hela K., 113
Helena K., 20–21, 97, 107, 116, 133–34, 174, 208, 226
Helen F., 126, 243–44
Helen P., 48–49, 59–60, 67–70
Helfgott, Sara, 137, *138*
Henlein, Konrad, 87, 88
Herzberger, Regina, 193
Herzog, Dagmar, 53–54
Herzog, Hanna, 200
Hillers, Marta, 233
Himmler, Heinrich, 31, 37, 49, 90, 94, 139, 153, 154, 156, 225, 284n35, 285n60, 286n65
Hitler, Adolf, 28, 82, 89–90, 167
Hoffmann, Regina, 214–15, 251
Hollander-Lafon, Magda, 124
Holocaust (as destruction of European Jewry): death marches, laborers' witnessing of, 222; forced laborers as only family survivors of, 146–47, 150–51; Gabersdorf as "heaven" in context of, 145; knowledge of Trautenau survivors about, 15–16, 38, 132–33, 147, 174; return home and realization of, 243–46
home. *See* families
Höß, Rudolf, 93, 284n35
Hrda, Anna, 107

"Hungarian girls" from Auschwitz, 37–38, 152, 165–79; knowledge of Holocaust conveyed by, 147, 174; labor supply and transport flows, 177–78; at liberation, 243–44; pregnant woman transported to Auschwitz, 133–34; reactions of forced laborers to appearance of, 165–66, 172–74; relations between forced laborers and, 174–77; selection as forced laborers and transport to Trautenau, 170–72; at smaller camps in Schmelt system, 136, 139, 147; testimony on transportation and Auschwitz selection process, 166–70
Hungarian Jews sent to Auschwitz-Birkenau (1944), 94, 95, 152
Hungarian state, multiethnicity of, 298n60
hunger, pervasiveness of, 26, 38, 110–11, 123, 141, 180, 183, 205, 220–21, 224. *See also* food and supplies

Ida G., 62, 106–7, 121, 157, 164, 172–73, 176, 207–8, 211, 219, 220, 221–22, 231, 238, 244, 245
IG Farben, 82, 117, 285n49, 299n81
illness and medical conditions, 129–34; abortions, 133; Auschwitz-Birkenau, ill, pregnant, or resistant laborers sent to, 33, 83, 115, 129–34; dysentery and diarrhea, 132, 184; families, ill, pregnant, or resistant laborers sent home to, 33, 83, 94, 99, 115, 129, 133; lice and bedbugs, 95, 178, 201; medical and dental care, availability of, 129–32; menstruation, 126–27; pregnancy, treatment of, 33, 115, 133–34, 186–88; prisoner of war, medicine provided by, 183–84, 252; TB (tuberculosis), 133, 250; threat of illness and death in forced labor system, 83, 114–16, 129; typhus, 115, 125, 129, 131, 132, 184, 242; work conditions leading to skin and

334

lung problems, 99–100, 106, 129, 184, 250
Inspectorate of the Concentration Camps (Department D-II), 36, 93–95, 152, 164, 287n81
International Tracing Service, 84
Irene W., 144, 147, 150, 189, 215–16

Jaworzno, 34
Jewish bodies, German access to, 50–54, 72, 83, 192
Jewish Claims Conference, 289n32
Jewish communal aid organizations, postwar, 242
Jewish Council of Elders, 58–61; Gross-Rosen concentration camp and, 156; Lajtner as medical doctor for forced laborers of Trautenau and, 130; mail/packages, facilitation of, 121, 202; mass roundup of 1943, participation in, 196; organization of, 58–59; provision of forced labor, involvement in, 30–31, 60–61, 63, 70, 75, 76, 77, 91, 93, 140, 142, 144; registering and tracking of Jews by, 59; social welfare services through, 29, 59; Wiederman working for, 47; young age of workers and coercion of, 23, 60
Jewish girlhood in Zagłębie, 35–36, 40–80; antisemitism and anti-Jewishness, rise of, 40–42; ban on relations between Jews and non-Jews, 53, 54; brother sent into forced labor, Helen P. smuggling message to, 67–70; family life, prewar, 43–45 (*See also* families); food and supplies, young females sent out to obtain, 54–57, 65–66; forced labor, selection for, 61–63, 70–72; German invasion and occupation of Poland, 42–48; Jewish Council of Elders and, 58–61; Jewish elders and communal institutions, Nazi treatment of, 48–51; male family members, attempts to hide/arrests of, 57–58, 64–65; new behaviors, taking on, 79–80, 281n157; passing as non-Jewish, 54–57, 66; relocation eastward, Jewish attempts at, 46–47; sexual/sexualized violence, 51–54; Sosnowiec sports stadium, mass roundup of Jews at (1942), 77–79; Sosnowitz *Durchgangslager* (*Dulag*), 34, 35, 70–77; Star of David, Jews required to wear, 51–52, 54. *See also* Gentile population in Zagłębie region
Jewish Historical Institute, Poland, 249
Jewish holidays and practices, efforts to observe, 27–28, 117–18, 121, 189–90
Jewish men on death marches, 83, 216–24
Jewish police (*milicja* or *milits*), 59, 61, 62, 71, 75–76, 77, 140, 143, 195
Jewish soldiers at liberation of Trautenau, 229, 233, 234–36, 241
Jockusch, Laura, 271n57
Judenältesten, 83, 113, 114, 120, 129, 207, 215. See also *Lagerältesten*
Jungbuch, 177

Kaczmarek, Ryszard, 276n49
Kaiser, Menachem, 34
Kamionka ghetto, Będzin, 79, 196, *197*
Kaplan, Marion, 40, 42, 79, 80, 234, 273n2, 281n157
Karay, Felicja, 24, 28, 95, 111, 123, 251
Katalin T., 167
Katowice, 90, 196
Kattowitz Gestapo, 2, 58, 91
Kirschner, Ann, 34, 122, 139–40
Kirschner, Sala, 139
Kirstein, Wolfgang, 28
Kleiman, Yehudit, 306n2
Kluge, Johann A., and J. A. Kluge textile factory, 33; Allied advance and closure of, 225; Barthel firm taken over by, 87, 137, 249; in forced labor system, 85–89, 94–95; postwar expe-

riences, 248; prisoners, formalization of laborers as, 157, 158; prisoners of war and other men working at, 214; smaller work camps and, 137; social relations, prisoner society, and ethics of care at, 108, 127, 198; testimony-givers' view of factory owners, 208–9
knitting and crocheting, 5–6, 7–8, 126, 127, 185–86
Kommando Trautenau, 139, 158–59, 287n84
Kraków, 48, 54, 164
Kratzau, 235
Kristallnacht (1938), 89, 284n45
Kryl, Miroslav, 32, 33, 136
Kubátová, Ludmila, 216
Kuczynski, Friedrich, 71, 75, 78, 195, 196
Kushner, Tony, 271n57

Lagerältesten, 109, 120, 171, 195. See also *Judenältesten*
Lagerführerinnen: coupon system and, 158; deaths of laborers and, 189–90; at Gabersdorf, 137; liberation of Trautenau, absence from, 228; negotiating with SS, 251, 252; prisoners, formalization of laborers as, 155, 156–58; red shoes given to, 191; responsibilities of, 82–83, 112–13, 120, 156–57; roll call, 156–57; selection of laborers by, 20; social relations, prisoner society, and interactions with, 127–28, 191–95; SS training for, 155, 157–58, 194, 296n19; theft of food and objects by, 21, 123, 191, 193; violence perpetrated by, 157, 193–94; visits/transfers between camps, allowing, 117–19; youth of workers and manipulation of, 23
Lajtner (Leitner, Laitner), Wolf, 130–32
Langer, Lawrence, 7, 10, 271n57
Lanzmann, Claude, 182
Laskier, Rutka, 34

The Last Ghetto (Hájková), 80
Laub, Dori, 7, 11
Lehnstaedt, Stephan, 29, 31, 93
Lena M., 5–6, 7–8, 27, 28, 113, 126, 127, 214, 221, 229, 231, 234
letters. *See* mail/packages/postcards
Levi, Primo, 182
Levitt, Laura, 182, 204
liberation of Trautenau, 4–5, 16, 38–39, 225–46; absence of guards and civilians, 228–29, 235; Allied advance, closing of factories, and transfer of laborers to outdoor work, 225–27; displaced persons camps, 246; Gentile population inhabiting former homes of returning laborers, 244–46, 308n75; "Hungarian girls" at, 243–44; Jewish soldiers at, 229, 233, 234–36, 241; lack of authority and control after, 241–42; looting, 238–40; number of women and girls at time of, 33; Parschnitz, transfers of forced laborers to/through, 227–28; partisans, arrival of, 229; pleasure and desire, experiences of, 238–41; remaining in Trautenau after, 242, 247; returning home after, 16, 39, 242–46, 247; Soviet troops, encounters with, 6, 23, 39, 227, 229–38, 240–41, 242
lice and bedbugs, 95, 178, 201
Lichtewerden, 139
Lili T., 104, 167, 170
Lindner, Heinrich, 71, 75, 78, 90, 285n60, 286n66
Livia R., 171, 228
local workshops, forced labor in, 30–31, 77, 81–82, 91–93, 178
Łódź Jews sent to Auschwitz-Birkenau, 95, 152, 176–77
Lola W., 56–57, 79, 127, 130–31, 159, 205–6, 209, 229
Longerich, Peter, 154, 252, 284n35
looting, after liberation, 238–40

Luba (pregnant laborer), 186–88
Lucy M., 61, 73, 99, 101, 109, 113, 120, 133, 161, 174, 207, 218
Ludwig, Alfred, 75, 79, 279n97, 286n66
Lusia B., 178, 230
Lydia B., 235–36

Magda F., 170
Magda-Madeleine F., 110, 121, 227, 230
Magdolna H., 167, 168, 170, 171
Mailänder, Elissa, 192
mail/packages/postcards, 195–99; allowance of, 11, 38, 121; barracks numbers, sent to, 114; brother sent into forced labor, Helen P. smuggling message to, 67–70; ceasing of, 121–22, 155, 156, 202; at *Dulag*, 74; families providing, 11, 38, 68, 74, 121–23, 155, 190–91; gendered construction of, 135; Jewish Council of Elders facilitating, 121, 202; objects, significance as, 182; prisoner society and ethics of care, 38, 182, 190–91, 195–99, 203; for prisoners of war, 183, 215; Regina H.'s poem compared, 203
Majdanek, 145, 216
Majstorović, Vojin, 241
Malá, Irena, 216
Mania R., 47, 54, 178
Mania S., 207, 230–31, 238
marches: factory work sites, marching back and forth from, 109–11. *See also* death marches
Marella (sister of Shoshana G.), 118–20
Marx, Karl, 89
Masha S., 41, 42, 71, 73, 99, 113, 130
Maurer, Gerhard, 94–95, 287n81, 287n84, 299nn81–82
Maus (Spiegelman), 34
medical conditions. *See* illness and medical conditions
medicalized naked selections, 159–62, 186–88

men and maleness, 38, 205–24; attempts to hide/arrests of male family members, 57–58, 64–65; Bernsdorf, abuses by male workers and staff at, 148; biological maleness, invocations of, 231–32; death marches, laborers witnessing, 83, 216–24; diary and poetry of Regina H. on "Antek," 202–3; elderly Gentile co-workers and factory personnel, as "uncle" figures, 206–10; facial hair, Nazis' public cutting of, 50; factory managers, men as, 97, 112; Geppersdorf, girls and women sent to work at, 139, 143; girls and women taking on male roles, 79–80, 101–2; girls passing as men, 64–65; guards at work camps, male, 163; information obtained from men at camps, 206–7, 213; Jewish elders and communal institutions, Nazi treatment of, 48–51; paucity of men in laborers' world, 206; prisoners of war, interactions with, 38, 183–84, 206, 210–16, 252; romantic liaisons, 206, 210–16; social relations in male camp environs, 135; Soviet troops, encounters with, 6, 23, 39, 227, 229–30, 240–41, 242; youthfulness of laborers and interest in, 205–6, 208, 212. *See also* gender; sex and sexuality
Mengele, Joseph, 169, 186
menstruation, 126–27
Merin, Moses, 58, 59, 60, 63, 93, 277n71
Michlic, Joanna Beata, 18
Michman, Dan, 60
Midwest Center for Holocaust Education, 14
Mina J., 149–51
Minnie W., 22–23, 122, 126, 163, 175, 189, 243
Minsk, 164
mobility: of forced laborers, 37, 91, 117–20, 224; of Jews in Będzin and

337

INDEX

Sosnowiec, 29, 31; of prisoners of war, 215; within Schmelt system, 37, 91, 117–20
Modrzejów, 34, 78
Moss, Kenneth, 41
Mühl, Maria, 296–97n28
Mühlhäuser, Regina, 53, 241
Murdock, Caitlin, 86, 87
Muselmänner, 181

Nache B., 249–50
naked selections, 37, 153, 159–62, 171, 186–88
Namysło, Aleksandra, 30, 47
Nazi Policy, Jewish Workers, German Killers (Browning), 29
Nesselrodt, Markus, 28
Nettie S., 1, 3, 11, 21–22, 54, 60, 63, 102, 110–11, 116, 117, 157, 158
Numbered Days (Garbarini), 8, 182
Nuremberg trials, 152–53

Ober Altstadt: as concentration camp, 26, 37, 136, 157–58; infirmary for, 129; Kluge factory base in, 89, 108; liberation of, 229; Łódź Jews sent from Auschwitz-Birkenau to, 176; naked selections at, 156; number of female forced laborers at, 33, 178; Parschnitz and, 32; as postwar detention center for suspected collaborators, 247; prisoners of war and other men working at, 183–84, 210, 212, 214; Shoah Foundation archive of survivor testimonies from, 10; slaps and hitting in, 51; Tola G. asking to join sister at, 79; as work camp, 32; Zaks postcards sent to, 198; as *Zwangsarbeitslager*, 152
objects and object exchanges, 5–6, 122–26, 182. *See also* food and supplies; mail/packages/postcards; photographs
Olga K., 211–12, 219

Olkusz, 2, 34, 59, 63, 65, 66
Operation Schmelt. *See* Schmelt system
Opole (formerly Sakrau/Zakrzów), 67, 68, 118
Ordinary Jews (Finkel), 30, 80
"organizing," 123, 125
Orth, Karin, 28
Osterloh, Jörg, 28, 87–88
Oświęcim, 56, 72, 90, 131, 277n66. *See also* Auschwitz-Birkenau
Ozick, Cynthia, 182

packages. *See* mail/packages/postcards
Pally, Marcia, 26
pamiętniki/Stammbücher (autograph albums), 38, 188, 200–202, *201*
Parschnitz: autograph album (*Stammbüch/pamiętnik*) from, 200–202, *201*; as concentration camp, 19, 26, 33, 37, 136, 152, 157–58, 200; death marches of Jewish males witnessed at, 83, 216–24; deaths of laborers at, 189; as Gross-Rosen subcamp, 287n85; infirmary for, 129, 130; labor supply/transport flows in late war and, 177–78; *Lagerführerin* at, 194; Łódź Jews sent from Auschwitz-Birkenau to, 176; naked selections at, 156, 186–88; number of female forced laborers at, 33, 178; Ober Altstadt and, 32; outdoor work at, after closure of factories, 226–27; prisoners of war and other men working at, 214; public hangings at, 50–51, 83, 188–89; Shoah Foundation archive of survivor testimonies from, 10; shooting of laborer observing death march in, 83; social relations in, 99, 108, 115, 117–20, 127–33; as transit camp, 19, 227–28; as work camp, 32
Passelman (relative of Sonia S.), 66
Patterson, Orlando, 273n2
Paula S., 110, 186–88

338

personal space, in barracks, 121, 124
photographs: discovery of confiscated photos, 190; Gentile co-workers giving photos of themselves to Jewish laborers, *128*, 186; Gentile co-workers hiding Jewish laborers' family photos from authorities, 109, 123, 190; in mail/packages from families, 11; value for laborers of, 190
Phyllis Y., 4, 53, 61, 104, 126, 155, 161, 212–13, 218, 219, 221, 240
Płowa Bestia (Wiederman), 47–48, 275n36
Plunder (Kaiser), 34
Pohl, Oswald, 93, 94, 287n81
Polenaktion, 40, 41
Pollin-Galay, Hannah, 9–10, 112, 143–44, 145, 215
Porat, Dan, 59
postcards. *See* mail/packages/postcards
postwar experiences, 246, 247–53; detention centers for suspected collaborators, 247, 309n4; displaced persons camps, 246, 248; emigration, 246, 248; ethnic German population in Czechoslovakia, 247–48; factories and factory owners, 247, 248, 249–50; monuments to forced laborers and concentration camp victims in Trautenau region, 248; prosecution of perpetrators, 34, 59, 132, 192, 248, 249–50; remaining in Eastern Europe/Trautenau region, 246, 248–49, 310n12; reunions between "camp sisters," 246; testimony, collection of, 248–53
potatoes, 124–25, 183, 189
pregnancy, 33, 115, 133–34, 186–88
pride in work: ethics of care and, 183; knitting project of Lena M., 5–6, 7–8; survivors' sense of, 16–17, 99–102
prisoner numbers, 128, 156
prisoners, formalization of laborers as, 152–65; combination of barracks and crowding, 154–55; conversion of work camps into concentration camps, 2, 32, 36, 37, 84, 152–55; coupon system, 158, 296n26; escapes, 163–65; factory owners and, 155–56, 157, 158, 162–63; forced nakedness and naked selections, 37, 153, 159–62; Gross-Rosen subcamp system, transformation of Schmelt system into, 152, 156, 157; *Lagerführerinnen*, SS training for, 155, 157–58; roll calls, 156–57; sexualized violence, subjection to, 152, 153, 159–62; SS, more direct contact with, 152, 155, 158–62; unregulated activities at work sites, efforts to end, 156, 162–63
prisoner society and ethics of care, 11, 180–204; behavioral ethics differentiated, 182; concepts of, 180–82; deaths of laborers, management of, 188–90; family members, concern for, 183, 184–85, 190; Gentile guards, interactions with, 191–95; mail/packages/postcards, 38, 182, 190–91, 195–99, 203; notes sent between laborers, *199*, 199–200, objects, role of, 182; *pamiętniki*/*Stammbücher* (autograph albums), 188, 200–202, *201*; performances, songs, and poetry, 180, 202–4; photographs, 190; relationality, concept of, 181, 192, 197–98, 203; substituting in naked selections, 186–88; support pairs or small groups, 181, 182–88; transactional relationships/reciprocity, 185–86, 191
prisoners of war: concentration camps for, 154; as forced labor, 28, 81, 87, 215; interactions of laborers with, 38, 183–84, 206, 210–16, 249, 252; mobility of, 215; Soviet versus Western European, 215
Proszyk, Jacek, 47

339

INDEX

public hangings, 50–51, 83, 188–89

questionnaire used by Shoah Foundation, 10–11

Radom, 176, 179, 243–44
Radomsko, 65
Ranz, John, 302n45, 305n41
rape. *See* sex and sexuality
Ravensbrück, 157, 296n19
reciprocity/transactional relationships, 5–6, 7–8, 25, 185–86, 191
Red Cross, 183
red shoes given to *Lagerführerin*, 191
Regina B., 141, 144
Regina G., 14, 50, 65, 99, 112, 121, 129, 155, 161–62, 220, 222, 226, 232. *See also* Regina S.
Regina H., 202–4
Regina P., 49, 62, 78, 232, 248
Regina S., 14, 50, 64–65, 73, 76, 100, 163–64, 220. *See also* Regina G.
Reichenbach textile cooperative, 178, 235, 282n16
Reichsautobahnlager (RAB) labor initiative, 81, 82, 139
Reichssicherheitshauptamt (RHSA) office, Katowice, 196
relationality, concept of, 26, 181, 192, 197–98, 203. *See also* prisoner society and ethics of care; social relations
Remembering Survival (Browning), 7, 29
Rena M., 100–101, 175, 222–23, 239
reunions between "camp sisters," 246
Rita R., 4, 16, 46, 75, 101, 126
Rittenberg, Dasha, 140
Ritterbusch, Fritz, 132, 158–59, 162–64, 249, 287nn84–85, 296–97nn27–28
Röger, Maren, 69
roll calls, 156–57
Rosalie S., 41–42, 78, 104, 113–14, 122, 173, 194, 217
Rosa S., 141–42

Rose B., 43, 176
Rose K., 100, 213–14, 244
Rose L., 83
Rosen, Alan, 27–28, 269n33
Rosensaft, Hadassah, 92
Rose S., 71, 72, 75–76, 100, 129, 130, 168, 217, 222, 223
Roskies, David, 203
Rossino, Alexander, 53, 278n36
Roth, John K., 182
Roza W., 92, 148
Rudorff, Andrea, 31, 136, 195
Rusia Y., 62, 74, 232–33
Ruth R., 178
Rutka's Notebook (Laskier), 34

sabotage, stealing, and subversion of camp rules, 123, 124–25, 126–27
Sádlo, Václav, 217
sailor suit, Mina J.'s story of, 149
Sakrau (Zakrzów, now Opole), 67, 68, 118
Sala B./Sally B., 155, *199*, 199–200
Sala K., 130, 142–44, 145, 253
Sala P., 190–91
Sala's Gift (Kirschner), 34, 122, 139–40, 142
Schatzlar: Bernsdorf, laborers moved to, 139, 155; description of site, 139–40; infirmary for, 129; *Lagerführerin* at, 194; number of female forced laborers at, 33, 178; selection and transport of laborers to, 140–43; Shoah Foundation archive of survivor testimonies from, 10; survivor texts from, 139–40; as work camp, 32, 37; work engaged in, at, 144
Scheck, Raffael, 304n19
Schindler (factory owner, not Oskar), 72
Schmelt, Albrecht, 2, 31, 36, 90–91, 93, 94, 152, 156, 158, 252, 277n71, 285nn59–60, 286n65
Schmelt system, 2, 31; age of laborers used by, 15; contextualization within

340

Nazi forced labor program, 6, 28–33, 81; creation of, 90–91, 93, 287n77; ghettoization of Sosnowiec and Będzin by, 196; Gross-Rosen subcamp system, transformation into, 29, 32, 34, 37, 86, 136, 139, 152, 156, 157; Inspectorate of the Concentration Camps (Department D-II), takeover by, 93–95; local workshops, use of, 30–31, 77, 81–82, 91–93; mobility of workers within, 37, 91, 117–20; replacement of ill, pregnant, or reluctant workers in, 33, 83, 94; Sosnowiec sports stadium, mass roundup of Jews at (1942), 77–79, 178, 195–96; Środula, mass roundup of 1943 in, 196; SS and, 2, 19, 26, 30, 31, 37, 75, 82, 195–96; state-run initiatives requisitioning labor from, 81–82; WHVA control, movement under, 154
Seidelmann, Else Herta, 285n60
Selbstschutz, 49, 52–53, 90, 196, 276n49
Service, Hugo, 267n4
sex and sexuality: armed forces interacting with civilian girls and women, 69; ban on relations between Jews and non-Jews, 53; barter and bribery, 69, 77, 234; concept of "sexualized violence," 152, 153; diary and poetry of Regina H. on, 202–3; forced nakedness and naked selections, 37, 153, 159–62, 171, 186–88; formalization of laborers as prisoners and exposure to sexualized violence, 152, 153, 159–62; gay and lesbian experiences, 7, 107, 184, 301n13; German occupation of Poland and sexual/sexualized violence, 51–54; interviewers' reactions to, 7; Nazi repression of sexuality, 53–54; romantic liaisons with prisoners of war and other males, 206, 210–16, 249; shaving, as sexualized violence, 169; Soviet troops, encounters with, 6, 23, 39, 227, 229–38, 240–41, 242; Steinert on, 19; at work camps and factory sites, 95, 107, 111–12; youthfulness and sexual naïveté of testimony-givers, 15, 23, 231–32; youthfulness and vulnerability to sexualized violence of testimony-givers, 51; youthfulness of laborers and interest in men/sexuality, 205–6, 208, 212. *See also* gender; men and maleness

Shandler, Jeffrey, 9
Shapira, Rina, 200
shaving. *See* hair
Shenker, Noah, 8, 10, 11
Shoah. *See* Holocaust
Shoah Foundation, 3, 8–9, 10–12, 14, 33, 34, 43, 56, 139, 142, 163, 246, 248–51, 269n35, 279n100
Shoshana G., 4, 98, 118–20, 174, 180, 209, 217, 220–21, 222, 233
Shoshana L., 42, 45–46, 55, 61–62, 73–74, 78, 107, 118, 177, 228, 231, 239, 241, 242, 243, 289n37
Siemens, 87, 137, 176, 177, 225, 248, 283n29, 289n32
Silesian weavers' uprising (1844), 86, 89
singing girl on Hungarian transport from Auschwitz, 172
Skarżysko-Kamienna camp, 123, 251
slippers made for Gentile co-worker, 185–86
Smoleń, Kazimierz, 171
Sobibor, 145
"social death" of Jews in German society, 40, 42, 273n2
social embedding, 123, 291n103
social relations, 36–37, 97–135; within barracks, 112–14, 120–21; beautiful setting, survivor memories of, 97–98; extremity as reference point in, 24, 25; with factory managers, 97, 112; gendered nature of, 135; Gentile guards and, 112–14, 120, 127–28, *128*;

341

Jewishness, retaining awareness of, 27–28; with local Gentile populations, 109–11; objects and object exchanges, 122–26, 182; performances, songs, and poetry, 120–21, 180, 202–4; personal space, in barracks, 121, 124; prewar relations with non-Jews, 42; pride in work, survivors' sense of, 16–17, 99–102; prison societies and possibility of, 38; production process shaping, 102–3; relational behaviors and choices, 26; relationality, concept of, 26, 181, 192, 197–98, 203; relatives in work camps, visiting/transferring to same camp, 98–99, 114, 115, 117–20; sabotage, stealing, and subversion of camp rules, 123, 124–25, 126–27; in spaces of persecution, 6, 24–28; support pairs or small groups, 25, 26, 181, 182–88, 205; transactional relationships/reciprocity, 5–6, 7–8, 25, 185–86, 191; in transportation to camps and selection process, 98–99. *See also* Gentile co-workers; illness and medical conditions; mail/packages/postcards; prisoner society and ethics of care; sex and sexuality

Sommer, Karl, 299n82

Sommer, Robert, 296n26

Sonderausweise/Sonders (labor passes), 91

Sonia S., 19–20, 41, 46, 47, 51, 57–58, 59, 60, 65, 66, 112, 120, 161, 162

Sosnowiec: closure of streets and areas to Jewish access, 54, 63, 196; Gabersdorf, transport to, 144; ghetto, creation of (1942), 4, 79, 91, 130–31, 196, *197*; Jewish Council of Elders, organization of, 58; Jewish population of, 2; Jews in hiding in, 196; liberation of Trautenau, returning home after, 16, 39, 242–46; map, *vii*; mobility of Jews in, 29, 31; Oświęcim Jews forced to move to, 56; prewar Jewish political organizations in, 41; Schmelt system centered in, 2; sports stadium, mass roundup of Jews at (1942), 77–79, 122, 178, 195–96; workshops of, forced labor in, 30–31, 77, 92, 93

Sosnowitz *Durchgangslager* (*Dulag*), 34, 35, 70–77, 93, 98, 140, 143, 149–51, 163

Soviet troops: laborers' encounters with, 6, 23, 39, 227, 229–38, 240–41, 242; as prisoners of war, 215

Soviet Union, prewar flight of Jews to, 46–47

Spiegelman, Art, 34

Spoerer, Mark, 69

Sprenger, Isabell, 136

Springer-Aharoni, Nina, 306n2

Šrámková, Helena, 310n12

Środula ghetto, Sosnowiec, 79, 130–31, 196, *197*

SS: during Allied advance and liberation of Trautenau, 225–26, 228, 235; Auschwitz, association with, 161; concentration camps and terror campaign of, 154; coupon system and, 158; death marches and, 216; escapes, response to, 251–53; forced laborers, selection/movement of, 2, 19, 33, 37, 45, 61, 62, 71, 94; forced nakedness and naked selections of laborers, 37, 153, 159–62, 186–88; Gentile guards as, 82–83; Gross-Rosen concentration camp and, 156; ill laborers selected for extermination by, 130, 131–32; Inspectorate of the Concentration Camps (Department D-II), takeover of forced labor system by, 94–95, 287n84; Jewish Council of Elders and, 2, 59, 61; Jewish police, disbanding of, 59; *Lagerführerinnen*, SS training for, 155, 157–58, 194, 296n19; liberation, withdrawal during, 38–39; local workshops and, 31, 82; at mass deportations, 19, 195–96; occupation of Poland and, 49, 53; Parschnitz, shooting of laborer observing death march in, 83; prisoner status of forced laborers and more direct contact with, 152, 155, 158–62; roundups by, 149; Schmelt system and, 2, 19, 26, 30, 31, 37, 75, 82, 195–96; Sosnowitz *Durchgangslager* (*Dulag*) and, 77; survivor perception of, 21; Trautenau Kommando, 139

SS-Wirtschafts- und Verwaltungshauptamt (WVHA), 29, 82, 93–94, 152, 154, 156, 164, 287n81

Stammbücher/pamiętniki (autograph albums), 38, 188, 200–202, *201*

Starachowice, 29

Star of David, Jews required to wear, 51–52, 54

stealing. *See* theft

Steinbacher, Sybille, 30, 285n52

Steinert, Johannes-Dieter, 19

Strzelecki, Andrzej, 30

Suderland, Maja, 25, 181

Sudeten German Control Centre, 284n35

Sudetenland: Allied advance and evacuation of German-speakers, 225; annexation of, 29, 36, 81; black market in food at border with former Czechoslovakia, 116; economic upswing and demand for labor in, 29; forced labor system, annexation and expansion of, 81; relocation of war production to, 87; Schmelt system in, 1, 2, 29, 30. *See also specific towns and cities*

Sulik, Alfred, 281n2

Survival on the Margins (Adler), 46

Suzan L., 99, 121, 160, 210–11, 238

synagogues, burning of, 48, 49–50, 89

Szternfinkiel, Natan, 74–75, 195

Telefunken, 178, 235, 289n32

Terezín/Theresienstadt, 25, 116, 281n158

testimony of survivors, 2–5; anecdotal approach, avoidance of, 13; citation of speaker by name, 13–14; "Hungarian girls" from Auschwitz, 166–70; interviewers, influence of, 11–12, 21–22; languages used by, 35; list of testimony-givers by surname, 255–63; postwar collection of, 248–53; postwar model of, 24; producers of knowledge, survivors' self-recognition as, 39; questionnaire, use of, 10–11; techniques and practices, 37; as text open to interpretation, 6, 7–14; visual impact of, 12–13, 269n35. *See also* forced labor system; Jewish girlhood in Zagłębie; prisoner society and ethics of care; social relations; youth of testimony-givers; *specific survivors by first name*

textile industry, forced labor in. *See* factory owners; factory work sites; forced labor at Trautenau; forced labor system; *specific manufacturers by name*

theft: *Lagerführerinnen* stealing food and objects, 21, 123, 191, 193; looting, after liberation, 238–40; sabotage, stealing, and subversion of camp rules, 123, 124–25, 126–27

Tola G., 78–79, 97, 98, 114, 214, 236–38

Tooze, Adam, 28

Tosia J., 145–47, 189–90

transactional relationships/reciprocity, 5–6, 7–8, 25, 185–86, 191

transit centers: Cosel, 93; Parschnitz, 19, 227–28; Sosnowitz *Durchgangslager* (*Dulag*), 34, 35, 70–77, 93, 98, 140, 143, 149–51, 163

Trautenau: beautiful setting, survivor memories of, 97–98; as concentration camp, 37; importation of Jewish girls and women as forced labor to, 1–6; infirmary for, 129; Kristallnacht (1938) in, 89; laborers remaining in, after liberation, 242, 247, 248–49, 310n12;

343

INDEX

looting in, after liberation, 238–39; map, *vii*; monuments to forced laborers and concentration camp victims in, 248; number of female forced laborers at, 33; Shoah Foundation archive of survivor testimonies from, 10; as textile center, 1; train station, 1, 19–20, 99, 143, 164; as work camp, 37; Zaks postcards sent to, 198. *See also* forced labor at Trautenau; Gentile population in Trautenau; liberation of Trautenau

Trautenau *Kommando*, 139, 158–59, 287n84

Treuhandler organization, 31, 65, 91

Trutnov. *See* Trautenau

tuberculosis (TB), 133, 250

Tuwim, Julian, 202

typhus, 115, 125, 129, 131, 132, 184, 242

United Nations Relief and Rehabilitation Administration (UNRRA) Central Tracing archives, 216

United States Holocaust Memorial Museum, 14, 139, 198

University of Michigan-Dearborn, 14

Usborne, Cornelie, 210, 212

US Joint Distribution Committee, 59

van Pelt, Robert Jan, 28, 139

Veprinska, Anna, 231

Visual History Archive (VHA), Shoah Foundation, 3, 136

Volksdeutsche lists, 51, 276n49

Wachsmann, Nikolaus, 154

Wagner, Richard, 90–91

Wałbrzych, 156

Walzel, Oskar, 310n10

Walzel Brothers, 33; Allied advance and closure of, 225; in forced labor system, 85–87, 89, 94–95; postwar experiences, 248, 310n10; prisoners, formalization of laborers as, 155, 157, 158; prisoners of war working for, 214; social relations, prisoner society, and ethics of care at, 100, 107, 121, 127, 198; testimony-givers' view of factory owners, 208–9

Wartheland work camps, 115

Waxman, Zoë, 7

West Upper Silesia: Jews expelled from, 2, 267n4; Nazi plans for, 1–2

Wichrowska, Elżbieta, 200

Wiederman, Paweł, 47–48, 74–75, 275n36

Wiener Library, 248

Wieviorka, Annette, 7

Wildt, Michael, 28

Wirtschafts- und Verwaltungshauptamt (WVHA), 29, 82, 93–94, 152, 154, 156, 164, 287n81

A Woman in Berlin (Hillers), 233

work camps, 84, 113; acquiring, making, and exchanging objects at, 5–6; barracks numbers, 114; concentration camps, conversion into, 2, 32, 36, 37, 84, 152–55, 157–58, 200; crowding at, 95, 154–55, 201; development of, 31–32; Gentile guards at, 82–83, 112–13; map of, *viii*; marching back and forth from work sites to, 109–11; personal space, in barracks, 121, 124; smaller work camps within Schmelt system, 136–37; social relations within barracks, 112–14, 120–21; terms for, 84; transition from work sites with barracks to *Zwangsarbeitslager*, 36, 84, 152; treatment of forced laborers at, 95–96. *See also specific camps by name*

Woyrsch, Udo von, 49, 276n39

Wulc, Pola, 61

Yad Vashem World Holocaust Remembrance Center, 202–4, 248

Yao, Xine, 13, 269n36

Yetta F., 47, 70, 73, 105–6, 110, 129
Yetta P., 23, 114, 117, 208, 212, 240–41, 244
Yiddish, 1, 9, 14, 22, 41, 59–61, 108, 165, 167, 202–3, 218, 235, 236, 270n54
youth of testimony-givers: effects of, 6, 14–24, 253; escape, prospects of, 164, 165; Gentile co-workers and, 108; German invasion and occupation, memories of, 45–48, 52, 58; girls under official age in work camps, 75; "Hungarian girls" from Auschwitz, 167, 168, 174, 175; interest in men/sexuality and, 205–6, 208, 212; at liberation of Trautenau, 238–40; pride in work felt by survivors and, 101; prisoners, formalization of laborers as, 155; self-awareness of survivors as young, 135; separation from family and, 141–42; sexual naïveté and, 15, 23, 231–32; Soviet Union, memory of fleeing to, 46; toilet-cleaning assignments and, 114; vulnerability to sexualized violence and, 51

Zagłębie region: impact of Nazi occupation on, 30–31; Jewish population of, 2, 267n1; liberation of Trautenau, returning home after, 16, 39, 242–46; mass deportations to Auschwitz-Birkenau from, 59, 77–79, 94, 122, 195–96; Trautenau, importation of Jewish girls and women as forced labor to, 1–6. *See also* Gentile population in Zagłębie region; German ethnicity in East Upper Silesia/Zagłębie; Jewish girlhood in Zagłębie
Zahra, Tara, 88, 269–70n43
Zaks family postcards, 197–99
Zalmanovich, Dov, 286n67
(Nie)Zapomniani (documentary film), 34
Zawiercie, 2, 34, 48, 146, 189
Żegota, 30
Zimmermann, Volker, 29, 87, 88, 304–5n35
Ziółkowska, Anna, 115
Zwangsarbeitslager (forced labor camps), 36, 84, 152
Zwieberge, 132

345